RED ROCK AND RAWHIDE

RED ROCK AND RAWHIDE

Ranching in the Grand Staircase,
Escalante Canyons, and Arizona Strip Country

JERRY D. SPANGLER & MARK E. DEGIOVANNI MILLER

THE UNIVERSITY OF UTAH PRESS
Salt Lake City

The Defiance House Man colophon is a registered trademark of the University of Utah Press. It is based on a four-foot-tall Ancient Puebloan pictograph (late PIII) near Glen Canyon, Utah.

Published in part with generous support from the College of Humanities and Social Sciences and the Department of History, Sociology, and Anthropology at Southern Utah University, and the Colorado Plateau Archaeological Alliance of South Ogden.

Library of Congress Cataloging-in-Publication Data

Names: Spangler, Jerry D., author. | DeGiovanni Miller, Mark E., author.
Title: Red rock and rawhide : ranching in the Grand Staircase, Escalante canyons, and Arizona strip country / Jerry D. Spangler and Mark E. DeGiovanni Miller.
Description: Salt Lake City : The University of Utah Press, [2025] | Includes bibliographical references and index.
Identifiers: LCCN 2024016368 | ISBN 9781647691233 (paperback) | ISBN 9781647691240 (ebook)
Subjects: LCSH: Range management—History. | Ranching—Utah—Grand Staircase-Escalante National Monument—History. | Ranching—Arizona—Arizona Strip—History. | Latter Day Saints—Utah—History. | Grand Staircase-Escalante National Monument (Utah)
Classification: LCC SF85.35.U8 S63 2024 | DDC 636.2/010979251—dc23/eng/20241001
LC record available at https://lccn.loc.gov/2024016368

Errata and further information on this and other titles available at UofUpress.com

Contents

Acknowledgments

This book provides important data and statistics that inform pressing debates about livestock grazing on public lands in southern Utah and the Arizona Strip. It also includes the voices of people who love this country: ranchers and farmers, politicians and pundits, conservationists and iconoclasts, scientists and historians.

To this end, we acknowledge the tireless work of Marsha Holland and the Southern Utah Oral History Project. Beginning in 2000 and continuing through the present, Marsha, a San Francisco Bay native with a bachelor's degree in history from the University of California, Davis, interviewed hundreds of local residents with deep ties to this region. She collected pioneer journals and photographs, all now archived in the Barbara A. Matheson Special Collections at Southern Utah University. Those interviews—the words of the people who created the human tapestry of Kane and Garfield counties and the Arizona Strip—are sprinkled throughout this volume.

We thank the College of Humanities and Social Sciences and the Department of History, Sociology, and Anthropology at Southern Utah University for supporting this book. The Colorado Plateau Archaeological Alliance of South Ogden, Utah, also made substantial financial contributions to bring this work to fruition. We also thank Dan Bauer, whose extraordinary photography captures the grandeur of the region in more than words. Lastly, we thank two anonymous reviewers, whose suggestions and insights were invaluable to a more robust consideration of the political, economic, and historic complexities that define this region.

FIGURE 1.1. Map of the Great Basin-Colorado Plateau with Mormon territory, as envisioned by Brigham Young in 1849, highlighted in green. Some major cities, like Phoenix, Denver, and Boise, were established long after the arrival of Mormon pioneers in the Intermountain West. Others, like Los Angeles, San Diego, and San Francisco, were established by Mexican settlers generations before the Mormons arrived.

1 Setting the Table

An Introduction

Mormon families have been raising livestock in southern Utah and northern Arizona for more than 170 years. For the first Euro-American farmers here, raising livestock was often the only feasible way to eke a living from the beautiful but unforgiving country. Frontier families generally had a rough road, yet the ranching culture that developed and life among family and friends brought its own rewards. Today several thousand of their descendants still work the land in southern Utah, including lands within the boundaries of the Grand Staircase-Escalante National Monument.

Non-Indigenous settlers moved into the red rock country of southern Utah during the age of expansion in the mid-nineteenth century by the Church of Jesus Christ of Latter-day Saints, commonly referred to as Mormons or Latter-day Saints. Church President Brigham Young sent thousands of Saints into the far-flung reaches of the American West during these years, mostly in the Great Basin and Colorado Plateau, but also into western Canada and northern Mexico.

The Southern Paiutes, a Numic-speaking people closely related to the Utes and Shoshones, long occupied the lands that beckoned Mormons in the early 1850s. Indigenous peoples lived, worked, and played in what is today southern Utah and northern Arizona for at least 10,000 years before the arrival of Latter-day Saint colonists. Early groups were hunter-gatherers, utilizing the bounty of the land's animal and native plant resources. Evidence of the earliest deer hunters anywhere on the northern Colorado Plateau is found in an unassuming rock shelter just outside of Escalante on the northeastern fringe of the monument.[1]

By about 1000 BC, maize farmers had migrated into the Kanab area, and by 200 BC farming of maize, beans, and squash was flourishing across the region. Some of these Indigenous farming communities were continuously occupied for hundreds upon hundreds of years. Archaeologists refer to these as Ancestral

FIGURE 1.2. Southern Utah has been home to families for at least the past 10,000 years. Photograph by Dan Bauer.

Puebloans and Fremont peoples, whereas their modern descendants call them the Hisatsinom—the "People of Long Ago."[2] An epic drought and resulting social conflict might have prompted many of the sedentary farmers to abandon the region about AD 1280.

But not everyone left. The ancestors of the Southern Paiutes remained, hunting and gathering in the harsh canyon environments, a few even planting crops along the permanent streams and rivers in the St. George Basin. The first Euro-Americans to encounter them were Spaniards taking part in the famous Domínguez-Escalante expedition in search of an overland route to missions in California in 1776. They found thriving communities of Southern Paiutes all along the southeastern margins of the Great Basin, especially in the Cedar City and St. George areas. When the 1776 friar-led Spanish expedition abandoned its quest to reach California, the party turned east, encountering yet more Southern Paiutes in the rugged canyon country of the Arizona Strip in places that today bear names like Moccasin and House Rock Valley.[3]

By the time Latter-day Saint settlers entered the Grand Staircase and Escalante River country, several bands of Paiutes lived in the region. The Antarianunts occupied the eastern edge, the Kaiparowits occupied the Escalante River basin into the upper Sevier River valley, the Panguitch band lived to the north at Panguitch Lake and the upper Sevier River valley, and the Kaibab band thrived along Kanab Creek, House Rock Valley, and Kaibab Plateau areas.

Ute bands also utilized the territory on occasion, but they were not always welcome visitors, preying on their linguistically-related Paiute neighbors. Long before Latter-day Saints colonized the area, the Paiutes were swept into Spanish-Mexican-Ute trade networks that would prove detrimental to their very survival. They were caught in a vortex of trade in horses, guns, and slaves at the same time European diseases were devastating local Indigenous populations. When the Old Spanish Trail penetrated the region in the early nineteenth century, herds of cattle and horses devoured the native plants they needed to survive. By the time Latter-day Saints migrated to southern Utah, the population of Paiute bands had been reduced to mere hundreds.[4]

The hoof prints of the Spanish friars' horses marked the first time domesticated livestock had trod these lands. To non-equestrian Southern Paiutes unfamiliar with horses or any other domesticated livestock, the massive beasts must have seemed oddly alien. Within a century, however, they would become all too familiar with the devastating impacts of livestock on their traditional homelands. In effect, the human history of this region spans ten millennia or more, whereas the history of animal husbandry here, at least in terms of cows, horses, and sheep, is a mere blink of 170 years.[5]

The first white settlers lived in crude dugouts and wagon-boxes. As they assumed the accoutrements of actual communities, stock raisers spread south in search of better grazing onto the isolated Arizona Strip, the part of Arizona north of the Grand Canyon. The entire region is now crisscrossed with highways leading to isolated villages and a cadre of national parks. Travelers can still see their descendants today living on picturesque homesteads tucked below brightly colored cliffs of red, tan, orange, yellow, slate, grey, and white.

Like generations before, stock raisers still rely on precious water from streams that plunge from the high country of the Colorado Plateau, small but reliable water sources that bear names like Kanab Creek, Paria River, Johnson Wash, Boulder Creek, Escalante River, Virgin River, and Short Creek. The home ranches of these families consist of modest farmhouses surrounded by fading barns, cedar post fences, corrals, and irrigated alfalfa fields. In the fall, cottonwoods lining the creeks adjacent to their fields turn to bright yellow and gold.

Today, ranchers work small parcels of private land primarily growing alfalfa or grass, but most of their stock graze public lands owned by the federal government and administered either by the Bureau of Land Management (BLM) or the U.S. Forest Service. This land tenure arrangement has proven an uneasy fit for local stock growers, as American culture has traditionally valued the independence that comes with owning your own land.[6]

Grudges from bygone generations also linger, and Mormon collective memory is still strong here. The nineteenth-century conflict between the Mormon Church and the federal government in Washington, DC, fueled mistrust of federal authority that runs deep. The fact the federal government still owns almost all of the land in the region means resentment is never far away.[7]

Area ranchers lease Forest Service lands that contain mountain pastures and vast stands of spruce, fir, pine, aspen, and oaks in the high country, with grasslands in the high valleys. The lower-elevation BLM lands consist of mountainsides covered by pinyon and cedar (juniper), mesas, and uplands dotted with sage and bunch grasses. Still lower are the barren flats and scrublands of the lower reaches of Glen Canyon country. Their ranches are often picturesque in a pastoral way, but they are not exceedingly profitable. Geographer Paul F. Starrs observed that ranchers stay because ranching is more of a way of life in the West than a profitable enterprise. To them, they are carrying on the ways of their ancestors; they often feel it is a dying way of life, but to them, it is one worth living. It is worth the struggles so they can pass along the land to their children and grandchildren.[8]

The ranching history of Kane and Garfield Counties in Utah and Mohave and Coconino Counties on the nearby Arizona Strip resembles the chronicle of stock raising in almost any part of the arid American West, with the notable exception of Mormon influence in the early decades. In southern Utah, the first cattle and sheep men moved into frontier-era grasslands that early Mormon

FIGURE 1.3. Ranching in the Grand Staircase-Escalante River country required determined men and women willing to withstand the droughts, floods, and vagaries of commodity prices. Photograph by Dan Bauer.

settler Levi Savage described as a "sea of grass," letting their stock graze and multiply on "free" government forage, theirs for the taking. Like elsewhere in the West, early settlers viewed the grass as endless, and their optimism knew no bounds.[9] Brigham Young preached that God owned the land, and encouraged his people to practice stewardship ideals in keeping with this beneficial "use" doctrine. But noted historian Thomas Alexander found that within a few decades after coming to Utah many congregants had disregarded his words.[10]

With no checks on herd numbers or their ambitions, the land was quickly over-grazed, and times got hard. Droughts were followed with floods; good spring seasons alternated with late-killing frosts. The most diligent ranching families survived. They grew proud of having toughed it out. Like all good Western traditions, they felt a sense of heroism in having "civilized" this corner of the American frontier, something that inspired a fierce sense of honor and love of country.[11] While ranching would never bring great riches, it brought a life one could be proud of—a life close to the land, to their animals, and to God. If they doubted this was "God's Country," all they had to do was look outside to see the beauty of the red rock canyon country, season in and season out.

Like settlers elsewhere in the West, Mormon pioneers had established a recognizable ranching pattern by the early twentieth century. They wintered their stock in the lower country on private plots or ranges owned by the federal government, feeding them with hay irrigated on small parcels of private land. In late spring they drove their animals to summer pastures in the high country. Later, these lands would be managed by the Forest Service and BLM through exclusive grazing permits.[12]

In the temporal scope of history, the establishment in 1996 of the Grand Staircase-Escalante National Monument is of fairly recent origin. As of 2024, heated debates still raged between environmentalists and livestock growers over the impact of the Monument on traditional grazing practices. Historian Jedediah S. Rogers has found that the tendency of both sides to demonize the other has scarcely helped promote rational discourse.[13] The fact that the drama has unfolded within the borders of Utah, often said to be the "reddest" of the red states with a strong conservative political tradition, means that political hay is there to be made by referencing the lightning-rod issue over the creation of the Monument. On one side, ranchers believe the Monument is slowly but surely strangling the livestock industry in the region. If the latter is killed, they say, a vital industry and the cherished frontier traditions that grew along with it will perish. On the other side, environmentalists and some local residents reliant on tourism argue the Monument has had little-to-no impact on the industry in southern Utah. They argue that cattle-raising on the public lands in the American West is a dying industry, destined to collapse from market forces that have nothing to do with the Monument or supposed grazing restriction on its lands.

The rhetoric on both sides has been white-hot since 1996, stemming, in part, from the fact environmentalists and ranchers both feel they are doing what is best for the land in southern Utah. In their own way, each sees the Grand Staircase and Escalante River country as a slice of paradise. As environmental historian William Cronon has written, "there is no clear right or wrong: both sides [are] merely defending their corner of Eden, trying to protect the nature they value so highly."[14] And as revealed in this work, it is not just "outsiders" from the East and West Coasts who are interested in these lands. The canyon lands and terraces of southern Utah with their monumental geological formations and epic scenery have become important natural landmarks for Utahns and other Americans, serving as symbols of a vanishing America.[15] The fact that both sides feel they are fighting to preserve a landscape and a way of life that is endangered makes them fight even harder.

Nathan F. Sayre, a geographer at the University of California, Berkeley, has concluded that ranching, despite its importance, has received scant attention by environmental historians.[16] This work provides a history of livestock-raising in southern Utah's Kane and Garfield Counties and the nearby Arizona Strip north of the Grand Canyon. It illuminates the struggles of Mormon settlers and their descendants to wrest a living from these beautifully scenic but harsh and difficult lands. Our goal is to provide factual knowledge and data on ranching in this corner of the American West to offer context for developments that transpired since the creation of Grand Staircase-Escalante National Monument by executive fiat in 1996. The Monument's existence has since overshadowed and, in the opinion of most local residents, endangered ranching in this once isolated Mormon region. The Monument's high-profile controversies have placed this area in the national spotlight. This book explores the conflicts between stock grazers, environmentalists, and average citizens over the future of lands in this part of the American West.

The Monument with its borders entirely within Kane and Garfield Counties contains landscapes and ecosystems of great contrasts. Bordering the Monument on the north are the high mesas of the northern Colorado Plateau, including landmarks such as the Pink Cliffs of the Paunsaugunt Plateau (and its famous Bryce Canyon National Park), the Sevier Plateau, the Escalante Mountains, the Aquarius Plateau, Powell Point, and Boulder Mountain, the latter studded with more than 100 pristine alpine lakes teaming with brook, rainbow, cutthroat, and brown trout, and even a few Arctic grayling.

These highest plateaus are the forested top rungs of the famous Grand Staircase, a series of sedimentary rock formations that crest at the Pink Cliffs on the north. Each lower "step" to the south reveals hundreds of millions of years of the Earth's geological history as it descends more than 7,000 vertical ft to the bottom of the Grand Canyon.[17] Pioneering geologist Clarence Dutton is typically credited with naming the Grand Staircase,[18] although he might

FIGURE 1.4. Geologists named this region the Grand Staircase for a series of ascending sandstone and limestone formations, starting at the Grand Canyon on the south and topping out on the plateaus around Bryce Canyon. The ascending "steps" of the Vermilion Cliffs, White Cliffs, and Pink Cliffs are visible here. Photograph by Dan Bauer.

have borrowed the term from late nineteenth-century surveyors working under the auspices of the landmark Clarence King and John Wesley Powell surveying expeditions. The Grand Staircase-Escalante National Monument, despite its name, actually includes only the northern portion of the Grand Staircase, specifically the Vermilion Cliffs, White Cliffs, Gray Cliffs, Straight Cliffs, and Pink Cliffs. The Chocolate Cliffs lie to the south of the Monument.

The oldest geologic formations in the Grand Staircase (the Chocolate, Vermilion, and White Cliffs) were deposited during the Jurassic period, or about 208 to 145 million years ago, an era of sand dunes, floodplains, beaches, and coastal plains. The Gray and Straight Cliffs were the result of subsequent Cretaceous period depositions (145 to 65 million years ago), when shallow seas invaded and retreated. The Pink Cliffs (the colorful formations that comprise Bryce Canyon) were the result of deposits during the Tertiary period (65 to 1.8

million years ago) that marked the final withdrawal of seas from this region. The Tertiary and Quaternary periods (1.8 million years ago to present) were times of deformation, uplift, and erosion that produced much of the topographic relief that now defines and demarcates the Monument.[19] This landscape is world-renowned for its geological wonders. It contains spectacular multicolor cliffs, buttes, terraces, and bluffs. Its small streams have carved otherworldly slot canyons, arches, natural bridges, and monoliths.[20]

The broken canyon country below the high plateaus contains vast tracts of dwarf pinyon and juniper forests, sagebrush, bunch grasses, and cottonwoods, willows, birches, and oaks along the stream courses. Lower still, are benches, mesas, rolling hills, and canyons, supporting more desert-like vegetation, with sagebrush, rabbitbrush, bunch grasses, stunted pinyons and junipers, yuccas, and various cacti predominating.

Some watercourses, such as Kanab Creek and Paria River, spill south and cut deep chasms into the lands of the Arizona Strip on their way toward the depths of the Grand Canyon of the Colorado River. This still-highly-isolated part of Arizona once contained bountiful grasslands that ascended to vast coniferous forests atop the Kaibab Plateau (first called Buckskin Mountain) that end abruptly at the North Rim of the Grand Canyon. Then as today, the Arizona Strip is much more tied both culturally and economically to Utah than to Arizona.

While the practice of livestock-grazing in southern Utah and northern Arizona is scarcely more than a century and a half old, its traditions evoke a sense of romanticism. Almost a hundred years ago, Walter Prescott Webb, a foremost Western historian, identified a unique cowboy culture that arose from the real-life work on the open ranges. Centered around traditions including roundups, rodeos, penning, lassoing, and branding, and the traits these engendered—rugged men (and a few women) with big boots and hats, chaps, jingling spurs, and six-shooters—a true American subculture emerged.[21] Truths and myths about cowboys and ranching were once mainstays of Hollywood; today they are enshrined by oral family histories that lionize and idealize cowboy ancestors as pillars of frontier spirit, hard work, faith in God, rugged individualism, and pioneer self-determination. Locals share a set of ideals often called the "Cowboy Code," invoking Old West values of independence, ruggedness, and manliness once popularly embodied by the Marlboro Man and the dashing figures of John Wayne and later Clint Eastwood in dozens of westerns, many filmed in

FIGURE 1.5. The ramshackle remains of the *Gunsmoke* television set are still visible along the road in Johnson Canyon. Hundreds of movies, most of them westerns, were filmed in the area, leading the town of Kanab to be referred to as Little Hollywood. Photograph by Dan Bauer.

Kane County.[22] The ramshackle remnants of the *Gunsmoke* television set just outside of Kanab are still a source of local pride, as if Marshal Matt Dillon was one of their own.

The culture of ranching, its facts and its myths, impacts the way people remember the past in this region, and it affects how some see the future of this beautiful but often remorseless landscape. The stereotype of the Western cowboy has become bigger than life. It has its own apparel: cowboy hats, shiny belt buckles, bandanas, and cowboy boots. It has its own musical style, now referred to as "country music" but known for more than a half century as "country and *western*." It has become a staple in movies about the Old West where gritty family stockmen stand their ground, usually against ruthless cattle barons or railroad tycoons. For decades this stereotype has defined the ideals and beliefs that motivate the modern descendants of the first cowboys to cling ferociously to the *idea* of ranching, a "cowboy zeitgeist," of sorts, driven by a spirit of time and place.

As with all stereotypes, elements of truth are woven throughout. The first cowboys and sheep men and their families were hardy and fearless folks, driven by faith and faithfulness, loyal to their church and their communities. Towns like Kanab, Panguitch, and Escalante bustle today because of a pioneer ethos rooted in sheer determination to defy the obstacles lined up against them: persistent droughts, repeated economic depressions, government intervention, and changing marketplaces where the value of their economic production continues to tumble. Given the plucky nature of ranchers, they might just surprise everyone and survive for generations yet to come. Often lost in modern debates about extractive economies, ranching traditionally has been the most stable industry in this section of Utah and northern Arizona. Even as other boom and bust industries such as timber-harvesting and mining came and went, locals could rely on raising livestock to make ends meet.

The peculiarly Western cowboy culture affects politics in the region to the present day. As famously invoked in the 1960s by Arizona conservative stalwart and presidential Republican candidate Barry Goldwater, and perfected by Ronald Reagan later in the 1980s, many leaders from the region celebrate the real and mythical attributes of the frontier cowboy past. Although quite aware of the bureaucratic realities of his home region, Goldwater chose to remember his youth in territorial Arizona by writing that "my mother spoke a lot about our country when we were kids—our heritage of freedom, how individual initiative had made the desert bloom." He wrote his life "parallels that of twentieth century America—raw energy amid boundless land and unlimited horizons."

Goldwater, a Westerner, and Reagan, a transplanted Easterner, understood power could be had from railing against the Eastern Establishment with its alien beliefs that ran counter to the Western gospel of opportunity and individualism.[23] These rhetorical tropes still resonate in the region today. Western historian Howard Lamar has concluded that protesting the region's colonial relationship with the eastern United States and high-profile confrontations against an overreaching federal government have played well in Western states such as Utah and will continue to do so in the foreseeable future. As with Goldwater and Reagan in the past, modern politicians have discovered that standing up for local interests can make one a hero.[24]

Yet, even without the issues caused by the Monument, the future of ranching in this part of Utah and Arizona is far from certain as the nation enters its third decade of the twenty-first century. Economist Thomas Power, a University of Montana researcher and perhaps the most widely published scholar on the economics of Western public lands, found that public lands contribute only 2 percent of the nation's total livestock feed. And the percentage of American beef produced from federal rangelands is less than 3 percent of the total. In other words, the public rangelands are an insignificant part of national beef production. Raw statistics tell the tale. Power found that the 17,989 jobs dependent on federal grazing amount to 0.06 percent of all employment in the eleven Western states, whereas the income generated from those jobs amounted to 0.04 percent of total job income.[25]

While ranching families of southern Utah and northern Arizona work hard to continue their way of life, they are aware of the precarious nature of ranching as a livelihood and their declining place in a regional economy increasingly dominated by tourism. According to census data compiled every five years by the U.S. Department of Agriculture, only 6 percent of Kane County households were engaged in agriculture in 2012; the average farm there lost $3,851 annually. In Garfield County, the percentage of households engaged in agriculture was slightly higher, at 14 percent, and the average net farm income amounted to $658.[26] In both instances, farm income contributed a tiny (or negative) amount to the household budgets.

According to U.S. Census Bureau estimates for 2019, Kane County had a median household income of $43,540 and Garfield County had a median household income of $54,565.[27] This disparity between farm income and non-farm income would seem to support a University of Arizona study that found rural communities are not dependent on ranching for their survival, but rather ranchers are dependent on full- or part-time employment in nearby towns to keep their ranches afloat.[28]

As discussed in the following chapters, the "cowboy zeitgeist" still prevalent in southern Utah and northern Arizona had its roots in events and developments generated elsewhere in the state, region, and nation. And pioneer ranch families of this region responded differently than did their contemporaries in other regions of the West. Noted geographer Terry G. Jordan identified a distinct agrarian village pattern and cultural landscape in Utah, where ranching was but a side note at first.[29] Chapter 2 discusses the initial settlement of southern Utah by Mormons heeding the call of church officials, the emergence of a village-based ranching model, the discovery of vast grasslands to the east of St. George, and the subsequent settlement of communities like Kanab where the entire economy revolved around livestock. In effect, these earliest settlers did not choose to come here, but rather they were chosen by church leaders to settle in the desert wilderness.

By 1870, years of hostilities with Navajos, Utes, and Southern Paiutes had ended, and as detailed in Chapter 3, this led to a new wave of Mormon settlement throughout the region. The environment was ideal for livestock grazing, but traditional agriculture was challenging, at best, and most of the early settlers in this day were stockmen. Cattlemen and sheep men began pushing their ever-growing herds south into the vast Arizona Strip country and into the high plateaus above Panguitch and Escalante. These were not small family herds. Instead, they were much larger aggregations of animals, referred to as cooperative herds and later as United Order herds for a communal system Brigham Young attempted to establish among the most faithful Saints. The United Order found its greatest success in the red rock canyon country here at Orderville, the classic "Arcadian Village," as Utah-born writer Wallace Stegner labeled the town.[30] There were also church-owned herds, often referred to as tithing herds. And collectively, they numbered in the tens of thousands. Management and arbitration of the open rangelands was under the direct control of ecclesiastical leaders, which served to further Mormon Church objectives that God's gifts should go to the benefit of all the faithful (and it created a closed economic system that served as a barrier to encroachment by non-Mormons).

By the mid-1880s, the cooperative herds had dwindled or been absorbed by United Order communal experiments. As seen in Chapter 4, once the United Order failed, herds were divvied up among individual church members. At the same time, the large church herds were sold off to surrogates (friends of the church) to avoid federal attempts to seize church assets, part of the government campaign to end polygamy in the territory. These actions led to a power vacuum in terms of livestock-grazing with no mechanism in place to arbitrate how the open ranges would be used. Into this void stepped two non-Mormon cattlemen, Preston Nutter on the western Arizona Strip and B. F. Saunders on the eastern Arizona Strip. Both were cattle barons in every sense of the word, running tens of thousands of head, closing off springs to small operators, and using questionable means to wrest exclusive control of the Arizona Strip grasslands. Under their control, the once-lush rangelands were denuded.

This work also discusses the emergence of the sheep industry in the region, from its birth as a homespun cottage industry in the 1850s through its existence as the dominant economic force in the Grand Staircase and Escalante country by the early twentieth century. Hundreds of thousands of sheep were brought to the region each spring, often by outsiders with no social or religious ties to the communities. The sheep (and later Angora goats) would eat the vegetation and shrubs to the bare ground, leaving the soils vulnerable to flooding and erosion. And the sheep men would turn out their flocks earlier and earlier in the year and just ahead of the cowboys in a race for forage.

Range "wars" erupted between cattlemen and sheep herders elsewhere in the West, including in eastern Utah and western Colorado along the Colorado River near modern Grand Junction, Colorado. There, Mormon sheep men had thousands of their stock shot by locals when they tried to bring their herds into the state in the mid-1890s.[31] But in Mormon-dominated southern Utah, range wars seldom erupted. Instead cattlemen largely bemoaned the destruction of what was left of the range, and their clamors for rangeland reforms finally reached the U.S. Congress, which in 1934 passed the Taylor Grazing Act during the height of the Great Depression and the great droughts of 1926 to 1936. By then, it was too late. According to oral histories of the first settlers in the region, the rangelands in 1934 were but a mere shadow of what they had once been, the native grasses generally replaced by less nutritious plants and weeds.

Historians Charles Peterson and Brian Cannon found that a strange historical convergence resulted in Utahns supporting increased federal management of public lands, just a few years after President Herbert Hoover had offered to grant all public lands to the Western states. Such an offer would be the Holy Grail to current and future politicians who still clamor for state control of federal lands. The agricultural economic crisis converged with the environmental range crisis to find Utah land users, including the cattle baron Preston Nutter who had played a huge role in the overgrazing of federal lands, supporting the Taylor Grazing Act. They drew the line, however, at new national parks or monuments, a trend that continues well into the twenty-first century.[32]

The end of free open range was welcomed by the ranchers in large part because the Taylor Grazing Act was weighted heavily in favor of those with a "home base"—a private ranch with water rights—which meant the legitimate ranchers who had historic ties to the area would always have preference to the grazing permits.[33] The fact local grazing boards were comprised of their friends and neighbors assured ranchers even more local control over range policy. But how to restore the rangelands? As discussed in Chapter 5, the Great Depression was also marked by the first serious attempts to improve grazing practices through soil conservation and stabilization, reseeding, water development, and seasonal grazing—all attempts funded entirely or in part through New Deal programs. Locals were overwhelmingly Republican and were outspoken critics of Democrat Franklin D. Roosevelt's policies, but they lined up nonetheless to take advantage of federal relief funds.

American entry into World War II in 1941 marked the onset of economic recovery and the reemergence of the cattle industry regionally, but it also engendered the greatest period of out-migration. Young men and women had left in record numbers to support the war effort, and a good share of them chose not to return. Better economic opportunities beckoned elsewhere.

The post-World War II years were characterized by growth in the cattle industry, the complete collapse of the sheep industry, a spike in nationalism during the Cold War, and fundamental changes in grazing policy that pitted grazers against other land users. In Chapter 6, we discuss the emergence of the modern environmental movement, courted by successive presidential administrations in the 1960s and 1970s. This movement promoted the principle that public lands belonged to all Americans and that each American had fundamental rights to clean air, clean water, and open spaces. Advisory boards were expanded to include mining, oil and gas, wildlife, and conservation interests, as well as grazers, and management of public lands increasingly was focused on multiple use principles.

Ranchers who had used the rangelands for nearly a century with little or no oversight or outside interference found themselves competing with other users who were afforded equal footing in the decision-making process. And with increasing regularity, other user groups, especially environmentalists, took to the courts to force better management of public resources. Beleaguered and legally outgunned in the 1970s and 1980s, ranchers across the West organized in opposition to federal policies and environmental activism, what is popularly referred to as the Sagebrush Rebellion.

The rebellion reached a boiling point in 1996 when President Bill Clinton, a Democrat, designated the 1.7-million-acre (expanded to 1.9 million acres through a land trade with the state) Grand Staircase-Escalante National Monument that encompasses much of Kane County and Garfield County. His action created by far the largest national monument outside of Alaska. Its total acreage was more than double the acreage of Utah's five national parks put together. Accomplished with no input from Utah lawmakers, the largely unilateral maneuver angered many local ranchers and townspeople, some of whom burned Clinton in effigy in public spectacles.

The anger never really subsided. In December 2017, President Donald Trump, a Republican, reduced the size of the Monument by almost half, to less than 1 million acres, and broke it into three distinct districts: the Grand Staircase, Kaiparowits, and Escalante Canyon units. This action opened up lands for resource extraction and other types of economic development.[34] Locals cheered while conservationists and Indigenous American tribes sued.

The election of Democrat Joseph Biden as president in 2020 reopened the possibility of a return to the pre-Trump Monument boundaries. And the next year Biden, in fact, did sign a proclamation restoring the pre-2017 boundaries. Even so, some conservative local politicians called for an end to the political seesaw and the uncertainties it brought. In Chapter 7, we discuss how the Monument's creation has impacted grazing practices in the region, the national and global economics that are contributing to the steady decline of public lands grazing throughout the West, and the economic future of local livestock operations that manage to survive modern economic trends toward centralized agricultural production. This chapter also details heated debates over the future of the Grand Staircase and Escalante River country. Fifth-generation ranching families have an obvious deep attachment to the land, a well-earned sense of place and love of the environment. But competing voices have gained power in arguing over what is the best and most beneficial use of the same landscape, many of whom arise from places far outside southern Utah.

FIGURE 1.6. The small towns of southern Utah were populated almost entirely by Mormons, many of them converts from distant countries. This unidentified Danish convert was 95 when photographed in 1936. He arrived as a boy and was probably among the first to settle Escalante in the 1870s. Photograph by Dorothea Lange, courtesy of Farm Security Administration/Office of War Information Black-and-White Negatives, Library of Congress, Washington, DC.

Recurring themes weave throughout this work. From the time the first wagons rolled into Kanab in 1870, almost all of the livestock operators have been poor, often barely surviving the vagaries of market fluctuations, droughts, and other widely fluctuating weather events. Utah ranks second in the nation behind Nevada in the percentage of lands owned by the federal government with 63.1 percent controlled by various federal agencies, excluding Indigenous American reservation lands held in trust by the government.[35] In southern Utah, the figures are much higher. In this light, very little private land remains for young people to start their own farms. In Garfield County, 96.5 percent of the land is owned by the state or federal government, while in Kane County, 89.7 percent of land is owned by the state or federal government, making them among the counties with the highest rates of public ownership of lands in the nation.[36] Ever since the second generation came of age in the 1870s and 1880s, these counties have experienced a steady out-migration of young people seeking economic opportunities elsewhere, a pattern that remains to this day. And those who remain feel a deep-seated resentment and distrust of the federal government, all fueled by a sequence of events, some related and others not, that challenged southern Utahns' sense of independence and self-determination.

This resentment was initially rooted in federal antagonism toward the Mormon Church that included the "invasion" of U.S. troops during the Utah

War of 1857, subsequent federal campaigns to break the Mormon Church as an economic force, and relentless efforts to arrest and imprison church leaders for their practice of polygamy. It would rear its head again and again whenever the federal government took actions that were perceived as threatening the settlers' traditional way of life: setting aside wildlife preserves and Indigenous American reservations, protecting landscapes through national monument and national recreation area designations, and, of course, new grazing regulations that limited the number of livestock and times of year they could be grazed.

In a very real sense, the conflicts generated by the creation of Grand Staircase-Escalante National Monument represent a collision of two very different cultures. One culture is rooted in its traditional use of the land and its embrace of conservative religious and political values; this cultural tradition imparts the belief that the best stewards of the land are those who have known and worked this land for generations. The other is rooted in the social and political ideals of the 1960s, that public lands belong to all Americans and must be managed for long-term sustainability and varied multiple uses for the benefit of future generations.[37]

The regional livestock industry today is slowly being suffocated by the combined effects of centralized beef production, high production and transportation costs, and lessening consumer demand for red meat—all market forces beyond the control of a rancher in Escalante or Kanab. On the other hand, the "cowboy zeitgeist"—the ideals and values that motivate people to action—remains loud and proud, mostly expressed through the rhetoric of politicians harkening to a time long past. Only a handful of full-time ranchers remain in business today, by some accounts only a few dozen in all of Kane County and Garfield County.

Instead most of the 462 "farming" households in both counties are comprised of "hobby" or part-time farmers and ranchers, raising a few cows or sheep, but with no expectation livestock will ever pay the bills. Many of these individuals, however, descend from families that once made their living exclusively from ranching. The fact that household income has risen steadily in both counties (it rose more than 100 percent in Kane County from 1990 to 2010) at the same time farm income has plummeted to less than $1,000 per farm suggests that agriculture in all of its different configurations is no longer the backbone of the rural economy here.

Each summer Kanab hosts several rodeos and the Kane County Fair where livestock raising, cowboy culture, and other Western traditions are celebrated. Cowboy life is still embraced by many of the region's youth. The Kanab High School mascot is the Cowboy. In the Grand Staircase and Escalante Canyon country, the image of the cowboy and the rancher still resonates. But as the number of people making a living as cowboys and ranchers declines, uncertainty casts a shadow over Kane and Garfield Counties, especially among the older generations. Can tourism provide a stable and proud way of life for their children? Can it offer a feasible way to make a good living in the future? Will the federal government, as they view it, continue to unilaterally "lock away" chunks of the land in this region without seeking input from people in southern Utah? These questions echo today across this red rock landscape.

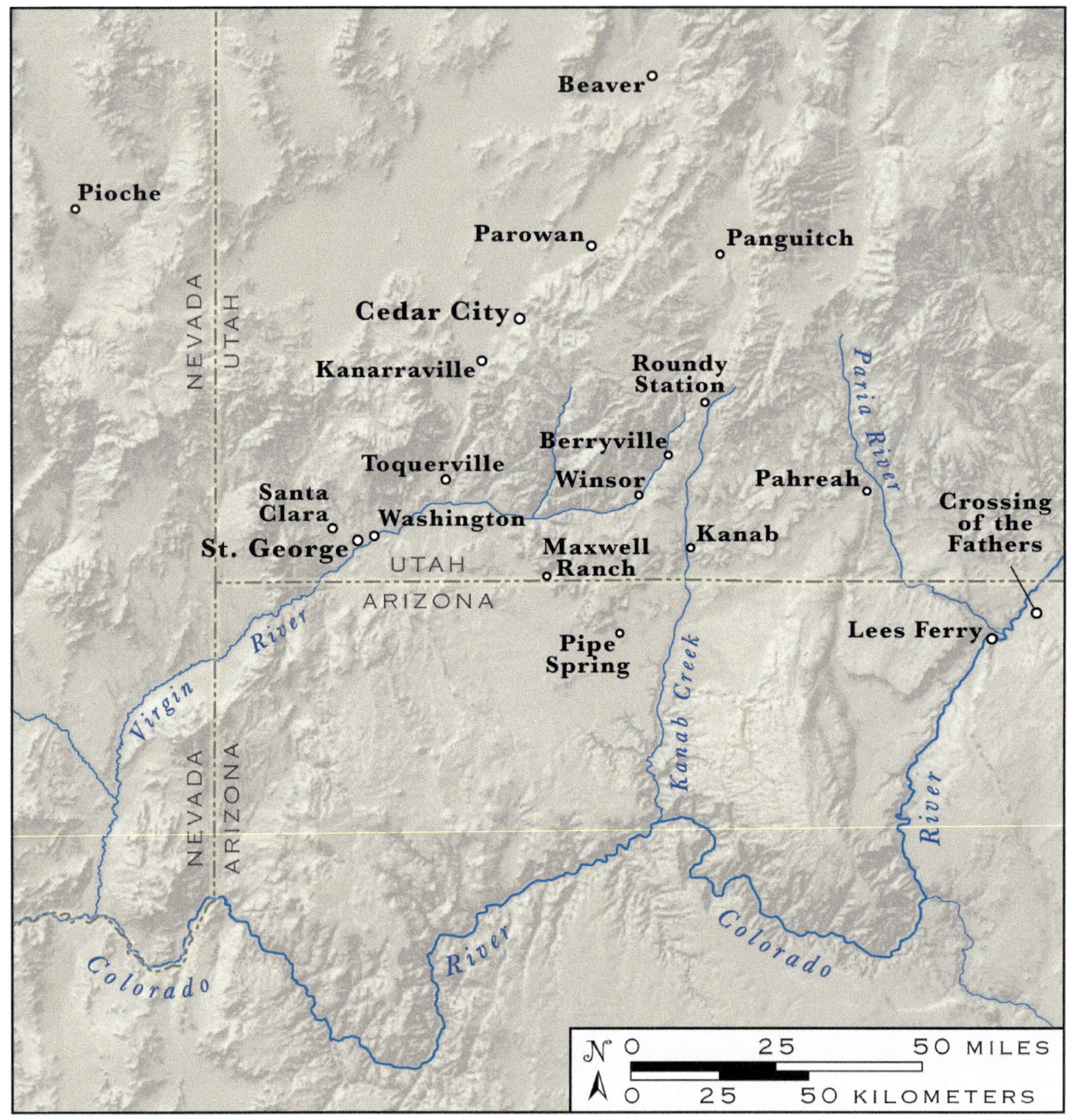

FIGURE 2.1. Map depicting southwest Utah and northwest Arizona with settlements, stations, and forts (1850–1870).

2 A Sea of Grass

Mormon Discovery and Settlement of Kane and Garfield Counties, 1852–1869

The origins of a livestock economy in southern Utah and the rest of the Mormon Cultural Area—a region from southeastern Idaho to central Arizona—are unique in the annals of the American West. Ranching here was not motivated by individual farmers seeking to carve out a piece of the wilderness they could call their own, as was the case with the tens of thousands of immigrants bound for Oregon Territory and California. Nor was it inspired by the often-romanticized model of isolated ranches amid tens of thousands of acres of open range, as was the case in southern Arizona, Wyoming, and Montana.

Rather, animal husbandry in this part of the West was rooted in the unflagging religious zeal of early converts to the Church of Jesus Christ of Latter-day Saints (Mormons) who answered the call of their church leaders to explore and settle the farthest reaches of their mountain refuge. The overtaking of the land and Indigenous peoples who already lived there was methodical and organized under the centralized authority of church leaders in Salt Lake City, often through local bishops and stake presidents.

Mormon settlers began moving to present-day Kane and Garfield Counties in the late 1850s and 1860s, migrating east from existing settlements in Iron and Washington Counties because of unabated population growth, a search for resources such as forage and timber, and the need for a buffer against threats from Navajo (Dine′) raiding parties from the east and potential invasion by federal troops from the south.

In her centennial history of Kane County, Martha Sonntag Bradley states that the area's

> settlement began humbly with the digging of crude dugouts by Jacob Hamblin and others starting in 1858. As small parties of settlers moved

> to the outpost in 1859 and later as part of the Mormon Church's effort to extend its domain, the most experienced pioneers led their fellows in the tasks of settlement.[1]

An earlier history by Adonis Findlay Robinson states that Jacob Hamblin led companies of men (actually missionaries bound for the Hopi villages south of the Colorado River) through modern-day Kane County in 1858, 1859, and 1860 and "found a few settlers who had come in search of good country for cattle raising and were living in dugouts near the willow-lined creek only a short distance from the present site of Kanab."[2] According to community boosters and non-scholarly sources, the name of the creek and the town derives from the Southern Paiute term for "place of the willows."[3] Other histories place the origins of permanent settlement in the area several years later, between 1862 and 1864.

At the time, the first Mormon settlers were creating a frontier culture and pioneer lore about real-life battles against Indigenous peoples and struggles to tame the land, stories that were passed on to subsequent generations. Their cultural blinders meant that they did not see themselves as invaders usurping the homelands of Indigenous peoples. Silas Hoyt, one of the founders of Parowan and Mount Carmel, recalled his early days in southern Utah: "At this time the country was swarming with Indians, so we had to fortify and be on guard both night and day. Wherever we went, either for wood or for stock or on business, we had our guns in our hands prepared for momentary conflict."[4]

In 1864 Hoyt was chosen by church leaders to find new locations for settlement. That year he established a farm and ranch at Winsor (now Mount Carmel) on the upper Virgin River. Hoyt recounted that "We raised one crop and started a second one when the Navajos attacked again and drove off a large number of sheep and other livestock." He remembered that local men raised a company of thirty militiamen and pursued the Navajos (unsuccessfully) all the way to the Colorado River in the Grand Canyon.[5] He noted that in his absence his entire crop withered and died, and coupled with the theft of his stock, Hoyt lost over $1,000 that year.

As elsewhere in Mormon-dominated Utah Territory, Latter-day Saint colonization of what would become Kane County and later Garfield County was motivated by several social and economic factors. Populations were increasing rapidly in Cedar City and other areas of Iron County, as well as in St. George and the earlier-settled villages of Santa Clara and Washington in Washington County. Mormon immigrants, many converts from Europe with no prior experience in pioneer life, were dispatched to the Iron Mission to work the iron ores near Cedar City, to the Cotton Mission to raise cotton in the hot, dry climes around St. George, or to the Southern [Utah] Indian Mission to preach God's word to the Indigenous inhabitants of the region. Census records indicate 1,701 white settlers were living in southern Utah by 1860, a mere ten years after the arrival of the initial vanguard.[6] The limited amount of arable and irrigable land in places like Parowan, Cedar City, St. George, and Santa Clara prompted settlers to seek out other areas suitable for homesteading, "each clinging to a stream that watered a small meadow, enabling oasis-like agriculture in the desert," say historians Douglas Alder and Karl Brooks.[7] Every nook and cranny with useable water attracted the attention of the first settlers.

Defense against a feared invasion by United States troops and raiding by Navajos also played a role in the Mormon expansion into the Grand Staircase. In 1857, anxiety was growing throughout the territory about a military campaign against the Mormons, commonly referred to as the "Utah War," when federal troops under the command of Colonel Albert Sidney Johnston began to approach Salt Lake City from the east to quell a rumored Mormon rebellion against the Union. At the same time, Lt. Joseph C. Ives was attempting to transport soldiers and supplies up the Colorado River by steamboat, a direct threat to the Mormons' exposed southern flank. Under mandates from Brigham Young, exploring parties were dispatched to locate suitable (and defensible) refugia in the mountains and canyons of southern Utah, including what is today Kane County.[8]

At the same time, Navajos were stepping up attacks on Mormon farms and villages, using the fords of the Colorado River at the Crossing of the Fathers and Lee's Ferry to escape into the maze of canyons of Arizona.[9] Southern Paiutes, who were largely friendly to their Mormon neighbors, also became increasingly disgruntled, and some took to raiding during the 1860s. Pushed out of their traditional foraging territories by unrelenting expansion of Mormon communities, small bands began making forays to appropriate stock of unprotected and comparatively isolated Mormon settlements on the outer flanks of St. George.[10] A protective buffer to the east of the larger communities was deemed a priority to deter further incursions, and faithful Mormons from as far away as Salt Lake City were dispatched on missions to bolster the frontier defenses.[11]

These major regional themes provide the context for the emergence of a local livestock economy in southern Utah and northern Arizona, beginning in the early 1860s and continuing in fits and starts until about 1870. Settlers began arriving in 1870 in what is today Kane County and Garfield County in even greater numbers after the cessation of hostilities collectively known as the Black Hawk War after its charismatic Ute leader Black Hawk, or Antonga.[12] The first livestock operators in the region were, by all accounts, isolated individuals or families living on the fringe of wilderness far removed from the protection of the territorial militiamen in Cedar City, Parowan, St. George, and Santa Clara. Permanent communities were eventually established, and they grew dramatically in size.

FIGURE 2.2. God's Country. Photograph by Dan Bauer.

Land and Livestock Policies

An understanding of the evolution of the livestock industry in southern Utah can only be appreciated within the broader context of Mormon Church policy regarding private land ownership and access to public domain rangelands. These policies were dictated by the Utah Territorial Legislature, which for all intents and purposes was under the control of the church leadership in Salt Lake City. Often at odds with federal law and policy, these rules were applied throughout the territory with only minor modifications by local church leaders. Almost all of Utah's frontier-era communities were designed under the same Salt Lake City master plan: building lots were surveyed and awarded (not sold) by drawing of lots, they were situated around a community square, and the size of the lots was determined by specific occupations. Farm fields surrounding the community were awarded by need, and water rights, including irrigation water, were held by the community at large and distributed under policies that benefited the community.[13]

When the Mormons first arrived in the Salt Lake Valley in 1847, most of the lands of Utah—and certainly all of southern Utah and northern Arizona—were part of Mexican territory. Mexican colonists never settled this far north, however, and the territory was the domain of several independent and loosely confederated Indigenous bands of Northern Utes, Shoshones, Paiutes, and Goshutes. Brigham Young and other Mormon Church leaders had intended to establish the independent "State of Deseret" in anticipation of the impending arrival of the Kingdom of God on earth. This massive territory was larger than Texas and included virtually all of Utah and Nevada, the northern two-thirds of Arizona, and portions of California, Oregon, Idaho, Wyoming, Colorado, and New Mexico.

In the 1840s, the relationship between the Mormons and U.S. government was an awkward one at best. Mormons had been forcibly displaced from their homes in Missouri and later in Illinois, and many had been murdered while the federal government ignored the atrocities and their pleas for protection. The church's charismatic leader, Joseph Smith, had been murdered, and faithful adherents had been pushed west onto the Iowa plains where they suffered unimaginable hardships during the winter of 1845–1846. Smith's successor, Brigham Young, had intended to send an exploratory expedition to find a new religious refuge in the far west in the summer of 1846. Those plans were shelved when the U.S. government came calling with its goal to muster 500 able-bodied Mormon men to march to Santa Fe in support of General Stephen Watts Kearny.[14]

It was common knowledge in 1846 that war with Mexico was imminent (war would be formally declared on May 13, 1846). Mormon representatives offered a deal: in exchange for the requested Mormon manpower, the government would assist the Mormons to establish a new religious refuge in either Oregon, Texas, California, or Vancouver Island. President James K. Polk flat-out rejected the idea. Instead he offered the Mormon soldiers a cumulative total of $21,000 in wages and uniform allowances—funds that could be donated back immediately to the cash-strapped refugees on the Iowa plains to assist their own journey westward starting in 1847. Brigham Young took the deal, and in July of that year, 543 men enlisted in what would become known in Latter-day Saint lore as the Mormon Battalion. Many of its members would go on to play prominent roles in the settlement of southern Utah and the Arizona Strip.

Once the Mexican-American War ended with the Treaty of Guadalupe Hidalgo in February 1848, Mexico ceded the lands that would become the states of Arizona, New Mexico, Utah, Nevada, and California, and Mormon Church President Brigham Young and his people were unwillingly swept back into the United States. With the Compromise of 1850 and its creation of Utah Territory, Young established what historians call a "theodemocracy," a semi-hidden government with church rule under the sheen of federal territorial status.[15]

As the first settlers spread south from Salt Lake City, they built their farms and communities on federal lands that had never been surveyed, and hence no legal mechanism was in place for farmers and ranchers to claim rightful title to this property. Brigham Young taught that all the land belonged to God, and he imposed a communal land stewardship doctrine upon the Latter-day Saints. During these years, a distinctive Mormon land ethic emerged that assigned natural resources to human use, an ethic that still resonates today in Utah.[16] The Mormon-run Perpetual Emigrating Fund allowed thousands of European converts to immigrate to Utah. By one account, in 1846, 40,000 converts in Great Britain alone were waiting to come to the Promised Land.[17] Converts arrived in the Salt Lake Valley by the thousands every year thereafter—colonists and refugees in need of food and shelter.

In short order, Mormon settlers had displaced Indigenous Utes and Shoshones who had lived along the Wasatch Front. Growing herds of Mormon cattle and sheep were also rapidly overrunning traditional Goshute lands in the

Tooele Valley and pushing deeper into Ute territories around the Sevier River in central Utah and Shoshone country in Cache Valley to the north. The settlers gave little thought that the grasses needed for their livestock forage were the same plants and seeds on which Indigenous Americans relied for their very survival. Like the beliefs of others of Anglo-American heritage, Mormon ideology held that only settled people who "used" the land in their manner deserved it, therefore providing a theological justification for Indigenous removal, as well.[18]

By necessity stemming from the lack of federal surveys, the responsibility fell to the church to administer the distribution of all lands, including open ranges. As early as 1852, Utah's territorial legislature passed a law allowing for local, legislatively-authorized surveyed lands to be claimed, privately held, and later sold. In 1861 another law was passed that stated that anyone who enclosed (fenced) any portion of unclaimed government land was the rightful owner of that land and any improvements they made. In 1865, land laws were expanded to include the right to claim lands that had not been formally surveyed.[19] Territorial lawmakers did not care that these tracts were federally owned and legally part of the public domain; the legislature simply created a uniform process whereby these lands could be claimed by private interests.[20]

The management of livestock also drew the attention of early lawmakers. Cattle, horses, and sheep were valuable assets that had to be protected from theft and "confused identity," and they presented potential problems in terms of trespass and damage to agricultural lands. Initially, the numbers of livestock did not create much of a problem, and in 1851 all unfenced lands were "hereby declared common pasturage, and all peaceable animals shall be free to run at large and graze thereon, except swine."[21]

But all that would soon change. As early as 1853, Brigham Young, then President of the Mormon Church and Territorial Governor of Utah, urged cattle owners to "group into fencing companies" and to enclose vast tracts of land in plots of about 50,000 acres until "all the vacant land is substantially enclosed."[22] Young urged the territorial legislature to pass strict regulations on herding and grazing. In effect, church leaders wanted all livestock not necessary for daily sustenance removed from the growing communities.

Although the area was theoretically under federal control stemming from its territorial status, Brigham Young continued to push church rule and theodemocracy. He established probate courts at the county level, with judges appointed by the governor, vested with both civil and criminal jurisdictions.

Later, Mormon bishops were elected as justices of the peace to handle local cases. Mormons were instructed to avoid federal district courts dominated by non-Mormon officials assigned to the territory from elsewhere.[23]

Regulating livestock was a central concern in rural communities. In 1854, the legislature passed the Herdsman Act, which required the licensing of a herdsman (the term cowboy was not yet in use) and gave county probate judges the authority to designate where livestock could be grazed and the size of a herdsman's designated rangeland. This law mandated that grazing areas could not be located "as to interfere with any previous rights, nor within the range necessary for the animals of any settler or settlement." In 1865, this law was expanded to include a provision that all livestock not needed on a daily basis—draft animals, milk cows, and in some cases horses—would need to be removed to more distant rangelands upon a two-thirds vote of the citizens.[24]

Historian Levi Peterson states the early territorial rangeland policies were effective because they allowed for the local resolution of grazing issues. He cites one 1866 example where the Kane County Probate Court warned the people of Toquerville to remove their herds from grazing lands belonging to another owner, and the Toquerville residents obediently and immediately complied. In fact, because the region was insular and almost entirely Mormon, rangeland disputes were virtually nonexistent prior to 1870. Between 1855 and 1857, more than thirty laws were passed granting public domain grazing lands to private citizens and the Mormon Church. Peterson said grants involving more than 100 mi^2 were common. To maintain the status quo, another law prevented non-Mormons, referred to as "Gentiles" by church faithful, from encroaching on rangelands necessary to settlements.[25]

For years, Mormons attempted to keep outsiders at bay by prohibiting them from owning land. Of course, it was not legal for the Territorial Legislature to sell off lands that were not theirs to sell. Lawmakers probably recognized changes were afoot when the first federal land surveyor, Captain Howard Stansbury, of the U.S. Army Corps of Topographical Engineers, arrived in 1849 to begin the first official survey of the Utah Territory. He reportedly was not welcomed by local settlers as he travelled through northern Utah.[26]

Utah Mormons had a system that worked without the meddling of Gentiles. Long-time Kanab Bishop William Derby Johnson Jr.'s journal provides a glimpse into the insular church legal process. On February 18, 1877, he recorded: "Brother Lundgren had his mare stole last night. Think one Charles Butler did it . . . Came up about 3 p.m., made out affidavit for Bro. Lundgren and issued a warrant for arrest of Butler." Within a few days Butler turned himself in and accepted the restitution required by church leaders.[27]

In 1869, the federal government finally established a land office in Utah. Formal federal procedures for securing title did not significantly change established patterns, however, as they allowed preemption claims for lands already settled. As elsewhere in the arid West, federal 160-acre homesteads were too small for viable farms on all but the most fertile, irrigated lands. Local settlers often still relied upon communally herded stock on public lands for subsistence.[28]

From the beginning, the church saw the importance of livestock to self-sustaining communities, although beef consumption was not a major factor in that realization. In 1833, Mormon prophet Joseph Smith announced a revelation, later known as the Word of Wisdom, urging faithful Latter-day Saints to refrain from strong drink and tobacco, and to use sparingly the "flesh of beasts and fowls."[29] Cattle were primarily used as draft animals and to supply dairy products to the community, and sheep were important for homespun wool clothing and meat. If a cow was to be butchered, it was as much for the leather needed for shoes and tallow for cooking fuel as it was for the beef, which was usually dried or "jerked" for later consumption.

But as herds began to increase, livestock served another purpose: a ready source of cash and trade with Gentiles. Historian Jeff Nichols has noted that cattle provided an ideal form of currency, being both highly mobile and highly profitable.[30] As early as 1850, Mormons were trading local livestock to throngs of California-bound gold miners, and by 1853, entrepreneurial Mormons were driving large herds—1,500 to 2,300 head at a time—west to sell in the booming California mining camps at greatly inflated prices.[31] Beef consumption was not all that common in Utah in the 1850s, but as one observer reported, "if the people of Utah were not a meat eating people, the workers in the new railroad towns and mining camps were."[32] Some early Utah entrepreneurs speculated in the livestock business in a big way. Cattle could be purchased in Texas at $3.75 a head, herded to Utah to be fattened, and then sold for $24 a head in California. Large-scale speculation was an exception, however.

Utah's draft animals were also highly sought-after by railroad and mining camps. The demand for draft animals, however, steadily declined after completion of the Transcontinental Railroad in 1869. In 1860, 27 percent of Utah's cattle were oxen, but by 1870 that number had dropped to 9 percent, and by

1880 it was down to 3 percent. As noted scholar of early Utah livestock economics Don D. Walker observed, "With this loss of market for oxen seemingly went a loss of interest in growing beef cattle, the demand for meat apparently being too weak to generate a new incentive."[33]

Within this context, the livestock economy of southern Utah likely followed the pattern established elsewhere in the Utah Territory. Mormons had a heavy focus on livestock that would make the community self-sufficient, such as oxen, dairy cows, and sheep, but beef consumption was a minor part of the motivation to keep livestock. Those with stock lived in established communities, but they were forced to keep their herds on rangelands distant enough not to interfere with local agriculture.

In southern Utah, individual livestock owners likely sold stock or traded with passing immigrants traveling to California along the Old Spanish Trail, acquiring cash and other goods otherwise unavailable on the Utah frontier. The public domain open ranges to the east of settled areas of Iron and Washington counties, such as the upper Sevier River, Long Valley on the upper Virgin River, and the Kanab Creek drainage likely were acquired from local Mormon civic leaders (e.g., probate judges) who also functioned as ecclesiastical officials. Coming from nearby towns like Cedar City, Parowan, St. George, and Santa Clara, these claimants rarely, if ever, lived on the land beyond seasonal camps while tending herds. Rights likely were determined by primitive means of fencing the range. Some individual rangelands were undoubtedly claimed by groups of community livestock owners, cooperatives in a sense that one herd might belong to multiple owners. New settlements were established on federal land through formal claims sanctioned by local civic and Mormon Church leaders, and these claims were subsequently ratified by the fencing of the claimed property.

During the last quarter of the nineteenth century, the Mormon Church became one of the largest livestock operators in Utah by default. Mormon faithful were expected to tithe—a contribution of 10 percent of their annual "increase" to the church. In those days, tithes were rarely paid in cash, but rather in cows, sheep, wheat, and other items produced by the faithful. For example, if a herdsman had one hundred cows and they produced fifty new calves in a year, five of those calves would be donated to the church. In short order, the church became the largest livestock operator in the entire Utah Territory. This most certainly held true in cash-strapped southern Utah. According to early

Kane County settler Brigham A. Riggs, tithing cattle from across southern Utah were driven to Pipe Spring and Canaan where it was Tommie Smith's job to brand them and keep records of them.[34]

Growing Pains

Although never discussed in detail in the various histories of southern Utah, the growing populations of Iron and Washington Counties resulted in an ever-increasing need for additional livestock forage for the rapidly increasing

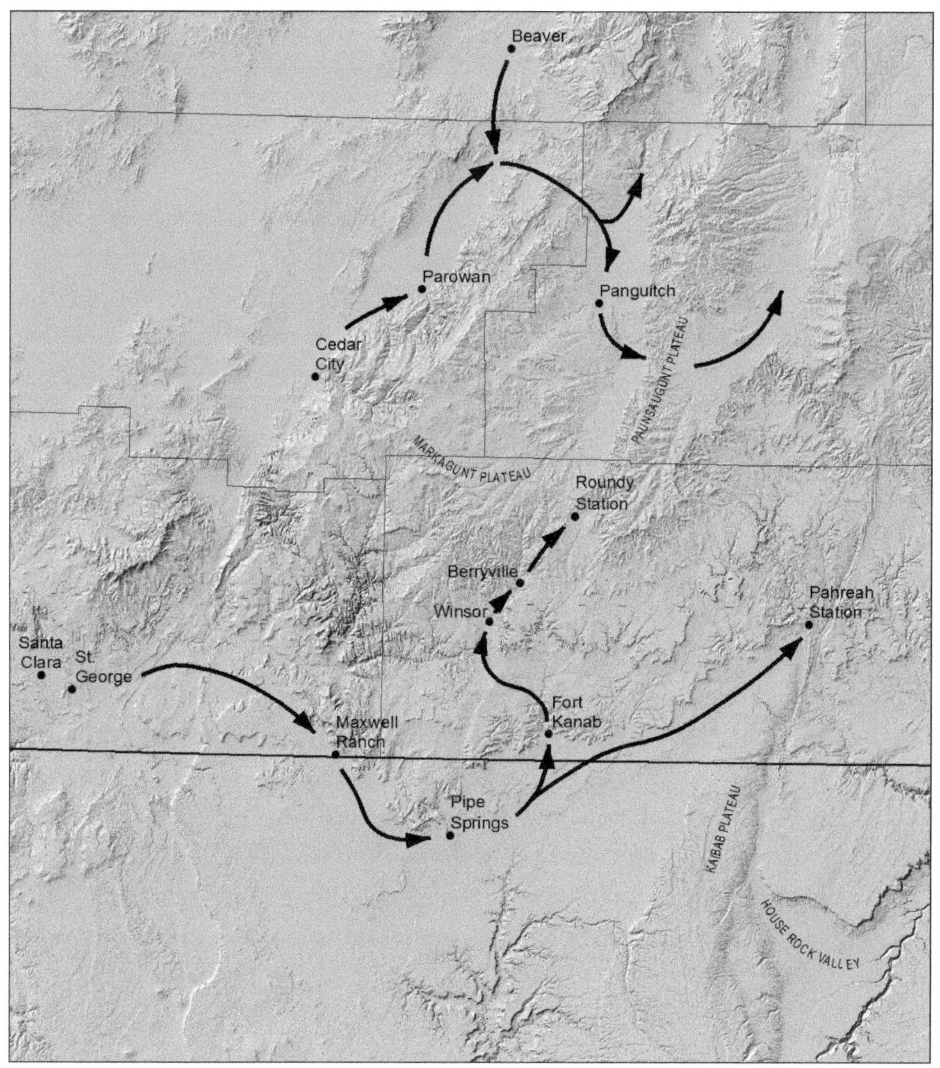

FIGURE 2.3. The initial settlement of Kane and Garfield Counties originated from two sources. Mormon cattlemen in the Santa Clara and St. George area accessed the region from the west, following the base of the Vermilion Cliffs to Pipe Spring and then north to Kanab and Long Valley. Pioneers from Parowan and Cedar City accessed the region from the north, arriving first in the Panguitch and upper Sevier River areas.

TABLE 2.1. Southern Utah Livestock Populations by Animal Type as Indicated in U.S. Agricultural Census Records for 1850, 1860, and 1870.

		Human Population	Horses and Mules	Oxen	Milch Cows	Other Cattle	Sheep	Total Livestock
1850	Iron	360				639	122	
	Southern Utah total	360				639	122	761
1860	Iron	1,010	239	341	445	336	1,855	
	Washington	691	162	165	382	320	1,303	
	Southern Utah total	1,701	401	506	827	656	3,158	7,249
1870	Iron	2,277	812	173	933	1,008	4,502	
	Washington	3,064	927	90	1,193	1,917	3,170	
	Kane	1,513	357	85	557	743	909	
	Southern Utah total	6,854	2,096	348	2,683	3,668	8,581	24,230

Note: Data derived from USDA Census of Agriculture Historical Archive, 1850–1870. The 1850 agricultural census does not distinguish between types of cattle.

numbers of cattle and sheep brought by the new arrivals. Initially, adequate forage was not much of a problem. In 1850, U.S. Census records indicate there were only 639 head of cattle in Iron County—a manageable number within the environmental constraints of the area. But ten years later, the number had nearly doubled to 1,122, and by 1870 it had almost doubled again to 2,114 (see Table 2.1).

The 1860 U.S. Census indicates only 867 head of cattle in the St. George area. But ten years later, the number had grown to 3,200. Some ranchers migrated to the newly created Kane County, established by an act of the territorial legislature in 1864 and named for Mormon ally Thomas L. Kane, a Pennsylvanian military officer and lawyer. In 1870, Kane County included the Virgin River area in the eastern portion of what is today Washington County, which reported an additional 1,385 head of cattle. In all, there were nearly 7,000 head of cattle by 1870 and simply not enough forage around the established communities in Iron and Washington counties. Furthermore, the percentage of arable lands that could be farmed in the Mormon pattern was extremely limited—certainly not enough to accommodate the hundreds of new arrivals every year.

The open lands around Cedar City and St. George were suitable for winter range, although limited in spatial scope and quality. Good summer range could be found immediately east of Cedar City on the Markagunt Plateau and in the Pine Valley Mountains north of St. George. But the Saints needed more rangeland, and they soon turned their attention toward the wild, unexplored

FIGURE 2.4. The Arizona Strip was once described as a vast sea of grass—forage that seemed endless for the growing herds of Mormon cattle and sheep. By the 1870s, tens of thousands of sheep and cows were grazing these lands, and within two decades most of the grass was gone. Photograph by Dan Bauer.

Arizona Strip and Kaibab Plateau (called Buckskin Mountain at that time) southeast of St. George, and to the Paunsaugunt Plateau in the upper Sevier River and upper Virgin River country.

The Arizona Strip was especially intriguing, featuring broad expanses of lower-elevation winter range and high plateaus with ample summer range. In 1869, while camped near Moccasin Spring, Edwin G. Woolley wrote, "this is the best stock range in this Southern Country. [The country] west from here [thirty] miles or more is a sea of grass, and running northeast from here thirty miles the same."[35] Even in the years that followed, livestock men in the region gushed that "grass was knee-deep all over,"[36] that it was common "to have grass brushing the stirrups,"[37] and that "grass was so high that you could hardly see the sheep for it."[38]

At least two lonely ranch outposts were established on the Arizona Strip frontier, first in 1862 when William B. Maxwell established a ranch at the point that Short Creek debouches from the Vermilion Cliffs, followed a year later by Dr. James Whitmore, who claimed Pipe Spring and Moccasin. Both men would play prominent roles in the region's livestock industry, but for different reasons.

William Bailey Maxwell joined the Mormon Church in 1845, a year before the then-24-year-old volunteered as a private in Company D of the Mormon Battalion that served during the Mexican-American War. He later arrived in Salt Lake City in 1852 as part of the Uriah Curtis Company. He would go on to become one of the first settlers of Santaquin in northern Utah from 1856 to 1859. In the fall of 1862, he was "called" to build up southern Utah, and after a short time in Rockville, he built a ranch at Short Creek where he "took care of his own and other men's cattle."[39] His original calling possibly was to work with Jacob Hamblin in the Southern Indian Mission. The official church account indicates "Brother Maxwell was an efficient Indian missionary and always sustained good influence with the natives."[40] He was, however, also a captain in the Nauvoo Legion, the name for the Utah militia at the time, and according to one family history, "took an active part in tracking down the lawless element that infested that wild frontier. He acted as scout against the renegade Indians of eastern Nevada and western Utah."[41]

It is not clear how long he lived in Short Creek (now the twin towns of Hildale, Utah, and Colorado City, Arizona), but it probably was not more than a few years. One family history indicates he had moved his growing family to Eagle Valley, Nevada, in 1865, at which time he secured the contract to provide beef to the silver mines in Pioche. Possibly he also kept the Short Creek ranch, which provided the inventory for his Nevada beef contract. Scattered references to the Maxwell Ranch at Short Creek date as late as 1869.

While in Nevada, he married his third wife, Jacob Hamblin's daughter Marietta (or Maryiete) Megdoline Hamblin, a young widow at the time. Maxwell would be directly associated with Jacob Hamblin for much of the rest of his life, even traveling on two occasions on Hamblin's missionary expeditions to the Hopis. In 1877, he moved his family to Panguitch, then to Long Valley, and finally to a new cattle ranch in House Rock Valley. But again he did not settle down. Within two years, he had moved on to the White Mountains of Arizona near the Little Colorado River in and around St. Johns where he bought out the original rancher to secure access to "many thousands of acres of the finest grazing lands in the southwest." But this area was also Apache land that would require all his fighting skills.[42]

To avoid prosecution for his continued practice of polygamy, Maxwell joined other Mormons fleeing to Mexico in 1887 to help build a refuge there called Colonia Díaz. Many frontier-tested men and women from Kanab ultimately were called by church leaders to establish the Mexican colonies, including William Derby Johnson who served as first bishop of Colonia Díaz, and later Anthony Ivins who served as stake president of the colonies before being called to serve in the First Presidency of the Mormon Church.[43] Maxwell returned to St. Johns, Arizona, within a couple years, and he died in 1895 in Mesa, Arizona. He fathered at least twenty-seven children during his lifetime, and had adopted at least two Indigenous children, one Mexican child, and one African American child. The veteran frontiersman was fluent in Lakota, Hopi, Navajo, and various Ute dialects. He was a cattleman to the very end.[44] The size of Maxwell's Arizona Strip herds in 1862 cannot be ascertained from the available histories, but it was certainly large enough that it capitalized his beef-selling venture in the Nevada mining camps.

James Whitmore, his neighbor at nearby Pipe Spring, was probably the largest operator in the area. In 1863, he brought 11,000 sheep and 500 cattle to the region. Along with his ranch hand, Robert McIntyre, he staked out corrals, built a dugout, fenced off ten acres, and planted apples and grapevines.[45]

Whitmore had been a Texas cattle rancher and frontier doctor, but he found himself ostracized by his friends and neighbors when he, his wife Elizabeth Carter Flaherty, a brother, and a sister all converted to Mormonism. The Whitmores drove 1,300 head of cattle with them to Salt Lake City, arriving in 1857 as part of the Homer Duncan Company of converts.[46] In 1861, the family was "called" to serve in the Cotton Mission, taking up residence in St. George. Family histories indicate he took 400 head of Texas longhorns with him (no mention of sheep is made, nor is it explained how the family cattle herd had dwindled from 1,300 head to 400). He filed a claim on 160 acres at Pipe Spring in 1863 and began improvements there while still maintaining his residence in St. George.[47]

In January 1866, during the Black Hawk War, Whitmore and McIntyre were both killed at Pipe Spring during a confrontation with a Navajo raiding party. The killings prompted retaliatory strikes by the Mormon militia and counter strikes by Indigenous warriors that plunged the region into violence for the next three years and led to the temporary abandonment of Kanab,

Berryville, and Panguitch. The Mormon Church later purchased Pipe Spring from the Whitmore estate and it changed hands over the years. In the 1920s, the National Park Service acquired the property and established a national monument here, in part to serve as a rest stop for tourists driving between the Grand Canyon and Zion National Parks.

Forgotten in the Pipe Spring tragedy is what must have been the remarkable story of Dr. Whitmore's widow, Elizabeth, who was arguably the first and perhaps only woman cattle baroness anywhere in the region. She had run her own 400-acre Texas cattle ranch after the death of her first husband, and she would run the Arizona Strip ranch after her second husband, James, was killed. She was listed as a thirty-nine-year-old widow with five young children in the 1870 Census, the oldest only sixteen years old.[48] Still a widow ten years later, she listed her occupation on the Census as "stock raiser."[49]

The family history states that Elizabeth was released from her church mission to southern Utah in 1883, and that she returned to Salt Lake City driving her substantial cattle herds ahead of her. It is probably not coincidence that her sons, successful businessmen and bankers, were soon thereafter running the largest cattle operation in eastern Utah, by some accounts 10,000 to 15,000 head.[50] Elizabeth is not even mentioned in the histories of the Arizona Strip, and the only reminder of her tenure there is the name Whitmore Canyon found in Parashant National Monument near the north rim of the Grand Canyon.

Ezra Strong, a resident of Rockville, might also have started a third isolated ranch in the Kanab area or perhaps in Long Valley. Robinson states that Strong settled on Kanab Creek at the same time Maxwell and Whitmore started their ranches on the Arizona Strip, which would have been in 1862 or 1863.[51] Bradley indicates the ranch was located on the upper Virgin River.[52] Very little is known about Strong's tenure in the region, but Ezra Strong and William Maxwell may have been previously acquainted, both having lived in Santaquin only a couple years before.[53] Perhaps relevant to a discussion of these earliest settlers, Merle H. Graffam, in his catalog of historic signatures in the region, references a Levi Savage inscription dated to the early 1860s,[54] although the earliest unequivocal pioneer inscription documented in the region so far is a John D. Lee inscription dated 1867. Levi Savage is listed among the first arrivals in Kanab sometime prior to 1865.

The expansion of these men onto lonely virgin grasslands was problematic to Mormon philosophy for two important reasons. First, the fundamental tenet underlying the Mormon settlement pattern was the establishment of tightly knit communities, not isolated ranches. As summarized by Douglas D. Alder and Karl F. Brooks, "ranching and mining were not the planned Mormon mode, the former because its people were more dispersed, the latter because they were congregated in what Mormon leaders considered the wrong kind of moral setting."[55]

These new rangelands were far distant from the Mormon settlements in Cedar City and St. George, and often they were located in environments where traditional agriculture would be risky if not impossible. This latter issue would mandate a modified community pattern oriented more towards isolated "stations" or outposts in closer proximity to vast rangelands rather than traditional communities surrounded by fields with vegetables and grains. In 1863, Mormon Apostle Erastus Snow, who founded St. George in 1861, was already acknowledging frontier realities in these marginal farming areas. That year he blessed the founding of a new ranching-oriented community at Hebron in northwest Washington County, envisioning the small settlement as a buffer against miners and their negative influence streaming in from nearby Nevada. Apostle Snow also encouraged these ranchers to trade with miners in the boomtown of Pioche, Nevada, in subsequent years, which probably led to Maxwell's profitable beef trade there in 1865.[56]

A second factor influencing expansion into the eastern frontier was the simple fact that these areas were already occupied by large numbers of Indigenous Americans. Kaibab Paiutes lived along Kanab Creek, in House Rock Valley, and along the base of the Vermilion Cliffs, and summered in areas of the Kaibab Plateau. The Panguitch Paiute were culturally and economically tied to fishing on Panguitch Lake and upper Sevier River country, and they maintained close kin connections to their Kaibab cousins to the south. Sanpits Utes at the time were entrenched in the Fish Lake and Sevier River areas.[57]

The Sanpits, named for the Ute leader Sanpitch, a brother of feared war chief Wakara, were especially distrustful of Mormon expansionism. They were closely related to the Timpanogos, and they had watched in horror as their relatives were slaughtered and forcibly driven from traditional territories in the Utah Lake country. Mormons had launched two retaliatory strikes in 1849, both instigated by allegations that Utes had stolen cattle, although the "thefts" were most likely desperate attempts to ward off starvation after settlers had blocked their access to traditional wild foods. By 1850, the Mormons had launched an all-out military campaign that by one account killed more than 100

FIGURE 2.5. The earliest Mormon arrivals to southern Utah found thriving Southern Paiute communities, many of which were reliant on farming the Virgin River floodplains. The Southern Paiutes and Mormons initially enjoyed a peaceful coexistence that included an alliance against Navajo and Ute raiders. Photograph courtesy of J. K. Hillers Collection, National Anthropological Archives, Bureau of American Ethnology Collection, Smithsonian Institution, Washington, DC.

Timpanogos; eleven who had surrendered were executed in front of their own families and some were beheaded in the name of scientific research.[58] Survivors joined the Sanpits Utes at reservations at Spanish Fork and the Sanpete Valley, but this solution was only temporary, and by 1861 their forced removal to the faraway wilderness of the Uinta Basin in northeastern Utah was inevitable.[59]

Triggered by disputes over livestock grazing and the impacts it had on native resources, the massacre of the Timpanogos in 1850 was not easily forgotten by the area's Indigenous peoples, who watched helplessly as Mormon cattle trampled the wild plants and seeds on which they had traditionally survived. Mounting tensions between Mormon settlers and Indigenous Americans extended into central Utah, beginning in 1853 with skirmishes now referred to as the Wakara (or Walker) War after the most famous of the Ute chieftains of that period. Compiled some sixty years after the fact by a one-time herdsman, a year-by-year catalog of "Indian depredations" in the Utah Territory suggests the Wakara War was overwhelmingly a central Utah event with armed conflicts commonplace in the Sevier River country that now includes Juab, Sanpete, Millard, and Sevier Counties.[60]

Fluent in Spanish and English, Wakara was a charismatic and cunning leader who rallied Utes in Utah and Colorado, as well as a few Paiutes and Shoshones, to his cause. His message attracted some Paiutes who were reeling from the impact of Mormon settlements that were moving ever deeper into traditional territories, disrupting local ecosystems and cultural practices. Jacob Hamblin, the well-known "Mormon Leatherstocking" and missionary, acknowledged as much in 1866, writing:

> When the natives resorted to gather seeds, they found they had been destroyed by cattle ... only the poor consolation was left them of gathering around their campfires and talking over their grievances ... I could not blame them, viewing matters from their viewpoint. I rather justified them in what they expected to do.[61]

Long Valley Explorations 1852

The first Mormon settlers to Southern Utah arrived in Parowan on January 13, 1851, under the leadership of Mormon Apostle George A. Smith, a first cousin of Mormon Church founder Joseph Smith; others included John Doyle Lee of later Mountain Meadows Massacre infamy and Priddy Meeks, who would play a prominent role in the history of western and southern Kane County. Meeks wrote in his autobiography that he arrived in Parowan in 1851 "to help strengthen the place against Indians; for they were very doubtful neighbors and committed some trespasses against us which was very hard to bear, such as killing our young calves on the range to eat."[62]

FIGURE 2.6. The isolated Maxwell and Whitmore ranches were both located at the foot of the Vermilion Cliffs where there are reliable springs. They were also on a transportation corridor between St. George and Crossing of the Fathers and settlements in Arizona. Photograph by Dan Bauer.

In January 1852, a party of twelve men led by John D. Lee explored the Virgin River country to the south.[63] And in June of that same year another exploring party set out from Parowan to investigate the unknown mountainous lands to the east. This expedition was led by John C. L. Smith, president of the Parowan Mission, and his counselor, John Steele, and they were accompanied by John D. Lee, John Dart, Solomon Chamberlain, Francis T. Whitney, and Priddy Meeks. One history indicates the expedition was initially part of a goodwill mission sent to meet with Paiute Chief Quinarrah, a meeting that did not go very well.[64] Meeks wrote that they ascended the Sevier River to its headwaters and then followed the "Long Valley" of the upper Virgin River from its headwaters south and west into the Orderville Narrows. This was followed by backtracking, getting lost, and suffering from thirst.[65] Meeks offered only minimal descriptions of Long Valley itself—a narrow but verdant valley that would become his residence a decade later. At the time, a band of about 100 Paiutes called Long Valley home.

The date of the arrival of the first livestock herds in Kane County is not known with certainty, and various histories display inconsistencies about when the earliest ranchers began to put down roots. Hearing the reports of the 1852 exploring party, Mormon settlers would certainly have recognized the critical importance of summer ranges and might have begun pushing livestock into the area at that time, although no one, it seems, actually lived there. If so, herds would not have been left unattended, but would have been watched by "herdsmen"—the early vernacular for "cowboys." These were usually teenage boys or young men who quickly became adept at riding horses and using firearms. William Adair, an early settler in the region, recalled that in 1877 the entire United Order herd, perhaps numbering in the thousands, was tended by two seventeen-year-old boys, Ed Lamb and Tom Stalworthy, who were left alone with rarely any adult company.[66]

Luella Adams Dalton offers some insight into this common practice in Parowan.

> Jimmy Clark herded and supervised the boys who helped with the regular community bunches of cattle and of sheep. Families who had no youngsters to send with Jimmy to help him had to pay a cent and a half per day, per cow to have them watched. If an animal was not brought back, the one responsible for it had to take a whipping, and if it did

> not come in the night someone had to hunt till it was found . . . The stock always had to be guarded. Indians and animal predators seemed to be always at hand.[67]

As forage around the established communities became overgrazed, the herds were pushed farther into the surrounding hills and unspoiled ranges, making it much more difficult to bring the herds back to the community corral each night. Dalton states this led to family cooperatives, "as each family owned a few of each but not enough to justify leaving other work to care for them."[68] It became a common practice for the teenage boys to spend the entire summer on the range tending the herds.

These forays were the stuff of young men's dreams. They typically involved camping under the stars, hunting deer, fishing, and enjoying life away from the strict social norms of their home community. Glynn Bennion, a one-time teenage herdsman in the Fish Lake area, wrote:

> The life of the cowboys in summer was little short of idyllic. Thousands of ducks and geese covered the surface of Fish Lake or waddled about on its shores feeding on berries, insects, and seeds. Fat deer and grouse were everywhere. Noisy little streams were alive with native trout. Certainly, in contrast to the deserts the boys were used to, this summer range was the Land of Beulah.[69]

In some instances, when the herdsmen returned to the same area repeatedly, they might construct crude shelters and dugouts.

Quite possibly the community herds from Iron County were pushed into the upper Sevier River and upper Virgin River country by the mid-1850s, and the young herdsmen might even have ventured as far as Kanab, constructing crude dugouts as protection against cold weather. If they did, the credit was instead assigned to a more famous personality. Bradley states that Jacob Hamblin and others constructed dugouts in Kanab in June 1858, the earliest reference to a structure in the region.[70] This reference is questionable because at that time Hamblin was in Santa Clara preparing for his first mission to the Hopi pueblos later that fall, an expedition that historical accounts generally agree was the first time Hamblin had ventured deep into the Arizona Strip (on the third day out of St. George, an Indigenous guide showed him Pipe Spring, which was apparently unknown to the Mormons before that time).

Robinson's earlier history contends that Hamblin "found a few settlers" living in dugouts in the area when Hamblin's missionary expeditions came through in 1858, 1859, and 1860. But Hamblin's journals and the more day-to-day descriptions of his devoted missionary companion, Thales Haskell, do not mention visiting Kanab or encountering settlers there. Also noteworthy, a party of twenty missionaries returning from the Hopi pueblos in 1862 camped on Kanab Creek. Hungry and exhausted, Lucius Miller rode 40 mi west to the William B. Maxwell ranch at Short Creek, returning with a fat sheep, flour, and bread to relieve the starving missionaries.[71] But Kanab itself would have been only a few miles north of their Kanab Creek camp. If indeed families were living there with livestock, it raises questions why Miller (or the entire party) did not instead make haste to ensure the safety and resupply of the ranches there. Either Hamblin had no knowledge that people were living there, which seems unlikely, or no one was living there at that time.[72]

Besides Jacob Hamblin, the names of others who might have been on the Kane County frontier looking for rangelands in 1858 or 1859 have gone unrecorded. The dugouts referred to might well have been temporary shelters used only occasionally by the herdsmen in the area. If families were here trying to establish a home, they did not likely come on their own accord, as the Mormon settlement pattern dictated centralized church control. They would have been sent here on a "mission" to establish an outpost that had a specific purpose to further the goals and objectives of the church. And the orders to go to Kanab would only have come from the church hierarchy in southern Utah. Likewise, those wanting to leave had to be "released" from their mission by church authorities. References to such a Kanab mission at this early date were not identified.

Into the Wild

What is more certain is that by 1862 families were settling lonely ranching outposts on the still wild frontier to the east of St. George, some of which defied the community-based Mormon settlement patterns elsewhere (see Table 2.2). William B. Maxwell had the previously-mentioned ranch at Short Creek by at least 1862, and James Whitmore began the earlier-mentioned ranch at Pipe Spring in 1863.[73] By 1865, Bradley indicates outposts had been established at Berryville (Glendale), Winsor (Mount Carmel), Pahreah, and Upper Kanab or Roundy Station (Alton), all part of a church strategy to protect the eastern flank of St. George and Cedar City. Robinson indicates there was another station at "Wah-wiep."[74]

Many of the new arrivals brought specialized skills such as masonry and carpentry intending to build permanent homes and other structures, but almost all also owned livestock, both for their own sustenance and as currency in their barter economy. These isolated outposts on the frontier did not reflect, at least not initially, the typical Mormon settlement pattern of symmetrical city blocks surrounding a town square and meeting house, with fields neatly placed around the outer edges of the community, each assigned to a family by drawing of lots.

FIGURE 2.7. Upper Kanab near the headwaters of the Virgin River was home to about one hundred Paiutes when the first Mormon explorers "discovered" it in 1854. It later became the site of Roundy Station near the modern town of Alton. Photograph by Dan Bauer.

Rather, they reflected small groups of families, often related by blood, clustered in a single area along a reliable water source. Agricultural fields, limited in most areas by narrow canyons, extended up and down the canyon bottoms rather than in grids. Cattle were loosed to graze open range nearby. These clusters were often referred to as "stations," perhaps a way for church leaders to distinguish temporary outposts from the towns established in the Mormon pattern and formally consecrated to the work of God.

The command of the stations was a church assignment, the leader being referred to as "President," and it was generally viewed as a temporary calling. Most if not all of the earliest settlers kept their established farms in more populous Iron County or Washington County. For example, in 1869, Jacob Hamblin developed a station at Pahreah for local Kaibab Paiutes, and Priddy Meeks was called to be its president.[75] Meeks had his own farm in Long Valley at that time and would return there after his unspecified tenure as president of Pahreah Station (it was later renamed Fort Meeks, a name that apparently never caught on because the site is still known as Pahreah to this day).[76]

Priddy Meeks was undoubtedly one of the most colorful characters of southern Utah. He was a frontier doctor, and much like Dr. James Whitmore, he was a practitioner of herbal medicine, as opposed to doctors who "bled" their patients. He was also renowned for his ability to see ghosts, apparitions, witches, and evil spirits, as well as for visions and prophecy. Born in South Carolina in 1795, he was among the early converts to the Mormon Church in 1840, enduring the expulsion of the Latter-day Saints from Nauvoo, Illinois, and making the overland trek to Salt Lake City in October 1847. Although older than most of the first emigrants at fifty-eight, he joined the first company of 167 Mormons to arrive in Parowan in the dead of winter 1851. He was part of the first exploring party into the upper Sevier River and upper Virgin River country the following year (and among the first non-Indigenous people to gaze on what would become Zion National Park). He also seems to have been a crusty sort, squabbling with his Iron County neighbors over water, among other things.[77]

According to the plaque erected in his honor along U.S. 89 near Mount Carmel, Meeks and two brothers, John and William Berry from Kanarraville, returned to Long Valley in the summer of 1862 in search of grazing and farmlands. Meeks staked a claim to an area in lower Long Valley he called Winsor, later changed to Mount Carmel, and the Berry Brothers claimed land farther

FIGURE 2.8. Dr. Priddy Meeks and his second wife, Mary Jane McCleave. Mary Jane gave birth in 1864 to what might have been the first white child born in what is today Kane County. Photograph courtesy of Uintah County Public Library, Vernal, Utah.

upstream, which they called Berryville, later changed to Glendale. Dugouts might have been built at that time, but according to the plaque, they did not stay. Rather, the Berry brothers and Meeks, who was seventy years old at the time, later returned in 1864 with their families, including two other Berry brothers, Joseph and Robert, and Meek's twenty-four-year-old second wife Mary Jane, who gave birth that same year to the first white child born in the area. Meeks fathered seventeen children before his death in 1886 at age ninety-one. Joseph Berry, Robert Berry, and Robert's wife Isabelle were killed during the Black Hawk War in 1866.

Residing at the outlying stations must have been a lonely if not terrifying experience, especially for families with no protection close to their homes. In 1865 and 1866, Peter Shirts was in charge of a remote station about 10 mi east of Kanab when Navajos raided all of his cattle.[78] He sent a rider to Kanab with word that Navajos were camped about 8 mi below the station, and that he wanted to return to the safety of Fort Kanab. Robinson indicated that Shirts and his family were pinned down by the presence of the Navajos for two weeks until Captain James Andrus, and thirty armed men arrived to rescue them and return them safely to Kanab.[79]

Peter Shirts, known as "the Daniel Boone of Deseret," was another colorful character who graced the landscape in Kane County, although he was in the area only briefly. Born in Ohio in 1808, he was among the earliest Mormon converts, joining the church in 1833 and helping to build the Kirtland Temple in Ohio and later the Nauvoo Temple in Illinois. He was a close associate of Brigham Young, and after his arrival in Utah in 1849, Shirts was sent on many missions to locate different parts of the wilderness that might make good settlements. By 1852 he had started a ranch in Iron County and had constructed a fort there called Shirts Fort. A colorful red buttressed canyon south of Cedar City still bears his name. Later in 1855, Shirts and Rufus Allen surveyed what would become Las Vegas. He returned to Salt Lake City (Mill Creek) and later moved to the Provo area where he constructed a sawmill. In 1861, he was in the pioneer company of three hundred families sent to reinforce the Cotton Mission in St. George.

According to the family history, "He was a man with a restless, eager spirit, a true Latter-day Saint who was also a lonely trailblazer. He penetrated into many remote, hidden valleys and mountain passes." By 1865, Shirts had staked a claim on land along the Paria River about 4 mi below what would later become Pahreah Station, constructed a stone shelter, and diverted water from the river to his new home. He lived there with his wife, two daughters, and a son. He indicated that Indigenous Americans had raided his ranch in the fall of 1865, taking all of his livestock and horses except one cow, making it impossible for him to remove his family to St. George for the winter. When the family never showed up in St. George, rumors swirled that they had been killed. After the spring snow melt, twenty men from the Iron County Military District in Cedar City set out to find them.[80]

FIGURE 2.9. Peter Shirts was known as the "Daniel Boone of Deseret." He was an intrepid explorer of the Great Basin and Colorado Plateau with a renowned sense of wanderlust. Photograph courtesy of Utah State Historical Society Classified Photo Collection (39222001360507).

The family history states: "they were surprised to see him tilling his fields with a group of men pulling his plow." He had survived the winter of 1865–66 by the following strategy:

> [He walled] up his windows and barricaded his door and kept his double-barreled shotgun with plenty of buckshot. He also kept his pitchfork, pick, and other tools ready for action, if needed. Although the Indians planned all winter to kill Peter, he gave them food to keep them from starving . . . The following spring, Peter told the Indians, "You have eaten my food. I must raise more for another winter. Because you ate my oxen, you must pull my plow."[81]

As late as 1951, reenactments of that event with people costumed as Indigenous Americans harnessed to a plow were being performed in Escalante.[82]

Peter Shirts then seems to have given up on his outpost on the Paria River and resumed his wanderlust. The family history reports that he returned to Kane County in 1868 and constructed a grist mill 35 mi east of Kanab, and later, while living along the San Juan River, he helped feed starving immigrants of the famous "Hole in the Rock" Expedition. In the spring of 1882, while again in Escalante, "Peter packed his donkey and headed out into the wilderness as he had done many other times. This time he didn't come back and no one heard from him again."[83]

The Forts

Another characteristic of the early settlements throughout southern Utah was the establishment of forts for communal protection during times of conflict with Indigenous Americans. This construction was typically done before a town was actually planned and plotted. In the early 1850s, Brigham Young exhorted his followers to "choose the best locations and erect the most functional, highest-quality, well-designed structures possible."[84] Five such forts were started in 1865 or 1866 in Kanab, Long Valley (Berryville), Panguitch, Pipe Spring (Winsor Castle), and Fort Sanford north of Panguitch, all of which were built specifically as places of retreat during times of conflict with Indigenous peoples. Of course, such fortifications are excellent protections for people, but they are much less suited to protecting large herds of unattended livestock, which could have been easily expropriated by Indigenous raiders. The enclosure at Fort Kanab was only 112 ft to a side.[85] In 1869, while settlers were holed up at Kanab and Berryville, Jacob Hamblin wrote that Navajo raiders stole 1,200 to 1,500 head of livestock from upper Long Valley alone.[86] In 1870, raiders absconded with another 2,500 head of livestock.[87]

The construction on Fort Kanab formally began in the winter of 1865–66. The town that took shape around the fort took its name from the Paiute term for the location meaning "place of willows."[88] Given that building a fort was the first order of business, the first Kanab residents can be assumed to have arrived at that time. The early families included the Judds, Johnsons, Hamblins, Mangums, Meeks, Stewarts, and Chamberlains. Indeed, the outbreak of hostilities with some of the area's Indigenous Americans earlier in 1865 made starting a new, unprotected settlement on the frontier extremely risky. This task was apparently undertaken by militiamen sent by church leaders in St. George to protect the eastern flank and by families sent on missions specifically to bolster the frontier defenses. Militiaman George Theobald indicates that the "posse" sent to apprehend the Indigenous Americans who had killed Whitmore and McIntyre in January 1866 continued on to Kanab and "stayed all winter. They built a fort and moved families in from out in dangerous places."[89] Among the early militiamen sent to build Fort Kanab was Charles Lowell Walker, the poet laureate of the Cotton Mission.

The construction occurred over several months in the winter and spring of 1865–66 before Brigham Young ordered the fort abandoned in response to increased attacks on outlying settlements during the Black Hawk War. Residents there retreated to a fort at Berryville, and in June of that year, Berryville was also ordered abandoned. The earliest Kane County residents then returned to their homes in Washington County. It should be noted that building forts seems to have been the primary purpose for these first arrivals, not specifically a call to permanently settle in Kanab or initiate ranches in the area. The builders of Fort Kanab all had homes and families in the St. George area, although some would later return at the end of hostilities (see Chapter 3). Kanab would not be reoccupied until 1869 when construction on the fort was resumed and a site for a town was planned and plotted. The names of the earliest Kanab "guards" are listed in Table 2.2.

Much more so than Kanab, the arrival of settlers in 1864 in what would become Panguitch appears to have been more motivated by desires for permanent settlement than actual construction of frontier defenses, at least initially. Fifty-four families from Beaver and Parowan arrived in March 1864 and immediately set out to fence fields, construct brush shanties and cellars, and build a log meetinghouse. The outbreak of the Black Hawk War in 1865 prompted the construction of a fort comprised of adjacent log houses with the doors and windows faced inward, all surrounding a five-acre enclosure. A guardhouse occupied the center, "and sentries watched over the safety of the community and its stock at night. A stockade made of closely set posts provided night protection for the animals and formed the fort's northwest corner."[90]

The Panguitch settlers found themselves surrounded on all sides by various bands of Southern Paiutes and Utes who already claimed this area as traditional hunting, fishing, and gathering territories. A town militia was organized in 1865, and the following year a second fort, Fort Sanford, was constructed at Lowder Spring 7 mi north of Panguitch, also with a 5-acre enclosure "with good grass so livestock could be protected."[91] Continued hostilities prompted Brigham Young to order Panguitch to be abandoned in May 1866. A few families retreated to Fort Sanford, but it also was abandoned a short time later. Most of those original settlers never returned.[92]

Beyond the fact the Panguitch settlers were moving onto lands important to Paiute survival, the frontier conditions took their toll on early settlers. In spring 1865 Alfred Whatcott and his wife Isabella, English converts to the Mormon Church brought herds of sheep and cattle to the Sevier Valley from their home in Parowan. They found trouble in the Sevier River swollen with snowmelt. Records show that while trying to cross a "herd of cattle," Alfred was swept away. Three weeks later after the river had dropped, his body was found on its banks. Isabella gave birth to her fourth child a few months later and named him after her dead husband Alfred.[93]

Scarcely mentioned in the Mormon histories of the region was that the neighbors of these first Panguitch settlers were Paiutes living around Panguitch Lake. For centuries if not millennia, the economy of the Panguitch Paiute had

TABLE 2.2. Names of Earliest Kane County Residents Prior to Regional Abandonment in 1866.

Earliest Kanab Residents	Year Arrived	Settled	Long Valley Residents	Year Arrived	Settled
William B. Maxwell	1862	Short Creek	John Berry	1862	Glendale
James Whitmore	1863	Pipe Spring	William Berry	1862	Glendale
Robert McIntyre	1863	Pipe Spring	Dena Hales Berry	1864	Glendale
Ezra Strong	1863	Kanab Creek (?)	Priddy Meeks	1862	Mount Carmel
George Staples	before 1865	Kanab	Joseph Berry	1864	Glendale
Henry Clark	before 1865	Kanab	Robert Berry	1864	Glendale
Levi Savage	before 1865	Kanab	Isabelle Hales Berry	1864	Glendale
Joseph Smith	before 1865	Kanab	Sarah Meeks	1864	Mount Carmel
George Petty	before 1865	Kanab	Mary Jane Meeks	1864	Mount Carmel
Amos Davis	before 1865	Kanab	Reuben Carter	1864	Mount Carmel
Hyrum Strong	before 1865	Kanab	H.B. Jolley	1865	Mount Carmel
Orin Clark	before 1865	Kanab	Silas Hoyt	1865	Mount Carmel
Charles Penny	before 1865	Kanab	Henry Gardner	1865	Mount Carmel
Joseph Macfate	before 1865	Kanab	William Jolley	1865	Mount Carmel
Thomas Adair	before 1865	Kanab	Louisa Stevens`	1865	Mount Carmel
Charles Partridge	before 1865	Kanab	Lorenzo Roundy	1865	Alton
James Powell	before 1865	Kanab	Susanna Wallace Roundy	1865	Alton
Widow Stokes	before 1865	Kanab	Jared C. Roundy	1865	Alton
Will Stokes	before 1865	Kanab	Myron Roundy	1865	Alton
Henry Stokes	before 1865	Kanab	Charles Partridge	1865	Alton
Byron Roundy	before 1865	Kanab	William Ford	1865	Alton
John D. Parker	1865	Kanab	Walter Smith	1865	Alton
Malinda Parker	1865	Kanab	William Smith	1865	Alton

Families Sent to Bolster Defenses	Year Arrived	
Joseph Hopkins	1865	unknown
Ann Hopkins	1865	unknown
Moses Harris	1865	unknown
John Harris	1865	unknown
James Maxwell	1865	unknown
George Spencer	1865	unknown
Hosea Stout	1865	unknown
Moses Farnsworth	1865	Kanab
Edward Pugh	1865	Kanab
John Rider	1865	Kanab
Allen Frost	1865	Kanab
George Mace	1865	Kanab
James Lewis	1865	Kanab
Louis Cram	1865	Kanab
Reuben Broadbent	1865	Kanab
John Standford	1865	Kanab

Paria River Residents	Year Arrived	Settled
Peter Shirts	1865	

Militiamen at Fort Kanab	Year Arrived	Settled
George Theobald	1866	
Charles Lowell Walker	1866	
Samuel Whittier	1866	
Warren Wilford Hardy	1866	
George Washington Ross	1866	
John Wesley Mangum	1866	
James Randle Wilkins	1866	
Willard G. McMullen (?)	1866	
Ammon Tenney	1866	
Clayburn Elder	1866	
William F. Pratt	1866	
William Wright	1866	

Note: Names derived from histories by Bradley (1999), Robinson (1970), and others. Name spellings were derived from U.S. Census and historical records and may not be consistent with family spellings used today. At that time, it was common for individuals to have multiple different spellings of their names.

revolved around fishing and collecting plants that flourished around the lake. The Paiutes were comparably friendly to the Mormons, but during the hostilities of the 1860s they and the Mormons were distrustful of one another. According to an account by Captain John Lowder, a detachment of thirteen or fourteen militiamen was dispatched from Fort Sanford to arrest all of the Paiutes camped above Panguitch and imprison them at Fort Panguitch until further orders even though there was no indication the Paiutes had done anything to warrant the eviction. At least one Paiute was killed in the ensuing scuffle; the arrested Paiutes were eventually released without charges or apologies.[94]

The abandonment of forts across the region offers some insight into Mormon populations at the time. Brigham Young's order specified that southern Utah residents were to gather together into groups of at least 150 men to protect families and livestock.[95] The fact that all of the forts were abandoned suggests the minimum threshold could not be met in either the Kanab or Panguitch areas. Our review of the names mentioned in the various histories suggests only about sixty adult men lived in the Kanab and Long Valley areas and perhaps only slightly more in the Panguitch area. In all, we estimate in 1866 fewer than three hundred men, women, and children were living in what is today Kane County and Garfield County.

As previously discussed, optimal locations in western Garfield County, western Kane County, and the northern Arizona Strip began to be occupied by small clusters of ranchers as early as 1862, and some of these livestock men brought their wives and children into the wilderness despite the dangers. With the exception of Panguitch, these were not communities in the traditional Mormon sense, but rather families clustered together for mutual defense. By 1865, a scattering of families lived in Long Valley, along the Paria River, and at Pipe Spring, Moccasin, Short Creek, and Kanab, but most of them were here for less than two years before the region was abandoned. The fifty-four families residing in Panguitch certainly constituted the largest community anywhere in the region.

For many, the decision to leave the frontier country would have been relatively easy. Even by arid Utah standards, the second- and third-generation Mormon settlers who made their way to the Grand Staircase and Escalante region found the environment daunting. Lowell J. Mecham, who was born in 1935 and lived most of his life in Tropic, relates a family story about his ancestors.

FIGURE 2.10. Water is scarce in this arid region, but where there is water there is life. This small stream originates on Canaan Mountain and feeds into Short Creek at the base of the Vermilion Cliffs. Photograph by Jerry D. Spangler.

> My great grandfather came here from Northern Utah and it was told he stopped his wagon, down probably just before Cannonville, and he took his lines and tied them and looked it over and wept, "What have I done coming to a place like this?"[96]

Mecham's great grandfather ended up staying and raising ten kids. His family adapted, as well. Lowell relates: "my grandfather started herding sheep in what we call the Lower Country, which would be the Rock Springs, Paria Creek area."[97] For families like the Mechams, sheep proved the most profitable way to make ends meet in the canyon country.

The "Indian Cowboys"

Jacob Hamblin was not the first to bring his family to Kane County, but he was certainly the most famous, having garnered considerable regional acclaim as a missionary to and peacemaker with Indigenous groups in Utah, Arizona, and Nevada. Hamblin had a fine stone house in the thriving community of Santa Clara and a summer ranch at Mountain Meadows, where he employed local Paiutes to tend his herds. In 1867, he decided to go into the mercantile business in St. George, putting up his large cattle herds as collateral. He was not much of a businessman, and when the business failed, he found himself almost penniless with a large family to feed. He informed his household they were moving to Kanab some 75 mi away on the edge of the Mormon frontier and in the middle of ongoing hostilities with Indigenous Americans. In his mind, as Hamblin biographer Hartt

Wixom concludes, "he was probably the only man who could resolve the mounting Indian problems in the Kanab region," and it would place him that much closer to his missionary work among the Indigenous Americans east of the Colorado River.[98]

Jacob Hamblin arrived in Kanab in early September 1869. Bradley states that John Mangum, George Ross, and James Wilkins moved their families to Kanab at the same time,[99] but it is not known whether they arrived in Kanab as a group. Another who probably arrived with them was Thales Haskell, Hamblin's closest and most loyal friend. He was also a veteran of more than a decade of living among and preaching to Indigenous Americans on Hamblin's many missionary expeditions.[100]

Hamblin might have thought his prestige among Mormons—he was known by the honorific title as Apostle to the Lamanites[101]—would allow some preference in where his family would live. But, as was the Mormon custom, building lots in Kanab were assigned by drawing of lots. According to Wixom's account, Hamblin returned from one of his many expeditions to find his portion of the farm fields had "the poorest soil of all." But he was not at home that much to tend to his fields. History notes that he was frequently elsewhere, establishing a farm at Pahreah and a ranch in House Rock Valley,[102] on missionary expeditions east of the Colorado River, and making trips to resolve the grievances of local Kaibab Paiutes.

As his practice had been previously, Hamblin probably employed local Paiutes to tend his farms and herds. He shared a sense of cultural superiority with other Anglo-Americans, believing Indigenous people had no future pursuing traditional hunting and gathering ways. He was an ardent believer in Brigham Young's mandate, sent to Hamblin in a letter dated March 5, 1858.

> The Indians should be encouraged in keeping and taking care of stock. I highly prove of your designs in doing your farming through the [N]atives; it teaches them to obtain a subsistence by their own industry, and leaves you more a liberty to visit others, and extend your missionary labors among them. A few missionaries to show and instruct them how to raise stock and grain, and then not eat it up for them, is most judicious.[103]

In Santa Clara and at Mountain Meadows, Hamblin also employed local Paiutes as herdsmen and domestic help.[104] And Hamblin maintained an open-door policy with them, often inviting them to dine with the Hamblin family. In all likelihood, Hamblin applied the same tactics after he moved to Kanab in 1869, where Kaibab Paiutes were well aware of his reputation for honesty and fairness. In December 1869, he was working shoulder-to-shoulder with local Paiutes to establish a farm at Pahreah to "help the Indians become self-sufficient."[105] By one account, 350 Indigenous Americans, presumably Kaibab Paiutes, were living alongside the settlers, "some planting and tending crops, helping guard the settlement, and clearing land." The Paiutes were paid in "church rations" distributed by John Mangum.[106] Some of the first cowboys in Kane County probably were Kaibab Paiutes.

Despite Hamblin's high hopes for Indigenous assimilation and Lamanite redemption (Lamanite was a contemporary term for Indigenous peoples from the Book of Mormon), white settlers came for "free" and open lands. Paiutes who lived at Kanab and other settlements were tolerated mainly because they were a source of cheap labor, often working on farms and ranches simply for a meal, a piece of clothing, or a basic manufactured item. Hamblin admitted to his people's role in their sad fate. Writing to John Wesley Powell in 1880, he noted: "The watering places are all occupide [*sic*] by the white man. The grass that product mutch [*sic*] seed is all et [*sic*] out. The sunflower seed is all distroyed [*sic*] in fact that thare [*sic*] is nothing for them to depend upon but to beg or starve."[107]

"Indian Wars": 1865–70

The threat of attacks was on everyone's mind in the mid- to late 1860s. Robinson wrote, "the Indians made raids at every dark of the moon and in every raid they succeeded in stealing cattle, horses and sheep. It seemed that they were so stealthy that the men were unable to capture them."[108] On March 1, 1866, Fort Kanab was ordered abandoned and the residents retreated to Berryville. And in June that same year, the settlers were ordered to "return to their homes" in Washington County. This latter statement suggests that the first occupants of Long Valley and Kanab were on temporary assignment to Kane County—probably a mission from church leaders to protect the larger settlements in southwestern Utah, collectively referred to as "Dixie." They left their fields in the care of friendly Paiutes, who apparently had become quite skilled in agriculture, later producing a harvest large enough that it took "several trips to haul all the produce to Dixie."[109]

Robinson's colorful description that Indigenous assailants came "every dark of moon" is likely an exaggeration, at least as far as the Navajos were concerned. The Navajos raided Mormon country from east of the Colorado River, crossing the river at Ute Ford, also known as Crossing of the Fathers near the location of modern-day Page, Arizona.[110] They returned with their booty the same way. The Colorado River at that time was only crossable late in the year. Jacob Hamblin knew this and always scheduled his missionary travels to the Hopis to coincide with low waters on the Colorado River. By late spring when the mountain snows began to melt, the river became a raging torrent. Any threat of Navajo raiders would therefore have been limited only to the late fall, winter, and early spring. Even if raiders succeeded in crossing the river at other times of the year, it would have been nearly impossible to get hundreds of head of cattle, sheep, and horses across the river. Jacob Hamblin hinted at the seasonality of the raids when he wrote, "I slept out many cold nights in the winter of 1869—70, watching and guarding with the Paiutes."[111]

FIGURE 2.11. This community on the banks of the Paria River started as a defensive "station" called Pahreah with Priddy Meeks as its president. Attempts to rename it Fort Meeks never caught on, and the ghost town is still known as Pahreah to this day. Photograph by Dan Bauer.

Much has been written about the conflicts between 1865 and 1870 collectively known as the Black Hawk War. Many accounts focus on the murders of Dr. James Whitmore and Robert McIntyre at Pipe Spring in January 1866, as well as the slaying of brothers Joseph and Robert Berry, and the latter's wife, Isabelle, in June 1866, also by Indigenous raiders. Gottfredson's biased catalog of Utah "Indian depredations" alleges that Isabelle was tied naked to a wagon wheel, raped, mutilated, and then killed, acts that would have outraged the sensibilities of Mormons everywhere and, in their own minds, justified their ethnic hatred.[112]

Much less has been written about Mormon atrocities against Indigenous Americans, including the murder of two "papooses" by Mormon militiamen and the shootings of peaceful Paiute allies (in their frenzy for retribution it appears some in the militia assumed all their Indigenous neighbors were hostile).[113] Gottfredson makes repeated and unapologetic references to the killing of Indigenous women and children, often with callous humor that mirrored the racism of the times.[114] George Theobald, a member of the militia sent to track down those who had killed Whitmore and McIntyre, revealed late in his life that the eight Paiutes initially thought to be responsible had all been captured, disarmed, and lined up, and that all were shot in the back when they tried to run. He wrote: "And shoot we did, shot till they were all still in their tracks. They fell head long and they lay there yet for all I know."[115] Historians agree these slain Paiutes were not the perpetrators of the killings at Pipe Spring.

The greatest atrocity of the entire Black Hawk War occurred in 1866 at Circleville just north of Panguitch. As spring arrived, Latter-day Saint settlers were on high guard, having lost much stock to raiding Utes and their allies. On April 21 of that year, news reached the townspeople that two Paiutes had shot a Mormon militiaman based in nearby Fort Sanford. A Paiute band living near Circleville had been generally on friendly relations with the townspeople. However, rumors swirled that "hostiles" had infiltrated the camp. After hearing the news of the wounded militiaman, Mormon Bishop William J. Allred ordered all members of the nearby Paiute band taken into custody. About thirty were rounded up, disarmed, and taken into the Circleville meetinghouse where they were bound by ropes. The Paiute men managed to loosen their makeshift handcuffs and attempted to escape but were cut down by bullets. Fearing retaliation by nearby hostile bands, local church leaders ordered the surviving Paiutes executed. Indigenous women and children were systematically led away and their throats were slit. The tragedy was largely swept aside. It took decades of soul-searching by local white residents, but eventually in 2016 a granite monument was erected in Circleville detailing the massacre.[116]

The Black Hawk War engulfed much of Utah from 1865 to 1872, and the military response directly impacted stock farmers in the Grand Staircase. First, continuing for several years after Ute Chief Black Hawk ceased his hostilities, the Navajo raids on Mormon settlements were primarily economic in nature in that the intent of the raiders was to appropriate Mormon livestock, something they did with remarkable success. Some Paiutes were also hostile to the Mormons (histories include repeated references to a feared Paiute named Patnish). But these Paiutes resided in the deep canyons and mesas of the southern Arizona Strip, and they had no escape across the Colorado River, making them more vulnerable to retribution from the Mormon militiamen and their friendly Paiute guides. Virtually every corner of the Arizona Strip as far east as Glen Canyon would have become known to the Mormon militiamen during these campaigns.

A second important consequence of this conflict was the Mormon response to the raids. On at least three occasions, Mormon militias were dispatched to chase down "hostiles." Intent on capturing or killing the famed Ute war chief Black Hawk, the first of these forays was in 1866 when Adjutant General Franklin B. Woolley and Captain James Andrus led an expedition east from St. George to Kanab, then north to the upper Paria River country, and east again to a point where they looked down on the Green River (probably near where modern-day Interstate 70 crosses the Green River).[117]

In February and March of 1869, the Utah Territorial Militia of the Iron County Military District (Cedar City), with Franklin's 24-year-old brother Edwin Gordon Woolley now as adjutant general and J. D. L. Pearce as commander, were dispatched to put an end to the Navajo raiding parties. Also led by Edwin G. Woolley, as well as Captain James Andrus, and guided by Jacob Hamblin, a second expedition was dispatched in November. Woolley's official reports of these two expeditions recount forays into largely unexplored regions of the upper Paria River and the Escalante River area in what would become Garfield County, as well as Fremont River country farther north, which would become Wayne County. In the process, they discovered as-yet unsettled areas that were ideal for ranching and farming.[118] After Jacob Hamblin's negotiated peace with the Navajos in 1870, the militiamen returned home to Iron and Washington Counties with tales of pristine valleys ripe for settlement. In the years that followed, the Mormon frontier would be expanded farther and farther to the east, and new communities were established with names like Cannonville and Escalante and Torrey (see Chapter 3).

Summary

As noted by Bradley, the initial settlement of western Kane County, perhaps as early as 1858 but certainly by 1864, was "driven by three motives: the extension of the Mormon empire into the Arizona Strip area, the need to obtain grazing land for the ranchers of Washington County, and the hoped-for conversion of Native Americans to the Mormon Church."[119] By 1864, a fourth priority had emerged: the establishment of a defensive barrier against hostile Indigenous Americans intent on raiding Mormon livestock on the Arizona Strip and Long Valley, which by that time numbered in the thousands. The current historical

FIGURE 2.12. Franklin B. Woolley was a commander of the 1866 campaign in southern Utah and might have been among the first to explore Wayne County. He was later killed by Indigenous assailants in the Mojave Desert of California in 1869 while returning to Utah. Photograph courtesy of Utah State Historical Society Classified Photo Collection (39222001421218).

FIGURE 2.13. Edwin G. Woolley, a commander of Mormon militia in Cedar City, led two campaigns to track down Chief Black Hawk that resulted in the Mormons' discovery of the Escalante Valley. Photograph courtesy of Utah State Historical Society Classified Collection (39222001421200).

record does not state whether these large herds represented aggregated livestock belonging to families living in more populous Iron County and Washington County, or whether they represented herds belonging to and brought by the first "missionaries" sent to the area, who constructed stations and forts up and down Long Valley and at Kanab, Pahreah, Panguitch, Pipe Spring, and perhaps as far east as Wahweap.

Population pressure was certainly a contributing factor as tens of thousands of Mormon converts arrived in Utah, many to be dispatched on missions to settle the frontier. Brigham Young sent settlers here on specialized missions aimed at Mormon self-sufficiency (mainly iron and cotton production) and as buffers against outside invasion. Many of these converts were sent to southwestern Utah where limited natural resources would have significantly curtailed settlement in the traditional Mormon agrarian model. And more immigrants arrived every year. In 1860, the combined population of Iron and Washington County was 3,755 souls, and by 1870 it had swelled to 5,341—a 42 percent increase.

Livestock grazing was, to a greater or lesser degree, a driving impetus behind all motivations to settle Kane County (it appears to have been less a factor in the initial settlement of Panguitch). Even with the missionary efforts among the Kaibab Paiutes, a primary focus was teaching them Mormon-style farming and animal husbandry, and in fact some Paiutes worked at these tasks alongside the new Mormon arrivals.

Traditional agriculture was greatly limited by the narrow floodplains, but grazing seemed to have unlimited potential—a virtual "sea of grass" extending 60–70 mi along the northern Arizona Strip and up Long Valley and into the upper Sevier River country. These open ranges, at that time, provided plenty of fodder for the large herds of cattle, sheep, and horses, all of which constituted currency in the barter economy of frontier Utah. Competition over rangelands was probably minimal given the seemingly limitless supply of free grass that can and did accommodate several thousand head of livestock.

Such large herds in a sparsely populated and poorly defended area proved to be an enticing target for Navajo raiders, who would cross the Colorado River in the late fall, winter, and early spring, and return with stolen Mormon livestock, sometimes more than a thousand head at the time. Ammon Tenney, a missionary who was fluent in many Indigenous languages, estimated the raiders had absconded with a million dollars worth of livestock in a single year,[120] an astronomical amount that suggests Mormon herds in southern Utah actually numbered in the tens of thousands, although these numbers are not supported by U.S. Census records.[121]

The Black Hawk War of the late 1860s that enveloped Mormon settlements across the Territory is appropriately discussed by historians within the context of Mormon encroachment on Indigenous lands. And Mormon livestock practices were at the very root of the bloody conflict. Livestock not only destroyed native plants and fouled water sources, these foreign beasts symbolized the loss of Indigenous American lifeways. Mormon livestock, especially cattle, represented an irresistible food supply to the starving and dispossessed to be justifiably expropriated. Surviving Latter-day Saint accounts reveal that Indigenous peoples felt they were owed a few cows and horses as a price for Mormon usurpation of their lands. Mormon settlers rarely died in the conflict (references account only six deaths at the hands of Indigenous Americans in all of southern Utah between 1866 and 1869), but the myriad newspaper dispatches and journal accounts of the times harp on the vast numbers of livestock lost to Indigenous raiders and the deadly retaliations that ensued. Hundreds if not thousands of Utes, Shoshones, and Paiutes—men, women, children, even babies in their cradleboards—died at the hands of the Mormon militiamen.

For all practical purposes, the end of the Black Hawk War eliminated any perceivable deterrence to the expansion of the regional livestock industry into every conceivable corner of the Utah Territory. But this expansion would bring its own unique problems and challenges. As detailed in the next chapter, elsewhere in Utah and in other areas of the West, the aggregation of large cattle herds led to the emergence of widespread cattle rustling, often by ruffians based at impenetrable enclaves like Robbers Roost and at times by otherwise honest ranchers known to alter a brand here and there. Historian Charles Kelly makes a case that "almost every small rancher in southern Utah was a rustler on the side,"[122] although this practice might not have been as widespread in the 1860s as it would become during the economic depressions of the 1880s and 1890s. Wixom makes the only mention of outlaws during the earliest settlement, stating that Jacob Hamblin worked at Pahreah Station with a rifle strapped to his back, "for there were outlaws about in such country with no established law enforcement in place."[123]

If outlaws were about, they would have been easily identifiable. All of the earliest settlers here were faithful Mormons answering the call of church leaders to protect the frontier. Their mission shared a commonality of purpose, along with a willingness to endure Indigenous attacks, scarlet fever, bone-numbing winters, starvation, and many other tribulations. Most of those first settlers never returned to Kane and Garfield Counties after church leaders ordered settlers to abandon the region in spring 1866, but some did. They provided the foundation for permanent communities that would be bolstered by the arrival of new immigrants.

Colonization of the Hinterlands 1870–1890

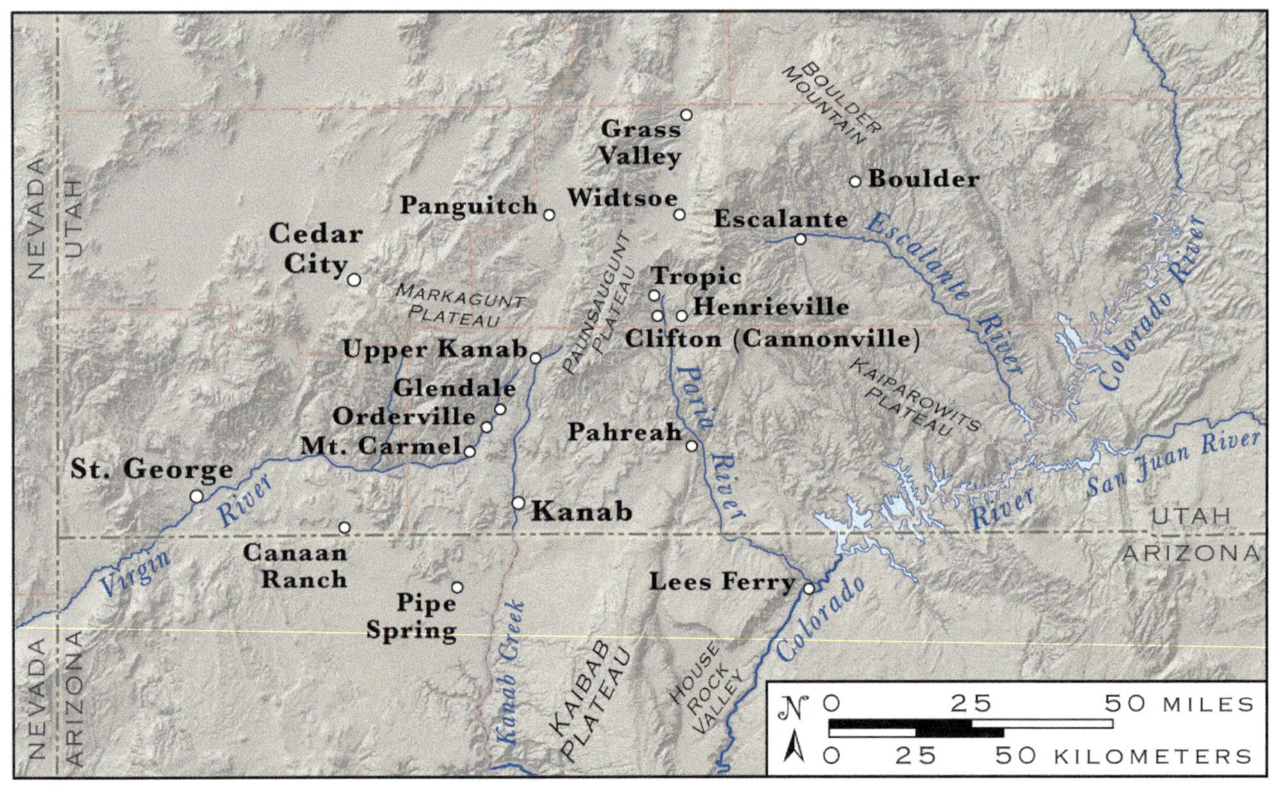

Figure 3.1. Communities established or expanded upon during the Mormon expansion era of 1870 to 1890.

3 One for All

Cooperatives and Communalism, 1870–1890

The last decades of the nineteenth century witnessed the birth of the modern cattle and sheep industries in southern Utah and northern Arizona, although they evolved out of very different Mormon precursors. Animal husbandry as a pioneer industry was predominantly focused on meeting the needs of individual communities, each operating under a mandate from Mormon Church leaders to become self-sufficient: sheep for wool, dairy cows for milk and cheese, chickens for eggs, horses for transportation, oxen and mules to pull plows. By and large, the settlers in this region came as tillers of the soil first and foremost, although the vast majority kept livestock for their immediate family needs. As previously detailed, most of the earliest settlers lived in organized communities, first in places like Parowan, Cedar City, Santa Clara, and St. George, and later in Kanab and Panguitch. A few exceptions included lonely outposts on the Paria River, Pipe Spring, Roundy Station, and Short Creek, but the existence of isolated ranches was anathema to the Mormon settlement ideal.

Mormons rarely ate beef, and southern Utah communities at this time simply had little or no local demand for beef cattle. In contrast, the mining towns of California and Nevada had a huge demand for red meat. As previously discussed, James Maxwell's cattle ranch on Short Creek probably provided the stock to fulfill his beef contract to the mining town of Pioche, Nevada. Cash-strapped Utah farmers soon discovered that beef cattle were a ready and renewable form of currency. They could be sold or traded for material items not readily available on the frontier, everything from needles and thread to household furnishings, china, and musical instruments. As early historian Julius S. Dalley observed, "The main business in the country was cattle and sheep, and practically every man owned one or the other or both in smaller or greater quantities."[1]

A series of events beginning in 1870 would radically change the traditional Mormon settlement model that had dominated community organization in southern Utah for the previous two decades. These developments prompted a rapid shift in the economies of Kane and Garfield counties away from cultivation of traditional food staples like wheat and oats to one focused predominantly on livestock, with beef cattle assuming even greater importance through time. As with the earlier Mormon village model, the changes were sanctioned and encouraged by church leaders in Salt Lake City, and the Mormon Church itself got into the cattle business in a major way. These changes also reflected a growing awareness among church leaders that southern Utah was simply too arid and arable lands were too limited to accommodate new generations of traditional farmers.

After 1870, at least four developments ensured that a livestock economy would predominate in the Grand Staircase, Escalante Canyons, and Arizona Strip country. First, in 1870 Brigham Young personally visited Kanab and dedicated the nascent community to "the work of the Lord." And he also took notice of the abundant rangelands that could accommodate large herds, the largest of which already belonged to the Mormon Church itself, acquired through tithe payments by church members. If the Mormon Church did not act first and decisively, these rich grasslands would inevitably be overrun by Gentile cattlemen unsympathetic to Mormon values. Second, in the early 1870s the federal government launched a series of law enforcement and punitive economic campaigns against the Mormon Church, as well as individual members, over the practice of polygamy.[2] While these campaigns began in the 1870s, they continued with on-again, off-again aggressiveness through the 1880s. A fundamental strategy of federal officials was to strangle the Mormon Church economically through confiscation of church property and the imprisonment of its leaders, who were also key business leaders in the Utah Territory. To protect their southern Utah livestock herds and thereby ensure cash flow, church herds were assigned to cooperatives operated by carefully selected and loyal, non-polygamous surrogates who were immune from federal prosecution.

A third development related to the nascent livestock industry was a religious movement in the mid-1870s called the United Order that was aggressively promoted by church leaders. It took hold strongly in the impoverished southern Utah settlements. Mormon families rededicated themselves to living divine principles, including one that mandated communal ownership of property. Within the structure of United Orders, individuals no longer owned and cared for their own livestock; livestock was now possessed and managed collectively, resulting in aggregated herds, some of tremendous size. At least four large United Order herds ranged throughout Kane and Garfield Counties and the Arizona Strip. This effort was short-lived, however.

Finally, a second generation of Mormon young men and women were coming of age by 1870, and in keeping with their agrarian values, they were in need of their own farms. Because of the arid nature of the country and its limited arable land in the valley bottoms, farm lands in and around Kanab, Long Valley, and Panguitch were extremely scarce, leaving no option other than to migrate somewhere else where land was available. Many of the young men were veterans of the Black Hawk War and had ridden deep into the previously unexplored southern Utah wilderness where they discovered new areas ripe for settlement. Along with their family members and friends, they would become the first settlers of eastern Garfield County, and statewide they would become the vanguard of the last great colonization of the Utah hinterlands. A few, most famously Robert "Bob" LeRoy Parker, better known as Butch Cassidy, left behind their religious upbringings in favor of an outlaw life.[3]

Cowboys in Context

The term "cowboy" became widely used by the early 1900s to describe men (and some women) who worked cattle. However, in the latter half of the nineteenth century when the first Mormon settlers came to Kane and Garfield Counties, the designation was merely "herdsman" or "stock man." The word "cowboy" actually had a derogatory connotation well into the 1890s. Its origins were in Great Britain as early as the 1820s, where its meaning understandably applied to young boys tending the cows owned by a family or community. In the New World, during the American Revolutionary Era, settlers used the word to denigrate young men who stole cattle from the Tory loyalists. And in the Deep South, "cowboy" was applied to slave laborers who cared for plantation herds. Even as late as 1881, then-President Chester A. Arthur spoke derisively of a band of desperadoes as "cowboys."

The term gradually evolved and became part of the American lexicon in the mid-1880s through dime-store novels that popularized the herdsmen-turned-cowboys as tougher-than-nails, working-class heroes. A cowboy was also called buckaroo, cowpoke, cowpuncher, wrangler, cowhand, leather pounder, saddle stiff, saddle bum, and waddy, among other names. The word origins for most of the cowboy's equipment—chaps, lariats, spurs—are derived from Spanish words for the same items that originated with the emergence of animal husbandry in Mexico, where cowboys are called *vaqueros*.[4]

The birth of a livestock industry in Utah was vastly different than what occurred simultaneously across the Great Plains from Texas to Montana. Charles Peterson makes the argument that there were no large ranches in the traditional sense anywhere in Utah in 1870. As previously detailed, faithful Mormons lived in villages, tended small farms on the outskirts of the village, and pooled their individual livestock—mostly sheep and dairy cows—into a community herd. Initially, each community maintained a cooperative corral used by all. As the human and livestock populations increased, the herds were pushed toward outlying rangelands. Most of these town herds were small, although there were exceptions.[5] As the size of the herds increased between 1870 and 1890, the price per animal dropped, from $25 a head in the 1850s and 1860s, to $10 a head in the 1870s and 1880s.[6]

Mormon herds served as the seedbed for the regional livestock economy. As Peterson observed:

> In the years after 1875, Indian and geographic barriers collapsed and livestock literally streamed from the crowded Great Basin settlements. In effect, the Great Basin played the same role in stocking the Colorado Plateau parts of Utah that Texas did in stocking the ranges of Wyoming and Montana.

The typical Mormon herd was tended by teenage boys, some of whom would be gone for two or three years moving cattle between summer and winter ranges before returning to their homes.[7] The boys came to relish the freedom and independence: plenty of time for fishing and hunting, no haircuts, no farm chores, no nagging from parents, and no attending church. Some returned with bad habits, such as smoking and a fondness for liquor, something that did not sit well with their pious mothers.[8]

The real life of a hard-drinking, hard-partying cowboy would not have been as foreign to early Mormon ranchers as one would suspect. When settlers established the first livestock operations, alcohol consumption was not forbidden, although drunkenness was a serious offense in local Latter-day Saint communities. George W. Adair was one of the earliest settlers of Kanab, a guide and wrangler for John Wesley Powell's famous geological surveys of southern Utah and northern Arizona, and a purported participant in the Mountain Meadows Massacre. He also had a fondness for "Dixie wine" that landed him before a local judge after a drunken celebration turned into a fight. Powell Expedition participant Stephen Vandiver Jones observed that Adair must have gotten the worst of it, that Adair "came in near night, looking considerably the worse for rough usage."[9] Adair dutifully stayed around for his trial, but was back working for the Powell Expedition by the following day.

Adair was riding with the Powell Expedition in May 1872 in the unexplored country below the Pink Cliffs of Bryce Canyon when the scouting party happened on Swallow Lake in upper Park Wash. Adair was so enamored with the area that he vowed to return to live there. He went so far as to write his intentions to claim the entire valley and post the notice next to a spring. His compatriots on the expedition called it Adair Valley.[10] It is now on the northern fringe of Grand Staircase-Escalante National Monument.

Given that Mormon proscriptions against alcohol were largely advisory, community celebrations or "jubilees" were often raucous affairs. Mormons of southern Utah commonly made their own beers and wines, and a few were blessed with the skill to turn corn into hard liquor. In 1865, to celebrate the one-year anniversary of the settlers' arrival in Panguitch, the bishop contributed forty gallons of beer to the festivities.[11] Cowboys were especially fond of hard spirits. Even some of today's cowboys in this area, faithful Mormons on Sundays, make sure that ample supplies of whiskey are packed away for their long sojourns into the wilderness, as their fathers and grandfathers had taught them.[12] Coffee, now prohibited by the Mormon Church, also was a basic staple in most southern Utah households and cowboy camps at the time.

Two types of cowboys emerged in southern Utah. One was the professional wrangler who hired out to cattle outfits, and if and when whimsy called he would drift from place to place. They tended to be older (in their twenties), rougher around the edges, highly skilled with lariats and guns, and legendary drinkers and rabble-rousers come payday. The other were Mormon herdsmen, mostly teenaged boys. They had been immersed in village life and church values from birth, and they had been given adult responsibilities to care for the herds upon which their entire community depended. Most were learning skills they would need to tend to their own farms and raise their own families. Mormons generally looked down on professional cowboys as being contrary to their core values.[13]

Another important point to consider in the early livestock industry in Grand Staircase country was the allocation of range lands. As previously noted, in the 1860s and early 1870s, the territorial legislature had granted county courts (the equivalent of a county commission today) and their Mormon-dominated leadership the authority to determine who had rights to which rangelands, and herdsmen were licensed accordingly. This practice was repealed in 1874, but territorial lawmakers could not agree on new regulations. In effect, no legal mechanisms were in place whereby one rancher or livestock cooperative could acquire secure title to open range. This "open range" policy generated considerable debate and conflict throughout the 1880s and 1890s, particularly as large cattle operations moved into the Arizona Strip. In 1890, Utah Territorial Governor Arthur L. Thomas appealed to the Secretary of Interior to do something about the problem.

> The title being vested in Government, they are looked upon as lands which may be used by anyone. The result is that the man who today may find a place where he can feed and water his animals, may tomorrow find himself surrounded by other men with their animals, and in a short time the forage plants sufficient to maintain a limited number of animals are eaten out, or completely destroyed.[14]

Utah cattle herds thrived on these unrestricted open ranges before the range lands were degraded. By 1878, Utah had become a major exporter of cattle to other states and territories. Between 1877 and 1881, some 180,000 head of Utah cows were driven or shipped by rail to Colorado, Wyoming, the Dakotas, and Nebraska, as well as to San Francisco and Chicago.[15] Given that most of these animals belonged directly or indirectly to the Mormon Church, these sales constituted a major source of revenue. At even $10 per head, the sales would have amounted to $1.8 million, or nearly $46 million in today's money.[16] And for many in southern Utah, livestock sales were the only source of income. As local rancher Frank Hamblin observed, "All the money we had came from cattle or sheep."[17]

Cattle only had cash value if they could be sold in markets where there was adequate demand. Massive cattle drives moved livestock for sale from Utah into Wyoming and the Plains states farther east. But with the arrival in Utah of the Union Pacific Railroad, in 1869, and its competitor the Denver and Rio Grande Western Railroad, (D&RGW) in 1882, Utah interests could ship their livestock by rail to markets in San Francisco and Chicago where higher prices would be paid. By this time, Chicago had become the entrepot of the cattle trade. Business innovators such as Gustavus Franklin Swift and Philip Danforth Armour had built massive industrial meatpacking plants in Chicago, providing store-bought products that were once raised on family farms.[18]

Geographically isolated southern Utah cattlemen still had to get their herds to a railhead, the closest being about 300 mi to the north in Salt Lake City. The town of Spanish Fork, 52 mi south of Salt Lake, became a major "cow town" and railhead for southern Utah communities after the arrival of the D&RGW railroad, although it was not as colorful as Abilene, Wichita, and Dodge City. Under optimal conditions with plenty of forage and water, cattle would be driven about 15 mi per day with two long breaks for the cattle to rest and graze. At a faster pace, the animals would lose so much weight they would become difficult to sell.[19] Prior to the establishment of railheads at Modena, northwest of St. George, and at Marysvale, north of Panguitch, it would have taken about three weeks or more to trail cows from Kanab to the nearest railheads along the Wasatch Front.

Filling the Void

The shift to a predominantly ranching way of life in southern Utah is inextricably linked to settlement policies that originated in Salt Lake City. By 1870, the influx of Mormon converts, along with internal population growth (families often had ten or more children), provided the human capital to fulfill Mormon Church President Brigham Young's vision of Mormon enclaves in every nook and cranny of the Intermountain West, not only in Utah, but in Nevada, Arizona, Southern California, eastern Oregon, Idaho, and western Wyoming. In Young's vernacular, each community was a stake holding up the expansive tent of Zion. The broader reality of the 1870s was that farmlands along the Wasatch Front—Salt Lake, Utah, Davis, and Weber Counties—had already been claimed by earlier arrivals. There certainly was not enough land there to accommodate the ever-increasing livestock herds or the number of young families in search of their own farms. As the Wasatch Front became increasingly urbanized, church livestock operations were shifted first to Tooele County to the west. By the 1870s, those rangelands also had been depleted, and Brigham Young began eyeing rangelands in central and southern Utah. As noted in the previous chapter, conflicts with Indigenous Americans during the 1860s had forced the Mormon Church to retract from its remote outposts, including Kanab, Pahreah, Panguitch, and Long Valley, into larger, more defensible settlements with armed militias. But with the end of those conflicts in about 1870, Young unleashed efforts to establish footholds in every remote corner of the territory. Jacob Hamblin, as well as members of his extended family and missionary companions, returned to Kanab in fall 1869, and by the time of the 1870 U.S. Census seventy-two white people were living in and around Kanab, none of whom self-identified as livestock operators (see Table 3.1). Hundreds more immigrants would follow over the next three years.

The impetus for the resettlement of Kane County was rooted, at least in part, by the Mormon Church's desire to establish new settlements in Arizona south and east of the Colorado River in places that now bear the vnames Mesa, Snowflake, Thatcher, and St. Johns. Young initially focused on settlement of the Little Colorado River country, a landscape so harsh that Andrew Amundsen, a scout on the initial 1873 exploring expedition, wrote:

> From the first we struck the little Colorado . . . it is the seam[*sic*] thing all the way, no plase[*sic*] fit for humg[*sic*] being to dwell upon . . . The moste[*sic*] desert lukking[*sic*] plase[*sic*] that I ever saw, Amen.[20]

Thousands of Mormons from across the Utah Territory answered the call nonetheless, many from overpopulated towns along the Wasatch Front. By the 1870s, two routes took settlers to Arizona. A longer, more circuitous one trailed south to St. George, then 75 mi or so east to House Rock Valley, and eventually south to the river crossing at Lee's Ferry. This route would later become known as the Honeymoon Trail as thousands of Arizona settlers returned this way to have their marriages solemnized in the St. George Temple, completed in 1877.[21]

The second, somewhat shorter route involved traveling up the Sevier River in central Utah to the headwaters of the Paria River, next down the river bottom to the Vermilion Cliffs, and then to House Rock Valley and Lee's Ferry. The Paria River is shallow and features a flat, compacted gravel bottom with minimal obstacles to wagon travel. This way might have been perceived as more direct, but the real advantage would have been a constant water supply for the horses, oxen, and other livestock. Hundreds, if not thousands chose the Paria River route, leaving testaments of their passage on the canyon walls.[22]

The first settlers of Kanab were frontier-tested men and women, such as David King Udall and his wife Ella Stewart, a daughter of Levi Stewart, the

TABLE 3.1. Names Listed on the 1870 U.S. Census for the Kanab Precinct, Kane County.

1870 Census (Kanab Precinct)	
Levi Stewart (farmer)	
	Margery (housekeeper)
	William
	Eliza
	Charles
	Margeary
	Heber
	Edward
	Lucinda
	Levi H. (farm worker)
Delweth Beintner (farm worker)	
Moses Farnsworth	
	Elizabeth (housekeeper)
	Franklin
	Edward
	Mary
	Reuben
	Louisa
James Mangren (farmer)	
	Frances (housekeeper)
	Mary
	John W.
	Heber
	Frances
	Jane
	Amanda
John Mangum (farmer)	
	Marian (housekeeper)
	Joseph
	John
	George
	Syeve
	Abigail
	Caroline
	David
	Ellen
	Harry
William Casiday (teamster)	

1870 Census (Kanab Precinct)	
Eli Stout (teamster)	
Edward Noble (farmer)	
	Annie (housekeeper)
Allen Frost (farmer)	
	Ann (housekeeper)
	William
	Daniel
	Ann
James Burt (Blacksmith)	
	Mary (housekeeper)
	Mary
	Christian
Edward Cook (Laborer)	
	Agnes (housekeeper)
	John
James Williams (farmer)	
	Sophia (housekeeper)
	Lorinda
	James
	Adda
	Jeddeah
	Fannie
	Frederick
Jacob Hamblin (farmer)	
	Louise (housekeeper)
	Joseph
	Benjamin
	Walter
James Wilkinson (farmer)	
	Adelaide (housekeeper)
	James
	Fannie
	Ada
	Indine
	Frederick

Note: Spellings listed here are per U.S. Census (1870) and may not be consistent with traditional family spellings or those found in other historical records.

FIGURE 3.2. The Paria River features a relatively flat, gravel bottom that proved to be an ideal travel corridor in the 1870s and 1880s. This route was one of two used by Mormons bound for the Arizona missions south of the Colorado River. Photograph by Jerry D. Spangler.

first bishop of Kanab. Ella, born in Salt Lake City, had moved with her family to Kanab in 1870 at the age of fifteen, stopping for six weeks in Toquerville to learn Morse Code at Brigham Young's personal request. In 1871, she moved to Pipe Spring as a representative of the Deseret Telegraph Company, becoming the first telegraph operator in Arizona. She also operated the telegraph in Kanab. She married David King Udall in 1875, but within weeks he was called to serve a mission in England. Upon his return, the family resettled among the Udall clan in Nephi, but soon returned to Kanab to begin a livestock operation in DeMotte Park on the Arizona Strip, an area controlled by Stewart. In 1880, Udall was called to serve as bishop of the Little Colorado Ward in Arizona on

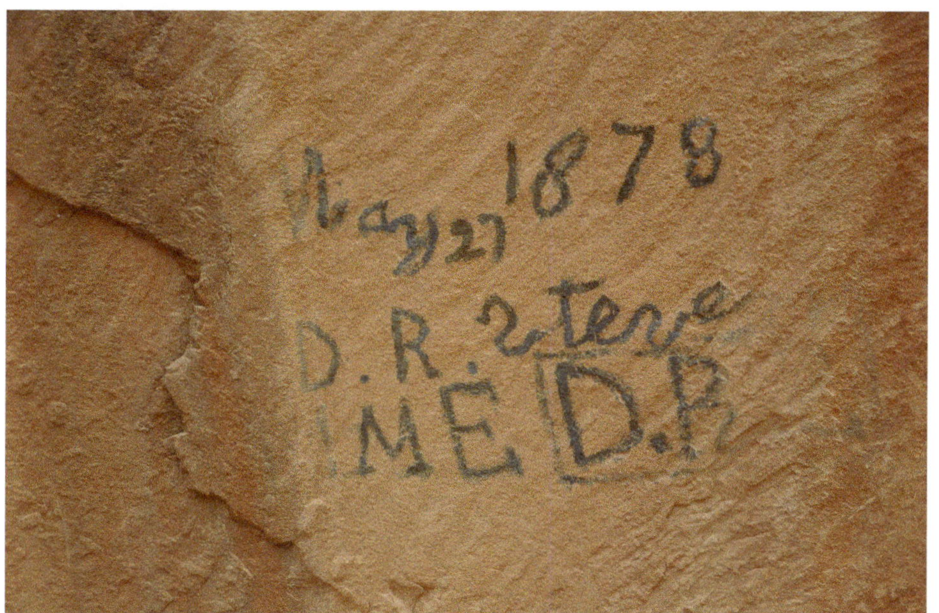

FIGURE 3.3. Arizona-bound immigrants would often leave their names scrawled in axle grease on the Paria Canyon walls. The first signatures date to the early 1870s. Photograph by Jerry D. Spangler.

the river of the same name. Among the Udalls' descendants were a Chief Justice of the Arizona Supreme Court, a Secretary of the Interior, a United States representative and presidential candidate, and two United States senators.[23]

Beginning in the early 1870s, the establishment of missions in Arizona was probably intended to diffuse population pressure in the increasingly urbanized communities in northern Utah where few, if any, opportunities remained to adhere to the Mormon agricultural model. Like their counterparts in southern Utah, these colonists were primarily ranchers.

On April 2, 1870, Brigham Young, George A. Smith, Erastus Snow, John Taylor, and other Mormon Church leaders visited Pipe Spring and then Fort Kanab, the latter occupied at that time by Jacob Hamblin and a few other families. John W. Mangum, who was present at the time, wrote that these included the families of Thales Haskell, Jehiel McConnell, Hyrum Judd, Ammon Tenney, and George Adair.[24] Levi Stewart recalled in his folksy way that Young casually asked if he wanted to "go on a tour of Southern Utah," and he said yes. The party crossed a divide into what is now Kanab where Young next asked, "if I wouldn't lead a band of Saints to colonize Kanab?"[25] Stewart said yes again, and church leaders consecrated the Kanab town site "to the work of the Lord." They recognized the area was ideal for the raising of cattle, horses, and sheep.[26]

They had come to Kanab by way of St. George and Pipe Spring, and Mormon leaders most certainly were looking south from Kanab towards the vast grasslands of the Arizona Strip when they made that recommendation; there is no indication the church leaders ventured north or east from Kanab at that time.

FIGURE 3.4. David King Udall. Photograph courtesy of The Church of Jesus Christ of Latter-day Saints (LDS) Historical Biographical Database.

The area around Fort Kanab must have seemed like an improbable oasis to President Young and his companions when they saw it for the first time in 1870. Kanab Creek watered a vast, wet meadow with a small channel that could be stepped across. Historic accounts indicate the meadow was a quarter-mile wide and extended 7 mi up canyon from where Kanab Creek leaves the Vermilion Cliffs and another 5 mi downstream. Unfamiliar with the hydrology of wetland ecosystems, the settlers set out to divert and dam the creek waters, setting the stage for disaster. A series of unusual floods between 1882 and 1885 not only destroyed the pioneers' water control measures, but also incised an arroyo 60 ft deep and 70 ft wide for a distance of 15 mi that is still visible today. The meadows never recovered.[27]

John Doyle Lee also was a Mormon frontiersman called to settle the Grand Staircase country. Lee converted to Mormonism in the East along with Levi Stewart, his childhood friend, and both would serve missions together and be called to settle southern Utah together. Young had invited Lee on August 16, 1870, to join a party set to explore the upper Sevier River country and lands to the east; for the purposes of the expedition, President Young assigned to Lee the title "Roads Commissioner."[28] After the twelve-day sojourn later that summer, Lee returned home and met with his family that included his many plural wives. As he told them:

> I shall not go into any detail about our trip, except to tell you that we must sell all our holdings here, in Kannaraville, and Washington, and move out to the headwaters on the Paria. There we will set up on a large tract of grazing land. We must lose no time if we get set up for winter.[29]

Both Stewart and Lee were charged with establishing a sawmill in the mountains north of Kanab in the area known as Skutumpah.

At the time, no one in Lee's family, including himself, knew that this move was a form of exile for his role in the Mountain Meadows Massacre of 1857. By 1870, Lee had been formally implicated in the massacre and was being hunted by U.S. marshals. Shortly before moving to the Kanab area, the Mormon Church excommunicated Lee. This excommunication might have been a preemptive move. President Young's 1870 exploring expedition—which included Lee, Jacob Hamblin, and William Dame—met up with and traveled with John Wesley Powell and his own expedition that was scouting resupply points for a second Colorado River expedition in 1871. Not only did Powell and Lee break bread together, but they discussed the Mountain Meadows Massacre.[30] Young must have known that Powell, a national celebrity at the time, would return to the East with stories of Lee operating openly on the southern Utah frontier, and with sanction from church leaders, including Young himself.[31]

The "excommunication" was merely for show, probably to placate the growing clamor in the East that Young himself had ordered the Iron County militia to destroy the wagon train of Arkansas immigrants bound for California that became known as the Mountain Meadows Massacre. In the years that followed his excommunication, Lee operated the sawmill at Skutumpah, built ranches at

FIGURE 3.5. The Colorado River crossing at Lee's Ferry was a strategic asset for the Mormon Church, controlling the movement of livestock and people into and from Arizona for more than sixty years until 1929 when the Navajo Bridge was opened. Photograph by Dan Bauer.

Jacob's Pools and House Rock Valley on the Arizona Strip, and constructed the ferry on the Colorado River that now bears the family name, all with Mormon Church sanction. He also had a fine cabin and farm in Panguitch.

One of his wives, Emma Batchelor Lee, would later famously run the ferry and adjoining ranch, including naming the outpost "Lonely Dell." She and Lee were living here in 1874, but her husband was absent when Deputy U.S. Marshal William Stokes came looking for him. Stokes followed a bunch of false leads before the trail led him to Panguitch and the home of Lee's fourth wife, Sarah Caroline Williams. Lee was found hiding in a pig pen; he was later executed for his crimes in 1877.[32]

Upon his return to Salt Lake City, Young dispatched a company of fifty-two settlers under the leadership of Stewart to settle Kane County and bolster the small group of returnees already there.[33] The 1870 U.S. Census records indicate these included the families of James Wilkinson, James Williams, Moses Farnsworth, Allen Frost, James Mangren (Mangum), Edward Cook, Edward Noble, William Thompson, and James Burt.[34] Robinson's history adds names not found in the census, including the families of John Morgan, Caleb Brinton, and John R. Rider.[35] Most of these settlers were from the Cottonwood area of southeast Salt Lake County, arriving at Fort Kanab in June 1870. A second group of about the same size, also responding to a call from Mormon Church leaders, came in April 1871, although many of these later arrivals were simply rejoining extended family already there. Others unaffiliated with Stewart's mission had arrived the previous fall (see Table 3.2).

Life in and around the fort at Kanab was very hardscrabble in the first years. A short autobiography of John Franklin Brown provides a view of those early days in the frontier outpost. His father was part of the Muddy Mission (on the Muddy River in southern Nevada), and with his two wives, he was later called to move to Kanab. Brown recalled as a youth:

> I went to the fort and was told where my father's first wife and family were. They were living in a tent we had got from Johnston's Army. At the time there were only two houses in Kanab; one was the rock house of Edward Pugh and the other was a little lumber one-room shack belonging to Abraham Windsor[*sic*], new to Kanab Fort.[36]

Eventually the town of Kanab with its fine pioneer-era homes took shape. David King Udall and Charles Shumway built rock homes. Long-time

Mormon missionary Ira Hatch built a large two-story adobe home during the 1870s. Zadok K. Judd Sr., who had served in the Mormon Battalion in the Mexican-American War, arrived with his family in the first group. They lived in a wagon box at first but later built a strong adobe house. Brick masons arrived by the 1880s, and many of the pioneer homes that survive today were built with this construction. Like in other frontier outposts, tragedy was never far from sight. In the first years of Kanab, a fire started in Stewart's makeshift quarters in the fort, and with no escape route, six of his children and one of his plural wives perished.[37]

TABLE 3.2. Male Heads of Families Associated with the Earliest Settlement of Kane County.

March/April 1871 Arrivals		
Priddy Meeks	Edward Pugh	James L. Bunting
James A. Little (?)	Francis M. Hamblin	Zadok K. Judd Sr.
William Crosby	Alma Spillsbury	Newman Brown
A.D. Young Jr.	Will Eager	Yance Anderson
Edwin Ford	Taylor Crosby	Guernsey Brown (?)
John Harris	James Leithead	Reuben Broadbent
Eli Stout	Zadok K. Judd Jr.	James William Wilson
Nathan Adams	Newman Brown Jr.	Daniel Stark
Late 1871 or Early 1872 Arrivals		
Byron D. Roundy	Andrew L. Siler	James Swapp
Gustavus Williams	Andrew Lamb	

Note: Names compiled from Kane County Histories by Bradley (1999) and Robinson (1970), as well as Works Progress Administration histories (Anderson, 1940; Dalley 1941). Spellings listed here may not be consistent with traditional family spellings or those found in other historical records.

The official records of the original Mormon settlers in the region are undoubtedly incomplete as some families were so isolated or lived in the area only seasonally that they ignored the census altogether. For example, in 1870, John D. Lee and his wife Rachel had built a ranch and sawmill at Skutumpah in the uplands northeast of Kanab, and they were joined by three brothers, Charles, Hyrum, and John Clark, who had all married Lee's daughters.[38] None of them show up on the 1870 census for the region.

Young returned to Kanab in September 1870 along with surveyor Jesse W. Fox, and the official town site was laid out and a lottery held to determine which families would get which building lots. This time, he arrived in Kanab by way of Panguitch, where he inspected the abandoned community there and its suitability for resettlement. He next went to Roundy Station in the Alton area, and then east to Johnson Canyon and south down the Paria River. He visited Peter Shirts' "fort," but was apparently unimpressed, declaring "there is nothing here desirable for us," before continuing on to Kanab.[39]

Moses Franklin Farnsworth, whose father had joined the Mormon Church in its first years, noted that in spring 1870 he was called to help settle Kanab. On September 10, 1870, the town site was surveyed. Stewart was appointed the first bishop, and he and his friend Tenney got lots near each other.[40] The surveying of a town site is important because it reflects the Mormon Church's intent to retain its model of cohesive communities rather than encourage isolated ranches closer to rangelands. As discussed later, the model would be modified to include dual residences, a winter residence in the village and a summer residence closer to rangelands.

Several families apparently defied this policy or exceptions were made by local bishops as to their residences. Byron Donalvin Roundy, his wife Matilda Ann, and a daughter moved to Upper Kanab (Alton) in the spring of 1872, reoccupying what had been previously known as Roundy Station. They lived there alone until other members of the Roundy clan began arriving the next year. That same year, Andrew LaFayette Siler, reported to have been nearly 7 ft tall, had a ranch on Kanab Creek, and Andrew Lamb started a ranch nearby. James Swapp started a ranch in Sink Valley about 3 mi south of Upper Kanab, and Gustavus Williams started a ranch on the upper Virgin River.[41]

The settlement of five brothers from St. George—George Washington Johnson, Joel Hills Johnson, Joseph Ellis Johnson, Benjamin Franklin Johnson, and William Derby Johnson—in Kane County also appears to have been an exception to official Mormon Church policy at this time.[42] Joel Hills Johnson was a missionary to the Paiutes and founder of Enoch, Utah (it was first named Johnson's Fort). Writing on January 23, 1871, he related that he was visiting with Young when the church leader offered him the Spring Canyon Ranch 12 mi east of Kanab

> for a stock ranch and for all family who wished to settle there.... We accordingly went out and found a beautiful canyon half to a mile wide and several miles long covered with grass with small springs coming out at the foot of the bluffs on each side and a small beautiful stream running from the mouth of the canyon, with plenty of building rock, fencing timber, and fire wood, and plenty of excellent grass for meadow and stock range extending for miles around. Therefore, we made arrangements for some of us to move there in the spring and start a cooperative stock association for herding stock and dairy purposes.[43]

Some of the Johnson family arrived in March 1871, although given the size of the clan, who came first and who arrived later is unclear.[44] Most of the brothers had entered into plural marriages, and these large, rambling families carved homes into the canyon terrain. Robinson's history says four of the five Johnson brothers made their way to the ranch, but her list of first arrivals included Joel

Johnson, at the time nearly seventy years old, his second wife Susan Bryant, and two teenage sons Joel H. and Almon B.; Joel's brother William Derby Johnson and his entire family; and Nephi, Sixtus, and Seth Johnson, Joel's three sons by first wife, Anna Pixley, and their families (Seth would go on to become one of the original settlers of the Cannonville area).[45] William Derby Johnson would later serve for years as bishop of Kanab. At its maximum, the ranch supported five hundred head of cattle.[46] Nephi and Sixtus Johnson were said to have brought Angora goats to the canyon.[47] Nephi Johnson had earlier played a role in the Mountain Meadows Massacre and is credited with being the first white man to see Zion Canyon. Within ten years, the isolated "family" ranch had evolved into a community of fifty people, nearly 40 percent of whom were members of the William D. and Nephi Johnson families.

In March 1871, a third wave of immigrants arrived in Kane County, this one from the abandoned Muddy Mission in the Moapa Valley of Nevada. Bradley states there were about three hundred immigrants from the Muddy Mission, about half of whom settled in Winsor (Mount Carmel) under the leadership of Daniel Stark and half in Berryville (Glendale) under the leadership of James A. Leithead.[48] Other families also moved into upper Long Valley at this time. A closer reading of Robinson's history suggests that isolated ranches were established up and down Long Valley spaced every few miles, and that there were no communities structured on the traditional Mormon model, although some areas certainly featured clusters of interrelated families, such as the Roundys in Upper Kanab and the Clarks in Skutumpah.

While Mormons were the first whites to settle the Grand Staircase and Escalante River country, they did not follow established Mormon patterns in the region. In effect, only Kanab and Panguitch were platted in the traditional Mormon model with square city blocks, wide streets, and central lots set aside for churches, schools, and community buildings. The other communities—Winsor (renamed Mount Carmel by the 1871 arrivals), Berryville (renamed Glendale by 1871 arrivals), Pahreah, Upper Kanab (now Alton), Skutumpah, and Johnson—were characterized by more lineal settlement patterns along dependable water sources. The scattering of ranches and farms along these water sources represented adaptation to limited access to water for culinary and irrigation purposes. As noted by Bradley, "Kane County's arid environment presented enormous obstacles to farming, and most settlers soon turned to stock raising. Implicit in any decision of where to settle was the identification of nearby sources of water for culinary purposes and for agriculture. Communities were all located near predictable water sources; if they were not, they did not survive for long."[49]

Conditions for many of the frontier settlers were rough. Jack Chynoweth recalled that his father was born in Pahreah Town in 1893. At the time, only small foot trails connected the houses stretched out along the small river. He remembers that a family with the last name Mangum lived in Dugout Canyon and "there were just places dug in the bank and a little cottonwood over the top of them and they would live in conditions like that." Even a good water supply did not guarantee permanence, however. Chynoweth remembers, "I think there were something like forty families that lived there." They abandoned it "around the turn of the century because of floods."[50] Today the Pahreah ghost town is a popular tourist attraction.

The country's scarce water resources could support only a limited population. By 1872 or 1873, there were roughly four hundred to five hundred individuals living in what is today Kane County, all scattered along water sources such as Kanab Creek, the East Fork of the Virgin River, the Paria River, and Johnson Creek. Occasional springs throughout the area supported one or two families, but certainly not insular, well-bounded villages in the preferred Mormon community model. And there was certainly not enough water to raise wheat, oats, and other grains. By 1874, 52 percent of Kanab's farm production was in animals and animal products, and only 14 percent was in the form of field crops. Of the assessed wealth, 72 percent was in livestock and "moveable goods." By 1880, there were 15,371 head of livestock, as Bradley concluded, "confirm[ing] that Kane County's open spaces had proven to be better suited for ranching than farming."[51]

Seeing their lack of beef consumption, Mormon settlers needed few cows for their subsistence. The reality, however, was these early settlers embraced cattle and sheep as their only form of currency to obtain foodstuffs from communities elsewhere that could not be grown locally. Even basic supplies like flour and sugar had to be purchased outside the immediate region. As historian Julius S. Dalley observed, in 1941, "local production does not provide for the needs of the several communities though families derive a substantial part of their living from that source. This county, among others, is not self-supporting."[52]

Several of the earliest residents got into cattle ranching on a large scale. Original settlers interviewed in the 1930s and 1940s as part of the Federal

Writers Project and the Utah Writers Project offered some insight into the size of the herds. Several agreed that John "Old Man" Kitchen ran as many as six thousand head of cattle in Kitchen Canyon, around Molly's Nipple, and on the Paria Plateau on the Arizona Strip, and by one account he ran more cattle than all the other ranchers combined who grazed east of Kanab Creek.[53] Ephraim Mansfield and James Andrus bought out John D. Lee and the Clark brothers, and they ran five thousand head in the Skutumpah area.[54] Frank Hamblin had as many as twelve hundred head,[55] and Brigham A. Riggs ran one thousand to two thousand head.[56] George Adams, William Swapp, Frank Farnsworth, William Hamblin, Taylor Crosby, Ed Woolley, Dan Seegmiller and the Negley brothers also ran large herds, although the sizes were not specified.[57] In the mid-1870s, the Orderville United Order had a large herd of dairy cattle that ranged

FIGURE 3.6. This rock cabin in the Grand Staircase is attributed to cattleman John Kitchen. Known today as "Monkey House," it was probably one of many temporary shelters on his vast ranges that extended all the way to the Paria Plateau in Arizona. Photograph by Jerry D. Spangler.

first in The Meadows and were later moved to Dairy Canyon, a tributary to Johnson Canyon known for its meadows and lakes.[58]

The Kane County herds in the 1870s likely had two origins: the overcrowded ranges around St. George and Cedar City, where other Mormons had taken livestock for protection during the "Indian wars" in the 1860s, and the Mormon Church herds from northern Utah being dispersed into central and southern Utah. Riggs, one of the earliest ranchers in Kane County, indicated that church herds were established at Canaan in 1870 under the supervision of James Andrus and at Pipe Spring under the direction of A. P. "Perry" Winsor.[59] These herds were probably moved there from Washington and Iron Counties, although later references are made to livestock being sent from Salt Lake City.

Levi Stewart brought a large herd of cattle with him from the Wasatch Front in the spring of 1870, enough that his herd might initially have been larger than the rest of the Kanab-area herds combined.[60] The 1870 U.S. Census lists Stewart's personal estate at $2,000—four times greater than any other resident at the time.[61] It is certainly possible the value of Stewart's estate was in livestock, but even if Stewart's wealth was entirely in cattle and even if he understated the value at only $10 per head, his herd would have been only about two hundred cows. And if that represented roughly half of the cattle on the local ranges in 1870, this calculation would reflect an aggregated herd in the Kanab area of only about four hundred animals. The numbers of cattle and sheep would increase exponentially over the next decade. By 1884, the Kane County assessment rolls listed 1,407 horses, mules, and asses; 3,491 cattle; 22,450 sheep; and 334 swine.[62]

Aggregation and Dispersal

The arrival of so many families in the area placed inordinate demands on available natural resources. The 1870 U.S. Census of Kane County listed only 1,244 acres of improved land in the entire county, which at that time included portions of what is today eastern Washington County. And early settlers estimated only about 20 acres more of river bottom could be developed.[63] The hundreds of immigrants who arrived in 1871 and thereafter would have found all of the well-watered areas along creeks already claimed. Those who were farmers by trade would have been forced by necessity to search out less optimal locations at higher elevations (with shorter growing seasons) and less predictable water resources (with springs instead of creeks). Settlers with industrial or commercial abilities successfully adapted to these realities by constructing sawmills, woolen mills, and grist mills, or by manufacturing shoes or blacksmithing, providing services not previously available on the frontier. A review of the 1880 U.S. Census data reveals that the vast majority of those living in what is today Kane County were not directly involved in agricultural production as their primary profession.

But many of the new arrivals were farmers with few other marketable skills. And with the development of new fields for planting no longer possible, these families generally became livestock ranchers, reflecting an adaptation to economic realities of the time. Raising livestock on unfettered open ranges was a relatively straightforward, inexpensive process. Rangelands were divided only in very general terms. Stockmen from Iron County and Beaver County laid claim to the high elevations of the Markagunt Plateau and Paunsaugunt Plateau as summer ranges, all under the name of the Kanarra Cattle Company, although these herds were actually aggregated ones belonging to many small operators. And stock owners in Kanab, Pipe Spring, and Canaan laid claim to the Arizona Strip and the rugged canyon country as far east and south as the Colorado River.[64] The vast sea of seemingly limitless grasslands in both regions was free for the taking. Ranching was a relatively low-cost endeavor requiring only sufficient brood-stock and enough young men (most often sons) to tend to the herds. Not surprisingly, family ranches had become firmly established by 1880.

An occupational identity as "stockman" was slow in coming in southern Utah. Kane County residents first began to list their profession as livestock men on the 1880 U.S. Census, although only about 3 percent of the population self-identified as such. Some thirty-four males used labels such as "rancher" or "stock man," implying they were involved in cattle operations. Another fourteen males identified their occupation as some variation of "sheep herder." Most of the cattlemen were living in Pahreah or Kanab, and most of the sheepmen were living in Long Valley. Johnson Canyon had one cattleman (Hyrum Clark) and one sheepman (German Buchanan). The Kanab cattlemen were probably associated with livestock operations on the Arizona Strip (see Table 3.3).

In what is today Garfield County, fewer men identified themselves as being in the cattle or sheep business, only about 2 percent of the total population. Twenty-three heads of household, all men, identified themselves as ranchers or raising stock, and seven men indicated they raised or herded sheep as an

TABLE 3.3. Kane County Residents (All Males) Who Self-Identified as Livestock Men on the 1880 U.S. Census.

Kane County Ranchers (1880 Census)					
	Census Precinct	Listed Occupation		Census Precinct	Listed Occupation
Hyrum B. Clark	Johnson	stock man	**George W. Hicks**	MountCarmel	stock man
German Buchanan	Johnson	shepherd	**John W. Clark**	Kanab	stock dealer
Thomas W. Smith	Pahreah	rancher	**Elmer Johnson**	Kanab	stock man
Silas Brinkerhoff	Pahreah	stock man	**Lucius Fuller**	Kanab	dairy man
Francis Hamblin	Pahreah	rancher	**Albert Riggs**	Kanab	stock man
William F. Hamblin	Pahreah	stock man	**Nathan Adams**	Kanab	stock man
Taylor Crosby	Pahreah	rancher	**Nathan Adams Jr.**	Kanab	stock man
John Kitchen	Pahreah	stock man	**George J. Adams**	Kanab	stock man
William Grice	Pahreah	stock man	**Francis H. Little**	Kanab	rancher
Nathaniel Riggs	Pahreah	rancher	**William T. Stewart**	Kanab	stock man
Dagbert S. Young	Kanab	stock man	**Alonza L. Stewart**	Kanab	stock man
James Emett	Kanab	stock man	**Alexander Findlay**	Kanab	rancher
Joseph Sawyer	Kanab	ranch worker	**James M. Clark**	Glendale	stock man
Arthur Sawyer	Kanab	ranch worker	**Alonza Harris**	Glendale	stock man
William Hasting	Kanab	ranch worker	**Warren Harris**	Glendale	stock man
Charlie Griesser	Kanab	ranch worker	**Leroy Harris**	Glendale	stock man
James Clark	Orderville	shepherd	**Martin Cutler**	Glendale	shepherd
Lars D. Jensen	Orderville	shepherd	**George Johnson**	Glendale	dairy worker
John R. Young	Orderville	shepherd	**Benjamin Black**	Orderville	shepherd
Jesse M. Palmer	Orderville	shepherd	**John Pearson**	Orderville	shepherd
Lorenzo S. Young	Orderville	shepherd	**Cyrenus Fackerel**	Orderville	shepherd
Joseph F. Fackerel	Orderville	shepherd	**John J. Covington**	Orderville	shepherd
Jesse Billingsley	Orderville	shepherd	**Carmi Porter**	Orderville	shepherd
Henry T. Stolworthy	Orderville	stock man	**Edward Lamb**	Orderville	stock man

Note: Spellings listed here are per U.S. Census (1880) and may not be consistent with traditional family spellings or those found in other historical records.

occupation (see Table 3.4). Most of these were in the Panguitch and Hillsdale area, although four cattlemen resided in Escalante.

Of course, these conclusions, taken at face value from census data, are subject to several biases, perhaps the biggest being how southern Utah residents viewed their occupations in 1880. They might have been raising cattle but considered themselves first and foremost farmers. This is certainly the case with Jacob Hamblin and Levi Stewart, two of the biggest cattle operators in the Kanab and Arizona Strip regions who listed their occupation as "farmer," as did noted ranchers Ebenezer Bryce (for whom Bryce Canyon is named) and John Sevy in Garfield County. Like many early stockmen, Bryce did not romanticize

TABLE 3.4. Garfield County Residents (All Males) Who Self-Identified as Livestock Men on the 1880 U.S. Census.

Garfield County Ranchers (1880 Census)					
	Census Precinct	Listed Occupation		Census Precinct	Listed Occupation
Joselina Riddle	Escalante	stock raising	**Theodore Asay**	Hillsdale	stock farmer
Isaac J. Riddle	Escalante	stock raising	**Amos Asay**	Hillsdale	stock farmer
Archibald Hunter	Escalante	stock raising	**Eleazer Asay**	Hillsdale	stock farmer
James Ganes	Escalante	stock raising	**James Little**	Hillsdale	shepherd
Joseph Haycock	Panguitch	shepherd	**John F. Jones**	Hillsdale	shepherd
Francis R. Owens	Panguitch	shepherd	**Meltier Hatch**	Hillsdale	stock raising
Oliver Lewis	Panguitch	stock raising	**Elias Hatch**	Hillsdale	stock raising
Timothy Robinson	Panguitch	sheepraising	**Francis Alger**	Hillsdale	stock raising
Joseph Woods	Panguitch	stock raising	**William Lefevre**	Panguitch	shepherd
John D. Norton	Panguitch	stock raising	**James Veater**	Panguitch	ranching
Ira Hatch	Panguitch	stock raising	**Robert P. Woolley**	Panguitch	ranching
James Prince	Panguitch	shepherd	**Joseph Kesler**	Panguitch	ranching
Matthew McEwen	Panguitch	stock raising	**James W. Marshall**	Panguitch	ranching
Abin Fatheringham	Panguitch	stock raising	**Joseph Marshall**	Panguitch	ranching

Note: Spellings listed here are per U.S. Census (1880) and may not be consistent with traditional family spellings or those found in other historical records.

ranching or the harsh wilderness country. He reportedly said of the beautiful eroded rim-country he ranched: "it is a helluva place to lose a cow."[65] Some residents apparently saw a distinction between farming and ranching and noted such on the census, while others saw farming and ranching as the same thing.

To arrive at a better understanding of how many early residents might have been involved in raising cattle and sheep, we looked at households where the head of the household or an adult son living at home listed his occupation as farmer or farm laborer (women were never listed in such categories even though they certainly worked on the farm). In Kane County, there were 257 total households, of which thirty-two were in the cattle business (12 percent), fourteen in the sheep business (5 percent), and 103 in farming of some kind (40 percent). In total, 57 percent of the households were involved in agriculture of some kind, of which animal husbandry (beef cattle, dairy cattle, and sheep) constituted a major portion of the economy (see Table 3.5).

In Garfield County, there were 318 households, of which twenty were involved in cattle-ranching (6 percent), seven in raising sheep (2 percent), and seventy-eight in farming of some kind (25 percent). In total, only one-third of

TABLE 3.5. Kane County Residents Who Self-Identified as Farmers in the 1880 U.S. Census.

Kane County Farmers (1880 Census)								
	Census Precinct	Listed Occupation		Census Precinct	Listed Occupation		Census Precinct	Listed Occupation
Charles W. Smithson	Pahreah	farmer	**Englebrat Englestead**	MountCarmel	farm worker	**Christopher Heaton**	Kanab	farm worker
Moroni Smithson	Pahreah	farm worker	**Thomas H. Keele**	MountCarmel	farm worker	**Joseph Croffs**	Kanab	farm worker
Alma Smithson	Pahreah	farm worker	**Henry B. Jolley**	MountCarmel	farmer	**Joseph Esplin**	Kanab	farm worker
Joseph Smithson	Pahreah	farm worker	**Haskel Jolley**	MountCarmel	farm worker	**Jessie Pearce**	Kanab	farmer
Hyrum Smithson	Pahreah	farm worker	**Aaron Asay**	MountCarmel	farm worker	**Boyd Stewart**	Glendale	farm worker
David R. Smithson	Pahreah	farm worker	**William Jolley**	MountCarmel	farmer	**Melvin Swapp**	Glendale	farmer
Henry Smithson	Pahreah	farm worker	**John A. Jolley**	MountCarmel	farm worker	**James Swapp**	Glendale	farmer
Francis Kirby	Pahreah	farmer	**Bryant H. Jolley**	MountCarmel	farmer	**John Brinkerhoff**	Glendale	farmer
Robert A. Smith	Pahreah	farm worker	**Robert Moncur**	MountCarmel	farmer	**Hyrum Brinkerhoff**	Glendale	farm worker
Robert Smith Jr.	Pahreah	farm worker	**Jacob Heirsiger**	MountCarmel	gardener	**Homer Boughton**	Glendale	farmer
James E. Smith	Pahreah	farmer	**Robert B. Moncur**	MountCarmel	farm worker	**Silas Harris**	Glendale	farmer
John S. Adams	Pahreah	farmer	**William F. Moncur**	MountCarmel	farm worker	**Warren Foote**	Glendale	farmer
William Crosby	Kanab	farmer	**Harvey Moncur**	MountCarmel	farm worker	**George A. Foote**	Glendale	farm worker
Moses S. Emett	Kanab	farmer	**Silas Hoyt**	MountCarmel	farmer	**John Hyatt**	Glendale	farmer
Robert J. Howell	Kanab	gardener	**Henry A. Jolley**	MountCarmel	farmer	**Swain Anderson**	Glendale	farmer
Brigham Y. Baird	Kanab	farmer	**Jerome Asay**	MountCarmel	farmer	**James Watson**	Glendale	farmer
William S. Lewis	Kanab	farmer	**John W. Reid**	MountCarmel	farmer	**John Carpenter**	Glendale	farm worker
Zadock K. Judd	Kanab	farmer	**Isaac Black**	Orderville	farm worker	**Royal Cutler Jr.**	Glendale	farm worker
Zadock Judd Jr.	Kanab	farm worker	**Simeon Allen**	Orderville	farm worker	**Andrew Gibbons**	Glendale	farmer
Henry Judd	Kanab	farm worker	**George Gale**	Orderville	farm worker	**Abinadi Porter**	Orderville	farm worker
James Carpenter	Kanab	farmer	**George H. Black**	Orderville	farm worker	**Joseph Croffe**	Orderville	gardener
Joseph G. Brown	Kanab	farmer	**John Esplin**	Orderville	farm worker	**Levi Hampton**	Orderville	farm worker
Leonard Nuttal	Kanab	farmer	**Jacob Fisher**	Orderville	farm worker	**Amos Cox**	Orderville	farmer
Thomas G. Smith	Kanab	farmer	**Alvin Heaton**	Orderville	farm worker	**John Esplin**	Ordervile	farm worker
James Halliday	Kanab	farmer	**Charles Carroll**	Orderville	farm worker	**Henry Esplin**	Orderville	farmmanager
Daniel Washburn	Kanab	farmer	**George A. Palmer**	Orderville	farm worker	**Charles Carroll**	Orderville	farm worker
Samuel Haycock	Kanab	farmer	**Mads Sorensen**	Orderville	farm worker	**Willard Carroll**	Orderville	farm worker
Edward Pugh	Kanab	farmer	**Hans Sorensen**	Orderville	farm worker	**John C. White**	Orderville	gardener
John E. Riggs	Kanab	farmer	**Isaac Losee**	Orderville	farm worker	**Lars R. Jensen**	Orderville	farm worker
David Udall	Kanab	farmer	**William R. Butler**	Orderville	farm worker	**Allen Orval**	Orderville	farm worker
James H. Lewis	Kanab	farmer	**Pear Pearson**	Orderville	gardener	**Theodore Orval**	Orderville	farm worker
Alfred D. Young	Kanab	farmer	**Jacob Heirsiger**	Orderville	gardener	**John Schwartz**	Glendale	farmer
Adolph Young	Kanab	farmer	**James W. Palmer**	Orderville	farm worker	**David Foote**	Glendale	farmer
Royal J. Cutler	Glendale	farmer	**Ben Leithead**	Glendale	farmer			
Allen R. Cutler	Glendale	farm worker	**Erastus Carpenter**	Glendale	farm worker			

Note: Spellings listed here are per U.S. Census (1880) and may not be consistent with traditional family spellings or those found in other historical records.

the households of Garfield County were involved in agricultural activities of one kind or another (see Table 3.6), a percentage far less than in Kane County. This quantity also seems inconsistent with the statement by historians Newell and Talbot that "stock raising became the dominant occupation, and along with this the dairy industry also grew" shortly after the resettlement of Panguitch in 1871.[66] This statistical oddity cannot be explained by census data alone.

Thus the census data probably understates the number of individuals actually engaged in ranching activities. Oral histories conducted in the 1930s and early 1940s with original settlers of both counties indicate that cattle and sheep ranching was the dominant economic activity in the region, and that ranching was the only consistent source of cash for southern Utah families.

As early as the 1870s and 1880s, residents witnessed the loss of scarce farmlands caused largely by human actions. Powell Expedition topographer Frederick Dellenbaugh remarked on the gullying of regional streams in the early 1870s. In 1881 settlers formed the Kanab Irrigation Company, selling shares to raise capital for a dam and canal system that could irrigate 269 acres. Just a few years later, a flood in 1883 washed out the dam and crops were lost. Approximately 100 acres were swept away, and the channel dropped 40 ft, making access to water even more difficult.[67]

Oscar Judd—a grandson of pioneer Zadok K. Judd Sr., a founder of Kanab—grew up in Johnson Canyon on the western border of today's Grand Staircase-Escalante National Monument. Like Kanab Creek, in the 1870s Johnson Canyon was a lush meadow with a series of small lakes and a small meandering creek. The Judd family ran a dairy using flood irrigation for their hay fields, getting water from a large reservoir built by early settlers. He noted that the impoundment never went dry until new neighbors upstream changed the flow of the creek. As he recalled, after the diversion we "had floods, and it just cut that creek right out down to nothing. Cut it down [20 ft] in two years." Before this, he remembers the creek was wide and shallow, and people did not need a bridge to cross it.

> Mother says when she first went down there, the whole valley was just one big meadow clear down to the old town. And they couldn't get the hay in the field cut. So they took a plow and went down through the middle to drain it and then that started the erosion.[68]

A handful of the small lakes survived the arroyo-cutting, but Johnson Creek did not.

TABLE 3.6. Garfield County Residents (All Males) Who Self-Identified as Farmers in the 1880 U.S. Census.

Garfield County Farmers (1880 Census)								
	Census Precinct	Listed Occupation		Census Precinct	Listed Occupation		Census Precinct	Listed Occupation
Samuel Mecham	Cannonville	farmer	**Joseph C. Lay**	Escalante	farmer	**Reese Evans**	Panguitch	farmer
Mansel H. Thompson	Cannonville	farmer	**Joseph H. Spencer**	Escalante	farmer	**Henry Lauer**	Panguitch	farmer
Edmund R. Thompson	Cannonville	farmer	**Andrew J. Lamb**	Escalante	farmer	**Joseph C. Davis**	Panguitch	farm laborer
William J. Henderson	Cannonville	farmer	**William Cottam**	Escalante	farmer	**Thomas Woolsey**	Panguitch	gardener
Niels B. Nielson	Cannonville	farmer	**Josiah Barker**	Escalante	farmer	**James Houston**	Panguitch	farmer
Joseph L. Thompson	Cannonville	farmer	**Peter Barker**	Escalante	farmer	**John Clark**	Panguitch	farm laborer
James B. Thompson	Cannonville	farmer	**Reuben Collett**	Escalante	farmer	**James Henrie**	Panguitch	farm laborer
William S. Thompson	Cannonville	farmer	**Hyrum F. Norton**	Escalante	farmer	**Neils Clove**	Panguitch	farm laborer
John O. Thompson	Cannonville	farmer	**John F. Moody**	Escalante	farmer	**William T. Owens**	Panguitch	farm laborer
Joseph Ingram	Cannonville	farmer	**Jo. Cameron**	Hillsdale	farm laborer	**Elijah Elimer**	Panguitch	farmer
Ebenezer Bryce	Cannonville	farmer	**John H. Hatch**	Hillsdale	farm laborer	**James H. Emplay**	Panguitch	farmer
Evan Greene	Escalante	farmer	**Niels P. Clove**	Hillsdale	farmer	**Truman Libbee**	Panguitch	gardener
Philo Allen	Escalante	farmer	**Seth Johnson**	Hillsdale	farm laborer	**Danilson Barney**	Panguitch	farm laborer
Perry M. Liston	Escalante	farmer	**David Frederic**	Hillsdale	farm laborer	**John L. Sevy**	Panguitch	farmer
David W. Campbell	Escalante	farmer	**James A Wilson**	Hillsdale	farmer	**Edwin M. Owens**	Panguitch	farm laborer
Lison Laramie	Escalante	farmer	**Brigham Knight**	Hillsdale	farm laborer	**Robert Talbot**	Panguitch	farm laborer
Andrew P. Schow	Escalante	farmer	**Plesant Minchey**	Hillsdale	farmer	**Thomas H. Cope**	Panguitch	farm laborer
David Stevenson	Escalante	farmer	**William Talbot**	Panguitch	farmer	**Squire Reynolds**	Panguitch	farm laborer
Isaac Goodwin	Escalante	farmer	**Henry Lynn**	Panguitch	farm laborer	**Samuel Henrie**	Panguitch	farmer
George Coleman	Escalante	farmer	**Enoch Reynolds**	Panguitch	farm laborer	**Francis Cherry**	Panguitch	farm laborer
Thomas Heaps	Escalante	farmer	**John L. Butler**	Panguitch	farm laborer	**Sheriff Marshall**	Panguitch	farm laborer
James Schow	Escalante	farmer	**John W. Butler**	Panguitch	farmer	**David Shakespeare**	Panguitch	farmer
Edwin Twitchell	Escalante	farmer	**James Butler**	Panguitch	farm laborer	**David Shakespeare Jr.**	Panguitch	farm laborer
Joseph F. Barney	Escalante	farmer	**James Henrie**	Panguitch	farmer	**Allen Miller**	Panguitch	farmer
Charles Hall	Escalante	farmer	**Samuel Q. Henrie**	Panguitch	farmer	**Mark Burgess**	Panguitch	farmer
Edward Wilcock	Escalante	farmer	**Royal Proctor**	Panguitch	farmer	**Alma Barney**	Panguitch	farm laborer

Note: Spellings listed here are per U.S. Census (1880) and may not be consistent with traditional family spellings or those found in other historical records.

Because of the hardships involved in making homes in a harsh landscape and the lived experiences of many settlers, it is not surprising that a ranching "culture" emerged in all aspects of community life. As summarized by Bradley, cattle round-ups became community affairs involving men, women, and children. Families would drive cattle to a public square in Kanab for branding, and when the herds became too large, they moved the public corral to the outskirts of town. As related by Bradley:

> Cowboys would ride horses over the range in search of cattle that had wandered from the herd. They brought along a mess wagon, as they might be gone for weeks. After the cattle were branded, they were driven to the ranges located to the south and west for months of grazing.[69]

Mormons had a very high birth rate and the ever-growing population was a serious problem by the mid- to late 1870s, not only in Kane and Garfield counties but throughout the Utah Territory. Population pressure was exacerbated by a continued influx of Mormon converts making their way to Zion. By the mid-1870s—some two and a half decades after the arrival of Mormons in the Salt Lake Valley—a second generation of Mormons born and raised in Utah were in need of their own farms. F. A. Hammond, writing in *Deseret News* in 1885, observed:

> I find the settlements crowded up to their utmost capacity, land and water all appropriated, and our young people as they marry off have no place to settle near home . . . the resources of the people are about exhausted, unless they go into manufacturing.[70]

They also were taking a toll on the delicate arid landscapes all along the Wasatch Front.[71]

The demographic makeup of Kane County certainly reflects this trend. The 1880 U.S. Census indicates at least 1,396 people were living in what is today Kane County, and seven out of ten residents had been born in Utah. About 10 percent were born in Europe (mostly Denmark, Sweden, Scotland, Wales, England, and Switzerland) and these people almost certainly were Mormon converts who immigrated to Utah. About 20 percent were born in other states or in Canada, some of which were older, first-generation converts who had survived persecution in Ohio, Missouri, and Illinois, while others represented more recent converts from the Deep South. Some were skilled tradesmen, but most were not.

The Mormon Church's economic principles were deeply rooted in agriculture, and the church responded to the population crisis by establishing additional agricultural-based colonies throughout the West. At least one hundred new communities were established in the mid- to late 1870s, some as far away as Alberta, Canada, and others in the neighboring territories of Idaho, Wyoming, Colorado, Nevada, and Arizona. More colonies were established "closer to home" on lands "discovered" by Mormon militiamen during the Black Hawk War, lands that were later organized as Garfield, Wayne, and Emery Counties. Historian Leonard Arrington called it the "greatest colonization movement in Mormon history" second only to the initial settlement of Utah in the 1850s.[72]

From first settlement, families in the Grand Staircase and Escalante River region have rarely felt a sense of permanence. Shortly after the founding of Kane and Garfield Counties, children of the original settlers were often forced to move elsewhere. Out-migration was a natural response to population pressure and limited resources. Bradley's analysis of census data revealed 88 percent of children born in Kane County died elsewhere between 1870 and 1910, and in Washington, Iron, and Kane counties, 72 percent of those born there moved elsewhere before they died.[73] In other words, plenty of young men were available to tend herds, but when it came time for them to marry and establish a place of their own, they were forced to look elsewhere. Local leaders to this day decry the out-migration of their young people who go off to find work in Provo or Salt Lake or some other city, that there are no jobs to keep them close to home. But this has been the case in Kane County since the 1870s when seven out of every ten young people moved away.

By the mid-1870s, Kanab and Long Valley had already reached capacity and less optimal agricultural areas such as Pahreah, Johnson Canyon, and Upper Kanab had already been claimed, leaving the next generation to seek out farms in even more marginal areas where agriculture was even more risky. Not surprisingly, many of these latest communities failed within a few years. Some of newly settled areas included the upper Sevier River and upper Paria River country, and the upper Escalante River basin at the foothills of the Aquarius Plateau and Boulder Mountain. By 1880, more people were living in present-day Garfield County (1,715) than in Kane County (1,396).

The major settlements of both Garfield and Kane Counties were in marginal areas from the start, even by the standards of the frontier-tested Mormon settlers of the Great Basin. The settling of Panguitch (initially called Fairview, but the name was later changed by the Utah Territorial Legislature) on the upper Sevier River occurred in 1864, or roughly the same time as the initial settlement of Kanab to the south. Fifty-four families migrated from the Beaver and Parowan areas into the valley that first year, planting fields and erecting makeshift shelters. At 6,624 ft elevation, agriculture there was at the upper margin of viability, and they found themselves "at the mercy of short growing seasons and harsh winters."[74] As previously noted, the burgeoning town was abandoned during the Black Hawk War.

The permanent settlement of what would become Garfield County can be attributed in large part to the previously mentioned 1866 military expedition to track down Black Hawk and other warring Indigenous peoples. Captain James Andrus split his command, sending one group under Lieutenant Joseph Fish north to Parowan and then across the pass to the upper Sevier River country where they discovered the valleys that would become the sites of Tropic, Henrieville, and Cannonville.[75] His own command traveled east from St. George across the Arizona Strip to Johnson Canyon, then north to rendezvous with Fish's company in the upper Paria River country. They then proceeded east into Potato Valley, now Escalante, where an official report estimated the valley could support a settlement of 150 families.[76]

Several veterans of this expedition returned to their homes with stories of virgin lands ripe for settlement. Many more families, friends and relatives of the veterans heard the stories and, oppressed by crushing poverty common at that time, dreamed of having their own farms, or at the very least better farms than ones they already had. Once Black Hawk sued for peace in 1869, these families began migrating to these unknown places to establish farms and ranches. Five veterans of the Andrus campaign were among the first to resettle Panguitch in 1871. While challenging to farm, Panguitch Valley proved to be ideal winter range for livestock, which were later trailed to Beaver to be sold.[77]

In 1871, refugees from the Muddy Mission in Nevada, who earlier had also settled Long Valley, established small communities south of Panguitch at Hatchtown and Hillsdale.[78] Grass Valley, also known as Coyote Creek and later as Antimony, was settled in 1873, Cannonville (and its predecessors Clifton and New Clifton) in 1874, and Escalante in 1876. Philo Allen Sr. and his son Edmund

FIGURE 3.7. Escalante River country has even less permanent water than Kane County, and arable lands suitable for irrigation are limited in scope and by shorter growing seasons. But it did have Boulder Mountain, a lush summer range with hundreds of small lakes. Photograph by Dan Bauer.

brought the first herd of cattle to Escalante the year before, in 1875, and left them to winter in Main Canyon. The Escalante settlers that followed the next year brought milk cows, oxen, horses, mules, pigs, a few sheep, chickens, dogs, and cats, but no mention was made of cattle at that time, only that "later, Joe Lay and the Liston brothers, Martin, Rufus, and Joseph, brought herds of cattle."[79]

The first sheep apparently did not survive. Early settler E. A. Griffin wrote that he brought the first herd of sheep to the area in 1879. The initial flock, which numbered 1,500, was first grazed in North Creek and later herded to the Griffin Top high on the Aquarius Plateau at over 10,600 ft where Griffin, his father, and a brother built cabins. As was the practice in the day, Griffin said:

> [we] bedded our sheep nearby each night. About this time this country was getting a real reputation for its wonderful range so by about 1885

> there were about 15,000 head of cattle owned here, besides a couple thousand head of wild horses.[80]

As these new waves of immigrants arrived, they discovered in no short order that growing food crops at such high elevations was extremely risky. But the valleys were ideally suited for cattle and sheep. Grass Valley was so named because the first riders who passed through said the grass was so lush that it brushed the underside of the horses' bellies.[81] They also discovered that alfalfa could be cultivated at these higher elevations, minimizing the effects of cold winters when open rangelands were covered in deep snows.

Cooperation and Cooperatives

Economic cooperation and self-sufficiency had always been fundamental tenets of Mormonism, as much out of necessity as theology. As a religious entity, the Mormons were geographically isolated, politically targeted by federal policies, and economically dependent upon one another for their survival. If they needed clothing they would raise their own sheep, build and operate their own woolen mills, and distribute their wool clothing to their own people. This mandate for cooperation assumed even greater importance in the late 1860s when the Mormons' socioeconomic isolation was threatened by the arrival in Salt Lake City of non-Mormon businessmen more interested in profiteering than community welfare. Just as important, the Salt Lake Valley had become increasingly urbanized, making it difficult for individual families to be entirely self-sufficient. And business endeavors were limited by the scarcity of capital, almost all of which was controlled by non-Mormon banks. To cut economic ties with outsiders, Brigham Young sought to establish an economic system not dependent on Gentiles and instead bolstered by the collective wealth of his people. Arrington noted that virtually

> every important enterprise organized by the Mormons after 1868 bore the name "cooperative." Mercantile cooperation was but the first step in a movement which saw the establishment of cooperative institutions in almost every realm of economic activity.[82]

This certainly included livestock cooperatives in southern Utah, which were central to the growth of the cattle and sheep industries in the Grand Staircase and Escalante country. Sanctioned and promoted by Young, the cooperative movement also had spiritual objectives. Mormon leaders believed it would create a sense of oneness of purpose, that all Saints were working together to build the Kingdom of God. And through the economies of scale, cooperation would increase production and lower operating costs. The movement was part and parcel to a regional campaign, as Arrington states, "to develop a completely self-contained Latter-day Saint community, with emphasis on local production of every needful thing, without financial or other aid from outside the realm of the church."[83]

The officers of the cooperatives were exclusively church leaders. In many instances, Young himself was an officer of larger cooperatives (usually president), whereas smaller, more distant cooperatives were placed in the hands of local church leaders, such as Erastus Snow of St. George. The Mormons themselves were expected to patronize the cooperatives, and in some instances failure to do so resulted in excommunication. As Arrington observed, "Utah's cooperative concerns were unique, not because they were cooperatives, but because of the ecclesiastical participation and influence and the broad basis of public support." The cooperatives rarely failed because the Mormon Church, with its own financial resources, refused to allow them to fail.[84]

As already noted, Young had recognized the importance of southern Utah and northern Arizona rangelands during his 1870 tours of Kanab and nearby Pipe Spring. In April 1870, the same month he led the delegation to Kanab, President Young and other prominent Mormons from the St. George area organized the Canaan Cooperative Stock Company with assets owned jointly by the Mormon Church and selected individuals.[85] Young then purchased Pipe Spring from the Whitmore estate and assigned Anson P. Winsor[86] to improve the spring and manage the livestock, all of which were derived from tithing payments by church members. In the fall of 1870, when Young returned to outline the headquarters for the ranch, about five hundred cattle and a number of horses were already at the ranch,[87] probably the largest cattle herd anywhere in the area at that time. Many of these animals were possibly dairy cows. Robinson stated three hundred milk cows were at Pipe Spring when Young returned in the fall of 1870.[88]

In 1870, under Mormon Church direction, ranchers built a ranch house and fort directly over Pipe Spring, naming it "Winsor Castle" as a play on words for the royal residence in England, but using the spelling of the Winsor family, among the very first to arrive in Kanab in 1870 to manage the church's livestock interests there. Winsor had been the bishop in Grafton in what is now eastern Washington County in 1866 when he was tasked with writing the official letter to Young informing him of the killings of Robert, Joseph, and Isabelle Berry (discussed in Chapter 2).[89] While managing the Mormon Church's operations at Pipe Spring, Winsor was also a Kane County postmaster in 1871,[90] although he probably was the postmaster at Pipe Spring, which the U.S. Post Office merely assumed to be in Kane County.

Young's decision to get into the cattle business was a pragmatic one. The construction of the St. George Tabernacle and St. George Temple, the first temple started in Utah, commenced in 1867, was undoubtedly a driving force behind the involvement of the Mormon Church in regional cattle ranching. Both were, in a sense, "public works" projects providing employment to young men whose fathers were away on church missions.[91] The workers were paid from tithing receipts, which at that time consisted primarily of livestock and farm produce paid by members. With rangelands around St. George already at or near capacity, Young recognized the potential of the Pipe Spring area to accommodate the Mormon Church's growing cattle herds and thereby maintain the supply of food necessary for the temple workforce. And it appears that most (but not all) of his interest in rangelands was directed at the Arizona Strip, not farther east in Kane County.

According to noted Utah historian Juanita Brooks, Winsor Castle was the source of butter and cheese delivered to the temple workers weekly, as well as the source of beef cattle to be butchered. Lumber from the Arizona Strip proved suitable for the large floor and roof beams of the temple, and the longer, heavier beams of ponderosa pine could only be harvested on Mount Trumbull. Lesser woods from the Pine Valley north of St. George were adequate for flooring and casings.

Around the same time, Ebenezer Bryce, who had settled Pine Valley prior to moving to Garfield County, was charged with designing and overseeing the Pine Valley Chapel. A shipbuilder, he designed the upper sections as an upside-down ship. Completed in 1868 with local ponderosa pine, the chapel has the distinction of being the oldest continuously operating Latter-day Saints chapel in Utah.[92] Beyond the easier to access Pine Valley timber, Brooks acknowledged the transportation obstacles for the St. George Temple, noting:

It is eloquent of Mormon persistence and ingenuity that the 80-mile desert, the difficult mountain roads, the lack of water both at the mill and for the teams enroute, did not deter them. The building must go up, at whatever sacrifice.[93]

In 1871, the older company was reorganized as the New Canaan Stock Company, with James Andrus as superintendent, and the headquarters were moved to Canaan Spring about 10 mi northwest of Short Creek (and closer to St. George). As Altschul and Fairley observed, "For the next six years, the New Canaan Stock Company subsidized the temple work by contributing beef and dairy products to sustain the massive labor force."[94]

In 1873, the Winsor Castle Stock Growing Company was organized as a subsidiary to New Canaan and headquartered at Pipe Spring. Like its parent company, it was owned by the Mormon Church and selected local officials. The reason for the subsidiary is not indicated, but it may have been to better

FIGURE 3.8. Among the original settlers and a militia leader during the Black Hawk War, James Andrus managed the Canaan Ranch about 50 mi west of Pipe Spring. The Canaan Ranch became the headquarters for Mormon Church livestock operations in the western Arizona Strip. Photograph courtesy of Carl Weeks photograph collection, J. Willard Marriott Library Special Collections Repository (p0207n01_06_05), University of Utah, Salt Lake City.

manage herds on the eastern portion of the Arizona Strip that were far removed from the new headquarters. In January 1879, Winsor Castle Stock Growing Company was also absorbed into New Canaan.

The geographic scope of New Canaan was massive. The company appropriated open ranges around Canaan Springs and Pipe Spring at the base of the Vermilion Cliffs, and its directors also pushed south into the high plateau country. In 1874, New Canaan purchased House Rock Valley and Kane Springs from Jacob Hamblin, allowing them to move herds onto the Kaibab Plateau in the summer and into House Rock Valley in the winter. New Canaan ran its sizeable herds in tandem with those of the Orderville United Order (OUO). In fact, there appears to have been little practical distinction between the two cooperatives. New Canaan also had holdings elsewhere in the region, including Long Valley and Upper Kanab (Alton), where it had an upper ranch and a lower ranch. New Canaan's ranches were separated by a private ranch operated by the Roundy brothers.

The Mormon Church also ran a dairy in Upper Kanab. Sarah Blanche Robinson recalled years later that her father Richard Smith Robinson was called to the area to run the operation. Her reminiscences provide a glimpse into pioneer life at the time. "We just burned the midnight candles" all the time, she wrote, "sewing, patching, darning and running the spindle to keep the men clothed." Her father and brothers milked the cows from which the women and girls made cheese and butter. She recalled that these products and vegetables were brought via wagon by her father to Salt Lake City in the fall and exchanged for dry goods, clothing, and Christmas toys. Sometimes as many as twenty people lived in the old ranch house in Upper Kanab. Sarah later was elected to the first all-woman city council in America in Kanab in 1912.[95]

New Canaan was a profitable operation, at least in the early years when it returned dividends of 33–50 percent annually.[96] But it was first and foremost a Mormon Church company, and the herds were referred to as "church cattle." The stock was continually augmented by "tithing" livestock paid by church members, and the herd managers would disperse the animals throughout the territory to the poor and needy as directed by church leaders.[97] New Canaan was running more than three thousand head of cattle in the region by the early 1880s, and according to one account the herd actually numbered ten thousand.[98]

In 1882, Edwin D. Woolley, who would later become stake president in Kanab, was called by Erastus Snow to take charge of the church's ranching

FIGURE 3.9. Edwin D. Woolley, who became the Kanab stake president, took over the management of the Mormon Church's livestock herds in 1882. Photograph courtesy of J. Willard Marriott Library Special Collections Repository (P0050n01_04_35), University of Utah, Salt Lake City.

operations. He then moved his family from St. George to Upper Kanab, where the Woolley ranch became famous as a hideout for Mormon polygamists on the run from U.S. marshals, part of an underground network of safehouses. Church leaders came from as far away as Salt Lake City to lay low here, some staying weeks at a time.[99]

By 1883, New Canaan had begun selling off its ranches, first the Oak Grove Ranch to non-Mormon businessman B. F. Saunders of Salt Lake, and later the Upper Kanab ranches to Woolley and others loyal to the Mormon Church. As discussed later in this chapter, the divestiture of ranches was probably related to the Mormon Church's efforts to divest its assets before they could be confiscated by the federal government during its strident anti-polygamy campaign against the Mormon Church.[100]

In these years, other Mormon livestock cooperatives expanded into the area. Most of the grasslands of southern Utah technically were open ranges owned by the federal government and in the first decades the population was overwhelmingly Mormon. These tracts were theirs for the taking. Kanab-area ranchers had a cattle cooperative, referred to as the "K Herd," which ranged in House Rock Valley in the Two Mile Spring area. Two or three cooperatives operated to the north in upper Sevier River and upper Paria River country. Whereas New Canaan was logistically located to support St. George,[101] these other, smaller cooperatives were connected socially and economically to Beaver, Parowan, and Cedar City. In Panguitch, local residents established their own cooperative under the management of Meltier Hatch shortly after the resettlement in 1871. The cooperative's ranch house and headquarters were about 20 mi south of Panguitch at the confluence of Mammoth Creek with the Sevier River.[102]

The Kanarra Cattle Cooperative (formerly Company) had a ranch a few miles northwest of Bryce Canyon that was managed by William S. Berry, which was reportedly in operation before Panguitch was resettled.[103] According to a Daughters of the Utah Pioneers history, the Kanarra Cattle Cooperative represented the combined herds of families living in Kanarraville, Old Harmony, and Cedar City. Forage in any single area was insufficient, so cattle and sheep were continually moved, first to mountains above Cedar City and Kanarraville in the summer, then to the upper Sevier River in the fall, and then into lower Paria River and Wahweap country for the winter.[104] Another livestock cooperative was operating in the same area under the management of Isaac Riddle of Beaver.

Raymond D. Pollock provides some perspective on how settlers naturally moved east into today's Kane and Garfield counties. His great-grandfather was a leader in the Kanarra co-op and was looking for new winter range. "So, a group of them saddled up and rode across Cedar Mountain down across the east fork of the Sevier up here and down into the Tropic Valley," Pollock recalled. They liked the land so much they ended up staying.[105] So many livestock cooperatives operating in the same area eventually resulted in disputes over who had rights to what rangelands. These conflicts were arbitrated by Mormon Church leaders. In one instance, a settlement was reached between Berry and Riddle whereby Riddle's outfit would have rights to run livestock north and east of Flake Bottoms and down the Sevier River (Johns Valley and Grass Valley) and Berry would have the rights to the upper Sevier River country—the Markagunt Plateau and the Paunsaugunt Plateau to the south and west, as well as the upper Paria River in the area of what would eventually become Cannonville.[106]

The larger aggregated herds, while reducing individual costs, were also vulnerable to catastrophic losses. One such event occurred during the winter of 1879–80 when massive snowfalls—the largest in anyone's memory at that time—blanketed much of the West and buried all forage until the middle of April. Livestock everywhere began dying off in record numbers, and hay prices doubled, forcing small operators to let their animals die or sell them for pennies on the dollar to opportunists. In the upper Virgin River country, a Cedar City stockman lost all but twenty head of a herd that numbered about six hundred before the snow.[107] But their herds rebounded. By 1890, there were 278,313 cows in the territory, or 1.32 cows per person, the highest ratio of cows per person ever recorded in Utah.[108]

Communalism and Millennialism

The cooperative efforts of 1868–69 were actually a harbinger of an even grander plan, what Brigham Young would call the "Order of Enoch, but which is in reality the Order of Heaven."[109] This radical experiment in communalism would not be initiated until 1874, and by and large it was a failure, although it would have profound impacts on the livestock industry in Kane County (and to a lesser extent in Garfield County). Young needed a motivating event to elevate the practice of cooperative economics into a communal system where all possessions were held in common. And such an event presented itself in 1873 when international financial markets collapsed, sending the world economy into a great depression, now called the Panic of 1873.

Different events around the world converged to create the collapse, but in the United States it was fueled largely by over-speculation in railroad construction and a chain reaction of failed banks that had invested heavily in those projects. Other factors included soaring unemployment in newly established and untested industries, devastating fires in Chicago and Boston, labor strikes, waves of immigration from Europe at a time when jobs were increasingly scarce, and changes in monetary policies that gutted demand for silver. This latter event had direct consequences to Mormons in southern Utah because it resulted in mine closures throughout the West, including mining camps where Mormon men worked for cash wages and where Mormon families sold their produce.[110]

Arrington noted the typical nineteenth-century response to economic disaster was to insulate one's community through greater self-sufficiency. In the Utah Territory, the Mormon response also was shrouded in religious idealism, where, as Arrington noted, "under the stimulus of the church, each community was asked to extend the cooperative principle to every form of labor and investment, and to cut the ties which bound them to the outside world."[111] As applied to communities in southern Utah, the United Order, as it came to be known, required each person to contribute all property and possessions to the order in return for equivalent capital stock, under the theological principles that each individual was only a steward of his or her property and that they were obliged to utilize it for the general good.[112] Or as Arrington summarized it:

> The resources of ward members were pooled, and an attempt was made, under the aura of religious sanction, to root out individualistic profit-seeking and trade, and achieve the blessed state of opulent self-sufficiency and equality.[113]

Making the commitment to consecrate property and surrender one's independence to join a United Order was often a difficult decision. William Derby Johnson Jr., a notable bishop of Kanab, recorded he and his wife Lulu's initial reaction in 1874.

> John R. Young came from St. George, where President Brigham is, with a letter from him to organize the Order of Enoch, or the United Order . . . It was a sore trial for Lulu and I, as we had just got our house

fixed up, comfortable, and beginning to live. After much thought and prayer, we concluded to turn everything we had into the Order and work in it. Which we did in March.[114]

Across Utah, communities pooled their assets and created an environment where they "would eat together, pray together, and work together."[115] In Kane County, orders were created in Kanab, Johnson, Pahreah, Glendale, Mount Carmel and nearby Orderville, and in most instances the entire adult population added their names to the United Order rolls, beginning in 1874.[116] Most of the 150 United Orders that were created during this period, including the ones in Kanab and Glendale, failed within a few years. The United Order of Orderville survived the longest and was not formally disbanded until 1900, although it had ceased as an economic force by 1885.[117] Wallace Stegner traced the upward arc and ultimate demise of Orderville in his classic study *Mormon Country*.[118]

Orderville was founded in Long Valley in 1875 when twenty-four families, mostly refugees from the abandoned farming endeavor on the Muddy River, broke away from the Glendale United Order in a dispute over management. The Orderville families were the most zealous of all practitioners of the communal lifeway. As their assets increased, their steadfast devotion to its principles garnered respect (especially among some members of failed orders) and, in some circles, jealousy. Each member was given capital stock, but it was formally decided the stock did not entitle the owner to dividends or profit sharing, but that it would all belong to God. Adherents built a store room, shoe shop, bakery, blacksmith shop, carpentry shop, cooper shop, tannery, school house, telegraph office, woolen factory, dairy barns, garden house, and sheep sheds.[119]

The Orderville United Order's aggregated livestock herds were soon ubiquitous. Livestock was initially grazed in Long Valley, but the herds grew too large. OUO cattle were moved to House Rock Valley in 1877 and placed in the care of two teenaged boys, Ed Lamb and Tom Stalworthy. And in January 1878, a flock of 2,500 sheep was also moved to House Rock Valley under the care of William Adair, John Covington, Jesse Billingsly, Thomas Chamberlain, Henry W. Esplin, and Charles Black. The flocks were sheared at Jacob's Pools, and in the summer they were pushed onto the Kaibab Plateau to join the OUO cattle herds that were moved there at the same time.

Earlier in May 1872, John Doyle Lee had established a small ranch where he set up one of his wives, Rachel, and her children at Jacob's Pools, a strong spring located in a protected cove in the midst of miles of prime grazing lands. At the time he also filed claims on smaller springs at Soap Creek and House Rock as part of his cattle operation. At "Doyle's Retreat," as the Lee family called it, Rachel and her kin set about building corrals for the cows and calves and putting up a cheese press so that they could utilize all the milk not needed for the calves. Lee and his family spent months building a large stone house here, with three rooms complete with windows, doors, and a cupboard before he was soon called to established Lee's Ferry that year.[120]

William W. Adair, an early settler of Kane County, recalled that corrals were built at Crane Lake and Pleasant Valley, a house was built at a place called "Look Out," and claims were made on Snipes Lake and Frank's Lake, all in the high country of the Kaibab Plateau. In his account, "we put up logs—four logs high—to indicate priority claim rights. We secured water holes, springs, and lakes everywhere in that way for the Order."[121] Adair's history also states that the 1879 shearing took place at Frank's Lake. After that, the Order's sheep operation was put under the management of John R. Young, who pushed the flocks "across the Buckskin" to the "brink of Pahreah Creek and sheared in that place. The idea of the move seemed to be to secure the territory."[122]

The OUO used the same process to secure priority rights throughout the region. Historian Mark A. Pendleton wrote:

> They early recognized the country afforded for stock and sheep raising, and lost no time in controlling the range by acquiring possession of watering places in southern Utah and northern Arizona. These ranches included House Rock, Jacob's Pools, Cane Springs, Castle, Elk and [150] acres on the Pahreah River.[123]

As the OUO became increasingly successful, and as other local United Order experiments failed, Mormons in surrounding communities still loyal to the principles then joined the OUO, subsequently contributing their own personal ranch holdings and water rights to the effort.[124] Many of these adherents moved to Orderville. By 1880, the population of Orderville had swollen to 513 people (four or five times its original size), making it the largest community in the region, according to 1880 U.S. Census data.

By 1877, the Order apparently was grazing cattle herds on the Kaibab Plateau (summer range) and in House Rock Valley (winter range), a move that reflected the rapid expansion of the Order's cattle operations into the Arizona

Strip. In its beginning, in 1875, the Orderville United Order owned only a small band of sheep and fifty cattle. Six years later, the Order paid taxes on five thousand sheep and five hundred head of cattle.[125] The importance of sheep to the Orderville community is reflected by the fact that twelve of the fourteen sheepmen in the entire region lived in the Orderville Census Precinct; only two identified themselves as cattlemen.[126] Seeing the centrality of sheep, Orderville had its own woolen mill.

Not everyone, it seems, joined the United Order, but most did. Warren Foote of Kanab wrote in his journal:

> All who joined the order put in their improved lands, farming utensils, horses, cattle, wagons, harnesses, etc. All the property was appraised by a committee and each one was credited as capital stock. There were a few in the ward who did not join the order.[127]

And the rapid growth of the OUO from 1875 to 1880, as well as its priority claims on limited water sources, "led to a growing unease among neighboring communities that the OUO might eventually absorb the whole region, since it alone had the financial resources at its disposal for the purchasing of property and water claims."[128]

The OUO also controlled most grazing lands in Long Valley and perhaps the nearby Markagunt and Paunsaugunt plateaus seeing that these highlands were adjacent to the lands where most of OUO members lived and where they had ranch properties that would have been deeded to the Order. William Adair recalled that all of the sheep in the Long Valley area belonged to the OUO and to a man named "Cutler."[129] An early Garfield County history states the aggregated herds in the upper Sevier River country were United Order herds, although it is not specified which United Order (it might have been the order in Panguitch).[130]

On public ranges in this Mormon region, little distinction was made between the New Canaan cooperative herds and the OUO herds, which grazed in tandem, and the Mormon Church certainly had two ranches in Long Valley at the time. It might have been about this same time that OUO and church herds were pushed east into the Paria River drainage as the earliest historic inscriptions here are in the mid- to late-1870s.

Some evidence suggests ranchers who were not Mormon Church members began to operate on the Arizona Strip during the 1870s. Several authors who have written about livestock raising on the Arizona Strip in the 1870s and 1880s have concluded that a non-Mormon outfit using the VT brand was operating in this region, but this seems doubtful. The OUO was clearly the greatest economic force at play in the region in the 1870s, although in terms of livestock, grazing came to be focused more on the Arizona Strip than it was on Kane County. The events surrounding the VT brand in the 1870s are confusing and may never be resolved. Gregory Crampton believed the OUO acquired cattle in the mid-1870s from non-Mormon ranchers in the House Rock Valley who had branded their cattle with "VT," which stood for VT Park, an alternate name for DeMotte Park, a summer headquarters on the Kaibab.[131] DeMotte Park is just before the entrance to modern-day Grand Canyon National Park's North Rim and was claimed by Kanab Bishop Levi Stewart in the mid- to late 1870s. F. M. Hodgin suggested two men named Thompson and Van Sleck purchased the cattle from the Order and then branded them with the first initial of their surnames.[132] Robert Cleland and Juanita Brooks, quoting early settler Walter Hamblin, suggested VT stood for "Valley Tan," a reference to a Mormon Church-owned tannery in Long Valley.[133] R. E. Gery and John A. Smith believed the VT brand was used by local ranchers operating in the area alongside the United Order,[134] and Byrd Granger suggested that Van Slack and Thompson were both members of the Orderville community, but that the VT brand referred to Valley Tan.[135] Altschul and Fairley concluded that the VT brand came into existence in the mid-1870s or early 1880s, and that the VT operation coexisted for a time with the United Order. They state:

> The VT outfit apparently concentrated their winter operations in the lower portion of House Rock Valley, south of Kane Springs, and used the southern portion of the Kaibab Plateau during the summer, while OUO dominated the northern areas.[136]

There is some support for the idea that other, perhaps non-Mormon cattle ranchers were operating in the Arizona Strip area during the latter part of the OUO's tenure in the region in the 1880s, but there is no evidence of this in the 1870s. John Franklin Brown indicated he was hired by the "VT Ranch outfit" in 1884 to fence in the DeMotte Park Ranch. He stated the ranch was then owned by J. B. Elsie, a Mr. Gibson, W. E. Kennison and H. J. Jillett, all from Missouri and Indiana.[137] Adair stated the "VT cattle men[*sic*]" arrived on the Kaibab in 1877, or the same year as the OUO cattle arrived there.[138]

Researchers have been reluctant to accept the "Valley Tan" explanation of the VT brand, citing a lack of evidence for a tannery in Long Valley. This hesitancy seems ill-founded inasmuch as tanneries were clearly operating in both Kanab and Orderville at the time of the United Order experiment, as was a shoe manufacturing concern. One of the first ventures of the Kanab United Order, initiated in 1874, was the creation of a tannery, among other projects. The tannery and shoemaking shop were operated by Edwin Ford, Lyman E. Hamblin, and James Bunting.[139] Arrington stated the Orderville United Order (OUO) built a tannery, and that shoes manufactured there were referred to as "valley tan" shoes.[140] Furthermore, when the OUO was dissolved in 1885 under the direction of Kanab Stake President Edwin D. Woolley, "the order retained ownership of three entities: the tannery, the woolen factory and the sheep enterprise," all of which were leased to individuals who managed them.[141]

In view of the available evidence, non-Mormon ranchers probably did not operate on the Arizona Strip during the 1870s and 1880s. Any encroachment by non-Mormons into their ranges would have been greeted by hostility and suspicion that would have been noted in the historical record. This was certainly the case when non-Mormon cattle baron Preston Nutter moved into the region in the 1890s. But references to non-Mormon cattlemen are glaringly absent in the 1870s and most of the 1880s. The only evidence for non-Mormon stock raisers in the area is Brown's account of building a fence for a non-Mormon operation in 1884. Given that DeMotte Park was part of the Levi Stewart family holdings in the mid- to late-1870s when the brand was instituted, and the strong opposition of Mormon culture to non-Mormon economic interests, the VT brand, if derived from non-Mormon ranchers, would have been unlikely to be retained by church interests.

Also unresolved is the relationship of the OUO operations and the Levi Stewart ranch operations in the same area. Stewart, the Mormon bishop of Kanab, was part of the Kanab United Order, deeding his cattle operations on the Arizona Strip area to the Order in 1874. After the Kanab United Order failed, Levi Stewart regained ownership of his ranch holdings, which were later passed on to surviving members of the family, who in 1880 deeded them to the OUO.[142] Given Levi Stewart's ecclesiastical role in the community and the dedication of his family to Mormon Church principles, his cattle were likely to have grazed side by side with OUO cattle. Also possibly Stewart's operation was one and the same with the United Order operations there.

United Order operations in Garfield County are poorly represented in the early histories of the region. A "family" United Order was started by Thomas Rice King in Circle Valley, although this was later subsumed by a United Order settlement at Kingston, which was populated by arrivals from Millard County. Some residents of Grass Valley (Antimony) participated in the Kingston United Order, and United Order cattle and sheep herds were also grazed in the Grass Valley area.[143] The Panguitch United Order was established in December 1874 by Stake President Joseph A. Young with George Sevy as its president and John W. Newton as vice president. The Order managed stock-raising, dairying, freighting, smithing, milling, and farming. The Order failed within two years amid internal dissension. One resident observed the Order "took thrifty, energetic men and made lazy men of them."[144]

End of an Era

Mormon Church founder and prophet Joseph Smith had first envisioned a communal utopia for his followers as early as 1831, something later sanctified through revealed scripture in 1834 in Section 104 of the *Doctrine and Covenants*, a sacred tome to the Mormon faithful. Smith's vision anticipated a future Millennium. But his successor, Brigham Young, deftly mixed theology and private enterprise in the present. As he told the faithful: "My policy is to get rich. I am a miser in eternal things. Do I want to become rich in things of the earth? Yes, if the Lord wishes."[145]

After arriving as refugees in the alien landscape of the Great Basin, Young had introduced concepts of land stewardship and communalism. But in the professed need to develop timber, water, and grazing resources, the Mormon Church hierarchy granted control of almost all the Wasatch Mountains' canyons and forests to a select few. Brigham Young himself took possession of City Creek Canyon, the early primary water supply of Salt Lake City. When he died in 1877, Young was the richest man in Utah Territory, with an estate valued at approximately $2.5 million dollars. In the far-flung reaches of the territory in Kane and Garfield Counties, this same pattern of entwined church and business elites was also evident.[146]

The federal government's anti-polygamy campaign hastened the formal transfer of Mormon Church properties to individual elites. The church's formal dominance of territorial industries began to wane in the mid-1880s in the wake of the federal crackdown on polygamy. Passage of federal laws—

in particular, the Edmunds Act of 1882 and the Edmunds-Tucker Act of 1887—allowed the government to seize church property not linked to religious practices, as well as the holdings of practicing polygamists, if their value exceeded $50,000. In this political climate, church leaders advised the dissolution of the Orderville United Order, and in 1885 it began selling its commercial holdings, although in most cases the property was acquired by faithful members of the Mormon Church who served as *de facto* trustees for the church's interests. The U.S. attorney certainly took notice that $268,982 of church livestock and produce had been transferred to corporations operated by stake presidents,[147] thereby splitting the value of herds among dozens of local surrogates, the individual value of which was below the threshold for confiscation.

Edwin D. Woolley was clearly a *de facto* trustee at this time; the title to the Mormon Church ranches in Upper Kanab was transferred to Woolley in the mid-1880s. In fact, Woolley, who had arrived here in 1883 and was named the Kanab stake president in 1884, was a "committee of one" assigned by the church in 1885 to dissolve United Order holdings in southern Utah and northern Arizona.[148] Woolley's heirs retained ownership of former church properties on the Arizona Strip as late as 1931.[149] Two other *de facto* trustees at that time appear to have been John W. Young, a son of Brigham Young, and Anthony Ivins, who would later rise to prominence in the First Presidency of the Mormon Church.

Documents from 1887 show the intertwining of church businesses and chosen surrogates. For example, John Young was to purchase a ranch on the Strip and then contract Woolley and his associate, Dan Seegmiller, to run it. The Salt Lake City firm, Cannon, Grant & Company—with its board dominated by Heber J. Grant, George Q. Cannon, and other high leaders of the Mormon Church—was still working with Ivins to run horses and other stock with Woolley and Seegmiller in the mid-1890s.[150]

The passage of the Edmunds-Tucker Act of 1887 had long been viewed as inevitable by the Mormon Church hierarchy, and this certainty prompted a preemptive move by the church to avoid confiscation of its assets by divesting direct ownership at least two years before the law was passed. The church ranches in House Rock Valley were listed for sale in 1885, but no one bought them, and finding a buyer took two or three years. That buyer, however, was none other than John W. Young. The purchase price was $5,000, for which Woolley was paid a $1,500 commission.[151]

FIGURE 3.10. Brigham Young's son, John W. Young, became the largest livestock operator in the region after the failure of the United Order experiments, acting largely as a surrogate for the Mormon Church. Photograph courtesy of Utah State Historical Society Classified Photo Collection (39222001410625).

In 1876, John W. Young already operated a massive cattle operation, by some accounts 30,000 head in size, in the San Francisco Peaks and Little Colorado River area of northern Arizona. But by 1885, "polygamy and other troubles" had pushed him out of that area.[152] Young may indeed have been operating as a *de facto* trustee for the Mormon Church, or at least in close cooperation with church authorities. When the Edmunds-Tucker Act accelerated the divestiture of cooperative assets, some of those assets were passed to individual shareholders, one of whom was John W. Young. He acquired several hundred head of cattle from New Canaan and OUO that he used to stock his newly created Kaibab Cattle Company. Anthony Ivins also acquired six hundred head of cattle from New Canaan to start his Mohave Land and Cattle Company, headquartered at the Oak Grove Ranch. Both cattle companies were started in 1887 or 1888.[153] In 1891 the Kaibab Cattle Company was contracting with James S. Emett, who ran stock near Lee's Ferry, to deliver hundreds of horses to the outfit.[154]

Range conditions in the late 1880s did not portend well for new cattle ventures. A series of droughts in the 1870s had devastated the ranges. In addition, throughout the decades Mormon ranchers maintained an open policy toward the limited water sources. Ranchers who assumed responsibility for the maintenance of the springs were considered to be the rightful owners and had priority use of the water. But other ranchers were not barred from the springs if the supply was sufficient to support additional use. Altschul and Fairley state:

> This informal and open policy not only encouraged overuse of the range, but it also left the water sources and the surrounding range, open to use by stockmen from outside the area, some of whom did not share the local ranchers' time-honored approach towards range and water use rights.[155]

John W. Young embraced the new cattle enterprise with enthusiasm. In addition to House Rock Valley, he acquired major holdings on the Kaibab Plateau. He soon embarked on a major expansion that included a log cabin summer headquarters at DeMotte Park, and two new stone buildings, one at Jacob's Pools and the other at Kane Springs. Dan Seegmiller was placed in charge of operations and Woolley was designated foreman of the herds.[156] Apostle Erastus Snow had earlier called both men to Upper Kanab in 1882 to manage church herds and ranches.[157] The only difference this time was a new JWY brand, a modification of the church's Y brand, which had stood for Brigham Young.[158]

Both Woolley and Seegmiller were experienced veterans of the New Canaan and OUO cattle operations. The new outfit was apparently based out of Kanab with local wranglers hired to actually move the herds. Larson maintained the New Canaan cooperative was reorganized (in about 1887) as a quasi-private enterprise and that it maintained its House Rock Ranch headquarters and brand until 1895, when it sold out to B. F. Saunders.[159] The headquarters of John W. Young's cattle operation was also the House Rock Ranch, constructed earlier by the Canaan and Orderville cooperatives. This suggests that New Canaan was operating herds alongside Young's Kaibab Cattle Company on the same range, although New Canaan, as a business of the Mormon Church, was but a shadow of its former size and power.

The failure to find investors apparently resulted in financial difficulties for Young, who reorganized the company as the Kaibab Land and Cattle Company using money borrowed from New York bankers.[160] Another account suggests that Young was bought out by "Grant and Cannon" of Salt Lake City through the redemption of bonds, and that Anthony W. Ivins was assigned to manage the operation.[161] It seems likely that Ivins, whose first cousin was Mormon Apostle Heber J. Grant, was acting on appointment by the church.[162]

A biographical sketch prepared by the Utah State Historical Society confirms that Ivins became involved in the regional cattle industry in 1884, and that he was a manager of the Mohave Land and Cattle Company and also an "owner" of the Kaibab Cattle Company.[163] He certainly was acting as an agent of the church-dominated firm Cannon, Grant and Company in the mid-1890s, contracting for livestock-related services with local leaders such as Ed Woolley and Dan Seegmiller.[164]

B. F. Saunders, a non-Mormon Salt Lake businessman friendly to the church, also was probably working behind the scenes with church leaders to protect church assets. Ivins had earlier worked for Saunders, who arrived in the area in 1883 when he purchased the Oak Grove Ranch from the New

FIGURE 3.11. Anthony Ivins, a close relative of many leaders in the Mormon Church hierarchy in Salt Lake City, was also a surrogate for the church, working in tandem with John W. Young to protect church herds from confiscation by federal authorities. Photograph courtesy of Utah State Historical Society Classified Photo Collection (39222001352454).

FIGURE 3.12. The higher-elevation valleys in the upper Paria River country in the Cannonville and Henrieville areas were among the first settled after the cessation of the "Indian wars" in the 1870s. Photograph by Dan Bauer.

Canaan cooperative. Acting as a surrogate for the church, Ivins later purchased the Oak Grove Ranch from Saunders in the 1890s. Saunders then acquired the Pipe Spring Ranch, which was later reacquired by the church.[165] Saunders also employed Antoine Ivins, Anthony's son, as his agent for the purchase and sale of cattle; the younger Ivins was also prominent in the church hierarchy and would later become a church general authority himself.

Anthony Ivins was clearly among the most prominent of Mormon officials in the region, serving as mayor of St. George in 1890, being elected to the Utah Territorial Legislature in 1893, and serving on the Utah State Constitutional Convention in 1894. He was raised in frontier Arizona and Mexico, becoming a true cowboy and renowned hunter along the way. In 1907, he became a member of the Mormon Church's Quorum of the Twelve Apostles, and in 1921 he was named second counselor to Mormon Church President Heber J. Grant.[166] Given his ecclesiastical responsibilities and relationships with the Mormon

Church hierarchy, Ivins' involvement in the Kaibab outfit, however peripheral, suggests that John W. Young was a "front man" for Mormon Church ownership to avoid the complications of anti-polygamy laws that targeted church-owned property.

When asked to speak at the September 15, 1928, dedication of the Grand Canyon Lodge, Ivins said he came to the Kaibab Plateau in October 1875, where "I too became a tender of flocks and herds, first for others and later for myself." He indicated he became the representative of the "people who were the owners of the entire Kaibab Mountain and the Great House Rock Valley which lies to the east."[167] Ivins did not specify who those owners were.

Disillusionment and Defiance

The period from 1870 to 1890 was characterized by tremendous population growth. In 1870, the Kanab Census Precinct, the only one in what is today Kane County, logged seventy-two people; no one was yet living in what is today Garfield County, at the time part of Iron County. Ten years later, 1,396 people were living in what is today Kane County and another 1,715 living in what is today Garfield County. By 1890, Kane County, which had by then assumed its modern boundary, had 1,685 residents, a modest increase of 20 percent over ten years. In Garfield County, which had existed for only eight years and represented entirely new communities, there were 2,457 people in 1890, an increase of about 43 percent, suggesting most growth was associated with new settlements far north of Kanab, the one-time center of social and economic activity in the region.

The vast majority of these residents were faithful adherents to Mormonism. But the area also held a growing number of people who had become disaffected or disillusioned with the church, especially in the wake of the unsuccessful United Order experiments that did not sit well with some independent types. In addition, thousands of young people born and raised in Utah had not experienced the hardships their parents endured at the hands of mobs in Ohio, Missouri, and Illinois, and were less than enthusiastic about some of the increasingly tightening mandates of church leaders, especially proscriptions on tobacco and alcohol. These individuals identified themselves as Mormons culturally but were less than diligent in participating in church activities and spiritual initiatives.

Through at least 1890, very few non-Mormons lived in the region. In the 1870s, Southerner and Civil War veteran Lige M. Moore trailed a herd of horses from Arizona to Utah by way of Lee's Ferry to trade for cattle and was one of the few non-Mormons in the Grand Staircase and Escalante area. Once there he decided to put down roots in Georgetown and later Henrieville. He remained a beloved member of the community for nearly six decades. The McCarty Brothers, Bill and Tom, are identified in various histories as non-Mormons, but they had also married into Mormon families in Sanpete County. Tom married Teenie Christianson, the sister of Willard Christianson, who would later become famous as the outlaw-turned-lawman Matt Warner.[168]

The McCarty brothers had come to Utah with their father, a cattle trader, in search of unspoiled rangelands, and by 1874 they had a ranch in Grass Valley, perhaps in partnership with others, one of whom was reported to be Orrin Porter Rockwell, a former bodyguard of prophet Joseph Smith. Rockwell was known as the "Destroying Angel of Mormondom," the most feared lawman in Utah Territory. On a trading expedition, one of the McCarty brothers (the histories do not specify which one or if it was both) killed three Navajos who had broken into their cabin and either slaughtered a calf to keep from starving or stole a horse, depending on the account.[169]

The killings resulted in Navajo demands for retribution and threats to resume raiding Mormon settlements. Jacob Hamblin led a Navajo delegation to Grass Valley so that Hamblin could demonstrate the Mormons were not responsible for the killings. The McCartys soon left the area and eventually became adept cattle rustlers in San Juan County. Later, they organized a family outlaw gang responsible for bank holdups in eastern Oregon and western Colorado. Bill and his son were killed during a holdup in Delta, Colorado. Tom lived out the rest of his life as a respected cattleman in Montana.[170]

At the time, as the McCarty family business indicates, both non-Mormon and Mormons utilized kinship bonds to raise livestock in the region. Mormon families were traditionally very large, and most of these residents were young (under age eighteen). Many were headed by a patriarch with several plural wives, with the women often managing specific parts of family businesses in the absence of their husbands.[171] Large families were needed to work the farms, and children participated in all aspects of farm life from an early age: plowing, planting, irrigating, milking cows, and keeping rodents and other varmints at bay. Most males tended livestock from their early teens, learning to ride, rope, and shoot rifles (pistols were rare at the time). During the early era of cooperative herds, the cooperative or United Order would designate a manager of herds, sometimes one manager for sheep and another for cattle. And given that most families were working toward the common good, it stands to reason that many if not most families would contribute teenage sons toward the tending of the large livestock herds.

As beef cattle became an important cash crop, families not involved in livestock cooperatives or United Order livestock operations probably ran some cattle on their own, although they would have felt the pinch of shrinking rangelands due to the larger aggregated herds in the prime grazing areas of the upper Sevier River and upper Virgin River. Some of these "independent" ranchers had resources to hire laborers, often local teenagers and sometimes professional wranglers who drifted from one ranch to another. Some of these teenagers turned to rustling cattle to get in on the lucrative beef business, a "trade" that would prove highly detrimental to livestock ranchers in the region.

Typical of this scenario is the story of Maximillian "Max" Parker, who had migrated to Utah as a child after his family converted to Mormonism in England. In 1865, he met and married Ann Gillies, a Scottish woman who had also come to Utah as a child by way of England. Both the Parker and Gillies families had been sent by church leaders to settle in Beaver. Their first son, Robert, who went by "Bob," was born in 1866. In 1879, Max had put together enough money to purchase an existing 160-acre farm and two-room cabin in Circle Valley, which Max had determined to be a fine place to raise their children (the old homestead has been developed into a historical site today). The family, which had by then grown to six children, was poor, and Max left frequently and for long spells to work at various silver mines, returning with cash wages and a new smoking habit that irritated his wife.

Robert, then only thirteen, hired out as a ranch hand to Patrick Ryan, who taught him the fundamentals of handling cattle. Robert worked on the Ryan ranch for two years before taking another ranch hand job closer to home. With the combined wages of Robert and Max, the family was able to purchase brood stock, but the cruel winter of 1879–80 effectively wiped out their new herd. Other setbacks and apparently some disputes with neighbors were resolved by the local bishop in favor of the neighbors. The results of these conflicts left Max disenchanted with what he viewed as the overbearing dictates of the church. Robert, and later Robert's brothers, followed their father's example and, as Robert Parker's biographer Richard Patterson observed:

> side-stepped [the church's] strict covenants when possible. Even before moving to Circleville, while living in Beaver, Bob would find endless excuses not to go to services, and eventually his mother gave up trying to force him to go.[172]

With the family left destitute by the loss of their herd, Max returned to work at various mining towns and Ann took a job running the dairy on the Jim Marshall ranch 8 mi away. Two of her sons were hired to help with the dairy, and Robert was hired as a cowhand. It was there that Robert met another cowhand, Mike Cassidy, who was only a few years older but already a seasoned wrangler with a knack for rustling on the side. As Patterson notes:

> Rustling was an ongoing problem in and around Circle Valley, especially the picking off of mavericks (unbranded calves separated from their mothers), which would be whisked away from the herd as soon as they could feed on their own.[173]

Mike Cassidy probably taught Robert a thing or two about rustling unbranded calves. He also gave Robert a pistol and taught him how to use it.[174] When Robert LeRoy Parker turned eighteen, he rode away and into the history books as Butch Cassidy.

Historian Charles Kelly makes a case that the era of cattle rustling in Utah's hinterlands began about 1875, or the same time as the ongoing economic depression that devastated small farmers and ranchers across the West. It also coincided with the emergence of large cattle operations that had claimed most of the public domain for themselves. He said, "If some misguided cowpuncher with a few months' pay in his pocket planned to start a ranch of his own on a small scale, he found his efforts violently opposed by the large ranch operators."[175] A common response of the upstart rancher was to round up unbranded calves and put his own mark on them; a few calves here and there from a large herd would never be missed. Kelly argued that many small ranchers in southern Utah were rustlers on the side.

Stealing cattle from church-owned herds presented moral dilemmas, even for "Jack Mormons" who had stopped attending services. The herds owned by cattle barons seemed fair game, but the stock run by the New Canaan and

FIGURE 3.13. Butch Cassidy's childhood home just south of Circleville has become a tourist attraction. Photograph by Dan Bauer.

the Orderville United Order seemed different. These were aggregated church herds, and rustling cows from the church that were intended to feed poor people would incur not only the wrath of your neighbors but God himself. But apparently enough Jack Mormons overcame these moral dilemmas, and cattle rustling became a problem beginning in the 1870s, not only in Kane and Garfield Counties but throughout the territory.[176]

As a result, rustling was pervasive in some areas of Garfield County in the 1870s and 1880s. Kelly claims an outlaw band was based out of a ranch in Bryce Canyon. In 1882, the *Salt Lake Tribune* reported that Kane County was "being overrun with cattle and horse thieves. It appears that there is an organized band in that locality who steal cattle and rebrand them so as to cover up the old brand, and then sell to others." The rustlers conducted a "big business" in stock theft for two years. As *The Salt Lake Tribune* wrote, they were a rough bunch of "blood atoucrs [*sic*] of whom the people fear to come in contact or excite their ire. This appears to be a good place for some [illegible] detective to operate in."[177]

Part of a national trend,[178] local ranchers in 1883 organized the Southern Utah and Northern Arizona Stock Protective Association, incorporated in Kanab for "the protection of the interests of the stock owners of Southern Utah and Northern Arizona from the raids of Cattle thieves and other unprincipled persons who may seek to destroy or injure the stock interests in the region."[179] It was the first stock association of its kind in Utah.[180] Kane County formally sanctioned the association and even covered its expenses. Such bodies were given quasi-legal authority to enforce rustling laws through the hiring of "stock detectives," some of them ex-lawmen, some of them former outlaws, and all of them ruthless. Rustling in those days was a felony that carried up to ten years in prison and a $5,000 fine.[181] Stock detectives were notorious for eliminating the problem using their own means. One detective, an ex-Texas Ranger and on-again-off-again outlaw, casually noted in a letter to a family member that he had killed six rustlers during his short employ with cattleman Preston Nutter.[182]

While cattle rustling is rarely mentioned in local histories, Kelly related a story (undated) where outlaws Tom McCarty, Matt Warner, and Josh Swett, the latter a young man from Panguitch, stole a herd of cattle in Mexico and fled north. They were chased by federal lawmen and were forced to leave the stolen herd behind in a shootout with deputies. Swett was shot three times in the exchange, but continued riding just ahead of the posse. The outlaws crossed the Colorado River on Lee's Ferry and made their way to Kanab, where Swett was left to recuperate in the care of friends.[183] Matt Warner later wrote: "That was the last we ever saw of him. He got well and quit the outlaw life."[184]

Pearl Baker relates another story of a notorious Robbers Roost outlaw named Jim Wall, who went by the name Silver Tip because of gray hair around his temples, whose exploits got him into trouble in the Grand Staircase region. After years of thievery, Silver Tip was finally arrested by lawmen in an abandoned cabin about 40 mi north of Lee's Ferry. He was shackled and transported first to Kanab and then sent to the district court in Beaver. After a trial and conviction, old Silver Tip's days of freedom and robbery ended when he was finally locked up in the state penitentiary.[185]

Other outlaws plagued the canyon country around Kanab. According to Frank Hamblin, local cattleman James "Jim" Emett was sent to spy on one group of horse rustlers, "men named Smith," but the accused became suspicious and killed the horses. "These men were [later] arrested for stealing cattle and served time to pay for it," Hamblin recounts.[186] John Wesley Mangum related another account of four robbers who stayed the night in Cannonville at the home of Kanace Fletcher. An Arizona sheriff arrived before the men arose and arrested two of them; the other two escaped to Coal Bench where they hid among a flock of sheep. The sheriff arrived the following morning, and, as Mangum recalled, "one man refused to surrender so his horse was shot out from under him. The sheriff put both men on a train, but the rebellious one jumped off and got away."[187]

Certain outlaws were afforded a measure of respect, especially those who reportedly played the role of "Robin Hood" and were of Mormon heritage with genealogical ties to rural communities. As Matt Warner, a Mormon from Sanpete County, later wrote:

> Like lots of cowboy outlaws in them days Butch and me liked to give lots of our money to the poor, the needy and the deserving. In this way we made sort of Robin Hoods of ourselves in our own eyes, gained a lot of popularity and protection from the public, and squared ourselves in our own estimation.[188]

Butch Cassidy and his outlaw bunch entered local folklore in tales that celebrated his cowboy-outlaw heritage and debated death in South America in 1908. Butch Cassidy counted local ranchers among his family and friends, and multiple stories recount various instances when Butch stopped to visit them well into the 1940s. His brother, Bill Parker, eventually settled in Fredonia just south of Kanab, where Butch reportedly visited in 1941. John Kitchen, who had a ranch in the Paria River country, was a close friend,[189] as was Lige Moore, who invited several local residents to visit with Butch during a purported visit in 1937 or 1938.[190]

Besides rumored visits by former outlaw Butch Cassidy, rustlers were still a dangerous and feared presence in southern Utah well into the 1930s. When a young traveler named Everett Ruess—later well-known as a desert explorer, poet and artist—vanished from a side canyon near the Hole-in-the-Rock Road in 1934, some believed Ruess was the victim of mistaken identity, killed by local cattle thieves who believed he was a covert government agent.

During the latter decades of the nineteenth century, few accounts reference non-Mormons, malcontents or otherwise, in the area. When John Wesley

Powell's survey crew arrived in Kanab in the winter of 1871–72, the presence of non-Mormons in their midst provoked considerable excitement, especially among "a swarm of children peeping through every crevice of the logs to get a view of the Gentiles, a kind of animal they had seldom seen."[191]

Erased from History

There is little doubt that the chroniclers of the early histories, faithful Mormons themselves, were biased in that they only told the stories of their faithful ancestors to the exclusion of others outside the fabric of Mormon culture. This was certainly the case with the dearth of references to Indigenous Americans after 1870. As previously noted, Jacob Hamblin worked closely with Southern Paiutes in the Kanab area to teach them Anglo-American agriculture and animal husbandry in the early 1870s, and many herdsmen at that time were probably Paiutes. But no further mention of Southern Paiute herdsmen occurs in the years that followed, along with very few references to Indigenous Americans in any context other than occasional hostilities and confrontation.

One of the primary reasons the first Mormon colonists were sent to southern Utah in the 1850s was to convert the Lamanites, as the Mormons referred to all Indigenous groups. According to the Book of Mormon, the ancestors of Native Americans, the Lamanites, had fallen into wickedness and were cursed by God. Their redemption through Mormon conversion would be a sign of the imminent Second Coming of Christ. As such, converting Indigenous peoples was considered a sacred responsibility ordained of God, especially among the first generation of Mormons who had settled among them in Utah. Such idealism faded quickly. The three years of violence that characterized the Black Hawk War ended in 1869, and hostilities with the Navajo ceased over the next two years. The termination of warfare also seems to have ended any serious interest by Latter-day Saints in converting their Southern Paiute neighbors. No references to the Southern Indian Mission are made after the Black Hawk War, and local county histories and journals make few references to Paiutes.

By and large, the Southern Paiutes had not participated in the Black Hawk War, and in the few instances when a Paiute turned to raiding, other Paiutes were more than willing to guide the Mormon militias into the forbidding Grand Canyon country where the raiders had taken refuge. When the defeated Northern Utes were forced onto the Uinta Basin reservation in the 1870s, the

Southern Paiutes, what few remained, adamantly refused to join the Utes who had preyed upon them for generations.

Instead, the Southern Paiute stayed, living and surviving alongside their Mormon neighbors. Some persisted on "Indian farms" near Cedar City, while others retreated deep into the Mt. Trumbull country of the Arizona Strip where they hunted and gathered in their traditional ways. Many lived among the Mormons in the Kanab area well into the 1930s when they were first interviewed by famed ethnographer Isabel T. Kelly. She observed at that time that many traditional Southern Paiute bands were extinct and others nearly so.[192] But no formal treaties protected reservations in their homeland, and their population numbers were too small to command attention.

The paucity of favorable references to the Southern Paiute after 1870 is noteworthy and likely reflects a regional antagonism that emerged in the wake of the Black Hawk War. When interviewed decades later by Peter Gottfredson, many of the Mormon militiamen who participated in the conflict described the Indigenous Americans in extremely racist terms, and they repeatedly expressed beliefs they should have been exterminated.[193]

In the last two decades of the nineteenth century, many Mormons called for the removal of the remaining Paiute groups and the creation of small reservations for them well outside local Mormon communities. Rancher and future apostle Anthony Ivins became a leader of this effort. Ivins grew up alongside Indigenous American cowboys as he learned to rope, ride, hunt, and wrangle, becoming so skilled as a cowboy that he was posthumously elected to the National Cowboy Hall of Fame.[194] Ronald Holt noted that Ivins had a reputation as a "friend of the Indian." The existing documentation, however, presents a more complicated picture of Ivins' role in their ultimate removal and relocation. More than the average Mormon, Ivins was given special church callings to minister to Indigenous Americans. When called to work in Mexico, Ivins received a blessing from Apostle Moses Thatcher that Ivins would be doing important work and become an "instrument in the hand of God to do great work among [the Lamanites]."[195]

In the 1880s as manager of the Mohave Land and Cattle Company, Ivins often came into contact with the Shivwits Paiutes of the Kaibab Plateau. Starving Paiutes sometimes even took Ivins' cattle for food. About these encounters, Ronald Holt notes that Ivins felt the Paiute men were "insolent," stealing his cattle and justifying the theft as a form of "payment" in return for the Mormons' taking Paiute lands and leaving them destitute.[196] By the 1890s, Ivins was working to have the Shivwits Paiutes removed entirely from the Arizona Strip, as we discuss in the next chapter.

Famed explorer John Wesley Powell also spent considerable time among the Southern Paiutes in the early 1870s, and proved an astute and sympathetic observer of their customs, beliefs, language, and way of life.[197] In 1873, the Bureau of Indian Affairs hired him and G. W. Ingalls as "special commissioners" to investigate the "conditions and wants" of the Great Basin tribes. Their trip brought them to St. George where they called a meeting attended by scores of surviving Southern Paiutes. Photographer John K. "Jack" Hillers accompanied Powell and Ingalls to this gathering where Hillers produced the earliest photographs of the Southern Paiutes, photographs that are widely seen today. Unfortunately, Congress never acted on their recommendation that reservations be established in Nevada.[198]

Like other Americans, Mormons were paternalistic toward the Paiutes, believing they knew what was best for them, and that meant conversion to Mormonism and eventual assimilation. Until plans for their removal came to fruition, Holt determined that whites tolerated their presence because they provided an inexpensive and docile labor force.[199] The Southern Paiutes see this period simply as a time of their "near destruction" at the hands of the Mormons.[200]

Summary

By 1870, the official Mormon settlement of what is today Kane County and Garfield County had begun with the arrival of hundreds of immigrants, mostly young families looking to establish a farm of their own. With few acres viable for farming, many of these families embraced raising livestock as a means to make a living. Between 1870 and 1890, the region probably had more sheep than cattle as the wooly animals were valuable commodities for Mormon Church mills and essential to home-based economies. Most families kept one or more milk cows for their own dairy needs and to produce milk, cream, butter, and cheese for sale or trade. A few got into the cattle business, not because there was a demand in the Mormon communities for beef, but because cattle represented an important source of currency in this part of the American West.

Through the implementation of Mormon Church cooperatives and later the United Order, Latter-day Saints merged sheep and cattle herds. Faithful church members were expected to contribute their herds to the greater community good, and as a result open ranges soon featured large herds of livestock run by United Orders, both sheep and cattle. These valuable animals seem to have attracted outlaw elements to southern Utah by the late 1870s, who preyed on the Mormon stock. In a real sense, the geographic barriers that had allowed the Mormon communities to prosper in isolation were collapsing by the 1880s.

By 1890, the Mormon Church was officially out of the livestock business, shuttering the livestock cooperatives and disbanding the United Orders. This decade also ushered in a new era of private livestock operations, including some large ranches but mostly family spreads that would shape the new regional economy within the context of homesteading laws and the emergence of federal grazing policies. The surnames associated with this new order would be largely the same as in the previous generation, along with a few new faces. The Mormon goals of social and religious isolationism would continue, but more as unofficial policy than church doctrine.

The transformation of cooperative livestock operations to individual family ranches might have occurred sooner in the Garfield County area where the dominance of church herds was limited to the upper Sevier River area (Johns Valley and Hillsdale) and the upper Paria River region. Vast areas of the Aquarius Plateau, Boulder Mountain, and the Kaiparowits Plateau were outside the range of the church herds, or at least the large ones. And as families flocked to new frontier communities such as Cannonville and Escalante, the cooperatives were less an influencing factor in their social structure. Rather, their geographic isolation required more individual self-reliance, which in turn promoted the dominance of family ranches.

FIGURE 4.1. Cottonwood Canyon, Grand Staircase. Photograph by Dan Bauer.

4 Death of a Frontier

Overgrazing and the End of the Open Range, 1890–1934

By the 1890s, the once-lush grasslands of the Grand Staircase and Arizona Strip country had been laid to waste by herds of cattle and flocks of sheep, with the livestock numbering in the hundreds of thousands. Their fabled bounty lived only in the memories of the first pioneer settlers. The overcrowding of the rangelands occurred on the heels of extended droughts in the 1870s that stubbornly refused to allow native grasses to regenerate under the onslaught of increasing herd sizes. Not a unique occurrence, drought was a persistent devil in this country, raising its head every five to seven years, some dry periods lasting a year or two, the longest persisting eighteen years. Two of the six worst droughts in southern Utah's modern history occurred between 1898–1905 and 1928–1936.[1]

During one dry spell in the summer of 1903, Lenora LeFevre wrote:

> The once rich meadows on the [Boulder] mountain had turned to dust beds. Herds of sheep were bedding by the streams and dying along the banks. Bones of cattle bleached on dry benches. The cattle lingered around the mud holes. Those in a weakened condition would flounder in the mud and die. Poison weeds that grew after the better feed was gone added to the death toll of the starving cattle.[2]

Historians Linda King Newell and Vivian Linford Talbot make the case that ranchers knew the rangelands could not sustain so many large herds, but many were hesitant, or at least they had no personal incentive, to reduce the size of their herds. The local economy was inextricably tied to cattle and sheep ranching. If fewer animals were on the range, less money would flow into their family businesses. Everyone would suffer, from the shopkeepers to blacksmiths and teamsters.[3] In a very real sense, what played out on Utah's open ranges was a case study of the economic theory known as the tragedy of the commons, where individual users of a shared resource acting in their own self-interests behave contrary to the good of all users by depleting that resource.[4]

Even with Mormon Church oversight of many areas of local life, there appears to have been no formal management of the rangelands for long-term sustainability in those times. If patches of grass were present, someone would be willing to push livestock onto it. Geographer John B. Wright has found that whatever deeply held, divinely-inspired land ethic that developed shortly after the Mormons' arrival in Utah quickly gave way to the typical American pattern of land exploitation. Many faithful came to believe that God condoned economic exploitation and the accumulation of wealth as a sign that they were living godly lives.[5]

The Mormon Church was deeply involved in making sure the land's resources were used efficiently and profitably by its members. Prior to the 1890s, church leaders determined which parties had the rights to graze livestock, and likewise ecclesiastical authorities resolved disputes over certain ranges. But there were few conflicts among Mormon ranchers, at least not very many that were made public. Grazing in those days, for all intents and purposes, involved Mormon Church herds, owned and managed by faithful church members for the good of all.

The collapse of Mormon livestock cooperatives in the 1880s, however, resulted in an economic power vacuum throughout the region. On the Arizona Strip, where the best rangelands were located, this void was promptly filled by two massive non-Mormon cattle corporations: the Grand Canyon Cattle Company (also known as the Bar Z) on the east and the Nutter Livestock Company on the west. Both companies brought a ruthlessness and intense competition to their cattle ranching that contrasted with the traditional Mormon ethos of cooperation and shared use of God's gifts for the benefit of all. These companies presented a significant challenge to traditional Mormon dominance of the Grand Staircase and Arizona Strip region and its cattle and sheep economy.

By this time, a new industrial beef industry was in ascendance. Railroad links with eastern markets and refrigerated railcars had made Western cities, like Salt Lake City and Denver, and Chicago in the Midwest centers of the beef industry. Meat packing plants run by Swift and Armour made beef available to many Americans. Cookbooks and magazine articles dismissed the old American mainstay, pork, as unwholesome while touting beef as a "health food." Steak became a symbol of the "good life" for elites and newly arrived immigrants alike.

Per capita beef consumption peaked in the early twentieth century. Southern Utah stock raisers knew there was a ready market if only they could achieve a closer rail link.[6]

The cattle barons restricted their monopolies to the Arizona Strip, but farther to the north, in Kane and Garfield Counties, the collapse of centralized church control over stock operations resulted in a splintering of the large cooperative herds among a multitude of smaller family-owned ranches. In aggregate, these smaller outfits also had herds numbering in the tens of thousands—so there was little impact on the overstocking of ranges. As Charles Peterson observed, these smaller ranchers were the economic lifeblood of the region; as they "got rich, towns grew, and the country filled up."[7]

In effect, two livestock models competed in the region. One was large-scale and corporate, and the other smaller and family-based. The corporate, profit-driven approach was typified by a large operator who stocked the range with thousands of purebred cattle. Steers and heifers were fattened on the hoof, then shipped by rail to eastern markets in Chicago, Kansas City, and Omaha. After sale, shareholders were paid. These corporate ranches bred purebred heifers to the finest bulls money could buy. The viability of ranching corporations rested in the large scale of the operation wherein tens of thousands of high-quality animals commanded top dollar. Similar to a colonial relationship to outside capital, aside from local wranglers hired by the big outfits, local communities did not receive much direct economic benefit.

The other model was typified by individual families who capitalized their own small ranch operations. The biggest cost was acquiring enough breed stock, and most of these families had comparatively small herds. In the early twentieth century, the Utah family farm and ranching economy was still strong, but the size of the operations paled by comparison to neighboring states. In 1920, Utah ranchers had the second lowest number of cattle per farm in the Intermountain West at 7.9 cows per farm. In Nevada, the ratio was 40.9 cows per farm, and in neighboring Arizona, the count was 29.3 cows per farm.[8] Ranch employees were typically unpaid family members, and overhead was low.

Until the early twentieth century, ranchers rarely could afford the new cattle breeds that were in high demand, such as Herefords, so their inferior crossbred animals were generally of lesser value. Economic return was determined by the natural increase in their own herds that family outfits could either sell to feedlots for fattening, sell to other ranchers seeking to expand their own herds, trade for goods and services, or, in the case of heifers, retain to expand the size of the rancher's own herd. Family outfits saw cash money only if they sold some or all of their increase.

Often referred to as cow-calf operations, the hopes and aspirations of family ranching operations rested in the mathematics of natural increase and the potential to rapidly increase the scale of even the smallest operation. In theory, a small rancher with a herd of one hundred pregnant heifers would produce one hundred calves, roughly half females and half males. If the female calves were retained in the herd, there would be 150 female cows the next year, 225 the following year, 337 the year after that. Within five years, the rancher would have more than five hundred females—a 400 percent increase on an initial investment.[9]

Based on the theory of natural increase and exponential growth, cow-calf operations became the dominant method of raising cattle in southern Utah, a fact that continued into the Grand Staircase-Escalante National Monument era.[10] Oscar Judd, a long-time rancher in Kane County, describes the process of raising the "crop." As he relates:

> We'd take the cattle out in the fall. Then they'd calve in the spring and then we'd bring them back in the spring. And put them on private lands during the summer. And then the buyers would come down and we'd sell them in the fall. You'd keep the calves until they'd get a certain age and weight, as big as they can and then you'd sell them, like they do now. They just raise a cow and calf crop and sell the calf in the fall and breed the cow back and have another'n next year.[11]

Across the American West, the possibility of owning vast herds and getting rich from what was originally a small number of cattle lured thousands into the ranching business. Of course, the exponential increases did not take into account the effects of predators, rustling, disease, drought, freak weather events, and the cyclical demand for beef and wool. But the *potential* for profit with minimal capital outlay prompted hundreds of families to take up ranching, most of them poor, undercapitalized, and easily wiped out by a single catastrophic event. According to one account, during one bleak period from 1896 to 1900, half the cattle on the Garfield County ranges died of starvation.[12] But there was no shortage of would-be ranchers willing to give it a try, and with no limits on the number of livestock on the range and with so many individual ranchers getting into the business, it is not surprising the available rangelands dwindled rapidly in quality.

Writing of his own family's cattle operation in the Salina region, Glynn Bennion lamented that:

> This process under a regime of unlimited grazing goes on until in a tragically short time the vegetation left alive on ranges of six to twelve inches of annual rainfall bears little resemblance to the original forms. So when I remember how my father and uncles and their fellow herdsmen used to rave about how wonderful the ranges were in early days, and how fat the horses and cattle and sheep got on them, I feel only a bitter sense of irony of it all. Why did they have to wreck those ranges at a time when they gained so pitifully little from doing it?[13]

The period from 1890 to 1934, the year when Congress passed the Taylor Grazing Act, was a momentous era in the history of stock raising in the Grand Staircase, Escalante River, and Arizona Strip country. It marked a time not only of uncontrolled growth in the size and geographic reach of cattle and sheep operations, but also of early government attempts through the Forest Reserve Act of 1891 to curtail the unfettered exploitation of the nation's natural resources.[14] It witnessed the emergence of cattle barons throughout the West, including several in the local area. The era birthed an array of cattle rustlers who preyed on the massive herds of the day. And it marked the end of free grass when anyone who could muster some breed stock could become a rancher. In this period, sheep ranching also supplanted cattle in economic importance, at least for a time, and many local ranchers took to raising Angora goats. Ranching's halcyon days in the years leading up to World War I were to be followed by the Great Depression that strangled demand for rural Utah's livestock.

This forty-four-year period is best understood through a series of events and developments, some local and others regional, that changed the small, village-based livestock economy into a robust livestock industry of statewide importance. As America became more and more industrialized in the 1890s, the national demand for beef exploded, leading to the emergence of Chicago as the nation's meat-packing center. The high demand (and high profits) lured large cattle companies to run stock in every corner of the West, appropriating vast stretches of public lands as their own fiefdoms, often without valid legal claims. The size of herds in the American West increased exponentially. The

FIGURE 4.2. A sheep herder tends to his flock at Duck Lake, Kane County, in the late nineteenth century. Sheep ranching emerged as a major Utah industry at that time, only to crash spectacularly by the middle twentieth century. Photograph by R. D. Adams, Barbara A. Matheson Special Collections (ph11b1i257), Gerald R. Sherratt Library, Southern Utah University, Cedar City.

Grand Staircase and Escalante country was no exception. In Kane County, there were 2,745 head of cattle in 1880. By 1890 there were 12,490 head, a 355 percent increase in ten years. In Garfield County, there were 5,382 head of cattle in 1890; ten years later that number had swollen to 11,323 head, a 110 percent rise.[15]

In addition to the vast increase in cattle herds, overgrazing of the public ranges was exacerbated by the growing number of sheep men in the region with flocks typically five to seven times greater than those of cattle. The Utah Territory had 1 million sheep in 1885, and 1.5 million in 1890. By 1900, the total had soared to 3.8 million head. Numbers declined sharply by 1910 to 1.6 million head, but then rose to 2.3 to 2.4 million head through 1934.[16] The 1890s and early 1900s also were characterized by growing conflicts, in some areas violent ones, between the cattlemen and the sheep men.[17] These clashes led cattlemen to band together under the umbrella of livestock associations to demand legislative solutions to protect their interests from the "odious" sheepherder.[18]

The 1890s marked the emergence of federal laws and policies that restricted some uses of the public domain. A growing conservation movement in the 1880s and 1890s resulted in the passage of the Forest Reserve Act of 1891 which had mechanisms by which the president could protect critical forest lands. The law was by no means purely "conservation" oriented. The timber industry backed the measure out of alarm over the economic instability of its markets. Decades of small-operator competition, reckless cutting, and boom and busts in timber markets led industry leaders to back the measure to have federal agents provide some measure of order and stability to lumbering. Joined by the American Forest Association and noted forester Gifford Pinchot, these parties often used the conservationist rhetoric of democracy and the general good to push for federal forest reserves. They worked to bring technical expertise and scientific management to rationalize the exploitation of timber resources.

Republican President Benjamin Harrison supported the Forest Reserve Act, along with urban leaders concerned about their water supply due to erosion and runoff from denuded slopes. He created the first federal forest reserves, totaling more than 3 million acres between 1891–1892. His successor, Democratic President Grover Cleveland, used his executive power to set aside more than 21 million acres. Republican President William McKinley established millions more acres of forest reserves until Congress ended a president's power to set aside forest lands. The 1891 legislation failed to specify how these reserves were to be managed and in the short term, they were off-limits to use. This caused an outcry among some Western timber, grazing, and mining interests. As such, the wide array of groups that supported the original 1891 forest law—including miners, livestock interests, timber companies, preservationists, the American Forest Association, and the National Academy of Sciences—backed a new law, dubbed the "Organic Administration Act" of 1897, that provided some guidance as to overseeing federal forest lands. The act made it clear that the primary purpose of the forest reserves was to provide a steady supply of timber products for the growing nation. Western senators almost to a one supported the measure, seeing it opened forest reserves to managed uses. This mandate would provide the basis for federal lands management for the next sixty years. Most national forests were established under this law.[19]

The Mormon Church hierarchy likewise supported the establishment of managed forest reserves. Church leaders could see the destruction caused by unrestricted grazing and timber cutting in Wasatch Mountains canyons and forestlands near their Salt Lake City headquarters. Flash floods ripped through long-established Mormon towns; once dependable streams began to dry earlier in the season. A 1902 federal forest study found that scarcely an oak sapling or tuft of bunch grass could be found in many mountain ravines. Against vocal opposition, the Mormon Church supported President Theodore Roosevelt's establishment of the states' first United States Forest Service reserves in 1906. While having the public health in mind, much like other supporters of federal intervention, church leaders liked the idea of exclusive use rights.[20]

Albeit in the interest of industry, this trend toward scientific management of federal lands led to the first grazing limits on forest tracts, including lands that are now part of the Kaibab and Dixie national forests. The conservation ethic promoted by President Theodore Roosevelt also included the designation through presidential proclamations of national monuments to protect treasures like the Grand Canyon, to establish game preserves, and to regulate grazing on tribal lands by non-Indigenous Americans. These conservation policies led to organized local opposition to any and all federal land designations.

By 1900, the geographic isolation of Kane and Garfield Counties from urban markets was ameliorated by the establishment of rail depots at Marysvale, about 50 mi north of Panguitch, and at Modena, about 65 mi north of St. George. These railheads eliminated the need for long cattle drives that could last a month or more, lowered the costs of other goods needed and desired by local communities, and allowed stock growers in the region to compete more equitably with ranchers in northern and central Utah who had long enjoyed more convenient rail access. The railroads also created a perception among many local ranchers that the larger U.S. market for their cattle, sheep, and wool was limitless, and if they simply produced more they would sell more.

The evolution of a livestock economy in Kane and Garfield counties decidedly contrasts to what occurred on the Arizona Strip at this time. Both areas would remain culturally intertwined, but their livestock economies would diverge after 1890. The reason was simple: non-Mormon cattle operators moved into the Arizona Strip, wresting control of the land and water from Mormon ranchers. These cattle barons never established a foothold farther to the north in the well-populated Mormon villages, thereby allowing family ranchers to proliferate and a family ranching subculture to emerge. Utah-based ranching would not expand onto the Arizona Strip until the 1930s and 1940s after the

Cattle Barons of the Arizona Strip

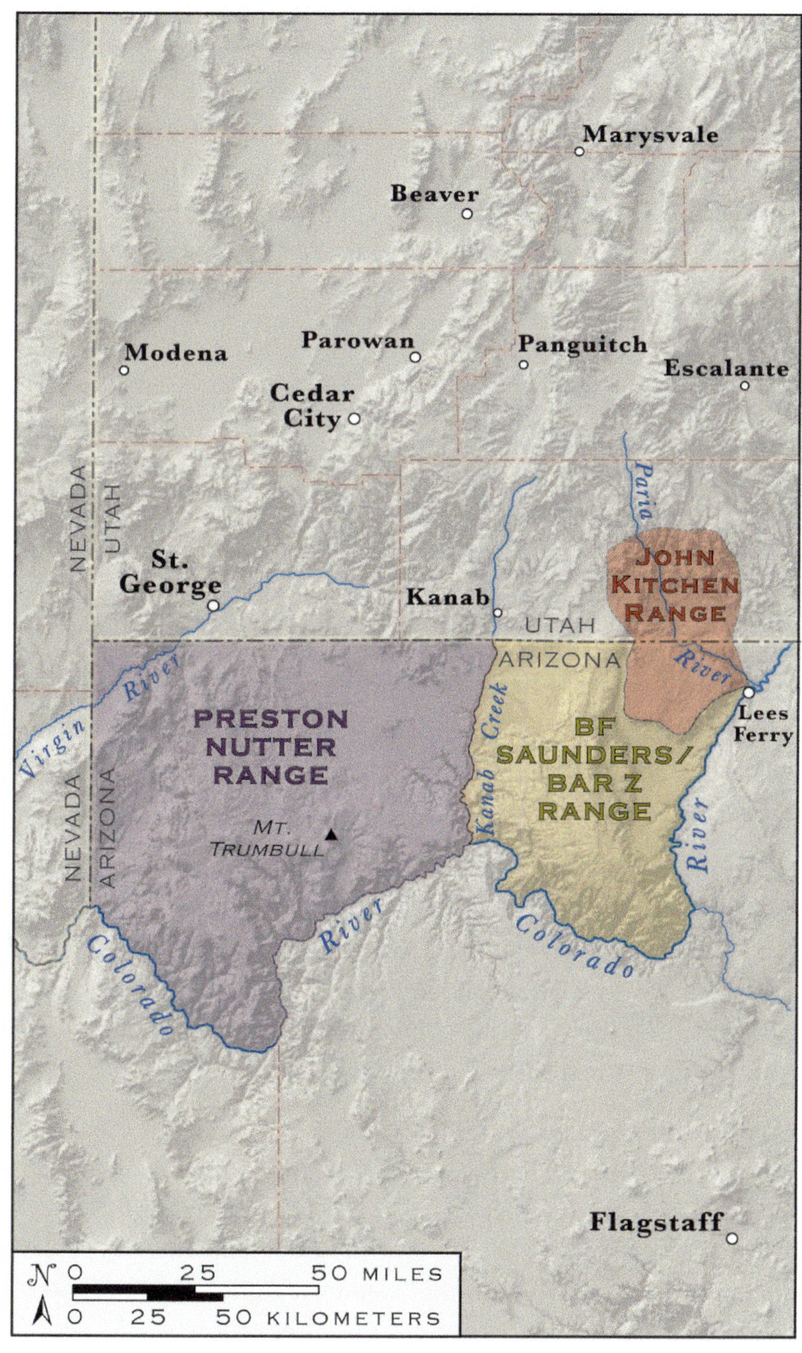

FIGURE 4.3. The 1890s saw the emergence of cattle barons on the Arizona Strip and small family ranches in southern Utah as cattle and sheep men pushed ever deeper into remote regions in search of grass.

big cattle outfits had sold out, mostly to Kanab and St. George ranchers, and long after the range had been devastated.

In an early 1970s study, the Council for Agricultural Science and Technology reported the "exploitive grazing practices prior to 1930 were nearly catastrophic," and the depletion of the ranges resulted from decades of grazing too many animals for too long and at the wrong times of the year. The report found that scientific management of rangeland had begun by the turn of the century, "but the accumulation of knowledge and its application advanced slowly." Not until after World War II would principles of controlled grazing of rangelands take root.[21]

Filching the Water

Throughout the 1870s and 1880s, Mormon ranchers maintained an open policy toward the limited water sources on the Arizona Strip. Ranchers who assumed responsibility for the maintenance of the springs were considered the rightful owners and had priority use of the water. But other ranchers were not barred from the springs. As noted by Altschul and Fairley:

> This informal and open policy not only encouraged overuse of the range, but it also left the water sources and the surrounding range open to use by stockmen from outside the area, some of whom did not share the local ranchers' time honored approach towards range and water use rights.[22]

The new arrivals to the Arizona Strip—B. F. Saunders and Preston Nutter—did not share this "time-honored" approach, and both men, bona fide cattle barons of the day, promptly set out to control all access to springs. As Nutter later explained in 1935 in a letter to J. N. Darling, chief of the U.S. Biological Survey, by controlling the water, he could control the surrounding lands by merely holding title to the springs. Nutter wrote:

> The Strip country was public domain and unsurveyed and there was really no way to obtain title to lands until Congress passed a law, known as the Forest Reserve Lieu Selection Act, which allowed citizens to locate 40-acre legal subdivisions on the public domain. This was a great benefit to the cattleman as it gave a person the right to locate springs or water holes. The speculators entered into this game and sold "scrip"

> covering these lands. I purchased a lot of this scrip and applied it on various selections, and as Arizona began to survey that country, made application for surveys, thus through patents I acquired title to twenty-one 40-acre tracts, all covering springs. Then there were other means of acquiring title. I purchased Sioux Half Breed scrip and in later years bought two 640-acre proven up homesteads, also 80 acres of cultivated land known as Parashant Field, and in more recent years a purchase of land from the Santa Fe Railroad. This gives me more than 7,000 acres patented land and practically all of the living water on that range.[23]

While Nutter's approach to land acquisition was legal, locals viewed it with dismay. Wrote historian Juanita Brooks, who grew up in southern Utah:

> Just as the Mormons had filched the water from the Indians, so he [Nutter] in turn filched it from the Mormons. They had paid for it, they thought; they held the springs, and in this country possession was all ten points of the law. But they had not taken time and trouble to have their claims surveyed and recorded.[24]

Reed Mathis, whose father ran cattle in competition with Nutter, indicates that Nutter "never did shut the waters off from other cattle ... But he owned it and he let you know it. This country wasn't fenced; the waters weren't even fenced; it was all open range."[25] Saunders' Grand Canyon Cattle Company was more parsimonious, restricting all access to their springs.[26]

How local Mormons responded to this enclosure movement is unclear. In 1903, Edwin D. Woolley reported that he had recently served as an agent for a New York company that had bought all the water rights around the North Rim of the Grand Canyon.[27] He clearly benefitted. It is certainly plausible, however, that the smaller ranchers of Kane and Garfield counties watched in horror as their Mormon brethren to the south and southwest were dispossessed of their rangelands by Gentile outsiders. But if they did, they failed to adopt preventative strategies to protect their own rangelands.

In terms of non-Mormon encroachment, there was an important distinction between the Arizona Strip and nearby Kane and Garfield Counties in Utah—the Strip was far less protectable, only having tiny populations at a handful of small settlements such as Moccasin, Fredonia, and Pipe Spring on its northern periphery. A few cabins and ranches were scattered across the Strip, but otherwise it contained wide open spaces used only seasonally. Kane and Garfield Counties had thriving villages, all situated on the area's few springs or creeks. It was one thing for the cattle barons to push out a few isolated ranchers, but displacing entire well-established communities would be far more difficult.

Mormon ranchers to the north of the Arizona Strip never did adapt the Nutter-Saunders strategy of locking up water sources, even if only to protect their own traditional use of the springs. Even on remote ranges like the Kaiparowits Plateau, lower Escalante River, and upper Paria River, the springs were recognized for the beneficial use of all. The remote rangelands of Kane and Garfield Counties managed to avoid the designs of cattle barons that had wrested control of most of the American West in the 1890s.

The Kane-Garfield livestock economy evolved differently than other areas of southern and eastern Utah. Cattle and sheep ranches in the Grand Staircase and Escalante River country were almost islands in a sea of ranches owned by large cattle barons. Some of their Mormon neighbors were large operators themselves with herds numbering as much as six thousand head, but these operations were small compared to those on the Arizona Strip. The barons controlled the Arizona Strip to the south, the Abajo Mountains above Blanding to the southeast, the Fishlake country to the north, and the Moab, Tavaputs Plateau, and Browns Park areas to the northeast.[28]

The Bar Z

Most historical accounts agree that Benjamin Franklin Saunders, who generally went by "B. F.", a non-Mormon businessman from Salt Lake City, purchased House Rock Valley and the VT Ranch on the Kaibab Plateau in the mid-1890s, perhaps under the name Grand Canyon Cattle Company, and that he instituted the famous Bar Z brand. However, the accounts vary on the specific details.[29]

B. F. Saunders was born in Missouri in 1847 and raised in Texas where he became a "cattle trail man." According to a biographical sketch in the *Salt Lake Telegram*:

> The old Texas cattle trail has passed into history, but many young men encountered difficulties and privations along the trail in the early days that taught them valuable lessons in self-reliance and endurance, and such was the early experience of B.F. Saunders.

Saunders arrived in Utah in 1882, and by 1906, he had become the "largest sheep dealer in the world" with a herd of 760,000 head in six Western states. The article noted that Saunders had run more than a million head of cattle during his tenure in the livestock industry.[30]

B. F. Saunders and the Mormon Church had a close business relationship prior to Saunders' acquisition of House Rock Valley and the VT Ranch. In 1883, he purchased the Oak Grove Ranch from the Canaan cooperative, which he later sold to Anthony Ivins. He also purchased Pipe Spring when the church put it up for auction, and he acquired financial interests in at least three ranches in the western part of the Arizona Strip. When the New Canaan cooperative liquidated the last of its holdings in House Rock Valley in 1895, Saunders sold Pipe Spring and his other holdings to the west, and the following year he acquired the cooperative's ranch headquarters (House Rock Ranch), followed later by his purchase of the VT Ranch from John W. Young.[31] He gained a reputation among local Mormons as a reliable purchaser of excess stock.[32]

A review of the limited historical information available suggests that B. F. Saunders purchased the Kaibab Land and Cattle Company holdings in House Rock Valley and the Kaibab Plateau, probably in 1896. He also clearly had a partner, Ara Farley of Laramie, Wyoming, and that the partnership was known in official court records as Farley and Saunders. Possibly Henry S. Stephenson of Los Angeles was a silent partner in Saunders' original 1896 venture. Stephenson acquired these properties in 1907. Rowland Rider, a wrangler for the Bar Z outfit, insists it was a Stephenson who bought out the Mormon Church's holdings.[33]

Saunders was a shrewd businessman, and like his rival on the western Arizona Strip, Preston Nutter, he employed a variety of legal strategies to acquire control of permanent water sources in the area. Saunders hired local wranglers and utilized the House Rock Ranch as one of his home bases. Saunders also began acquiring water rights soon after his purchase of the property from John W. Young. As Gretchen Younghan and Katrina Rogers noted:

> Until that time, the range had been used in common, and watering places were not restricted to individual ranchers. Most of the watering places on the Kaibab Plateau became legally entitled to Saunders, though the nature of this legality was questionable.[34]

A good example of questionable legality was Saunders' filing in February 1904 of a placer mining claim on the lands around Kane Springs. The U.S. Forest

Benjamin Franklin Saunders

MEN WHO HAVE MADE UTAH FAMOUS

This Will Be a Series of Pictures of Utah's Big Men | No. 24 | Short Sketches of Men Who Built Up the State

FIGURE 4.4. B. F. Saunders had been operating in the Arizona Strip country since the 1880s working hand-in-glove with the Mormon Church. By the 1890s, he owned and controlled the entire eastern Strip. Image courtesy of *Salt Lake Telegram*, July 16, 1906.

Service disputed the mining claim and its inherent implications for ownership of Kane Springs, but in September 1905 it granted Saunders a permit to maintain a pipeline from the springs to the Kane Ranch. The permit was renewed in 1908, a year after Saunders and Farley sold out to Henry S. Stephenson. In 1935, Stephenson challenged the Forest Service ruling that Kane Springs was federally owned, but the Kaibab Forest supervisor successfully argued in court that the springs were non-flowing seeps not subject to Arizona water law and therefore held in reserve by the federal government.[35]

Given that all the springs in the eastern Arizona Strip are non-flowing seeps like those at Kane Spring, the argument made by the Kaibab Forest supervisor would seem to apply to all Bar Z claims made under mining claims. However, no legal challenge to the other mining lands appeared, and it is unknown if the federal court ruling in the Kane Springs case was ever applied to other holdings. In fact, "mining" claims recognized as valid today (e.g., Sunset Lode, Emmitt Lode) appear to be remnants of Saunders' legal efforts to acquire land patents to the springs needed for his cattle operation. These mining lands became part of the rights transferred during subsequent sales. Saunders left the Arizona Strip in 1907, probably because of the deteriorating condition of the range and increased federal restrictions on grazing. He died two years later in Salt Lake City.

During the 1890s when both Saunders and Nutter were expanding their operations onto the Arizona Strip, the clear environmental degradation of the region's forests and grasslands brought calls for conservation steps in the area. The historical record is clear that the Arizona Strip had suffered considerably from overgrazing by Saunders and Nutter, who ran a combined herd of perhaps a hundred thousand head of cattle on the Arizona Strip.[36] The overgrazing, as well as a growing public awareness of the unique scenic and wildlife attributes of the region just north of the Grand Canyon, prompted increased scrutiny by federal authorities, who sought tougher grazing restrictions even before Saunders acquired House Rock Valley and the Kaibab Plateau. The Kaibab forests had first been set aside as forest reserves in 1893, and a game preserve was established in 1906.

The widely publicized scenic wonders of the Grand Canyon led to a strange tug-of-war between Utah and Arizona over the fate of the Arizona Strip that was culturally tied to Mormon-dominated Utah. In 1903, local leaders such as Kanab Stake president Edwin D. Woolley worked with powerful Utah Senator

Reed Smoot to have the Strip annexed by Utah. They wanted Utah to offer to reimburse Arizona's Coconino and Mohave Counties for the lost lands. Among other issues, Arizona Territory clearly was not going to willingly surrender the Grand Canyon. Woolley then proposed allowing Arizona to retain the canyon itself, but to allow Utah to secure all the territory north of the North Rim. The scheme came to naught.[37]

By this time many Utah political leaders, including Governor Heber Wells (1896–1905), and prominent business leaders came to believe federal forest reserves were needed to protect water supplies from overgrazing and its consequences. In a trend that started in northern Utah, the Dixie and La Sal National Forests were established by 1908 in southern Utah, bringing the total state acreage in national forest lands to 7.5 million acres.[38]

The trophy bucks of the Kaibab mule deer herd had become famous by this time. President Theodore Roosevelt, an avid hunter, desired to protect the herd for fellow hunters. Federal officials earlier had created the Grand Canyon Forest Reserve in 1893, encompassing lands on both sides of the Grand Canyon. In 1906, President Roosevelt succeeded in establishing the Grand Canyon Game Reserve. A few years later in 1908, officials proclaimed the timbered lands north of the Grand Canyon, including the game reserve, the Kaibab National Forest. Officials estimated the mule deer population on the Kaibab Plateau at the time was about 4,000 animals.[39]

Utilizing the best contemporary scientific management ideas, federal land managers launched a campaign to boost mule deer numbers. The first step in increasing the Kaibab deer herd was to reduce livestock numbers. Tens of thousands of sheep and cattle were removed from the range because they competed with deer for browse. However, C. John Burk found that the trend of reducing cattle and sheep herds predated the federal game reserve. He estimated that between 1889 and 1908, as many as 195,000 sheep were removed from the Kaibab. Animals that preyed on mule deer were the next targets.[40]

What happened next on the Kaibab National Forest became a well-known conservation parable taught in classrooms across the nation, as the federal government sponsored a campaign to exterminate predators that had unintended consequences. At the time a growing number of well-heeled sportsmen supported the predator extermination campaign. They were joined by stock growers. Eager to please these interests and local politicians, the newly established U.S. Forest Service entered into cooperative agreements with the Territories

FIGURE 4.5. Predator control programs were wildly popular among ranchers who blamed coyotes, wolves, and bears for their livestock losses. But without predators, the deer and elk populations exploded to the detriment of the range. Photo courtesy of John David Morrill Collection (morrilli70), Barbara A. Matheson Special Collections, Gerald R. Sherratt Library, Southern Utah University, Cedar City.

of Arizona and New Mexico to utilize forest guards to trap predators. Local trappers came to the Kaibab for the government bounties.

In 1914, the United States Congress established the Predatory Animal and Rodent Control (PARC) bureau within the U.S. Biological Survey in the United States Department of Agriculture. At the time, grizzly bears and grey wolves still roamed the Arizona Strip. Between 1907 and 1923, on average 176 coyotes, forty mountain lions, seven bobcats, and one wolf were taken annually on the Kaibab. The last wolf was taken from the Paria Plateau about 1928, the last grizzly sometime earlier. Native American hunting had been eliminated decades before. With predators decimated, or in the case of Indigenous hunters expelled, deer numbers exploded by 1918.[41]

Federal investigators warned of the looming catastrophe, but nothing was done. In a famous study by pioneering conservation writer Aldo Leopold he estimated that the deer herd increased to 100,000 by 1924. Later scholars questioned these figures, estimating the deer population much lower at 30,000. In any case, tens of thousands of the prized mule deer died of hunger and disease. Leopold reported that the deer herd had been reduced to 20,000 animals by 1931. The *New York Times* ran a story, calling the Kaibab "the range of death." What had once been the country's most heralded deer herd had been devastated. Leopold, as well as famed conservationist Rachel Carson, wrote plenty about this collapse. Although the statistics were debated long afterwards, land managers' disruption of the predator-prey relationship on the Kaibab became one of the most-taught environmental lessons of the twentieth century.[42]

In a national movement, states began to create game laws and state game commissions to regulate hunting, treating wild animals as a "natural resource." Early wildlife conservationists led by George Bird Grinnell decried the market hunting of wild animals that had led to the extinction of the passenger pigeon and near extinction of the American bison. Others placed a market value on wild game animals for recreational purposes.[43] An elite organization, the Boone and Crockett Club established record books, while also promoting hunting as a manly and noble pursuit sorely needed in a rapidly urbanizing and industrializing America. Club leaders argued that teaching boys to hunt would instill in them the virtues of outdoor life. At the same time, other pursuits in nature—including wildlife viewing, walking, painting in the open, or nature writing—became feminized. The latter social construct still exists in the modern era. Overall, desirable wildlife species such as elk and deer became "animals of leisure" with their own value and whose grazing put them at odds with the value placed on livestock by local ranchers.[44]

Acting on behalf of the "better men" of Kanab, local stake president Edwin D. Woolley lobbied for what became the Kaibab Game Reserve. He complained that Navajo hunters were killing hundreds of deer annually, selling their tanned hides in the area. Lorum Pratt, forest supervisor of the Dixie Forest Reserve out of Fredonia, backed the idea. Once the reserve was established, Woolley asked Senator Reed Smoot for funding to stock the area with bison, elk, and pronghorn antelope. Apparently a big dreamer, he envisioned the Kaibab as a breeding ground for game to restock all of the nation's national parks, especially Yellowstone.[45]

The increased federal intervention on the Arizona Strip, Grand Staircase and Escalante country convinced many local ranchers that additional federal restrictions were inevitable, with many selling out in the face of increased challenges to their open range practices. According to Coconino County land records, Saunders and Farley sold a portion of their holdings in House Rock Valley, specifically Two-Mile Spring and Jacob's Pools, in December 1907 to the Grand Canyon Cattle Company. Less than a month later, on January 11, 1908, Theodore Roosevelt created the Grand Canyon National Monument. The following May, the Grand Canyon Cattle Company acquired the remainder of the Farley-Saunders assets in the Arizona Strip, including the mining claims, water rights, and Kane Ranch. This was the same year the Kaibab National Forest was created and expanded, bringing even more restrictions on open range cattle outfits.

Exactly who owned the growing Grand Canyon Cattle Company is unclear. No signature was recorded for the new owners, but both deeds were "recorded at the request of E. J. Marshall." It does appear that little changed with the new ownership. The company retained the Bar Z brand and either

FIGURE 4.6. Marble Canyon, just upstream from Lee's Ferry, became the site of the first bridge, opened in 1929, to allow automobile traffic to flow freely between Arizona and Utah. Marble Canyon was designated a national monument by President Lyndon Johnson in 1969. Photograph by Dan Bauer.

instituted or bought the rights to the name Grand Canyon Cattle Company, with E. J. Marshall as president and Harry E. Way as vice president. Rowland Rider even referred to the outfit as the E. J. Marshall Company. Rider stated the Bar Z outfit ran 100,000 head of cattle on the Kaibab Plateau at this time, although other accounts place the number at 20,000 to 60,000.[46]

Buying out the Competition

The new owners of the Bar Z apparently inherited a problem that proved a fundamental challenge to all ranchers in the region: moving their livestock to market. Although the Bar Z controlled most of House Rock Valley and the Kaibab Plateau, it did not control Lee's Ferry on the Colorado River above the Grand Canyon or the small family cattle outfit there. And the crossing at Lee's Ferry was the most direct route to move Bar Z cattle to railheads in Flagstaff. The Atlantic and Pacific Railroad (later Santa Fe) tracks had reached modern Flagstaff in 1882, and the town soon grew into the major shipping center for the region.[47] Lee's Ferry had been an important cattle crossing for years prior. Jacob Hamblin first used the crossing in 1864, noting it was the only place in the canyon country where a wagon could be driven down to the river. Mormons utilized wood cut on the Kaibab to build the first ferry here in 1870. A few years later, in 1872, church leaders exiled John D. Lee and his wife Emma to the site to run the ferry, in part to hide him from federal authorities who were hunting Lee for his role in the Mountain Meadows Massacre of 1857.[48]

In the 1870s, the Mormon Church established dozens of settlements in Arizona, and cattle was the currency used to buy out the previous claimants. Thousands of church cattle were driven across the river at Lee's Ferry on their way to Arizona. Mormons living in Arizona used the same trail to travel back and forth to the St. George Temple for marriage ceremonies, for decades the closest temple to Arizona, with the old trade route taking on the new name "the Honeymoon Trail."[49]

Years after John D. Lee was arrested for murder, Lee's Ferry was operated by James Emett, acting as agent for the Mormon Church. With no access to summer range in the mountains, Emett ran his cattle year-round along the Colorado River. He had acquired the rights to operate the ferry in 1895 after Warren and Permelia Johnson sold it to the church. Travelers using the ferry would pay Emett in cows, Navajo blankets, or other supplies. Most of the livestock were "scrub" cattle not needed by the immigrants. Over the years, Emett had built up a

FIGURE 4.7. Lee's Ferry at the mouth of the Paria River was the only practical crossing for people and cattle to be moved to rail heads in Flagstaff. The Bar Z later purchased the ferry when it was denied use of the ferry. Photograph courtesy of Utah State Historical Society Classified Photo Collection (39222001655765).

considerable herd, but he had no place to run them other than lower House Rock Valley, which also happened to be Bar Z winter range.[50] Emett had to do many jobs to make ends meet in this hardscrabble county; in 1894, he contracted with the Kaibab Cattle Company to deliver horses and other stock to the company.[51]

The Bar Z cowboys suspected Emett of allowing his inferior cattle to roam and to graze among their high-quality breed stock. These suspicions were given added weight after Emett "produced a herd of white-faces that were just about as good and looked about as good and were the same breed as the Bar Z stock." The Bar Z subsequently invested $30,000 in a barbed wire drift fence—something that was illegal on open ranges at the time—to separate the two herds. It ran from the base of the Paria Plateau near Jacob's Pools to the head of North Canyon, a distance of about 7 mi. Emett reportedly would stampede bison through the fence, followed in short order by his own drifting herd. As a result, Rowland Rider said, "the Bar Z and the Emetts were bitter enemies. They carried guns."[52] On two occasions, the Bar Z accused Emett of rustling, but the charges were dismissed for lack of evidence.

The new owners of the Bar Z soon initiated efforts to buy out competing landowners in the area, with a central goal of acquiring Lee's Ferry to facilitate quicker access to railheads in Flagstaff rather than the long route to Modena in southwestern Utah. In August 1909, the Grand Canyon Cattle Company purchased what was left of the Mormon Church holdings at Lee's Ferry from Church President Joseph F. Smith (an event to which Edwin D. Woolley was an official witness) for the sum of $1,750. For the cattle company, the purchase was a way to kill two birds with one stone. The acquisition of the ferry deprived Emett of his primary source of income and would hopefully persuade him to leave the area. It also ensured Bar Z access to the railheads in Flagstaff.[53] On the same day, the Grand Canyon Cattle Company paid $1,000 for Emett's water rights, water improvements, and mining claims in House Rock Valley, including a spring 4 mi north of Jacob's Pools. In a separate transaction, the company also bought out Emett's ranch improvements. Rider indicated he personally travelled from Kane Ranch to Lee's Ferry to finalize the deal and filled in a blank check from Grand Canyon Cattle Company to the Emetts for $65,000.[54] Rider noted that it was a man named "Stevenson, one of the main owners of the company" and "president of the Board of Directors of the Grand Canyon Cattle Company" who was personally on hand during the sale negotiations who gave Rowland Rider written instructions on how to fulfill the terms of the contract.[55]

Lee's Ferry remained a valuable river crossing until the end of the 1920s when the new "Grand Canyon Bridge" (later renamed Navajo Bridge) was constructed, spanning the river a few miles downstream. At some point in the preceding years, the Grand Canyon Cattle Company sold its Lee's Ferry holdings to Coconino County, who continued to operate the ferry that by the 1920s was carrying automobiles. The grand opening of Navajo Bridge, a large steel-arch structure that at the time was the highest in the world, enabled car and truck traffic to flow smoothly between Utah and Arizona and eliminated the need for Lee's Ferry altogether.[56]

Several records note that the Grand Canyon Cattle Company sold out and left the Arizona Strip in 1924, but many sources indicate this was not the case. A review of land patent records reveals the Grand Canyon Cattle Company was aggressively acquiring lands in House Rock Valley, often through intermediaries, for nearly a decade after. For example, Congress, through the *in lieu* provisions of the Forest Reserve Act, allowed those with lands inside forest reserves to exchange their properties for public domain lands elsewhere. In September 1930, F. A. Hyde & Company, a firm involved in land speculation throughout the West, exchanged their Sierra Forest Reserve parcels in California for lands in House Rock Valley. That same day, F. A. Hyde and Company sold their House Rock Valley holdings to the Grand Canyon Cattle Company. Similarly, Mary E. Coffin owned lands in the Gila River Forest Reserve in New Mexico. On June 18, 1930, she applied for an *in lieu* exchange for lands in House Rock Valley, and in September of the same year she sold the parcels to the Grand Canyon Cattle Company. As Nutter had done, the company also used Indigenous scrip to buy multiple properties.

While buying up most of the private land, the new owners of the Grand Canyon Cattle Company apparently did allow some small cattle outfits to use the range and watering holes. Rider, his father, and his brother ran their own cattle among the Bar Z's stock, using the Bar JR and Bar DR brands.[57] The Bar Z, however, found itself in disputes with other smaller cattle operators on the Kaibab Plateau, who complained their permits to run cattle were reduced by the U.S. Forest Service due to overgrazing. Ranchers in turn blamed the overgrazing on the heavy drifting of Bar Z cattle onto their ranges. At a grazing summit held in late 1908 and early 1909, the U.S. Forest Service agreed to construct a drift fence to keep Bar Z cattle away from other operators.[58]

During the 1920s, at the same time as some large operators were downsizing on the Arizona Strip, the last wave of hopeful homesteaders arrived north of the Grand Canyon, with almost all "busting" during the next decade. The family of Ruth Cunningham was among this last group of settlers to try their luck on the Strip. Her parents Amos and Lorinda Kent had moved to Yuma, Arizona, from Illinois in 1904 because one of her siblings had "lung fever" and a doctor advised the dry air would improve his health. After establishing a successful dairy, she recalled that her father's health started to fail and the family sought a cooler climate.

Of her ten siblings, her older brother Walter had fallen in love with Arizona Strip country in 1927. When her parents visited in summer 1927, she recalled, "the summer rains had been good, the grass was high, the weather pleasant and everything looked wonderful except the roads which were, of course, terrible." As she noted "the decision was made to take up a homestead and build up a cattle ranch." The government was offering 640-acre grazing land homesteads, and several siblings and their families also established ranches in the Tuweep Valley in 1928. Her father drilled several wells, but after failing to find water, had to rely on a neighbor's cattle tank at Nixon Springs, a source that was miles away.

Life was often hard, and residents soon found themselves regularly praying for rain. Like her brothers, Ruth learned to rope and ride, and the siblings were often sent miles away to tend the family's herd of cattle. Ruth's family grew vegetable gardens, corn, and peaches near the four-room clapboard houses they built, and they had to do odd jobs to make ends meet. She remembered that a good period occurred when her father worked for an area mine: "for two years dad butchered two or three beaves [beefs] each week for the Grand Gulch Mine and mom cooked for the cow men."

Since mail was sent from faraway Short Creek, her family petitioned for a new post office at the new village of Tuweep, and family members received what was a lucrative paycheck for handling the mail. A dispersed community developed. They would often have dances and other social gatherings with residents of Nixon Springs and Mount Trumbull (Bundyville) farther away. When the Great Depression began, ranching, with its regular droughts and widely fluctuating prices for cattle, got too hard for Ruth's "tribe" and their neighbors at Tuweep Valley. During the 1930s, the post office closed and everyone moved away. Her brother Walter, who was the first to pioneer the area, was "the last to give up the dream and leave," Ruth reported.[59]

As Ruth Cunningham's tale reveals, federal laws were encouraging settlement of marginal lands at the same time other federal policies were seeking to limit ecological damage to these very lands. Despite some early support for federal management, Utah politicians with their traditional utilitarian views started to see red flags as the government took tentative steps to manage public lands. As historians Charles S. Peterson and Brian Q. Cannon conclude, "conflict was bitter throughout the early decades of statehood (after 1896), as the pioneer culture of wilderness conquest gave way before the centralizing national pressure of conservation." Governors William Spry (1909–17) and George Dern (1925–33) took strident "states' rights" stands, opposing any further federal regulations and restrictions.[60]

Federal grazing limitations were apparently too much for the Bar Z owners, who, as Rider recalled:

> sold and moved all their cattle off of here . . . They wouldn't pay the grazing fee that the Forest Service imposed on them. They drifted to Arizona through House Rock, across Lee's Ferry to New Mexico where they had a range. That was the end of the Bar Z.[61]

Altschul and Fairley place this event in 1924, although Coconino County land records indicate otherwise.[62]

The actions of the Bar Z through its various incarnations had direct impacts on the livestock industry in Kane County. When these lands were controlled by the Mormon Church or its surrogates, Kanab-area ranchers were able to utilize House Rock Valley and the Kaibab Plateau. The Kane County livestock economy at this time was focused predominantly to the south toward the Arizona Strip. But once the Bar Z arrived on the scene, the "public" springs were closed to them, and the sheer number of Bar Z cattle made it difficult, at best, to compete for rangelands.

The Bar Z hired some local wranglers, such as Rider, but the corporate interests were generally hostile to local Mormon ranchers encroaching on their territory. Historic photos from that time depict wranglers armed with rifles and pistols. The Kanab ranchers were forced to look elsewhere for unencumbered rangelands—the Wahweap country to the east, the labyrinth of side canyons of the Paria River, and probably the southern Kaiparowits Plateau in the Warm Creek, Last Chance Creek, and Rock Creek drainages. Particularly troubling was the loss of the Kaibab Plateau summer range. The other summer ranges—the Markagunt Plateau to the west and Paunsaugunt Plateau to the north—were already claimed and crowded.[63]

Preston Nutter

Preston Nutter arrived on the western Arizona Strip in about 1892, at the same time he set out to acquire exclusive grazing rights on Ute reservation lands in the Strawberry Valley of northern Utah. The U.S. government attached a condition to that lease that stated Nutter was not allowed to hold title to or financial interests in any other holdings in the Utah Territory. But he could own land just south in Arizona, and he promptly set out to control the entire western Arizona Strip. Some accounts assert Nutter had herds of as many as 100,000 head of cattle between his spread on the Arizona Strip and his operation in northern Utah—claims that were probably exaggerated. A legend suggested that his herds were so large that he had no idea how many cattle he actually owned, something that is unlikely given his meticulous attention to business details.[64] Another account claims that at one time Nutter owned more land and ran more cattle than any other rancher in the West.[65]

Nutter was a self-made man, a future cattle baron who had come west from Virginia in 1863 seeking his fortune. He ended up in Colorado (he was even a star prosecution witness in the case against Alferd Packer, the notorious cannibal who killed and ate his traveling companions in the San Juan Mountains), served in the Colorado legislature, was friends with the great Ute Chief Ouray, and became moderately wealthy freighting supplies to the gold and silver mines. He sold out of that latter enterprise to become a cattleman in the rugged canyon country called the Triangle on the Utah-Colorado border.

The railheads at Thompson Springs, Utah, proved most fortuitous to Nutter's operation, and the railroad helped cement Nutter's legend as a canny cow man. The winter of 1886–87 was exceptionally harsh, with blizzards blanketing available forage in deep snows. Cattle died by the thousands. Instead of spreading the herd, as was the custom in the day, Nutter concentrated his animals at Thompson Springs and shipped in hay to feed them through the winter. As noted by his daughter, Virginia Nutter Price, "there is every indication that it paid off because his losses were small and receipts show him buying more cattle throughout the entire bleak winter."[66] Plenty of livestock were available for purchase as the harsh weather, coupled with poor cattle prices, had devastated family farms throughout the region and small ranchers everywhere were selling out.[67]

Nutter was certainly opportunistic. According to historian Charles Peterson, he bought cattle in the Mormon settlements at less than ten dollars a head:

> fattening cattle on virgin ranges and selling for fantastic profits in the burgeoning mining country of Colorado. It is difficult to know how many cattle were trailed from the Great Basin to eastern Utah, but it is certain they numbered in the hundreds of thousands.[68]

Nutter's obituary states that he bought out Anthony W. Ivins's Arizona Strip holdings in 1892,[69] whereas his daughter asserts that occurred in 1896.[70] Ivins was himself a large-scale cattle operator, and later a prominent Mormon apostle and territorial politician. He was also widely recognized as a surrogate for the financially distressed Mormon Church during its federal anti-polygamy trials.[71]

FIGURE 4.8. Preston Nutter was one of the great cattle barons of the robber baron era, running hundreds of thousands of cattle on ranges from northern Utah to the Arizona Strip. He was a friend of Mormon Church leaders, but no friend to the southern Utah ranchers. Photograph courtesy of Uintah County Public Library, Vernal, Utah.

Based on the available historical evidence, Nutter initially purchased existing use rights that were not necessarily patented lands. And he recognized a legal loophole of which he took full advantage: he requested formal government surveys and then acquired legal land patents centered on the springs. As noted previously, the western Arizona Strip at that time was open range used in common by a multitude of small ranchers, mostly from the St. George area, who shared the limited water sources. Some springs had been claimed by Ivins as representative of the Mohave Land and Cattle Company. But seemingly no one held valid title to the lands where the springs were located. As could be expected, Nutter's legal strategy to control the springs generated considerable animosity with his Mormon neighbors.

Nutter's daughter hints that his relationship with local ranchers was not just strained but downright hostile, forcing him to hire Texas "deputies" to protect his interests—a euphemism for hired guns. She wrote that "the Arizona Strip range war against Nutter might have continued on much longer if he had not, after legally acquiring title on all the springs, bought out the opposition."[72] This approach was the same one used by the Bar Z to eliminate competition from small operators.

Nutter also got hauled into court for his use of Indigenous scrip to acquire title to springs. Indigenous scrip was, in effect, a government voucher for 40 acres of federal land given to Native Americans who had been displaced by white settlers from their homes in the Midwest, usually as part of a treaty. Through a loophole in the law, the scrip could be bought and sold.[73] Speculators would "purchase" the scrip from Indigenous owners and in turn sell it to entrepreneurs like Nutter who would then file a claim to springs they needed. The practice was rife with fraud and eventually landed Nutter in the courtroom as a defendant accused of swindling the U.S. government. He was never convicted, and by most accounts he was an unwitting purchaser of allegedly bogus scrip.

Utah ranching historian James H. Beckstead also emphasized a simmering feud between Nutter and B. F. Saunders, who had tried and failed to run Nutter out of business. But, ever the shrewd businessman, by 1894, Nutter was subleasing to Saunders a portion of the Strawberry Valley, at the time part of the Ute reservation, to run several hundred head of his own cattle there.[74]

With Arizona Strip winter range locked up and the lease secured on the Strawberry Valley, Nutter set about restocking his herds. He put the word out in southern Arizona that he was buying cattle, and by September 1893 he had amassed a herd of five thousand head. The problem was how to get the herd across the Colorado River. One of the legendary stories of Nutter's sheer force of will has it that he swam the herd across the river at Scanlon's Ferry south of Mesquite, Nevada, without losing a single head or rider. Nutter was always proud of this feat, but in recounting it in later years would say, with a twinkle in his eyes: "It is possible we lost a few spectators lined up to watch from the banks. I was too busy to keep an eye on them."[75]

Over the next several years, Nutter's wranglers moved cattle back and forth between the summer ranges in Strawberry Valley in northern Utah and winter ranges on the Arizona Strip. His Strawberry Valley lease expired in 1898, and although he was able to get a one-year extension, the pressure to open the Ute reservation to homesteaders was mounting, as was the clamor to open the Strawberry Valley to sheep men.[76] Most accounts agree that the end was in sight for cattle grazing on tribal lands in the Uinta Basin. The traditional history holds that Nutter responded to that imminent reality by searching out a new base of operations, especially a new summer range for his 25,000 head of Utah cattle. In 1902, he found it on the West Tavaputs Plateau with a headquarters in Nine Mile Canyon and outlier ranches in Range Creek and Desolation Canyons.[77]

Unfettered by the previous lease stipulations, he no longer needed to move large herds back and forth from northern Utah to Arizona. Nutter retained the Arizona Strip ranch primarily as breeding grounds to stock his Utah herds. He died in 1936, and a year later his widow sold the Arizona Strip holdings. Like many other large operators, Nutter was an advocate of increased federal management of public lands, knowing both that the land needed better oversight and that his greater capital and leverage would prove an advantage over the numerous small operators on the public domain. In fact, Nutter had hoped his holdings on the Arizona Strip would become a massive game preserve, but that never happened because of the failure of the Department of Interior to act on his offer.[78]

Nonetheless, Nutter's livestock operation on the Arizona Strip further constricted the small family ranchers in the area. Those pushed out of House Rock Valley by B. F. Saunders and his successors could not move their herds west without bumping up against Nutter's stock, reportedly even larger than Saunders's herds. And Nutter's wranglers were known as rough, Texas saddle veterans with little affinity for the Mormons. Between Nutter and the Bar Z,

TABLE 4.1. Cattle Populations in Kane-Garfield Region and on the Arizona Strip.

Cattle Populations							
	1890	**1900**	**1910**	**1920**	**1925**	**1930**	**1935**
Kane County	12490	7697	13187	n/a	6451	10102	3480
Garfield County	5382	11323	19858	n/a	25806	13656	9230
Eastern Arizona Strip	n/a	n/a	n/a	n/a	89490	92935	23598
Western Arizona Strip	n/a	n/a	n/a	n/a	6357	22558	34

Note: All totals derived from USDA Census of Agriculture Historical Archive records from 1890 to 1935. The 1920 totals are not broken down by county and could not be determined.

TABLE 4.2. Sheep Populations in the Kane-Garfield Region and on the Arizona Strip.

Sheep Populations							
	1890	**1900**	**1910**	**1920**	**1925**	**1930**	**1935**
Kane County	39433	46552	106534	n/a	46880	55321	80346
Garfield County	86696	91884	116488	n/a	122529	130946	100571
Eastern Arizona Strip	n/a	n/a	n/a	95113	297869	350965	145161
Western Arizona Strip	n/a	n/a	n/a	n/a	6357	22558	34

Note: All totals derived from USDA Census of Agriculture Historical Archive records from 1890 to 1935. The 1920 totals are not broken down by county and could not be determined. The 1920 Eastern Arizona Strip (Coconino County) number is derived from the number of sheep shorn and reflects a minimum number for that year.

the only options left to the Kane County ranchers were to move their herds east into Glen Canyon country, where there is minimal summer range, or north into the already crowded Paunsaugunt, or onto the Kaiparowits Plateau, by then already filling up with Escalante herds. Many of the Kane County ranchers likely just gave up, or they moved north to Garfield County.

The possibility of a south-to-north shift in family ranching operations is illustrated in the 1890 and 1900 U.S. Census data. In 1890, the number of cattle in both counties totaled 17,872. Ten years later, the total number of cattle was 19,020, or a modest 6 percent increase. But the number of Kane County cattle had actually plummeted from 12,490 in 1890 to 7,697 by the turn of the century, a drop of nearly 40 percent. During this same time, the number of cattle in Garfield County had increased from 5,382 to 11,323, a rise of 110 percent (see Table 4.1).[79]

A south-to-north shift is not as evident in the sheep populations for the region. Sheep numbers increased in Kane County and Garfield County in each agricultural census between 1890 and 1925. In Kane County, the sheep population more than doubled from 1900 to 1910, and on the eastern Arizona Strip (Coconino County), it more than tripled from 1920 to 1930 (see Table 4.2). The record-high sheep populations evident in the 1930 census throughout the region probably reflect national economic trends where wool production was more profitable than cattle ranching. The numbers probably do not reflect the total sheep populations inasmuch as "transient" sheep brought to the region each spring by nonlocal sheepherders would not have participated in the census.

Lawlessness and Poverty

As discussed in Chapter 2, the presence of rustlers and other outlaw elements in the Grand Staircase-Escalante area appears to have been a minor nuisance in the 1870s. One band of rustlers reportedly operated out of the Bryce Canyon area, some outlaws of the day like Butch Cassidy of Circleville had blood ties to the region, and outlaws were frequent visitors to friends and family in southern Utah. Lige Moore, a Texas cowboy who settled in Henrieville, was friends with many outlaws of the time, including Matt Warner, Silver Tip Morgan (Jim Wall), Tom McCarty, and Butch Cassidy.[80] The close-knit social structure of the 1870s and early 1880s seems to have been a deterrent to lawlessness. Most communities did not even have a lawman because Mormon communities handled matters themselves through church-dominated institutions. The closest court was in Beaver, Utah. That situation changed dramatically in the late 1880s and continued throughout the 1890s and into the early 1900s.

At the national level, two stereotypes emerged from this period that had variants in Grand Staircase-Escalante country. One trope regarded the Gilded Age "robber baron," an extremely rich man who engaged in shady and monopolistic business practices, manipulated politicians and the democratic process, and amassed enormous wealth at the expense of the working poor. Taking on the robber barons was the "Robin Hood" outlaw type who preyed on the symbols of economic oppression, especially banks, railroads, mining magnates, and cattle barons, and in the process became folk heroes to the masses.[81] In the West, this outlaw tradition was represented by the Wild Bunch, the Robbers Roost Gang, and the Hole-in-the-Rock Gang. As with all stereotypes, nuggets of truth are wrapped in a blanket of embellishment.

One nugget of truth was that rustlers and bandits found safe haven in rural Utah, passing through various communities with impunity and on occasion doling out their loot to beleaguered farmers and ranchers.[82] Even a $500 bounty offered by the Utah governor for the arrest of the most notorious outlaws failed to land the miscreants behind bars. The poor—and almost all rural farmers and ranchers were poor—did not share the same views of the outlaws as the governor and his cronies in business and mining. They found at least some of the outlaws to be honorable men. Plus, the payouts they received from the Robin Hood-types served to buy their silence.

Old West historian Charles Kelly related an account of Harry Ogden, a fourteen-year-old at the time, who had been riding near Robbers Roost in 1898 when he was relieved of his horse and saddle. A few weeks later, several visitors showed up at the Ogden home in Escalante. One was Butch Cassidy, arguably the most famous outlaw of the day, and with him was a companion riding the stolen horse. According to Kelly:

> When Cassidy asked Ogden if he had lost a horse, the boy quickly identified it. Butch then ordered the outlaw off the horse and told him "to start walking toward a gap in the hills and keep on going." He then said, "we don't have any room in this country for a man who will mistreat a boy."[83]

Stories like this only served to perpetuate half-truths about men like Cassidy. Matt Warner, also one of the most famous outlaws of the day (he rode with the McCarty brothers and Butch Cassidy before becoming a respected lawman), acknowledged that the outlaws themselves encouraged the largely false perception that they were stealing only from the robber barons who were foreclosing on small farms, manipulating commodity prices, forcing miners to work in deplorable conditions, and in general contributing to their poverty.

The canyon country of eastern and southern Utah became a natural haven for some outcasts who felt economically oppressed, as well as many others who were simply criminals. Old West historians make the case that as many as three hundred outlaws were living at Robbers Roost in the San Rafael desert—enough of them that lawmen never dared venture into the area.

At the national level, the Panic of 1893, the country's first major industrial depression, exposed the often-harsh realities of the new urban, industrial America, while making an easy target of seemingly heartless robber barons of the age. The canyon country of southern Utah, however, had a dearth of wealthy elites in the 1890s. There were no rich bankers, no railroad developers, and no mines.

But two cattle enterprises came to symbolize the wealthy elite: the Bar Z and the Preston Nutter outfit. Thus it is not surprising that most of the outlawry in this region was directed at these big outfits.

Nutter was well acquainted with the criminal element from his earliest ranching days on the Triangle, and like other ranchers he adopted a strategy of hiring them. His daughter maintains, and there is no reason to doubt her, that her father:

> often found it more practical to hire the outlaws to work as cowhands during their cooling off periods. Most of them were cowboys at one time or another and made top hands, but what was more important their code prevented them from rustling from an employer.[84]

In the early twentieth century, Nutter's ranch foreman in eastern Utah was Pete Nelson, who had earlier been a Robbers Roost outlaw under the name Pete Logan.[85]

To cattle barons like Nutter, rustlers remained a persistent threat, as did the sheep men. "I am plagued by rustlers, bootleggers, and sheepmen," Nutter once wrote.[86] From outright theft to altering cattle brands, rustling remained a problem well into the twentieth century. The Southern Utah and Northern Arizona Stock Protective Association met at the Lyceum Building at St. George in January 1906, with President James Andrus reporting that brands of members were being changed by thieves in eastern Kane County.[87] The association offered rewards of $500 for the identification and conviction of rustlers. B. F. Saunders offered an additional $500 reward at times. The association noted that a cattle thief in Garfield County had recently been convicted and sentenced to four years in the state prison.[88] Cattle thieving caused hard feelings between Saunders and Edwin Woolley and other Kanab cattlemen. But ultimately they decided to collaborate. As Saunders wrote to Woolley in 1905: "we should pull together to get rid of this petty thieving that is going on constantly in this section of country."[89]

A common myth about Preston Nutter is that he was different from the cattle barons of Wyoming and Texas in that he did not resort to violence to deter the rustling of his herds or the encroachment onto his range by sheepherders, but rather preferred to use the court system. He indeed loved to litigate, but he also was not above hiring tough men to do very nasty deeds. In 1896, through his friend, Sheriff Cyrus "Doc" Shores of Montrose, Colorado, Nutter employed one of Shores' deputies, John A. "Jack" Watson, as a "detective" to put an end to the rustling. But Watson was not just any detective. He was an ex-Texas Ranger, a violent drunk who was in and out of jail, an on-again-off-again outlaw, and by his own accounts a stone-cold killer.[90]

According to a Watson biography, the scarred and grizzled enforcer looked every part an outlaw, and he easily blended into the criminal underground. He reportedly worked undercover as a blacksmith and came to know the outlaws quite well. Watson made periodic reports to Shores, but apparently never met Nutter personally.[91] By 1898, he had become so effective in ridding the country of outlaws that Nutter requested a personal meeting with the shadowy character. In a May 28, 1898, letter to his brother in Tennessee, Watson claimed to have killed six men while working for Nutter. The cattle baron pleaded with Watson to remain in the area to discourage the return of the outlaws, but Watson responded by going on a drunken bender. By July of that year he was dead, killed by two bullets during a gunfight in a saloon in Price, Utah.[92]

Nutter's daughter only hints that rustling got so bad that her father hired "Texas deputies" to put a stop to it. Regional histories make several references to Nutter's Texas wranglers, apparently because they were tough enough to deal with the outlaw element and could intimidate small operators and sheep men who ventured onto "their" ranges. They were also heavily armed, as were the Bar Z cowboys.

Little, however, has been written about the rustlers of the Arizona Strip, and their refuges are not known with certainty. Some sources reference Paria River country as a hideout, as well as the Glen Canyon area and the many side canyons of the region. Outlaws were known to cross the Colorado River at Lee's Ferry, and the most logical trail to Robbers Roost from this point would have been the wagon route along the east flank of the Kaibab and then north up the bottom of the Paria River to Cannonville and then east. The outlaws who preyed on the Bar Z and Nutter herds apparently never became famous enough to become entrenched in Old West outlaw lore.

Family Affairs

Historian Martha Sonntag Bradley insists the 1890s were times of optimism for ranchers in the region, even if they were being squeezed out of their Arizona Strip ranges and the rest of the nation was gripped by economic depression. The demand for cattle and sheep products was strong and would continue to be so through at least World War I.[93] Populations were stable if not growing steadily, variety was increasing in the goods and services available to local residents, and herd sizes were growing and profits better than any time before.

The various regional histories do not mention how local ranchers were impacted by the depression of 1893, but they likely responded as they always had, through greater self-sufficiency, a barter economy, and community cooperation. If the demand for locally produced livestock was less, that decrease, for

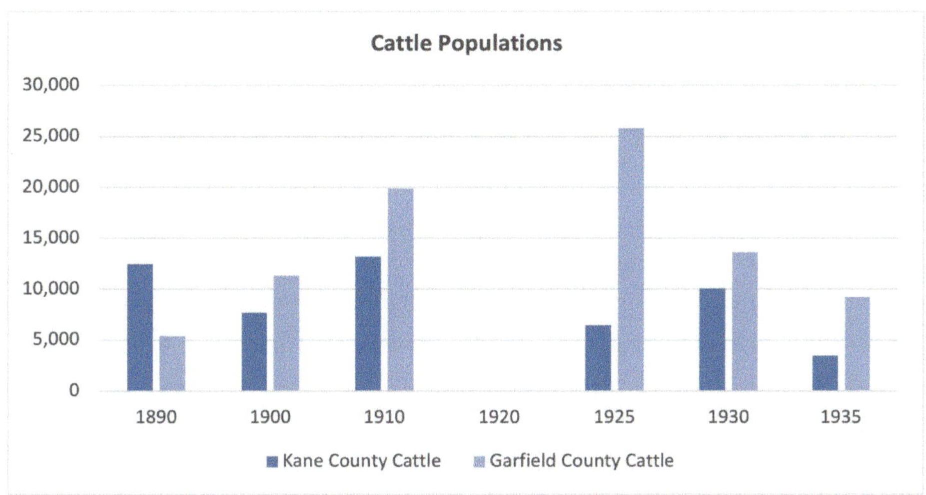

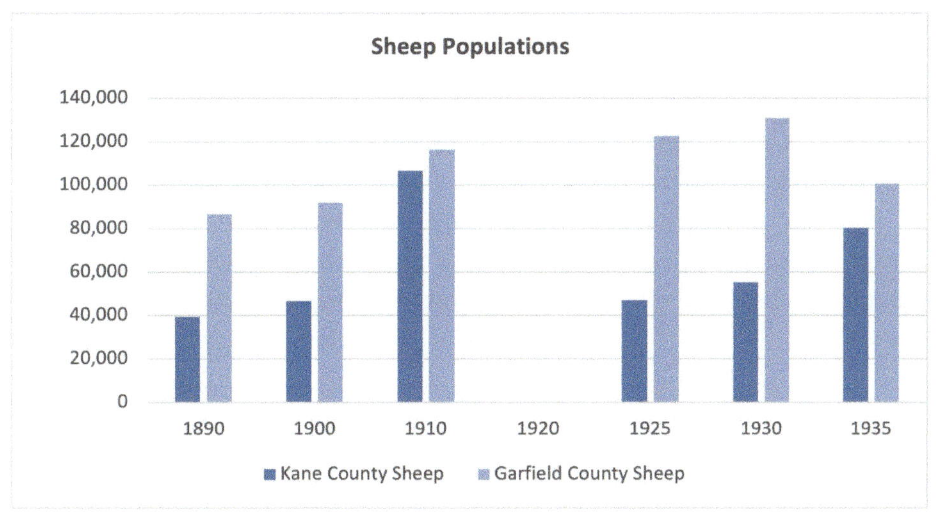

FIGURE 4.9. Trends in cattle and sheep populations in Kane County and Garfield County (combined) from 1890 to 1935. Data derived from USDA Census of Agriculture Historical Archive. The 1920 data not broken out by county.

the most part, was not reflected in the numbers of cattle and sheep on the range (see Table 4.3). As summarized by historian Adonis Robinson:

> From the early history of Kanab, the cattle industry has been outstanding... The ranges in the vicinity afforded fair grazing the year around. Although animals maintained through the year on the open ranges did not bring as good prices as those that were winter-fed, the expense of keeping them on the range was so much less that cattle and sheepmen have found such practice profitable.[94]

By the late 1890s the cattle industry in southern Utah had developed certain contours and rhythms. Pioneer ranchers like Kanab-founder Levi Stewart worked hard to care for their stock, and as his daughter Clarice Stewart Anderson recalled, "he was constantly improving the strains of his cattle by careful breeding."[95] Untended herds tended to wander or "drift," so herdsmen likely were employed to run the cattle regularly. Otherwise the high number of livestock on the open range would have led to unintended mixing of herds and undesirable interbreeding. A rancher who had invested in high-quality Herefords would be livid to find his prized stock mixing with low-value crossbreeds. Mixed-breed herds on the open range resulted in many unbranded calves with debatable ownership.

For ranchers, competition and threats to their livelihoods appeared on every horizon. As a result, they had an incentive to make sure their own herds got to the best grasslands first and were moved consistently to new grasslands ahead of the competition. Untended herds were also vulnerable to predators. Ranchers declared war on any animals that preyed on their livestock; bounties were placed on coyotes, cougars, and wolves, the latter of which were eventually extirpated. Untended herds were also vulnerable to the waves of rustlers that rolled through the Utah Territory in the 1890s.

Ranchers had to have someone guard their livestock at almost all times. Writing about his father's experiences with a large herd, Glynn Bennion recalled that teenage boys and unmarried young men watched the herds, sometimes for years on end. They were not always good at protection, losing hundreds of head every year to rustlers, predators, and cows wandering off never to be seen again.[96]

Apart from the larger spreads on the Arizona Strip, ranchers in Grand Staircase and Escalante River country followed what historians refer to as a village-based approach. Rather than isolated ranches, the ranchers' primary residences were in small towns or small communities like Escalante and Tropic. During the summer they would move to an outlying ranch in the nearby canyons or well-watered mountain meadows. Stockmen and women also employed a strategy known as "transhumance," moving livestock to lower elevations in the winter and higher mountains and plateaus in the summer.[97] As historian George W. Rollins noted:

> In Utah, a stockman usually required a winter and a summer range, the former in the protected valleys and the latter in the foothills of the mountains. Because of this system it was necessary for the stockman to have control of two grazing areas instead of one. Under the laws, he was assured of neither.[98]

The Yardley brothers—James Heber, William Edward, and Daniel Alfred—provide a good example of the practice of maintaining a summer and winter range. Beginning in the late 1800s, the Yardleys possessed a winter ranch in Beaver, and Al Yardley would winter part of their herd on the Wahweap and sometimes at the foot of the Kaibab Plateau south of Fredonia, living in a tent and subsisting only on salt bacon, potatoes, and coffee. In 1908, the brothers partnered to buy a summer ranch on Asay Creek, which they own to this day; it would take three and a half days to trail their herd from Beaver to Asay Creek, a task made longer and more difficult if deep snows lay on the land. They also secured the first permit to run four hundred cattle on the Dixie National Forest, which according to Dick Yardley, is "some of the finest summer country on earth." They bought a couple of farms in Panguitch and several meadows in Hatch, which provided hay to feed the cattle in the fall and early winter before the return trip to Beaver. Additionally, James Gilbert Yardley homesteaded another ranch a mile west of Hatch.[99]

Ranching in southern Utah was made more precarious by the virtual absence of grazing laws in the 1890s. As noted previously, the public domain was open range available on a "first-come, first-served" basis, and there were no prohibitions on encroachment by anyone who might come later. The open range could not be fenced, and any improvements would be shared by one and all. Until implementation of national forest regulations in subsequent years, no legal limits were put on the number of livestock. Individual ranchers had simply no incentive to improve the ranges or develop springs because of the uncertainty about their tenure.[100]

Old-timers interviewed in 1941 almost unanimously blamed the deterioration of the range on too many sheep. William Adair, who ran sheep in southern Utah, noted that:

> Sheep men tried to see which one could get to the spring range first so that they could hold it. The only restriction of territory were these squatters' claims and the first ones to get on the ground or at the watering places. Unrestricted grazing and bad droughts ruined the country.[101]

Chidester and Bruhn suggest that the arid environment of southern Utah's canyon country, which is punctuated by a drought occurring about every five years, made the situation worse, "causing dryland farmers to leave their farms, ranches to discontinue their summer ranching and dairying, sheep and cattlemen to suffer great losses, and even whole towns to vacate."[102]

Over time, family ranchers in Grand Staircase and Escalante River country who made it through drought cycles continued to follow the dual strategy of moving herds between summer and winter ranges. Those living in the Boulder area ranged their cows on Boulder Mountain in the summer, and when fall arrived, they would herd them into the deserts around the Henry Mountains. In the Tropic area, the summer range was the eastern fringe of the Aquarius Plateau and the winter range was the lower Paria River and Wahweap areas near modern Lake Powell. In the Panguitch region, the summer range was the Paunsaugunt Plateau, but in the winter herds would be pushed far to the west in the Escalante Desert west of Cedar City or south into Wahweap country.[103]

Christian Moosman, one of the earliest settlers of Boulder, owned a 160-acre homestead on upper Boulder Creek and also had another place in the town center. His daughter Veda Moosman Behunin recalled: "We moved to the ranch in the spring and then we come down in the fall to go to school. We run on the Boulder Mountain in the summer-time[*sic*] and then Steep Creek and Lower Bowns or the Little Bowns in the wintertime."[104] The sheep men followed the same pattern. Horace Hall owned a quarter section in Salt Gulch called the McGath Ranch that served as a winter base, and in the summer he herded his flock of 3,500 ewes onto the Aquarius Plateau and Escalante Mountain.[105]

In the Kanab and Long Valley areas, the mountain meadows of upper Virgin River country, the Markagunt Plateau, and the breaks below Bryce Canyon were summer ranges. In the winter, livestock would be pushed east toward the Paria River and Glen Canyon. Escalante was situated between two upland ranges—the Kaiparowits Plateau on the south and Boulder Mountain on the north; local ranchers viewed lower Escalante River country as ideal winter range, as was the wild Colorado River country around Hite.

FIGURE 4.10. A sheep herd at a waterhole in the Dixie National Forest, date unspecified. Photograph courtesy of U.S. Forest Service.

The Railroad Cometh (Sort of)

Boosters in southern Utah long dreamed of having a railroad built to their part of the territory. They knew all too well that a cow had cash value only if someone was willing to pay for it, whether owners of feed lots, butchers, packing plants, or other ranchers. Wool growers needed buyers in the mills in the industrialized Eastern states. A rail line to outside markets would help them sell their produce to these purchasers. As noted previously, in southern Utah, there was minimal local demand for beef and only somewhat more for wool. In the early decades of settlement, markets were elsewhere, and southern Utah ranchers were forced by necessity to transport their products to those markets.

In the 1870s, that required massive cattle drives, first to St. George and then north to Salt Lake City—a process that required a month or more on the trail. Sheep were processed closer to home. Ranchers sheared them twice a year, and each shearing required shipping the wool by wagon to mills in St. George, giving rise to a thriving freighting business throughout the region. The freighters would return with commodities otherwise not available in the isolated communities of Kane and Garfield Counties.

The region's transportation infrastructure improved dramatically in the 1890s with the arrival of two different rail lines. On one hand, local residents found they could acquire basic goods cheaper, as well as heretofore unavailable luxury items. On the other hand, lower transportation costs also allowed them to market their own products—cattle, sheep, and wool—more competitively. Rail access also intertwined the local economy with Utah as a whole and linked ranchers more directly to the Midwest stockyard and processing cities of Omaha, Kansas City, and most importantly Chicago. With the railroad, gone were the days that local ranchers were captive to buyers like Preston Nutter and B. F. Saunders offering up a paltry $10 a head; now they had a nation of potential buyers.

The Union Pacific arrived in Ogden in 1869 and a spur line soon connected Ogden to Salt Lake City. In the early 1880s, the competing Denver and Rio Grande Western Railroad arrived in Spanish Fork, later pushing north to Salt Lake City. Both events had profound effects on Utah's economy. For all intents and purposes, they shattered the traditional Utah model of agricultural self-sufficiency where all goods and services were exchanged within Mormon social networks. Competition between the Union Pacific and Denver and Rio Grande railroads kept the costs of imported goods reasonably low, and for the first time Utahns had ready access to luxury goods uncommon on the frontier. They also had the means to ship Utah products to markets elsewhere. Quickly, the urbanizing Wasatch Front became part of a national trade network that included the export of cattle, not only to meat packers in Chicago but also to ranchers in Wyoming and Montana to stock the ranges in those territories.

In the 1870s, southern Utah ranchers were required to drive their herds to Salt Lake City. The arrival of the Denver and Rio Grande in Spanish Fork shortened the distance and briefly transformed that community into a wild cow town. Railroad speculators, including prominent Mormon businessmen and the church itself, entered the railroad building frenzy with plans to build extensions or spurs to other communities. Particularly attractive were potential lines to mining towns such as the silver boomtown Frisco in Beaver County and the vast coal deposits in eastern Utah. As historian Leonard Arrington noted, "in each case, companies were formed, capital was solicited in the East, and the developmental and surveying work was financed by the church."[106] Seeing that railroads had sparked an economic renaissance along the Wasatch Front, southern Utah community leaders hoped a rail link to their region would be a way to improve the economies of geographically isolated smaller communities of the Utah backcountry.

Their hopes were realized when a rail line was extended from Spanish Fork south to Nephi and later to Milford, shortening the distance southern Utah drovers had to trail the herds. But the biggest boon to Garfield-Kane ranchers came in 1891 when the Denver and Rio Grande Western Railroad constructed its tracks to Salina only about 100 mi north of Panguitch. By 1900, another spur was constructed south connecting Salina to Marysvale, then a booming gold mining town that later busted, a fact that was attributed more to high transportation costs than the quality of the ore.[107]

The rail line to Marysvale, only 50 mi north of Panguitch, may have been constructed because of mining, but it also lowered transportation costs for farmers and ranchers throughout the region. Ranchers in Garfield County certainly benefitted from of this new railhead. Escalante resident David M. Woolsey recalled watching herds of cattle stretching 10 mi long travelling the trail from Escalante to Marysvale.[108]

Kane County ranchers also drove their cattle and wagonloads of wool north to the railhead at Salina and later Marysvale after the tracks reached

FIGURE 4.11. Kane County sheep men with wagonloads of wool being loaded onto train cars at Marysvale. Photograph courtesy of John Esplin Collection (p165n01_01_08), Utah State Historical Society.

there. Even so, Marysvale was still about 115 mi north of Kanab.[109] In Kane County and the Arizona Strip, this solution was not particularly ideal, but better than what they had known before. While some ranchers preferred to drive their herds across the Colorado River at Lee's Ferry and then to Flagstaff, the nearest railhead, swimming the cattle across the river was dangerous to both man and beast. Others on the Strip drove herds to St. George and then north to Nephi and later Salina, the latter a long, onerous drive of more than 200 mi. This situation improved in 1899 with the arrival of the Utah and Pacific Railroad (six years later it would become the Los Angeles and Salt Lake Railroad) in Modena west of Cedar City and only 65 mi north of St. George.

The arrival of the Utah and Pacific Railroad was an economic godsend to the people of southwestern Utah, greatly reducing the costs of goods and facilitating the shipment of local products north to Salt Lake City and south to Las Vegas and Los Angeles. A continuous rail line connecting Salt Lake City and Southern California was the brainchild of several of Utah's wealthiest entrepreneurs: David Eccles, A. W. McCune, and Thomas D. Dee, among them. As *The Salt Lake Tribune* reported at the time, Modena was created out of thin air specifically as a "shipping point for freight and cattle."[110] It also became the preferred railhead for Arizona Strip drovers, as well as many cattlemen in the Kanab area.

The movement of tens of thousands of cattle to and from rangelands on the Arizona Strip and Kane County to the Modena railhead was an annual spectacle in Kanab and St. George. For the Bar Z, it was closer to move herds south to Flagstaff, but until 1909 they were effectively restricted from using the Lee's Ferry route. Given the precariousness of swimming cattle across the Colorado River, the Modena railhead remained a preferred hub for cattle shipping through the 1920s.

Donald Kraack offered one particularly colorful description of the annual cattle drives in the early 1920s from southern Utah ranches to the railhead at Modena.

> The cowboys, or drovers, carried sale-guns and revolvers, and we kids would ride our ponies to the outskirts of town to meet them—a sort of self-appointed escort. We were awed at the riders in their chaps, scuffed boots, leather wrist cuffs, battered Stetsons and stubble beards, and at hearing them holler and swear at the herd.[111]

The railroad never did come closer to Grand Staircase country than Marysvale on the north and Modena on the west, and hence the people's sense of isolation, although diminished, remained. Remote communities throughout southern Utah lobbied the railroads and capitalists to build tracks to their towns to no avail. Even boosters in comparatively densely populated St. George and Cedar City pushed aggressively to lure a rail line, but as Alder and Brooks note, "the capitalists in Salt Lake City were not moved. The rail line was laid farther west, skirting Washington County; thus the commerce and outside capital that usually accompany the iron horse went elsewhere."[112]

The preeminent area booster, Edwin D. Woolley, even held public meetings about building a railroad to the North Rim of the Grand Canyon to promote tourism in the region.[113] He lobbied continuously, often using his ties to Mormon leaders, to have a line extended south to bring tourists to a planned resort on the North Rim that would offer not only lodging, but also horse rides, hunting, and other leisure activities.[114] In 1913, Woolley seemed close to securing a branch of the San Pedro, Los Angeles and Salt Lake Railroad to come to southern Utah by promoting its timber and coal, and, of course, tourism potential to the North Rim of the Grand Canyon.[115] As late as 1930, the Denver Pacific Railroad, based in Salt Lake City, entertained plans for a rail line to Kanab. Coleman Crenshaw, the president of the company, went so far as to inquire about the number of Kane County cattle being shipped at other railheads and how far the ranchers had to drive their stock.[116] Nothing came of either proposal, however.

Because of the hardships of transporting their products to markets and their general isolation, residents of Grand Staircase and Escalante River country developed a mixed subsistence and market economy that persisted well into the 1940s. Dixie Shakespear, who was born in Boulder in 1923, told an interviewer in 1999 about her life as a girl growing up on a ranch in southern Utah.

> We used to have chickens that we fed, and turkeys and the boys pretty well fed the pigs and things that way we had all kinds of animals. And then we helped Mother quite a lot around the yards and the house. But I remember Mother made cheese, she always made cottage cheese, butter, and all those things ... We had quite a few horses. A lot of cattle, sheep.

Kept in cool, dark root cellars, her family sold the milk products in nearby towns for much needed cash.[117] Like many others, Shakespear lived on her family's ranch outside of town, residing in town for school in the winter. Another local woman, Veda Moosman Behunin, grew up near Boulder Mountain. While some families had girls do herding and work in the fields, she had nine brothers. She recalls girls pulled their weight by "scrubbing floors and washing dishes and peeling potatoes."[118]

Neal Liston, who was born in 1909 in Escalante, would spend weeks out on the range tending cattle that consisted primarily of Herefords mixed with Angus and what he called brown cattle. During these decades Herefords became the most desirable breed in the West.[119] He remembers that "Good horses and good dogs [were essential]. Good dogs because cattle them days, if they would drift out away from the main places, you know, they'd get wild. Then you'd have to have good dogs to get the cattle."[120]

Despite their isolation, local cowboys and cowgirls had their own sense of style, and bought manufactured goods that they could not make themselves or simply desired for personal reasons. Liston remembers that Leo Munson had a mercantile store in Escalante. It sold "just merchandise. He just had anything you needed to buy. If you needed a new saddle, you could order it from him,

FIGURE 4.12. A general store and gas pump constituted the "downtown" Tropic business district. Photograph by Russell Lee, courtesy of Library of Congress, Washington, DC.

he'd order it for you ... [we] used to buy our boots there." Liston always wore Nocona Boots bought from Munson and Levis jeans that cost 90 cents a pair. Cowboys, he remembers, "they had to have the Stetson hat." He bought his first one for $10.[121] Long-time Kanab bishop William Derby Johnson Jr. regularly purchased goods through the Montgomery Ward catalog during the 1870s.[122]

Long cattle drives would remain a fixture of the region through the 1920s. Oscar Judd, who secured his father's livestock and federal permits after serving in World War II, recalls: "We'd trail from Johnson [Canyon] out to Wahweap both ways; six days out in the fall and seven days back in the Spring ... The Heaton Brothers (from Alton) would have [five] or [six] hundred head on their trail when they would come down through here," going to Mount Trumbull on the Arizona Strip. "I thought that was the only life there was," he added, "work, work, work [laughs]. The kids now days, I don't think they could stand it."[123] As Judd's comments reveal, he was in a dying group still trailing cattle on horseback after World War II. By the end of the 1920s, the region already was laced with roads connecting to the outside world. A new means of transporting livestock had emerged: cattle trucks with internal combustion engines.

Goats and Cattalo

Beef cattle and wool production dominated the local economy of southern Utah by the 1890s. But other forms of animal husbandry also were present. Many families kept swine for personal use, and many if not most families had at least one dairy cow. Several larger-scale dairy operations existed in the area, producing milk, cream, butter, and cheese for sale and trade in the various communities. Some ranchers started experimenting with more nontraditional breeds, as well as promoting hybrids to improve the quality of stock.

In 1905, Kanab-area ranchers and entrepreneurs Edwin D. Woolley Jr. and Dan Seegmiller organized the Utah Cattle Company specifically to improve breeding practices. They even sponsored an experiment with Persian sheep.[124] Many others preferred goats, banking on a growing national market for mohair. The Utah Angora Goat Association was organized in 1906 with Benjamin Hamblin as president. In 1912, the *Kane County Independent* reported that 13,000 head of goats had been sheared.[125]

Beginning sometime between 1900 and 1910, goat ranching was apparently a much larger enterprise than the 1912 report indicates. It would prove one of several boom and bust industries in the area. In a 1941 interview, local rancher

TABLE 4.3. Goat Populations in Kane-Garfield Region and on the Arizona Strip.

Goat Populations					
	1900	1910	1925	1930	1935
Kane County	8	10087	9700	13667	5
Garfield County	0	2777	2503	2902	2
Eastern Arizona Strip	n/a	n/a	50392	11050	506
Western Arizona Strip	n/a	n/a	6357	22558	34

Note: All data derived from USDA Census of Agriculture Historical Archive records for 1900 to 1935. The 1920 numbers were not available.

Neaf Hamblin recalled that Kane County once had 25,000 head of goats (the U.S. agricultural census data reveals a lower number). And there was more than double that amount on the Arizona Strip, where Coconino County reported a high of 50,392 goats in the 1925 agricultural census and Mohave County reported a high of 22,558 goats in the 1930 agricultural census (see Table 4.3). By 1935, goats had all but disappeared from the region.

Neaf Hamblin attributed the decline to breeding practices that led to goats with poor "vitality" that made them ill-suited to the climate and rough range conditions. He also attributed it to the deleterious effects of goat grazing on the range itself. Hamblin observed:

> They say the goats graze too low and too high. They eat trees as high as they can reach and take the grass and brush, as well . . . A goat eats a greater variety of feed than any animal I know of, but he resorts to close picking only when he is held on one place too long at a time.[126]

A review of U.S. agricultural records for that era suggests that Kane County produced the second most mohair in the state, second only to Washington County. In fact, Kane County accounted for nearly a fourth of Utah's entire mohair production with 68,814 lb clipped in 1929 and 47,116 lb in 1934. In Garfield County, 3,000 lb were clipped in 1929, none in 1934.[127]

Today an isolated herd of bison grazes north of the Grand Canyon. It resulted from one of the more unusual experiments in exotic breeds that occurred in the early 1900s courtesy of Edwin Woolley. In 1905, Woolley, B. F. Saunders, James T. Owen, Frank Ascott, Ernest Pratt, and Charles Jesse "Buffalo" Jones hatched a plan to crossbreed bison and Galloway cattle. Saunders was likely involved because he owned or controlled all of the rangelands

FIGURE 4.13. Goat farming became a huge business in Kane County, but the mohair industry proved to be a passing fad. Photograph courtesy of Barbara A. Matheson Special Collections (376c), Gerald R. Sherratt Library, Southern Utah University, Cedar City.

in the eastern Kaibab and House Rock Valley at the time. Woolley acquired stock in the company in exchange for some of his own cattle, which he planned to trade for Galloway cows. In January 1906, Jones received a federal permit to allow fencing of a large area on the Kaibab for the experiment, and six months later the first bison arrived. The forest supervisor based in Fredonia, Lorum Pratt, had earlier supported bringing in "buffalo," feeling the range was ideal for bison.[128]

At one point local ranchers appealed to Utah Senator Reed Smoot for support in the venture, but the "cattalo" experiment failed after four years.[129] Sources vary on the cause, with some saying it was because the cows and bison failed to breed, others saying the resulting offspring had undesirable traits that led to the discontinuation.[130] In 1911, Sharlot Hall, the first woman to hold the office of territorial historian in Arizona, went on a ten-week expedition across the wild Arizona Strip. Her report suggests the cattle and bison indeed had offspring and that "they are lighter and smaller than the full-bloods, with sharper horns and without the beautiful manes."[131] What is clear is that the bison refused to stay on the Kaibab Plateau, preferring instead the open ranges of House Rock Valley, where Hall observed them. In fact, bison thrived in House Rock Valley for decades to come, and some survive to this day in Grand Canyon National Park. Officials proposed the establishment of a federal bison reserve, provoking consternation among local ranchers. They have also wreaked havoc on ranges in modern-day Grand Canyon National Park, with debates occurring over reducing the size of the herd.

One of the cattalo investors, James T. Owen, was purported to have been a member of the Jesse James Gang.[132] He later went on to become a game warden and well-known hunting guide who claimed to have eradicated 1,100 cougars from the Kaibab Plateau. Among his clients were Theodore Roosevelt and Zane Grey.[133]

"Buffalo" Jones bought out Woolley's and Saunders's interests in the bison and managed the herd on his own, apparently in House Rock Valley. Jones sold the herd to the federal government in 1934 for $10,000.[134] A short time after the failed cattalo experiment, in 1907, Saunders had decided to abandon the Arizona Strip. He liquidated his interests in the cattalo experiment two or three years after he sold his other holdings in the region.

FIGURE 4.14. Buffalo Bill Cody (center right) agreed to be part of a scheme to promote the Kaibab Plateau as a hunting playground for the rich and famous. This photo was taken at Kane Ranch in House Rock Valley. Photograph courtesy of Barbara A. Matheson Special Collections (ph18b01i0496), Gerald R. Sherratt Library, Southern Utah University, Cedar City.

As previously mentioned, Ed Woolley was attempting during these years to develop a tourism industry in southern Utah and on the Arizona Strip. In southern Utah, twenty-first century tradition holds that turning to tourism is a post-New Deal phenomenon, a last-ditch response to the decline of the ranching industry caused by federal overreach, but this is not the case. To Woolley and others, tourism was seen as a potential boon already in the first decade of the twentieth century. Decades earlier, the landscape paintings of Thomas Moran and photos of William Henry Jackson and John K. Hillers—all participants in the first great government surveys of the Rocky Mountains, Great Basin, and Colorado Plateau—had awakened an interest in the American West, from its grand vistas to the "colorful" Indigenous peoples who lived here. Southern Utah had these attributes in spades. At one point Woolley and John Young even hatched the idea of bringing British aristocrats to the Kaibab to hunt its famous trophy-size animals. In 1891 they got Buffalo Bill Cody to agree to guide a hunt. The first party was met at the railroad in Flagstaff amid much fanfare and celebrity, but the conditions they faced getting to and from the Kaibab were so rough the idea of a hunting resort and major tourist economy quickly faded.[135]

Government Intervention

Overgrazing of critical rangelands had occupied the minds of early Mormon Church leaders from almost the time of their arrival in the Salt Lake Valley, although the church's solution appears to have been to simply move livestock herds farther and farther away from its settlements. Mormon Apostle Orson Hyde lamented in one 1860s sermon:

> I find the longer we live in these valleys that the range is becoming more and more destitute of grass; the grass is not only eaten up by the great amount of stock that feed upon it, but they tramp it out by the very roots; and where grass once grew luxuriantly, there is now nothing but the desert weed, and hardly a spear of grass is to be seen.[136]

Like Apostle Hyde earlier, cattlemen in the 1890s certainly recognized the ranges were deteriorating, perhaps irreparably, but most placed the blame on the growing number of sheep that grazed the grasses to mere stubs, resulting in severe erosion and arroyo cutting. Some cattlemen even believed that the "poisonous" breath of sheep would kill the grasses.[137] Others blamed the large cattle outfits that ran tens of thousands of cattle with no regard for what the range could handle. They pleaded with the governor and other Utah elected leaders to take action, but they were powerless to do anything. The lands were open range under the jurisdiction of Congress, and federal lawmakers were reticent to tackle the problem. At that time, the General Land Office (the predecessor of the Bureau of Land Management) had no authority to manage the public domain, only to conduct surveys. Individual herdsmen, acting in their own self-interest in an unregulated environment, ran as many cattle and sheep as they could.

The deteriorating range conditions in the American West had also come to the attention of policymakers in Washington DC, including progressive reformers like Theodore Roosevelt, at the time a rising star in the nation's first large-scale conservation movement. In 1891, Congress passed the Forest Reserve Act, which allowed the president to "set apart and reserve, in any State or Territory, lands wholly or in part covered with timber or undergrowth, whether of commercial value or not."[138] The measure had bipartisan support. In short order, Republican and Democratic presidents alike set aside more than 45 million acres of forest reserves.

After the assassination of President William McKinley in 1901, vice president Teddy Roosevelt moved into the White House and elevated the protection of the public domain to an unprecedented level. Before he left office in 1909, he increased the amount of lands protected by federal reserves by nearly fivefold.[139] He used his presidential pen to designate three forest reserves in Kane and Garfield counties: Sevier, Aquarius (later renamed the Powell), and Dixie, encompassing more than 3.6 million acres of summer livestock ranges in Kane and Garfield counties and the Arizona Strip.

The Forest Reserve Act was amended several times to grant the federal government more authority to manage the public forests. In 1896, an amendment allowed the creation of a National Forest Commission with Gifford Pinchot as its head. Pinchot, a university-trained forester and first chief of the U.S. Forest Service in 1905, introduced the concept of "leasing" forest reserve lands to ranchers and allowing federal managers—called "rangers" at the time—to limit the number of livestock on those ranges. These limitations were more of a concept than a reality because there were too few rangers to patrol new forest reserves that covered millions of acres of wild, mountain country. Another limitation was that most of the rangers were hired from the local community, and they were particularly accommodating to their friends and family seeking grazing permits. Added to these facts was the truth that no one had any experience in evaluating how many animals the range could accommodate.[140]

As Charles Peterson observed:

> It must be understood that Utah's farm village stockmen were a class favored by both forest policy and forest personnel. They lived on locally owned land adjacent to the forests, thus qualifying as particularly dependent upon the forests. In addition, the small number of animals they owned came in well below the maximum limit cutoff prescribed by forest policy, so virtually all qualified for permits.[141]

In fact, there appears to have been no effort, at least not initially, to reduce the number of livestock on the Kane-Garfield forests. Ranchers were invited to apply for as many permits for cattle and sheep as they were already running there.

Because the first federal forest reserves lacked mandates for conservation, the 1893 Kaibab reserve, the first and only federal unit in the area until the early

FIGURE 4.15. Wallace Roundy, a local cowboy, was a ranger on the Aquarius Forest Reserve in 1918. Photograph courtesy of Herbert E. Gregory Collection (P0013n08>099_1498), Utah State Historical Society.

twentieth century, did not provoke much concern among small ranchers.[142] But new range policies directed by President Roosevelt changed the status quo. Rowland Rider asserts the forest grazing restrictions had a large effect on the extensive holdings of the Bar Z, whose owners bristled at the reduced numbers mandated by the newly created Forest Service under Roosevelt and the grazing fees they were required to pay. They left the Kaibab rather than pay the grazing fees.[143]

In 1905 during the Roosevelt administration, when new regulations and restrictions were implemented, ranchers started to take notice of federal grazing policies. Roosevelt and Pinchot, his friend and chief forester, were at the lead of the progressive movement's plans to administer the nation's public lands for maximum efficiency using modern science as their guide. They had egalitarian impulses as well, with Pinchot's famous statement "the greatest good of the greatest number in the long run" his guiding dogma.[144]

In the same era, the controversial efforts by Pinchot and Roosevelt to scientifically manage public lands were not seen as going far enough or in the right direction by other reformers. John Muir and his preservation allies regularly attacked their utilitarian viewpoint about wise use of lands in favor of preserving lands in parks and preserves.[145] At the local level, Chidester and Bruhn noted that several Garfield-area ranchers, seeking to run herds of more than three thousand head, were denied forest grazing permits.[146] In September 1912, the U.S. Forest Service ordered one thousand head of cattle removed from the Kaibab, and local residents erupted in outrage at the heavy hand of government.[147]

The 1912 decision was the proverbial straw that broke the camel's back for area stockmen. Federal land grabs seemed to be occurring in every direction. The clamor of opposition was very similar to the outcry of 1996 with the designation of Grand Staircase-Escalante National Monument. Locals in southern Utah charged that the federal government was riddled with ideologues with a preservation agenda, that preservationists in far-off eastern states were unduly influencing federal land policy to the detriment of locals who knew the land best, and that "locking up" the public domain in national forests, parks, monuments, and reservations was contrary to core American values and would lead to the demise of the livestock industry.

In many respects, the chorus of opposition was right on target. The federal government was intent on using presidential executive orders to conserve and to a lesser degree preserve as much land as possible, influenced by a nascent environmental movement, and openly embraced principles that natural resources were not limitless and should be managed and preserved for future generations.[148] The intertwining of these objectives was, of course, much more complicated than a straightforward federal land grab.

In the early 1890s, a national environmental movement had emerged, a central part of what was soon called the Progressive Movement, with two competing factions. On one hand, the conservationists, epitomized by Pinchot, sought to prevent unscrupulous robber barons from devastating the nation's natural resources. They believed natural resources should be used, but used efficiently in a manner that avoided ill effects and exploitation.

Advocated by preservationists, the other school of thought was rooted in the earlier writings of the famed transcendentalists Henry David Thoreau and Ralph Waldo Emerson. It held that nature itself was sacred and worthy of every protection humankind could afford, that nature benefitted the health and well-being of all.[149] This ideology was championed by John Muir, who founded the Sierra Club in 1892 and later in 1905 turned the Audubon Society into a national political force. Roosevelt was a self-avowed conservationist, but he was certainly not averse to using his presidential pen to accomplish the goals of the preservationists. In 1908, to preserve a stand of old-growth redwood forest near San Francisco, he even designated Muir Woods National Monument in California, in homage to the nation's preeminent environmentalist. Both the conservation and preservation reform movements promised to bring changes to regions like southern Utah and northern Arizona. They sought to significantly limit or eliminate grazing. The Forest Service was founded on multiple use principles, and it was pro-grazing so long as it was managed correctly. In contrast, preservationists believed managed wise use did not go far enough, and in the early 1900s they began lobbying for the creation of what would become the National Park Service (NPS), established by an act of Congress in 1916 and signed into law by President Woodrow Wilson. Unlike the Forest Service, grazing was anathema to NPS principles. The Forest Service and NPS became rivals as each sought to expand their own empires.[150]

An underlying current in this debate was the argument that national parks, especially parks with monumental scenery such as in southern Utah and northern Arizona, would foster a tourism industry that would diversify rural economies. At the forefront of efforts to create the NPS was Utah Senator and Mormon Apostle Reed Smoot, who unsuccessfully sponsored a bill in 1911 to create a National Park Bureau. Smoot was also vice president of the Western Pacific Railroad and a director of the San Pedro, Los Angeles and Salt Lake Railroad (later Union Pacific). As Wayne K. Hinton observed, "railroad executives, always seeking profits, believed that tourism would follow the creation of a National Park Service and thereby increase travel by railroad." Through Smoot's influence, the railroad companies committed to building lodges at the national parks and monuments to accommodate tourists.[151]

Smoot's collaboration with the environmental activists and his role in establishing the NPS is not well-known today. Smoot next sponsored the 1919 legislation that created Zion National Park, adding even more grazing restrictions on upper Virgin River country.[152]

Another character enmeshed in this political backstory is Republican U.S. Representative John F. Lacey of Iowa. He sponsored legislation for the creation of a National Parks Bureau in 1900, and when that failed he sponsored the Antiquities Act of 1906, a law granting presidents largely unlimited authority to designate national monuments to protect "historic landmarks, historic and prehistoric structures, and other objects of historic or scientific interest."[153] The new law was embraced enthusiastically by Roosevelt (eighteen national monuments), Taft (ten national monuments), and Wilson (thirteen national monuments).

In 1908, Roosevelt used the Antiquities Act to designate the 800,000-acre Grand Canyon National Monument, effectively adding new layers of restrictions to Utah grazers that had used the country to their south for decades. There was already a game preserve here, and a crescendo of voices called for the Kaibab itself to be designated a national monument. Led by Kanab Stake President Edwin D. Woolley, the "leading men of Kanab" lobbied Utah Senator Reed Smoot to reduce the size of the game preserve. They also had heard rumors that the Interior Department was planning to create a reservation for the Paiutes in the area and vociferously argued against it.[154]

A 1906 petition to Congress from the residents of Kanab and Fredonia gives a glimpse into the feelings of local ranchers and farmers at the time about federal land proposals. They protested the potential "taking" of area lands for a proposed Kaibab reservation for the Paiutes on the west side of Kanab Creek, asserting "that the people of Kanab and Fredonia were depending upon [this land] for arid farming under the Smoot Enlarged Homestead Act." Kanab-area residents noted that the proposed reservation "also deprives them of what little cow range the people of these towns have had and used and depended upon for their sustenance." Non-Indigenous residents wanted it known that the proposal would take their improved water sources, "the only living watering places for the livestock industry of the whole desert country." Showing how they viewed the "taking" of these lands for Indigenous uses, they noted that "our communities are small and depend principally on the livestock industry."[155]

In 1909, Republican President William Howard Taft designated Mukuntuweap National Monument (now Zion National Park), and in 1923 Warren G. Harding, also a Republican, designated Pipe Spring National Monument and Bryce Canyon National Monument, withdrawing even more grazing lands. There was even talk of a bison reserve in House Rock Valley to preserve the non-native herds brought to the area by ranchers themselves. Many of the stockmen's fears were confirmed when, in 1918, Grand Canyon was expanded and, through an act of Congress, redesignated as a national park, promising further restrictions on land uses.

Historian Hal Rothman has found that presidents such as Roosevelt used the Antiquities Act in its first decades to preserve Indigenous and early Euro-American historical sites that faced threats, as the wording of the law intended. In moves that would cause controversies for presidents in later decades, Roosevelt also established precedents by setting aside larger areas such as Grand Canyon and Mount Olympus National Monuments (later Olympic National Park), utilizing the "scientific interest" clause of the Antiquities Act.[156] Revealing how many residents in southern Utah felt about these withdrawals of the public domain, the *Kane County Independent* wrote at the time:

> The proposed [Kaibab] park would cut into the grazing area on the Forest materially, and this at a time when stockmen are facing a cut in their grazing permits because the range is already becoming overcrowded, and when beef is beyond any but the rich on account of their being so little public range left to raise beef on … The game on the Forest is already fully protected by the game preserve, and the natural wonders of the region are protected for all time by being set aside as a national monument. By these measures the Nation is already taking care of its scenic wealth.[157]

FIGURE 4.16. Bryce Canyon was designated a national monument in 1923 by President Warren G. Harding. Utah's sixth national monument did not evoke much controversy at the time. Photograph by Dan Bauer.

The Indigenous Ranchers

As local whites viewed it, the government added insult to perceived injury in 1912 when it announced that it would establish a Southern Paiute reservation (and therefore ignoring their earlier pleas) to be centered on major springs traditionally used by local ranchers: Pipe Spring, Moccasin Spring, Main Spring, Tunnel Spring, and West Cabin Spring. President Woodrow Wilson created it by executive order on June 11, 1913, and federal officials instituted new policies charging area ranchers fees of a dollar per head per year to graze cattle on the Indigenous reserve and two dollars per thousand sheep to cross the Kaibab Indian Reservation. The *Kane County Independent* again weighed in, stating "this is one of the grandest little schems (sic) to put cattlemen out of business ever hatched."[158]

The newspaper apparently missed or ignored the irony in its outrage. The last of the Paiutes had been pushed off the Arizona Strip only twenty-two years before when cattleman and future Mormon apostle Anthony Ivins successfully lobbied the Indian Office to have the Shivwits, the last largely unassimilated band of Paiutes that had been rustling his cattle, removed from the Mount Trumbull region to an Indigenous farm on the Santa Clara River west of St. George, as Ivins later said, "from the mountains to a place where they could be civilized." Ivins succeeded in gaining federal funds and was appointed special agent for the band.[159] The Shivwits band was formally recognized as a tribe by an act of Congress on March 3, 1891. Just west of modern-day Ivins (named for the church apostle), the land base is the current home of the Shivwits band. The Shivwits Reservation was formalized later in 1905 and enlarged to over 26,000 acres by President Woodrow Wilson by executive order in 1916. Ronald Holt wrote dismissively that the new reservation was too small and implied it was designed to keep them dependent; however, the record does not support this latter contention. Historical letters and reports reveal that with the ethnocentric blinders common at the time, Ivins and other church leaders hoped to provide safe homes and limited aid at Shivwits Reservation so the Paiute people could get back on their feet and become assimilated, self-supporting citizens.

For decades, the Bureau of Indian Affairs neglected the "scattered" and "landless" bands of Paiutes throughout southern Utah and along the Nevada border. The most isolated, Indian Peaks, received federal recognition by executive order on August 2, 1915, and Congress set aside areas of the public domain as a land base for the band in Beaver County. The Koosharem Band received recognition by Congress and acreage in the public domain on March 3, 1928.

The outrage expressed by Kane County residents about grazing restrictions at Pipe Spring probably had more to do with the denial of free water they had enjoyed for a half century than it did to the actual reservation. The official church policy of the era was to assimilate the Paiutes through Euro-American-style farming and the sedentary lifestyle that accompanied it, and the Kaibab Indian Reservation furthered those objectives. From the 1880s to the early 1930s, whites hoped to make over Indigenous Americans in the white image: individual land ownership, citizenship, and ultimately independence. Several factors converged in this era to make a church-led Latter-day Saints' role possible in the eyes of federal officials.

The government was "getting out of Indian business," so the fact the church took on the burden was a positive for budget-conscious bureaucrats. As Ivins often noted, he did not want to step on toes, but the agent assigned to Indigenous peoples in southern Utah and northern Arizona, Dr. A. B. Farrow, and others were glad the church was taking on the "scattered" landless Paiutes as wards. Neither Ivins nor Farrow envisioned permanent land-based reservations, and they likely would have seen it as their failure that Shivwits and Cedar Band lands are reservations today. As Frederick Hoxie noted in his landmark article, "From Prison to Homeland," these bases inadvertently created and served as vital cultural homeland for Indigenous peoples like the Paiute.[160]

The "landless" Cedar Band was one of the last to secure a permanent homeland. Beginning in 1924, with the help of a local college professor and others, William R. Palmer, manager of the Cedar City Mercantile and serving in the local stake presidency, used church funds and volunteer labor from both Paiutes and local ward members, to create a small farm and build eight homes on a new church-owned site for the local Cedar Band of Paiutes.[161] Through Ivins, the larger church aided the project. Both Ivins and Palmer repeatedly noted that church welfare work and development programs—such as an arts and crafts program Palmer spearheaded in the late 1920s—were directed, as Palmer said, "to the purpose of making white men of them" and "self-supporting." What these loaded terms meant to Ivins, Palmer, and other whites of the time can be surmised: Indigenous Americans would cease "roaming" and hunting and gathering and instead settle down as farmers, become educated, and live and act like white men and women.[162] Ivins later recalled his pride in establishing the Shivwits reserve: "this property had a tendency to dignify the Indians, it made them self-supporting."[163] Writing to the Bureau of Indian Affairs agent at Moccasin, Arizona, in 1925, Ivins reported the Cedar City land base was intended to allow the Paiutes to attend school, learn English, find jobs, be in closer contact with whites, and become active citizens.[164]

Officially categorized as "non-reservation Indians" in the late nineteenth century, the Kaibab Paiutes had begun drifting to Moccasin Springs near Pipe Spring by at least 1903 but perhaps as early as 1880. U. S. Indian Inspector Levi Chubbuck indicated the Kaibab Paiutes lived around Kanab, but many local residents found this "distasteful," so the Mormon Church then purchased for them a ten- or twelve-acre ranch and one-third water rights at Moccasin Springs. In 1903, Special Indian Agent James A. Brown wrote in an annual report the total Kaibab Paiute population was comprised of sixty-four men and forty-six women. They had a small farm where they grew corn and alfalfa, but mostly they hired out as laborers, the women as domestic help earning 25 to 60 cents a day washing clothes and the men as farm workers. They had been denied access to their traditional hunting territories on the Kaibab Plateau due to the establishment of a game preserve, and all were severely impoverished. By 1906, their population had plunged to only seventy-three individuals.[165]

In 1906, Congress appropriated $10,500 to "support and civilize" the Kaibab Paiutes and to purchase lands and water, along with farming implements, machinery, and livestock. Chubbuck filed another report in 1907, stating "stock raising must be the principal means of support for these people, as it is for the whites of this region, hence it is necessary that ample provision for grazing ground be made."[166]

In late 1907, Secretary of Interior James Rudolph Garfield approved a proposal to pipe water from Moccasin Springs to a reservoir site a mile and a half to the south, an appropriation of fifty to one hundred heifers and a suitable number of bulls, and a General Land Office withdrawal of 138,000 acres from settlement and entry, the first step toward creating a reservation. The withdrawal included all of Moccasin Springs and Pipe Spring and as far east as part of the town of Fredonia. In 1908, the Kaibab Paiute families were removed from the church farm to a new town site at the newly constructed reservoir called Kaibab Village. By 1909, when Kanab-area ranchers were vigorously protesting the size of the pending reservation, the Kaibab Paiutes had already embraced cattle ranching as "the best chance for many Native American communities to build a local economy and rebuild a society."[167] By one account, they had "the nicest bunch of cattle in the country."[168]

Political wrangling intensified, surveys were conducted to exclude the town of Fredonia, and water rights were secured. On July 17, 1917, President Wilson issued an executive order creating the reservation with a land base of 120,413 acres, much of which was already being grazed by tribal herds. The Kaibab Paiutes were also making good money leasing to non-Indigenous ranchers at a dollar a head per year. The Kaibab Paiute organized as a separate band with a formal government under the Indian Reorganization Act of 1934. As of 2000, 131 Kaibab Paiutes were living on the reservation.[169]

The Sheep Problem

The number of sheep and cattle on the Utah forest reserves steadily declined after 1910, although it is unclear whether the decline was due to Forest Service limits on livestock, deteriorating range conditions, fluctuations in the demand for beef and wool, or some combination of all these factors. In 1904, there were 75,000 head of sheep and 12,500 head of cattle on the Aquarius reserve. By 1907, there were 55,000 head of sheep and 11,000 cattle.[170] The reductions appear to have provoked little comment among Garfield County ranchers at the time, at least not to the extent found in Kane County. Local histories suggest that Garfield County ranchers knew that something had to be done, and might even have welcomed the Forest Service leases as a way to help the range recover; it may have given them an edge on sheep men, as well. In 1907, ranchers created the Escalante Cattle and Horse Growers Association to "promote and protect the business of raising cattle and horses upon and adjacent to the Powell National Forest." Other associations with similar goals were later formed in Boulder and Hatch-Hillsdale.[171] These professional groups fostered proper range stewardship, encouraged modern animal husbandry practices, and sponsored range improvements.

Garfield ranchers clearly recognized that their ranges were depleted. They also were aware that flooding was becoming more and more frequent and that arroyo cutting was more pronounced. Escalante-area rancher Joseph J. Porter recalled 150,000 sheep grazed in the Boulder Mountain area before the forest reserve was created, most of them "transient" or "tramp" sheep brought by outsiders. Porter stated, "the first flood I remember seeing come off the mountain was about 1887, but we thought nothing of it. Before that time it could rain for days and the streams never got muddy."[172] Sheepherder E. A. Griffin echoed Porter's observation, noting that flooding became especially severe after 1900. Previously about 12 ft across and lined with marshes and willows, the Escalante River eroded into a gully 400 ft wide and up to 20 ft deep.[173] Like elsewhere in the West, local cattle ranchers felt that federal intervention would favor them, allowing more local control over the transient sheepherders they believed were despoiling their lands.[174]

The cattle associations in the area also became politically active with two specific targets in mind: reining in the sheep men who "trespassed" on their ranges and opposing federal designations that impinged on their own grazing. In 1930, local ranchers traveled to Salt Lake City to participate in a protest against the proposed House Rock Valley bison preserve, a rally held in conjunction with the annual convention of the Utah Cattle and Horse Growers Association. The *Kane County Independent* wrote, "do we want to stay in the cattle and sheep raising business or be lackeys for big brewers, soap-makers and stock gamblers and their wives, for the wages a tourist agency would pay?"[175] This theme was repeated often in the decades ahead. As summarized by Bradley:

> The battle over public lands continued throughout the century, with ranchers resisting any government attempt to more strictly manage the public lands or increase grazing fees. Many area ranchers in Kane County, as elsewhere in the West, seemed to believe that their lengthy use of the land entitled them to permanently control it or at least not have any of their previous privileges reduced or eliminated.[176]

Forest lands and national monuments enjoyed some modicum of environmental protection during this period, but that was not the case with public lands outside the forests, monuments, and game reserves. These were still open ranges free to one and all on a first-come, first-served basis. Since the late 1800s, Congress had been debating the issue of grazing on the public domain with little consensus. One proposal was to amend the Homestead Act to allow ranchers to acquire patents on "Grazing Homesteads" of up to 3,000 acres. Another called for leasing of the public domain at ten to thirty cents an acre.[177] Nothing came of these proposals.

As public lands continued to deteriorate in the first part of the twentieth century, federal regulation of rangelands won over an unlikely ally: Preston Nutter. Always a pragmatist, he saw advantages in partnering with federal officials. Nutter probably had been responsible for more degradation of the Arizona Strip ranges than any other person. But, in his later years, he became active in various associations trying to deal with the pervasive problem of "trespassing" by sheepherders on established cattle ranges. Through these efforts, he also became an ardent supporter of the Taylor Grazing Act—the federal government's first attempt to regulate grazing on public lands through allotments. He apparently felt that the 1934 act "would put rout the itinerant sheepmen and allow the established, legitimate rancher to manage the feed and forage."[178] By some accounts he was instrumental in the passage of the legislation, but more likely he was an outspoken supporter whose opinions commanded respect even in Washington, DC.[179]

At the same time, some scientists, activists, and forward-thinking ranchers realized the limits of human usage of the environment. With the livestock industry in decline, ideas began to emerge as to how to maintain and promote the area's cowboy traditions and frontier culture for profit. As previously mentioned, Ed Woolley had hosted politicians for a tour of the area in 1905, and a few years later he took another delegation of dignitaries on a trip to the Kaibab and North Rim of the Grand Canyon, with noted author Zane Grey and Utah Governor William Spry treated to a cougar hunt. Woolley brought the first automobile to Kanab in 1909 and supported the development of auto roads to the Grand Canyon and Zion.[180]

Woolley firmly believed that outsiders would come to love the lands of southern Utah and northern Arizona if they saw them. But exposing once-isolated communities to an outside world came at a cost to local pride. In 1912, Zane Grey published his classic in Western fiction, *Riders of the Purple Sage*, set in southern Utah, wherein Mormons were portrayed as the evil antagonists in a story that revolved around the victimization of women in Mormon culture. By today's standard, its biases and prejudices still are jarring.[181] But the novel was a huge popular success, spawning a sequel, five movie adaptations, and an opera.

National stereotypes notwithstanding, Mormon locals were protective of their history and proud of their cowboy heritage. Kanab residents began to formalize frontier traditions to accommodate spectators. Between 1912 and 1916, they held the "KKK" for Kanab Kounty Karnival, with a rodeo, horse races, roping contests, bulldogging steers, and bronc riding. Woolley displayed some of his bison as part of the festivities. The Kanab Lion's Club later built a city rodeo grounds and horse track, where both it and the American Legion began sponsoring rodeos and races for prizes. Building upon their cowboy heritage, these events became lasting traditions.[182]

The Changing Landscape

Regional histories about the Grand Staircase and Escalante River country agree that the demand for local cattle and sheep remained consistently good from the 1890s through the end of World War I in late 1918. Federal tariffs worked to maintain high prices for sheep products during these years.[183] In fact, the war effort boosted the demand for beef to feed the troops and for wool to make uniforms. Some, like Preston Nutter, became even more wealthy through military contracts. But after the end of World War I, national demand for livestock products plummeted, and farm prices and production also declined, helping send the national economy into a recession. Bradley, however, argued:

> The agrarian lifestyle of most residents was less dependent upon national employment and economic trends and problems, and most residents were able to grow their own basic food. Since mining, industry, and tourism had never been important sources of revenue, the downturn of the cash economy did not impact Kane County as it did most other regions of the country.[184]

A similar scenario held true after the stock market crash of October 29, 1929, ushering in the Great Depression. Newell and Talbot noted that most farmers of Garfield and Kane Counties were not as adversely affected as most Americans because they could raise their own food. But when the few banks in the region began to shutter their doors, many lost their savings, credit was hard to come by, and they had to make due with old equipment. As Newell and Talbot concluded, "even if they could raise additional crops or animals, markets for them were scarce or nonexistent."[185] A barter economy thrived, harkening to the practices of the first pioneer settlers of the region.

It is often forgotten, but the first years of the Great Depression could have offered a final solution to what later became protracted and angry debates over the fate of public lands in the West. Republican President Herbert Hoover was a Westerner himself, having grown up on his uncle's cattle ranch in Oregon. Also a staunch proponent of "hands off government" and laissez-faire economics, Hoover offered in 1930 to transfer federal lands (minus underground mineral rights) to the states, but Western states governors refused, believing the economic costs to them were too high.[186] In Utah, Governor George Dern likened the proposal to giving his state a "squeezed lemon," seeing that public lands were in such poor shape and that the economic depression, especially in agriculture, resulted in thousands of people actually abandoning marginal lands. A few years later, a federal study confirmed his fears with findings that 61 percent of state lands were severely eroded. On the Colorado Plateau the number was between 89–100 percent.[187]

Warren Foote, who was raised in Long Valley during the Depression, recalled that

> times were lean, money was short. We did not deal much with money; we dealt mostly with produce. We always had food, we always had the things we needed. My father in his history mentioned that during the Depression they lost about a third of their property.[188]

According to Jean Bybee Syrett, a child during the Depression, "we didn't know we were poor, we just knew we didn't have any money."[189] The effects of the Great Depression are discussed in greater detail in the next chapter.

Adding insult to injury, the 1930s featured some of the worst drought years on record, causing grazing conditions to continue to spiral downward. Some ranchers quit the business, and others (or immediate family members) went to work for the Forest Service or the New Deal-era Civilian Conservation Corps (CCC). Many found construction work through other government programs, building schools and roads. William Isabell, a Canadian living in Garfield County, turned to moonshining.[190] By 1934, the economy was in tatters and rangelands were exhausted. The federal government's inaction on grazing reforms had left many livestock operators disillusioned. Contrary to popular perception, many area stockmen, like Preston Nutter, also praised the imminent passage of the Taylor Grazing Act of 1934 as long overdue. In fact, the law's sponsor, Edward Taylor, a congressional representative from Colorado, was a foe of Roosevelt and Pinchot's conservation agenda, but agreed that the land demanded some regulation. As envisioned by Taylor, the new grazing law would promote cattlemen's interests foremost.[191]

The CCC was the most popular New Deal work program with major impacts in rural Grand Staircase and Escalante country. The CCC boys (they were all male) worked throughout the arid West to rehabilitate damaged rangelands. In an effort that would surprise many modern residents of southern Utah, crews were hired by the government to kill Utah prairie dogs (currently listed as "threatened" under the Endangered Species Act) and burn cacti to make room for livestock. Government programs also reseeded grasslands in desirable species of sage and bluestem grass, fenced off sensitive riparian areas, and built reservoirs. An earlier federal effort, the Animal Damage Control Act of 1931, created new predator and rodent control branches in the U.S. Fish and Wildlife Service, with coyotes being the main target, to "improve" both the range and its valuable game species.[192]

Some eagerly welcomed the changes. Grazing lands had become what stockmen called ten-by-eighty ranges, as historian David Lavender explained, "a steer has to have a mouth [10 ft] wide and be able to run 80 mi an hour from one clump of grass to the next to get enough to eat."[193] All ranchers knew the problem: too many cows and sheep and not enough forage. Several original settlers of the Grand Staircase and Escalante country provided historical context. Many commented during interviews conducted in 1941 that the range at that time could only accommodate about 10 percent of the livestock that once grazed there. William McAllister observed that "bad droughts and overgrazing made the range poorer from year to year. There is [sic] not a hundred cattle now to where there was a thousand then."[194] In southern Utah, differences of opinion rested on how to resolve the situation. Some sought to break up the big cattle outfits, others to prohibit sheep on the range, and yet others preferred government regulations over the free-for-all that had destroyed the rangelands.

As historian Don D. Walker observed, "some overgrazed lands would perhaps never again revive to the pristine lushness; but more and more cattlemen knew that ranges, like the cattle themselves, must be protected if they are to have a continuing value."[195] As the effects of the 1930s droughts lingered, they also recognized it would take time for the ranges to recover from decades of overgrazing. As Neaf Hamblin concluded, "the Taylor Act will be a good thing for the range, but it will take a long time for the range to come back . . . [but] something had to be done to protect [it]."[196]

FIGURE 5.1. Lower Calf Creek Falls. Photograph by Dan Bauer.

5 Depression, Determination, and Recovery, 1934–1945

The mid-1930s was a period of despair across much of the nation. For many Americans, these years of economic deprivation were characterized by food lines, Dust Bowl droughts that prompted a mass exodus from the Great Plains to California, predatory bank lending that resulted in the loss of homes and farms, and the rise and fall of criminal gangs who terrorized communities from coast-to-coast. Rural southern Utahns shared in that despair, yet it was tempered by the fact that many could grow their own food and muddle through. The droughts hit Garfield County and surrounding areas particularly hard in 1933 and 1934 when the county had among the state's highest per capita distribution of welfare relief funds.

Utah's economic stress also exceeded the national rate. A supplier of bulk materials such as livestock, minerals, and crops, the state was directly impacted by volatile commodities markets as prices dropped precipitously after 1929. By 1933, per capita income in Utah had fallen to approximately half of what it had been before the Stock Market Crash.[1] Even with such dismal statistics, southern Utah residents were hardy stock, many self-sufficient and close-knit, most of them related by blood, marriage, or religion. They remained, for the most part, geographically isolated from rest of the world, a separation breached by only a couple of dirt or gravel two-track roads hastily constructed to provide tourists access to new national parks at Bryce, Zion, and Grand Canyon.

That isolation served many of the people struggling to survive in the Grand Staircase and Escalante River country better than those in cities unable to raise their own food and make their own clothing. Two years into the Great Depression, the *Kane County Standard* boasted "Kanab people drive good cars, have good homes, wear good clothes, and eat good food."[2] But not everyone shared that rosy view. Trevor Leach, who grew up in Kanab, recalled: "If we had anything to eat we were lucky. If we didn't we had Hoover's wheat,"[3] a reference to bags of raw wheat handed out by the government to starving families. The grains were cracked in a coffee mill and toasted, and "it made awfully good cereal."[4]

The small-town environment even allowed residents of the Grand Staircase and Escalante River country to make do without using federal currency. Clare Ramsay, who was raised in Long Valley, recalls how Hans Chamberlain, who ran a store in Orderville, found a way to continue operating in his cash-strapped corner of Utah.

> He was such a swell guy, he had a store there, and he made his own money. I don't know how legal that was; not paper money, but they had what was called Chamberlain Store Money, and it was probably a square or an oblong piece of metal that had Chamberlain Store written on it and says 25 cents, and that's what he'd give you back in change . . . I can remember hoeing weeds in the neighbor's garden for them . . . they'd give me 25 cents in Chamberlain Store Money for the pay![5]

While relatively isolated, residents of Garfield and Kane Counties had access to the news of the world via increasingly popular radio programs and newspapers. They played baseball in the town parks and certainly heard that Babe Ruth had finally retired in 1935. They likely knew Benny Goodman had introduced a new style of music called "swing" and that Germany was rearming and there were already whispers of war. They almost certainly heard that the notorious outlaws John Dillinger, Baby Face Nelson, Pretty Boy Floyd, Ma Barker, and Bonnie Parker and Clyde Barrow had all met their demise at the hands of G-men.

Kane County at that time was welcoming a steady stream of tourists traveling U.S. Highway 89, the north–south thoroughfare that initially was intended to connect Yellowstone on the north to Grand Canyon on the south, and some news of the outside world certainly found its way onto Kanab's main street. Some had access to the latest technological craze, a magical wonder called "radio," for the very latest news and entertainment. According to Helma Richards Haas, who was born in Tropic in the mid-1920s, a few residents had radios that even could receive signals from Salt Lake City stations.[6] Just as likely, what the locals knew of the outside world came from monthly magazines and movies. Every week, beginning in 1929, area resident Kay Heywood dragged a

FIGURE 5.2. The movie theater in downtown Escalante photographed in 1936. Photograph by Dorothea Lange, courtesy of Farm Security Administration/Office of War Information Black-and-White Negatives, Library of Congress, Washington, DC.

projector and gasoline-powered generator to screen films in Cannonville—tickets were purchased with produce and foodstuffs.[7] Escalante had a theater, and Kanab had its own establishment, the Star Theater, where residents could enjoy "talkies," introduced just a few years prior, and take in live entertainment. Some of the westerns had even been filmed locally using area cowboys and livestock.

National milestones were rarely, if ever, mentioned in the local newspapers of the day, further perpetuating a perception of social isolation. Local residents instead were fed a weekly diet of articles on how to properly can fruits and vegetables, marriage announcements (and surprise elopements), church conferences, weekly dances, community plays, and obituaries. On occasion, they read news about ranching, such as the new requirements of the federal Taylor Grazing Act of 1934 and the local committees charged with implementing the law.

The combined effects of the Great Depression and the crippling droughts certainly defined ranching life in the Depression years throughout the West. But several other watershed events, many of them interrelated, characterized the grazing history in southern Utah and northern Arizona from 1934 to 1945. The unrelenting droughts of the 1930s prompted the first serious attempts to address rangeland health and long-term sustainability through the Taylor Grazing Act. In Utah, 1934 capped the worst drought the state had experienced since 1856, with precipitation in the state roughly 35 percent of normal rates.[8] With the combined economic and environmental crises, local ranching became enveloped within broader statewide and national range policies focused on conservation.

The economic crisis of the Great Depression resulted in numerous New Deal efforts promoted by Democratic President Franklin Delano Roosevelt (FDR) to bolster the local livestock industry through direct payments to ranchers, loan programs, and financial incentives to embrace conservation techniques

FIGURE 5.3. Unrelenting droughts and federal conservation programs resulted in widespread water control projects. This 1936 project involved the construction of a reservoir near Tropic, Utah. Photograph by Dorothea Lange, courtesy of Farm Security Administration/Office of War Information Black-and-White Negatives, Library of Congress, Washington, DC.

and invest in range improvements. New Deal planners in Washington even extolled the virtues of the Mormon village-based model of self-sufficiency to the rest of the nation.[9] Although local ranchers were overwhelmingly Republican, they embraced the federal government payouts that came with those programs passed by a Democratic president and a Democratic-controlled U.S. Congress. As many as 70 percent of Escalante residents were on government relief in 1935 "due to depleted range and crop failure."[10]

Another trend witnessed in the 1930s was the collapse of the once-dominant regional sheep industry to the point that after World War II it became irrelevant, not only in southern Utah and northern Arizona but nationwide.[11] Throughout Utah, all families who made a living off the land struggled. Cash receipts from chickens, hogs, cows, and other animals, dairy products, and eggs declined more than 50 percent from 1929 to 1934. However, sheepmen suffered the most. By 1934, their income from sheep, lambs, and wool was only one quarter what it had been in 1929.[12] This collapse was due to national factors, mostly changing consumer preferences for synthetic fibers for textiles and for beef instead of mutton. The collapse also illustrated how Western livestock economies had become inextricably linked to the national and global markets.

World War II effectively ended the Great Depression, as it stimulated economic recovery and spurred an increased national demand for local wool, mutton, and beef to support the war effort. But with most of the young men gone to war, ranchers in southern Utah and northern Arizona were hard-pressed to meet the increased demand. Herd sizes were actually smaller during the war than they were in the years before the war, despite the increased demand.

Finally, conflicts between livestock producers and other competing uses of the public domain continued unabated during the 1930s. Livestock operators invariably found themselves at odds with wildlife advocates and those promoting tourism and conservation. Politicians created more national parks and monuments, and others were expanded. But conflicts with the federal government over grazing restrictions did not flare up during this period.

Droughts and Reforms

The vagaries of climate have always been a cruel mistress to farmers and ranchers everywhere. For millennia, farmers have religiously read the horizons for any hint of approaching storm clouds, pleading to the gods for rain. In the 1930s, during the height of the Great Depression, their prayers for rain were increasingly futile. Prolonged droughts across North America devastated farmlands, the most famous being the Dust Bowl, which reached its peak in 1934 and would eventually displace two million farming families in Texas, Oklahoma, Kansas, Colorado, and New Mexico. But these droughts were not limited to the Great Plains. In fact, 77 percent of the United States at that time was severely affected by droughts.[13] Noted historian Donald Worster found the Dust Bowl and other manmade "natural disasters" spawned new conservation-oriented ideals. Americans began to embrace concepts of limits, and they recognized that humans had overdeveloped the land. Franklin Delano Roosevelt, who idealized his distant cousin Teddy Roosevelt, developed his own national conservation policy behind goals of more scientific management, more federal intervention, and the idea that the public interest should preside over private welfare.[14]

FDR's conservation approaches were widely popular across great political divides. In Utah, Roosevelt's friend and fellow Democrat George Dern, was elected to the first of two terms as governor in 1924, even though Utah was a solidly Republican state and GOP candidates swept the other statewide races at the time. An advocate of environmental protections and rehabilitation of Utah's public lands, Dern later went on to serve as secretary of war in FDR's cabinet, a relatively minor position given the nation's isolationist tendencies at the time, but one that would have profound ramifications on public lands in Utah and elsewhere in the West. As secretary of war, Dern was in charge of the Civilian Conservation Corps (CCC), a New Deal program that hired unemployed young men to build rural roads and infrastructure, and to rehabilitate and protect the nation's natural resources.[15]

Decades of poor land use practices and the epic drought of the 1930s provided the CCC with plenty of potential rehabilitation work, especially in the American West. In particular, the American Southwest was among the hardest hit areas, even though it was an arid region accustomed to droughts every five to seven years. But this drought was unusual both in terms of its severity and its duration (1926–36). Certainly parallels can be made between what happened in the Great Plains and what occurred in southern Utah and northern Arizona at the same time. In the Great Plains, farmers had plowed under native grasslands to plant wheat. But once the droughts arrived, with no grasses to protect the soils from erosion, the unrelenting winds lifted the topsoil into dust clouds that reached 10,000 ft high and blew east as far as New York City.[16]

In the Southwest, the open range served the same role as the plow did on the Great Plains. The proliferation of livestock on the open ranges denuded the landscape and removed the fragile grasses, making the already marginal soils vulnerable to rapid erosion, both by winds and flash flooding. As a result, range forage quickly deteriorated in quantity and quality during the 1930s. In 1936, a U.S. Department of Agriculture report referred to Western range practices as representing "perhaps no darker chapter nor greater tragedy in the history of land occupancy and use in the United States."[17]

FIGURE 5.4. George Dern was an avid hunter and angler who used his position as Utah governor and later as commander of the Civilian Conservation Corps to foster rehabilitation projects on Utah public lands and develop critical infrastructure in rural Utah. Photograph courtesy of Utah State Historical Society Classified Photo Collection (39222001346183).

In Grand Staircase and Escalante River country, overgrazing led to widespread flooding and erosion of top soils. It also promoted the invasion of noxious weeds, some of them toxic to livestock. As early southern Utah historian Julius S. Dalley observed, native forage plants once abundant in the region were soon replaced by less nutritious types, and

> these in turn were killed out by continued excessive grazing and still poorer types succeeded. This process has been repeated on many of our ranges until the present vegetative cover is not natural to it at all, and bears no resemblance to that which the pioneers found.[18]

The unrelenting droughts of 1926–36 prompted similar responses across the nation: people picked up and moved elsewhere. Some farmers walked away from their farms to find work in urban factories or shipyards. Others loaded all their earthly possessions in the back of primitive pickup trucks and headed to California, which had assumed a mythical status as a destination for new beginnings. But this drought-induced exodus never really happened in southern Utah, despite the crushing local poverty and bleak prospects for the future. Historian Brian Q. Cannon addressed this oddity, noting that southern Utah farmers and ranchers, unlike their counterparts in Oklahoma or Kansas, were spiritually bound to the land through "callings" from their church leaders to settle specific areas. These leaders echoed the biblical prophet Isaiah's promise that through their faithfulness the desert would blossom as the rose. To abandon their farms was tantamount to admitting they had failed God.[19]

An example of this, Cannon pointed out, was the short-lived community of Widtsoe on the northern periphery of the modern Grand Staircase-Escalante National Monument. Settled by Latter-day Saints in 1908 under the name Adairville, the town was renamed Widtsoe after University of Utah President John A. Widtsoe, a prominent range scientist and proponent of dryland farming. Mormon Apostle Melvin J. Ballard dedicated the community to the work of God and promised the settlers that the high-desert valley would become a Garden of Eden if the residents kept God's commandments and stayed out of debt. In effect, the land was a spiritual and symbolic link to God. Even after the settlers succumbed to drought conditions and left, "some former residents of the area still remember that promise, speak of their valley reverently, make annual pilgrimages to it, and speculate that it may one day blossom."[20]

Amid the Great Depression, some local residents pled to government officials for help. Resident Orson Adair wrote to officials:

> It is fall—and the people have milk cows, some horses, chickens, pigs and in some cases a few sheep to feed this winter, and nothing to feed them . . . Will you please picture a community in a locality where practically no income is available other than forty dollars a month [in relief payments]? We have no gardens, no fruit trees, no pastures.

Ultimately, a New Deal agency, the Resettlement Administration, stepped in to aid the desperate residents of Widtsoe. It bought nearly 30,000 acres and gave financial assistance to former residents to move elsewhere. Most of the acreage purchased is now managed by the U.S. Forest Service.[21] The end of Widtsoe was chronicled in 1936 by Dorothea Lange, the most famous photographer of the Depression era.[22]

As Chapter 4 detailed, overgrazing of the open ranges of the American West had long been recognized as a growing problem, not only by the ranchers themselves but by policymakers in Washington, DC. Abuses were widespread, most of which were blamed on the hooves of the hundreds of thousands of sheep that grazed public lands at the time. Grazing on public forests had been managed since 1896 with the establishment of a National Forest Commission, which leased forest lands to ranchers and limited the numbers of livestock that could be grazed. But non-forest lands remained open range, free to one and all on a first-come, first-served basis. Lawmakers debated the merits of further grazing restrictions and their potential impact on states' rights to public lands for nearly forty years before passing the Taylor Grazing Act in 1934, landmark legislation in the American West. As early as 1902, Albert F. Potter, chief grazing officer of the Department of the Interior's Division of Forestry under Gifford Pinchot, lamented that Utahns had failed to see the relationship between overgrazing and deforestation and the deterioration of watersheds that directly impacted the water quality of local communities.[23]

FIGURE 5.5. Now a ghost town, Widtsoe once had its own mercantile store, gas station, and post office. Photograph by Dorothea Lange, courtesy of Farm Security Administration/Office of War Information Black-and-White Negatives, Library of Congress, Washington, DC.

The stated intent of the legislation was to "stop injury to the public grazing lands by preventing overgrazing and soil deterioration" and to "provide for their orderly use, improvement, and development."[24] The legislation created the U.S. Grazing Service, an agency in the Department of the Interior with the authority to create regulated grazing districts on unclaimed public lands, issue permits to graze on those lands, and charge grazing fees. Ranchers were eligible for permits if they met two conditions: (1) they had to own a nearby base property, and (2) they had to demonstrate a recent history of grazing on those federal lands. As such, the law gave preference to ranchers who lived on the land and had used those rangelands historically.[25]

The Taylor Grazing Act reversed nearly sixty years of open range practices in the West. In light of modern controversies, it might seem logical to assume that these restrictions were met with suspicion and hostility by ranchers in the Grand Staircase and Escalante River regions. But there is little evidence, at least not in Kane and Garfield Counties, that cattlemen opposed the law. In fact, little mention of the impending restrictions is made in the years leading up to the act's passage in 1934 (amended in 1936 and again in 1939). There are two fundamental reasons behind the absence of protest over the restrictions. First, local cattle ranchers believed the law could help keep itinerant sheepmen off their ranges. Second, provisions in the law meant that their own men would control land use practices.

On the first point, local cattle ranchers all recognized there was a serious overgrazing problem. But they did not see their own grazing practices as the source of the range degradation. They were the "legitimate ranchers." Instead, they attributed the problem to "tramp" sheep grazers who descended on the

FIGURE 5.6. Johnson Canyon, Kane County. Photograph by Dan Bauer.

open ranges every spring with tens of thousands of sheep, gobbling up forage before local cattlemen had turned out their herds. Cattle ranchers felt the new law would help curtail the activities of itinerant sheepmen. While displacing the primary source of blame, a legitimate gripe about sheep grazing versus cattle was the fact that sheep have a "prognathous" mouth, meaning they have teeth set at an angle that allows them to pull out grass from below the buds.[26] Prior to 1934, these conflicts, Dalley noted, resulted in a few "scrimmages" between cattlemen and sheepmen, and "the sheepmen won out by sheer numbers. Any sheepherder knows how easy it is to run out, or eat out, all the cattle in the country."[27]

In frontier Western tradition, epic battles need a good villain, and sheepmen provided one. Like many area cattle raisers, Arizona Strip cattle baron Preston Nutter, a supporter of the Taylor Grazing Act, believed the act "would put rout the itinerant sheepmen and allow the established, legitimate rancher to manage the feed and forage."[28] F. R. Carpenter, director of the U.S. Grazing Service in 1936, was more blunt, calling the sheepmen

> vandals of the rangelands, nomadic, tax-dodging operators who roam the great western grazing empire . . . [passing] over the public domain without outfits, without using proper methods of livestock operation, and devastated the lands the Government is now trying to protect.[29]

John Muir, founder of the Sierra Club, would have agreed with Carpenter's assessment. Years earlier he famously called sheep "hoofed locusts" and worked to have them banned from his beloved Yosemite, an early national park, decrying how they were "trampling the wild gardens and meadows almost out of existence."[30] A former rancher himself, Teddy Roosevelt also despised sheep, calling them "bleating idiots."[31] In other words, to many observers, local cattle ranchers were not the problem, and the implementation of a permit system would only eliminate a problem not of their making.

Neal Liston, who was born in a little log house in Escalante in 1909, recalled his family's desire for U.S. Forest Service regulation. "We had our own permits and our own cattle; we run them on the desert in the winter time and up on the Canaan Mountain in the summer." His father had grazed on Canaan Mountain for years, "but he went to Ogden to the office up there and had it put in the Forest Service to do away with the transients [from Fillmore and Parowan]." According to Liston, they just kept "coming in, just kept a crowding us off. So they had put it under the Forest."[32]

However, this account was not entirely accurate. Several large sheep operations in Kane and Garfield Counties were owned by local men. Clare Ramsay, who was raised in Glendale, recalled:

> there were two or three outfits in town, families I should say, that had sheep [and] all the men herded sheep for them. And it was pretty much the same in the Bryce Valley area and everybody worked for the sheepmen . . . They went out for months and stayed and didn't come home.[33]

The second reason for what appears to have been local support for the Taylor Grazing Act is that administration of grazing restrictions was to be placed in the hands of local grazers, the so-called "home rule" clause. "Eastern conservationists" strongly opposed this provision, believing ranchers could not be trusted to regulate themselves. But home rule was nonnegotiable to Western lawmakers who otherwise would not have supported the bill.

Ranchers learned of the basic tenets of the Taylor Grazing Act through articles placed in all local newspapers throughout the region, and immediate jostling ensued over who would get permits for the best ranges.[34] Arizona officials initiated an unsuccessful effort to prohibit grazing by Utah-based ranchers on the Arizona Strip even though, as one man observed in the local newspaper, "the roads, trails, and water holes of the section of Arizona north of the Grand Canyon have been developed almost entirely by Utahns during the past fifty years."[35] Later in 1934, Arizona formally protested to the Secretary of Interior about the livestock flooding into the state, not just from Utah, but Nevada, California, New Mexico, and Texas.[36]

Actual apportionment of the ranges did not occur until 1935 when much of the future Grand Staircase-Escalante National Monument came under some federal supervision. In May of that year, ranchers were notified of local elections to be held to choose "advisors" to each grazing district.[37] Three local representatives were initially chosen for each of three proposed grazing districts: (1) western Kane County from the Washington County line to Kanab Creek, (2) Kanab Creek to Warm Creek just east of the Paria River, and (3) Glen Canyon country to the east of Warm Creek as far as the Colorado River, including the Kaiparowits Plateau and eastern Garfield County.[38] These three districts were consolidated into a single unit, Utah District 4, which encompassed all of Washington, Kane, and Iron Counties, as well as much of Garfield County. Another grazing district encompassed the Arizona Strip (Arizona District 1).[39]

Ranchers had only a month to file their applications, and they worried about how the government would apportion permits. The *Kane County Standard* observed at that time, "Some heated disputes over certain claims of individual stockmen in these districts have taken place recently. It appears that it will be a hard matter to divide the range in a way that it will be satisfactory to all concerned."[40]

Interviews with stockmen in 1941 revealed only minor complaints. Some believed the administration of grazing permits was moving too slowly, and others suggested that those making the decisions were doing so to their own personal benefit and thereby denying equal participation by all.[41] In some cases, local and family ties did not aid aspiring permit holders. Arnold Alvey of Escalante recalled how his father had historically run livestock at Collet Top on the Kaiparowits Plateau. Alvey's uncle, Dee Haws, was on the board apportioning the grazing permits.

> He come to my dad and said, "now James, you don't need to go to that meeting. I'll see that you get that range out there. Don't worry about it." Well, he went to Kanab and got the range alright, but it was for himself, and [he] shoved us down into what we call Collets.[42]

The Utah District 4 Advisory Board, led by W. C. Gardner, held its first meeting in Zion National Park in September 1935, and it immediately passed fourteen resolutions. The very first expressed opposition to "the enlargement of Indian reservations, National Parks, and National Monuments in this district."[43] Others included a call for livestock numbers to be held steady at January 1, 1935, levels, a request that grazing disputes be heard by Utah officials and not the Division of Grazing (renamed the U.S. Grazing Service in 1939) in Washington, DC, and several petitions for a predator control program. One petition asked for a requirement that all agricultural properties be fenced.[44]

Three months later, the board passed a series of rules with the binding effect of law. One regulation mandated a 5-cent-per-head surcharge on cattle, 7 cents on horses, and 1 cent on sheep "to cover the cost" of administering the grazing district. Additional fees were imposed for trailing stock across public lands. Other rules regulated the amount of time sheep and goats could be bedded in any one location, required cattlemen to utilize only purebred bulls at a ratio of one bull per thirty heifers, and mandated that livestock have adequate salt. Another provision allowed ranchers to exceed the number of livestock authorized by their permits by 20 percent "to take care of the normal losses."[45]

One area where it was clear early government intervention favored local ranching interests was the long-standing predator control program subsidized from Washington, DC. The U.S. Forest Service and the U.S. Biological Survey, a predecessor of the U.S. Fish and Wildlife Service, paid bounties and federal employees to eradicate species deemed a threat to livestock.[46] In an interview recorded in 1964, Henrieville resident Sears Willis recalled his trapping work. "In 1919 I started working for the forest or government as a government trapper . . . I'd herded sheep before that, and trapped some around the sheep herds [for coyotes]." He was paid $95 dollars a month, including all supplies, a horse, food, and feed. A forest service newsletter provided incentives via contests.

> They give trappers that got 12 points or over . . . a coyote counted 1 point, a lion counted 10, a bear counted 10, and a wolf counted 10 points; well the ones that got 12 points or over their names would be in the news. They called it the "honor roll" . . . I started right off the bat. My name was right up at the lead.

Willis did this work for nineteen years, using poisons such as strychnine as well as snares. At the time it was common to shoot pronghorns, today a prized game species, as well as the lowly Utah prairie dog because they competed with stock for grass.[47] Willis recalled working on a campaign to kill one of the region's last wolves: "there was one down in House Rock Valley, called him Old Three Toe. Had this toe taken off his left front foot . . . and they're offering a $1,000 reward for anybody who could trap 'em." Willis did not get Old Three Toe. But overall, these efforts paid off for area ranchers, as all wolves were extirpated from the Kaibab and southern Utah by the 1940s.[48]

Environmental historians have identified ecological damage that resulted from the eradication of wolves and bears, particularly. With no predators to control populations, in some areas deer and elk populations exploded, resulting in overgrazing, gullying, and the inability of some tree species such as aspens to regenerate. This opened the door for invasive species like thistle and cheat grass that replaced desirable grass species like grama grass, bluestem, and Indian rice grass.[49]

Newspaper accounts from 1934 to 1938 generally lauded the reforms, and if any locals dissented it did not warrant much attention in either of the area newspapers, the *Kane County Standard* or the *Garfield County News*. Ranchers seem to have willingly embraced the idea of payment for permits to graze their livestock on the federal domain. Regulations were implemented slowly. The "first of its kind" Utah prosecution for improper grazing did not occur until 1938—nearly four years after passage of the Taylor Grazing Act—when Kane County rancher Sandall Findlay was fined $200 for grazing two hundred head of livestock without a permit.[50]

A New Deal

Accounts vary as to the effects of the Great Depression on farmers and ranchers in southern Utah and northern Arizona. Local rancher Lee Mace recalled that it really was pretty much life as usual, and since no one had much of anything anyway, the Depression meant only a little less of the little they

FIGURE 5.7. Rock house constructed in the 1920s west of Lee's Ferry. Photograph by Dan Bauer.

already had.[51] Yet others related stories of food shortages and losing their livestock to the banks when they could not make the payments. Edith McInelly Barker, born in Escalante in 1928, remembers her father and grandfather lost their entire herd of sheep when they could not pay the bank loan, a fate that befell dozens of area livestock men in the 1930s.[52] Throughout Utah, farmers and ranchers fell behind on their mortgages and taxes. In 1932, the Federal Land Bank, the state's largest holder of farm mortgages, reported that 43 percent of its state customers were behind on their loan payments. That year, rural Utah tax delinquency rates approached 40 percent. Thousands of farmers and ranchers faced the threat of losing their lands to bank and tax foreclosures.[53] Yet despite their Republican politics, which during the 1920s and 1930s tended to support free markets and laissez-faire economics, Kane and Garfield ranchers lined up to take advantage of several federal relief programs.

The unprecedented economic crisis led to a Democratic Party landslide in the elections of 1932, with generally conservative Utah following national trends. Church of Jesus Christ of Latter-day Saints' President Heber J. Grant had declared his support for Republican incumbent Herbert Hoover, but Utahns instead gave his opponent, Democrat Franklin Delano Roosevelt, 56.5 percent of their votes. They elected Democrat Henry H. Blood governor over his Republican opponent, and in the U.S. Congress, they turned out Republican incumbents Don B. Colton and Frederick C. Loofbourow in favor of Democrats J. Will Robinson and Abe Murdock.

In a shocking upset, voters turned against Latter-day Saint Apostle and U.S. Republican Senator Reed Smoot that year. First elected in 1903, Smoot was then the nation's longest-serving senator. In 1932, he was defeated by University of Utah political scientist Elbert D. Thomas. Smoot partly blamed his downfall on fellow Apostle Anthony Ivins, who as a vocal Democrat had promoted reform and change. The next year in state elections, Democrats captured almost 57 percent of the seats in the state senate and 86 percent of seats in the state house.[54]

For ranchers in Grand Staircase and Escalante River country, the Depression years presented a conundrum of sorts. They had plenty of sheep and cattle which reproduced every year, and in theory should have provided a steady income flow. But regional and national markets where they could sell their livestock were limited. Massive livestock surpluses occurred nationally, and the costs of shipping their animals to market were sometimes greater than any expected return. Claud Glazier remembered his father, who raised goats in Johnson Canyon, sold his entire year's bounty of mohair in Chicago for 18 cents per lb, "and the railroad took all that for freight. So he had a year's bills and a herd of goats that weren't worth anything."[55]

To survive, ranchers faced the very real prospect of having to increase herd sizes at the same time the ranges had been depleted. In addition, they had no money of their own to pay for feed, which would have prompted even greater reliance on grazing allotments. Jack Chenowyth, a cattle rancher in the Cannonville area, recalled the Depression "didn't affect us one bit. The only way it affected us is that Dad couldn't find a sale for his cows. So his calves each year just kept accumulating and getting bigger and bigger."[56]

Chenowyth's dilemma was not isolated. Overproduction was a national problem that eventually reached crisis proportions, and in June 1934, the U.S. Congress authorized the Drought Relief Service to purchase excess cattle in designated emergency areas where cattle were in danger of starvation. This and other New Deal relief programs often paid above-market prices for beef, a major short-term boon for local ranchers.[57] The entire state of Utah qualified as an emergency area. Under the government's purchasing schedule, ranchers received $12 for each cow over two years old that was unfit for food, each yearling in the same condition would bring $10, and calves useless for food were worth $4; these animals would be immediately slaughtered. Animals fit for human consumption brought $13 to $20 for two-year-olds and older, $11 to $15 for yearlings, and $5 to $8 for calves; these animals were then shipped to packing plants.[58] The program was also expanded to include sheep, to be purchased at $2 per head, and goats, to be purchased at $1.40 per head.[59] Willis C. Little and David Rider were put in charge of the appraisals in Kane County.

In the government planners' minds, the program served three purposes: reducing the number of animals on a depleted public range, lowering national livestock surpluses and thereby driving up prices to the benefit of producers, and providing canned meat for "emergency relief needs" across the nation. The rancher got rid of surplus animals he could not afford to feed anyway, and he had cash in hand—a rare commodity at that time. Banks benefitted because they were first in line to be paid if there were loans against the livestock.

How many surplus southern Utah cattle the government bought is unclear, but the program lasted from June 1934 to January 1935. One brief report indicated 1,700 head had been purchased in Garfield County by mid-August 1934, and additional purchases were to be made later that month.[60] Local newspapers reported that at least 386 cattle were purchased or condemned in Alton in early August 1934, but no mention was made of more sales other than a passing reference to the fact that Kanab cattlemen had not made any shipments under the program.[61] In December 1934, an additional allotment was made to remove 2,500 female goats from Kane County at $1.40 per head and 300 more from Garfield County.[62]

Chenowyth recalled his father sold all of his "big steers to the government for twenty dollars a head. And he had a lot of them you know, and woo! We were rich then." His father used the proceeds to buy a pickup truck, which he then used as a "taxi service" to haul Civilian Conservation Corpsmen from their Henrieville camp to town at a dollar a trip.[63]

The cattle-buying program was not without controversy. Ranchers complained the prices paid were too low, many questioned the wisdom of reducing food production when so many were going hungry, and some—mostly ardent opponents of anything to do with FDR's New Deal—thought the program was a veiled attempt by the federal government to take over the cattle industry. As one prominent Texas cattleman asserted at the time, the Roosevelt Administration promised "to come to our relief on condition that we surrender to the Secretary of Agriculture the right to manage our affairs."[64] Others, however, including the National Cattlemen's Association, praised the program.

When the federal purchases waned that fall, Utah livestock operators deluged the Secretary of Agriculture with letters to continue the livestock program, as the *Kane County Standard* reported, prompting a meeting in Ogden with Utah Governor Henry H. Blood, federal officials, and "sheep and cattle men from all over the state." Federal representatives made tentative promises that the government would buy as many as 80,000 more cattle and 100,000 sheep.[65] Whether these additional purchases were ever made is not known, but by January 1935 the program had ended.

The underlying premise of the federal cattle-buying program was revived four years later by a local Utah consortium that included the Utah Cattle and Horse Growers Association, the Utah Bankers Association, and the Utah State Agricultural College Extension, among others. That plan called for the culling of inferior stock across the state. These animals were to be replaced with animals with better bloodlines. One unnamed supporter stated at the time:

> Thousands of animals are allowed on the range each year and are carried through the winter months, which are not profitable meat producing animals and cannot make the necessary gains to create a profit for the owner. They do not dress out satisfactorily and the meat is of an inferior grade, but it sets the market price. Inferior cattle like all other inferior farm produce sets the farmer's price below the profit line and far below the cost of production.[66]

A second federal program also assisted southern Utah ranchers. It was implemented by the Agricultural Adjustment Administration (AAA), a New Deal agency under the Department of Agriculture that had been created through the passage of the Agricultural Adjustment Act of 1933 (revised in 1938). The AAA originally was charged with implementing Roosevelt Administration policies aimed at raising commodity prices paid to farmers and ranchers by reducing production. Farmers would receive subsidies for leaving their fields fallow, and ranchers would be paid for culling their herds (the AAA also had administered the cattle-buying program discussed above).[67]

By 1936, the agency had shifted its focus to implementing programs to promote soil conservation, enlisting the aid of the Utah State Agricultural College Extension and county administrative organizations. Kanab resident James A. Brown was the Kane County representative for the AAA. Under terms of the program, a range examiner would survey a grazing unit and make recommendations for contouring, water development, water impoundments, surface water diversions, range fences, sagebrush removal, building fire breaks, and reseeding projects. Ranchers would earn from 7 cents an acre up to a maximum of two dollars an acre for their voluntary participation in the program.[68]

William Peterson, director of the AAA program in Utah, assured ranchers, "the program is not one of limiting the number of livestock on the range, but one designed to bring the ranges back to their best economic carrying capacity and maintain them for future use."[69] By July 1937, Kane County ranchers had been paid $3,053 and Garfield County Ranchers $10,104 for their participation in the program.[70]

During the 1930s, the Rocky Mountain region, that included Utah, relied more heavily on federal relief programs than any other region in the country. In fact, by the end of the decade, Utah ranked third in the nation in percentage of its workforce employed by public agencies at 7.7 percent, trailing only Oklahoma (7.9 percent) and New Mexico (9.1 percent). Mormon Church leaders such as Apostle J. Reuben Clark warned members about becoming dependent on federal funds and programs that would "debauch us," and the First Presidency opposed Roosevelt's reelection in 1936. But the needed federal relief programs overcame Utahns' resistance to federal dependency during the decade.[71]

The New Deal offered other benefits to local livestock operators, and to a varying extent, southern Utah ranchers took advantage of the programs. In 1938, the Commodity Credit Corporation authorized government-backed loans to sheepmen in the area.[72] In 1937, $2,500 in rural rehabilitation funds were granted to area livestock owners in "urgent need of subsistence and without feed for their range sheep, milk cows, pigs, or chickens."[73] The Farm Security Administration provided long-term loans to help families purchase farms, and the Federal Surplus Commodities Corporation purchased and distributed surplus agricultural commodities to the local poor.[74]

At the national level, the most popular program of the era was the Civilian Conservation Corps (CCC), created in 1933 and comprised of otherwise unemployed young men from across the nation who were engaged by the federal government in public works projects. As mentioned previously, the program was headed by former Utah Governor George Dern, FDR's Secretary of War. Relevant to the livestock industry, their tasks involved a variety of water control, soil conservation, reseeding, and fencing projects.[75] Sometimes their efforts constituted simply lending a helping hand. In February 1937, Civilian Conservation Corp Company 4778 rushed heavy equipment to open snowbound roads and rescue 22,000 head of sheep and 3,000 head of cattle in the area, and as the *Kane County Standard* reported, "thus saving the people of this section thousands of dollars."[76]

At least five CCC camps were located in the Kane and Garfield County region and another ten in the St. George and Cedar City areas. Five other camps were on the Arizona Strip, working mostly on projects in the Kaibab National Forest and Grand Canyon National Park. At the state level, the CCC established 116 camps in rural areas. At least half of all CCC projects in the region were directly related to grazing improvements (see Table 5.1).

Although not part of its mission, the creation of CCC camps in southern Utah opened the region to outsiders, and initially their presence was not welcomed by conservative Utahns. In fact, while ultimately popular, the entire

Courtesy of US Forest Service. On loan to Sherratt Library, Southern Utah University.

FIGURE 5.8. Civilian Conservation Corps crews constructed the first road linking the tiny community of Boulder, Garfield County, to Escalante and the rest of Garfield County. The Hell's Backbone Bridge (Dixie National Forest) depicted here was an improbable feat and it remains a hair-raising adventure to motorists who travel it. Photograph courtesy of Barbara A. Matheson Special Collections (ph08b10i03206), Gerald R. Sherratt Library, Southern Utah University, Cedar City.

TABLE 5.1. CCC Camps in the Kane-Garfield Area and on the Arizona Strip.

CCC Camps Southern Utah-Northern Arizona				
Year	**Company**	**Project**	**General Location**	**Project Focus**
1933	1255	S-211	Widtsoe area	state forest
	1256	S-212	Alton area	state forest
	818	NP-1	Grand Canyon National Park	park improvements
	962	NP-3	Bryce Canyon National Park	park improvements
	1966	NP-2	Zion National Park	park improvements
	1339	F-18	Escalante area	U.S. Forest Service
1934	818	NP-1	Grand Canyon National Park	park improvements
	847	NP-4	Grand Canyon National Park	park improvements
	847	G-170	Fredonia area	U.S. Grazing Service
	961	F-27	Panguitch	U.S. Forest Service
1935	1980	F-44	Escalante area	U.S. Forest Service
	2557	DG-44	Fredonia area	public domain grazing
	2529	DG-33	Henrieville area	public domain grazing
1936	2833	NP-1	Grand Canyon National Park	park improvements
	3233	NM-1	Cedar Breaks	park improvements
	4429	F-44	Escalante area	U.S. Forest Service
1937	4778	F-44	Escalante area	U.S. Forest Service
	2833	NP-1	Grand Canyon National Park	park improvements
1939	4723	F-42	Escalante area	U.S. Forest Service
1940	1814	G-173	Fredonia area	U.S. Grazing Service
1941	2887	NP-4	Zion National Park	park improvements

Note: A comprehensive catalog is found in Hinton and Green (2008), Appendix A and Appendix D.

New Deal agenda was severely criticized by Mormon Church President Heber J. Grant. The prospect of thousands of once-unemployed young men descending on rural southern Utah alarmed many residents, especially because of its potential impact on community morals. Taylor C. Nuttall, one of only twenty-four Utahns employed among almost 200 New Yorkers at a CCC camp north of Bryce Canyon, reported that they were "an awfully scummy crew." A young Utah woman from rural Delta recalled that the CCC migrants were treated "like an epidemic of smallpox. Anyone who professed to be moral practically refused to walk on the same side of the street with any of the CCC boys. The Church preached against it, parents were alarmed, and stories were circulated to scare young girls." In time, many CCC workers reported that they found acceptance in rural Utah, and even a few married into local Latter-day Saint families.[77]

The CCC's work was instrumental in opening the Grand Staircase and Escalante River region to the outside world and, in the process, modernizing its economy. As the Great Depression began, Boulder was one of the most isolated towns in the United States. For part of the year, it still received its mail via mule teams from Escalante. The rugged canyons and terraces had long hindered transportation and the economic prospects of the area's farms and ranches. In 1933, CCC crews completed the Hell's Backbone Road from Escalante to Boulder, but it was closed in winter.

In 1935, work began on the Lower Boulder Road, which is incorporated in parts by Utah State Route 12 today. Nicknamed the "Million Dollar Road," the CCC boys used dynamite and backbreaking labor to carve the Lower Boulder Road from seeming bare rock. They blasted sandstone ledges down the Escalante River and up Calf Creek Canyon until they reached Boulder. On June 21, 1940 local residents held a celebration to commemorate the completion of the first all-season auto road into Boulder. The highway made transporting supplies and livestock much easier. It also opened this part of the Escalante River canyons to outside visitors. The modern highway helped lead to the "rediscovery" of the spectacular Lower Calf Creek Falls, a 126-foot waterfall on a tributary of the Escalante River. Named for the canyon that was used as a natural holding pen for cattle, the falls area was developed by the BLM as a recreation area, its popular trail and campground a highlight for many visitors to the area.[78]

The "make work" programs of various New Deal agencies were instrumental in creating the tourist infrastructure on public lands in the Grand Staircase and Escalante region and elsewhere in the American West. The CCC, Works Progress Administration (WPA), and Public Works Administration (PWA) workers made the trails, campgrounds, and park and forest service structures that enabled the "Western experience" for millions of Americans in the post-World War II era. The WPA completed the Bryce Canyon Airport in 1938, a rustic log structure still in use today. The PWA, along with the WPA, constructed the administration building at Bryce Canyon National Park. These entities also built employee cabins, a fee station, restrooms, and a ranger dorm. Utilizing the "rustic style" with its heavy-timber and intricate rock work construction techniques seen at other parks, the CCC boys built numerous other structures at Bryce Canyon, as well as planting trees, constructing erosion control dams, and doing work to control pine beetle infestations. They built the Rainbow Point overlook, the Fairyland Loop Trail, and the Under-the-Rim Trail still in use today.[79]

Also important during this period was the Utah State College Agricultural Extension offices (now Utah State University), which ushered in a new era of range management using emerging and, for that day and age, revolutionary scientific techniques. Experimental farms, ranches, and rangelands were acquired across the state, enhanced breeding practices were developed, soil conservation measures became standard practice, and livestock associations took a more active role in encouraging proper use of the ranges. These initiatives were funded in large part by New Deal dollars, and Extension officials functioned as the *de facto* representatives of the federal agencies.[80]

Overall, the federal government in the mid-1930s emerged as an important source of cash, jobs, and infrastructure development throughout rural Utah. Even if federal regulations stoked local resentment, as historian Martha Bradley observed, "like many in the state and nation who proclaimed the merits of self-sufficiency and limited government, when government programs were made available, county residents did not want to be left out."[81] Or as the esteemed Western historian and philosopher Bernard DeVoto summarized this attitude, "get out and give us more money."[82]

Although the predominantly Republican Utah ranchers appear to have been generally supportive of the New Deal programs, their tendencies continued to lean toward traditional Republican philosophies advocating unfettered free enterprise while opposing federal regulations of any type. As summarized by C. Roger Lambert in his history of the cattle-buying program:

> During the crises they were willing to go along with anything which offered immediate money and hope for the immediate future. But they viewed with extreme suspicion any long-range planning or guidance of their industry. Their traditional independent or uncooperative attitude was too strong, their inability to look beyond the present too great, and their fears of outside forces too engrained for cattlemen to join willingly in regulating their industry.[83]

Clearly southern Utahns embraced New Deal assistance with differing levels of enthusiasm. In 1934, Kane County received less federal relief than any county in the state with only 6.13 percent of the population receiving aid.[84] By comparison, their neighbors in Garfield County had the second highest per capita relief expenditures in the entire state.[85] A University of Utah study in 1938 examined the reasons behind that, and the researchers found Garfield County to be poorly suited to agriculture and unable to withstand long

FIGURE 5.9. Highways into the Grand Staircase and Escalante River regions were dirt or gravel-compacted roads vulnerable to the vagaries of adverse weather conditions. Winter snowstorms could leave the entire region inaccessible for weeks on end. Photograph by Charles Ford, courtesy of Ford Collection (Ph18B02F47i76), Barbara A. Matheson Special Collections, Gerald R. Sherratt Library, Southern Utah University, Cedar City.

FIGURE 5.10. Southern Utah businesses capitalized on tourism the best they could, but the three- or four-month seasonal nature of tourism made investment risky. Motels sprang up in Panguitch and Kanab, but they sat empty most of the year. Photograph by Charles Ford, courtesy of Ford Collection (ph18B02F46i27), Barbara A. Matheson Special Collections, Gerald R. Sherratt Library, Southern Utah University, Cedar City.

economic depressions due to "increasing competitive individualism, decreasing cooperation, unintelligent land use, very limited natural resources, and an excessively high rate of natural increase."[86]

At that time, tourism had not yet emerged as a major economic force in the region due in large part to poor roads and infrastructure, problems ameliorated somewhat by the CCC and other federal programs. Utah writer Wallace Stegner noted that the Mormon Country never caught the public's attention at the national level as a tourist draw as had other areas with a cowboy "frontier" heritage. Few people were willing to use their hard-earned cash to visit Mormon historical sites or the state's quaint agricultural villages. Locals would need to play upon their frontier ranching heritage to lure tourists to Grand Staircase and Escalante country.[87] During the Great Depression, New Deal federal relief programs built some of the infrastructure that helped maintain the public profiles of ranching and cowboy traditions in the area. Young men employed by the WPA constructed a new racetrack and fairgrounds in Kanab. In 1937 the town began holding its annual three-day rodeo at the site. Local youths in the Future Farmers of America displayed their animals at the fair each August for generations. The 4-H club also took part. Cowboy dinners with a barbeque, horse racing, and rodeo sports engaged local residents for decades.[88]

A Woolly Collapse

The meteoric rise and spectacular collapse of the sheep industry in Utah, as well as the United States generally, is a classic case study in the effects of changing consumer preferences and the failure of an industry to respond to those

TABLE 5.2. Cattle and Sheep Populations in the Kane-Garfield and Arizona Strip Areas, 1930–1950.

Cattle and Sheep Populations by Region 1930–1950										
Census Year	1930		1935		1940		1945		1950	
	Cattle	Sheep	Cattle	Sheep	Cattle	Sheep	Cattle	Sheep	Cattle	Sheep
Kane and Garfield Counties	20,866	192,808	25,276	180,917	19,463	109,779	24,342	83,667	23,718	40,733
Arizona Strip	42,385	383,955	86,441	188,546	67,596	187,174	72,649	97,728	74,014	95,567

Note: All data are from USDA Census of Agriculture Historical Archive.

changes. From 1890–1935, sheep raising dominated the Utah livestock industry.[89] Roughly 181,000 sheep grazed in Kane and Garfield Counties in 1935 alone, producing nearly 1.6 million lb of wool. By comparison, only 25,276 head of cattle grazed on those same ranges at that time, or roughly one cow for every seven sheep. By 1950, the ratio had dropped to one cow to less than two sheep, even though the number of cattle was slightly less than it was in 1935 (see Table 5.2).[90]

The dominance of the sheep industry prior to World War II certainly reflected national economic trends. Wool was a preferred fiber for clothing, blankets, rugs, and other woven items because it was abundant and relatively inexpensive. And sheep served a dual function at that time as an important meat source. The United States was an undisputed world leader in sheep production, and Utah was among the nation's leading sheep producers.

The heights reached by sheep-related businesses made the collapse of the industry more remarkable. The industry today is only about a tenth of what it was during World War II, and wool now constitutes less than 1 percent of all fibers used at U.S. textile mills. American consumption of lamb has dropped to less than 1 lb per person per year. Even as late as the 1960s, American consumption of lamb had averaged nearly 5 lb per person per year.[91] As discussed below, several factors contributed to this collapse.

Based on statewide numbers, the earliest years of the Great Depression (1929–34) appeared to have had minimal impact on sheep growers throughout Utah. In 1929, the total statewide sheep population stood at 2.5 million, and by 1935 the number had dropped by only about 6,000 sheep (see Table 5.3). But those overall numbers do not reflect the spatial variability in the industry during that time. In some areas of southern Utah, the overall sheep population actually increased dramatically during that same period, while in other areas it declined. In Kane County, the population increased from 54,808 in 1929

TABLE 5.3. Sheep Populations in Selected Regions from 1930 to 1959.

Sheep Populations by Region							
Census Year	**1930**	**1935**	**1940**	**1945**	**1950**	**1954**	**1959**
Garfield County	130,946	100,571	57,891	50,235	22,564	27,572	20,682
Kane County	55,321	80,346	51,888	24,432	18,169	20,425	23,291
Eastern Arizona Strip	350,955	145,161	174,966	92,775	96,501	109,966	75,150
Western Arizona Strip	33,000	43,385	12,208	4,953	66	188	340
Utah Statewide	2,458,652	2,452,196	1,597,346	1,672,392	1,101,324	1,396,981	1,290,950

Note: All data are from USDA Census of Agriculture Historical Archive.

to 80,346 in 1935—a 47 percent increase. In Garfield County, the numbers declined from 136,215 in 1929 to 100,571 in 1935—a 26 percent decline.[92]

A similar pattern was observed on the Arizona Strip. On the western half, in Mohave County, sheep populations increased from 33,000 in 1929 to 43,385 by 1935—a 31 percent increase. But on the eastern Arizona Strip, in Coconino County, the numbers declined from 350,955 in 1929 to 145,161—a 59 percent decline.[93]

The reasons behind these spatial shifts are not clearly evident in the historical record. Possibly the rangelands in the eastern Arizona Strip and in Garfield County had deteriorated during persistent droughts of the early 1930s, and some sheepmen simply moved their flocks to better rangelands in Mohave and Kane counties. Oral histories indicate that some sheepmen also switched to raising cattle at that time. The reduced sheep numbers also might reflect more aggressive management of Kaibab National Forest lands where forest rangers mandated flock-size reductions in response to the persistent droughts and deteriorating range. Another factor was likely the extreme volatility in wool prices, as discussed below.

If the four counties of Kane and Garfield in Utah and Coconino and Mohave in Arizona are considered collectively, the overall sheep population declined by 36 percent during the six years from 1929 to 1935, most of that coming in the eastern Arizona Strip, long considered by Utah sheepmen and cattlemen as the best open range in the region. This decline foreshadowed the complete collapse of the sheep industry in southern Utah and northern Arizona in the decades to follow (see Figure 5.11). And it also coincided with a resurgence in beef cattle in the four-county region, from 63,251 head in 1930 to 111,717 head in 1935—a 77 percent increase during this same time period.[94]

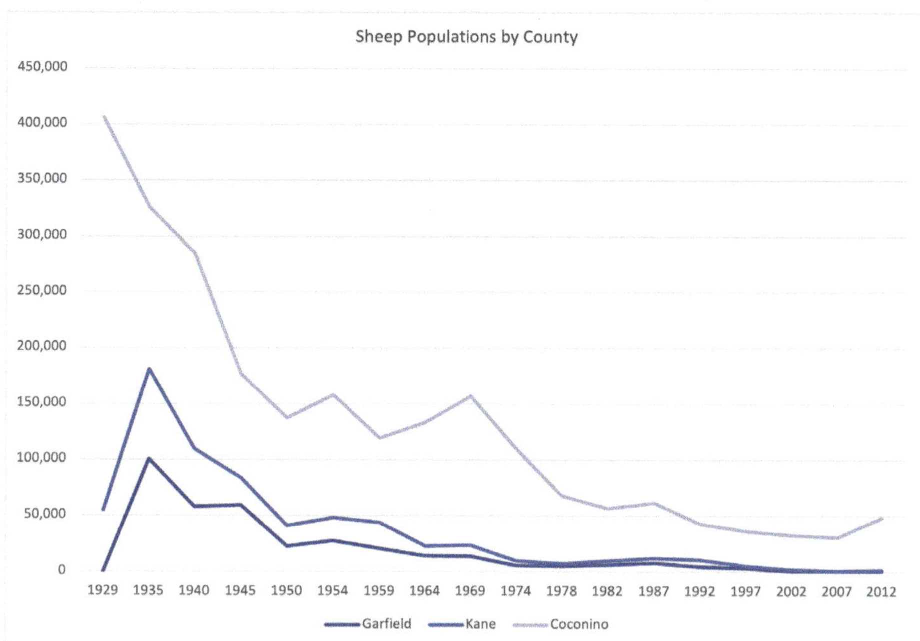

FIGURE 5.11. Chart depicting the collapse of the sheep industry since 1930. All data from USDA Census of Agriculture Historical Archive.

Nationally the sheep industry continued to expand throughout the Great Depression, reaching an all-time high by the end of World War II in 1945. But that upward trend was not evident in Utah where the numbers of sheep fell from a high of 2.5 million in 1929 to 1.6 million in 1940, a 36 percent decline. The numbers rose only slightly during World War II to 1.7 million, still well below the numbers reported at the beginning of the Great Depression.[95] Similar declines were evident in Kane and Garfield Counties during World War II (see Table 5.3 above), as well as on the Arizona Strip.

Despite the overall decline in sheep numbers, sheep raising remained the dominant livestock enterprise in the Grand Staircase and Escalante region and Arizona Strip throughout the Great Depression. A canny sheepman could make good money if he could weather the ups and downs of commodity prices. In 1931, ranchers were paid, on average, 12.9 cents per lb for wool, but a year later the price had dropped 29 percent to 9.2 cents a lb[96]—an all-time low. By 1933, the price had risen to 24.2 cents per lb—a 163 percent increase in a single year.

Clare Ramsay recalls his early life in a family who worked with sheep. Born in 1932 and raised in Glendale, like many others he remembers that "almost everyone was poor, but there were two or three outfits in town, families that had sheep and those that had the herds of sheep, all the other men (including his dad) herded sheep for them." The large flocks usually had between 1,000 and 1,500 head and were free ranged over the country, using horses and dogs to corral them. The fact that his father never had his own herds created hardships for the Ramsay family because he was often away for months herding for the big operators around Glendale. "It was a different lifestyle, so I mostly grew up without a father. He wasn't there very much and then he died when I was about twelve (from lung cancer due to smoking)."[97]

Clare describes the largely itinerant life of men like his father:

> At that time, they pulled the sheep wagons with horses, so whenever they moved camp, they'd hook on to the sheep wagon with a team of horses and move. It had one bed in there and then cabinets and benches where they'd store the food, and one little stove in the corner that would really get toasty warm in a hurry. They made sourdough biscuits and cooked mutton.

Clare's mother Bertha always made sure to keep a few sheep at their house, shearing them and using the wool to make her own quilts. Years later when he was interviewed in 2004, Clare still missed the sheep-raising life and still loved the smell of mutton. "Once a sheep herder, always a sheep herder," he said. "Even those people that had the big herds, and sold them out and went into cows or got clear out of it, they always kept a handful of sheep out in the back somewhere. They just never got over having sheep."[98]

The volatility of wool prices was a problem for sheepmen throughout the United States. It emerged as a political issue when the U.S. Congress implemented tariffs on foreign wool to artificially prop up domestic prices with the Agricultural Adjustment Act of 1933. This effort, strongly supported by Utah sheepmen, was intended to raise the cost of foreign wool imports (Argentinian wool was seen as a specific threat), thereby bringing "parity" to the prices of foreign and domestic wool.[99] The tariff was eventually deemed a failure because the policy, as M. Polasek concludes, "benefited U.S. growers at the expense of consumers of woolen products" and "it could neither stabilize farm prices of wool from one period to another, nor be relied upon to bring wool into a desired price parity relationship during any particular marketing period."[100]

The tariff approach proved entirely ineffective as the Utah and national sheep industry continued its remarkable death spiral after 1940. In Garfield

County, the number of sheep on the ranges fell to 59,235 by 1940, and to 22,564 by 1950. The numbers stabilized for a decade before resuming a precipitous decline. In 2012, the county had only 474 sheep.[101] Similar declines were observed in Kane County. By 1940, the numbers had fallen 35 percent from six years before to 51,888, and by 1950 they had declined to 18,169. The numbers stabilized in Kane County for a decade before plummeting to a low of 451 sheep in 2007. Similar declines were evident on the Arizona Strip.

As will be discussed in Chapter 6, the U.S. Congress again intervened in the 1950s, declaring wool to be a strategic material important to national security (half of the wool needed for military uniforms during World War II and the Korean conflict had to be imported).[102] The ten-year stabilization in sheep numbers (but not market prices) between 1950 and 1960 might have been partly the result of the the National Wool Act of 1954, which provided permanent price supports for wool and mohair. These measures were intended to boost domestic production through incentive payments to sheep raisers. This subsidy, which amounted to 62 cents per lb of wool between 1954 and 1960, encouraged producers to add more and more sheep to the range.[103] Census statistics indicate sheep numbers increased somewhat in 1954 in Garfield, Kane, and Coconino counties (sheep raising in Mohave County had dwindled to insignificance with fewer than five hundred sheep in any census after 1950).

By 1964 the wool industry in southern Utah had again resumed a steady decline towards irrelevancy. By 2012, only 1,543 sheep remained in Garfield and Kane counties combined—a 99 percent decline from the number of sheep in 1930. The Arizona Strip had slightly higher numbers with a 2012 sheep population of 47,104, but that total was still a far cry from the nearly 400,000 sheep that grazed there in the early 1930s. The reasons behind the collapse have intrigued economists for decades, and the debate has produced no real consensus. One study by the National Research Council maintains that numerous interrelated factors might have contributed to the collapse. One theory suggests that World War II depleted the labor force to a point where not enough shepherds were available to maintain large flocks. After the war, veterans might have been unwilling to return to menial farm labor after they had seen the world. Some scholars note that U.S. soldiers had been fed a steady diet of canned mutton during World War II, and they came to despise its taste. Their refusal to eat mutton or lamb upon their return contributed to a negative public attitude toward sheep consumption.[104] This, in turn, led American consumers to switch to beef.

Grazing regulations on public lands clearly were targeted to a greater degree at limiting the numbers of sheep, which were seen as more destructive to the open range than were cattle. Other factors in the decline included the repeal of wool tariffs and incentive payment programs that led to cheaper foreign imports. Added to this fact, there was a persistent problem with predators such as coyotes and wolves. Predators contributed to annual flock losses of 20 percent or more. Finally, the concentration of U.S. packing and feeding operations had increased economic efficiencies for large sheep producers, but this practice impacted the ability to compete for small family operations like those in Grand Staircase and Escalante River country that were especially reliant on public ranges.[105]

It is not debated that the rapid decline in wool production also coincided with the proliferation of cheaper, synthetic fibers such as rayon (1920s), nylon (1939), acrylic (mid-1940s), and polyester (1940s and 1950s). Some of these fibers were invented during World War II as part of national defense production. Not only were synthetic fibers cheaper to produce than wool, the fabrics were more comfortable, more convenient (e.g., wrinkle-free, easier to clean), and they often imitated luxury fabrics (e.g., silk) at a fraction of the price. Beyond clothing, everything from carpets to drapes to auto upholstery used less and less wool in favor of synthetic fibers and plastics.[106]

As such, domestic wool production also was a casualty of the shifting American preferences to synthetic fibers. And it continued its decline from the 1950s onward. According to a National Research Council study, wool accounted for only 0.6 percent of all fibers used in U.S. mills from 1995 to 2005.[107] The wool industry in southern Utah and the Arizona Strip thus seems unlikely ever to recover. It seems improbable that American consumers will radically alter their fashion preferences to again embrace wool as superior to synthetics. Instead, a new generation of synthetic fibers (e.g., lightweight, self-wicking, water-resistant, fire-resistant materials) will probably lessen demand for woolen fabrics even more.

A second, related factor that reduced demand for U.S. wool was the increased globalization of the textile industry. The sheep industry had spent decades lobbying for tariffs on cheaper imports and later for price supports to make domestic wool production more competitive. This effort inevitably led to higher domestic prices for wool products. Manufacturers responded by building textile mills in countries where raw material costs and labor costs were substantially less. Foreign manufacturing (and later outsourcing by American manufacturers) made U.S.-produced wool noncompetitive.

The collapse of the sheep industry in the Grand Staircase and Escalante River region was not an isolated phenomenon. On the world stage, the United States is now a minor producer of sheep products. In 2016, there were only 5.3 million sheep in the United States. By comparison, in 2013 China had 185 million sheep, and both Australia and India each had more than 75 million.[108] Most U.S. wool is now exported to China and India, countries that have vibrant textile industries and growing demand. Australia and New Zealand have seen steady growth in their sheep industries due to niche marketing of lamb meat.

Thus, there is little optimism that U.S. sheep production will ever grow again beyond its current role as a minor industry, in particular as a food staple among growing ethnic populations in major urban centers. Utah is currently the nation's fifth largest sheep-raising state with 305,000 head reported in 2012. But Kane and Garfield counties combined account for less than 1 percent of the state total.

Conflict and Resolution

While the mid-1930s was marked by radical reforms in grazing policies, evidence of outright hostility among different user groups in southern Utah appears to have been relatively muted. In contrast, ranchers in some parts of the country were vocally opposed to federal grazing reforms, viewing the changes as an overt attempt by federal officials to wrest control of private livestock operations.[109]

As discussed earlier, there was also an undercurrent of opposition to the designation of national monuments and their later designations as national parks, as well as opposition to the establishment of game preserves and the Kaibab Paiute Indian Reservation. The Utah District 4 grazing advisory board reflected this attitude by passing a resolution in 1935 opposing "the enlargement of Indian reservations, National Parks, and National Monuments in this district."[110] But when President Roosevelt used the Antiquities Act to designate Capitol Reef National Monument (now National Park) on August 2, 1937, on lands just to the north of Garfield County, southern Utah livestock men did not protest. Instead, 2,250 Utah residents, most of them southern Utah representatives, attended a dedication celebration featuring barbecues, musical numbers, prayers, and speeches that lasted much of the day; the Utah governor gave the dedicatory address.[111]

Support for the Capitol Reef designation flowed, in part, from a growing appreciation of the economic benefits of tourism in southern Utah, especially in Kane County, which is centrally located on Highway 89 between the North Rim of the Grand Canyon on the south and Bryce Canyon and Zion National Parks on the north. Tourists pumped badly needed cash into the local economy with minimal burden on local taxpayers. Tourism really expanded with the completion of the scenic Zion–Mount Carmel Tunnel connecting Kane County with Zion National Park in 1930. In the late 1950s, U.S. Highway 89A, a new alternative route to U.S. Highway 89 through Kanab, added an additional boost.[112] Along with several prominent community leaders during the 1920s and 1930s, the local newspaper championed tourism as the region's economic future. By the late 1920s, the railroads had followed through on their earlier promises to build posh lodges at Grand Canyon, Zion, and Bryce Canyon National Parks, which became premier tourist destinations.[113]

Much like modern-day developments, some proposals for land preservation and tourism originated far from southern Utah and northern Arizona. A year before the creation of Capitol Reef National Monument, members of the U.S. Congress proposed establishing "Escalante National Monument," a huge reserve that would have included the canyons of the Escalante River as well as most of southeastern Utah. As envisioned by hard-driving Secretary of the Interior Harold Ickes, it would encompass 6,968 mi^2, double the size of Yellowstone and approximately 8 percent of the land area of Utah. Planners in Washington, DC, worked in secret and did not seek public opinion. The proposed massive national monument caused alarm in Utah. A low-level park service official, David Madsen, was charged with meeting a group of eighty-seven concerned citizens in Price to explain the proposal, at one point admitting officials felt the highest economic use of public lands in the region was recreation, not ranching.[114]

Charles Redd was present at the meeting. A well-respected stockman who owned the Redd Ranches, one of the largest cattle and sheep operations in the American West from his base in southeastern Utah, summarized the feelings of many, saying we "have for a long time, recognized the value and importance, the unusualness of the scenery we have here," however, "the exploitation of these natural wonders is not inconsistent with the full and free use of the range by livestock."[115] Soon thereafter the U.S. entered World War II, and the proposed legislation never came to pass.[116]

Hollywood also had openly embraced Kane County and its scenery as backdrops to more than one hundred films, many of which employed local cowboys as wranglers, stuntmen, and extras. Historian Martha Bradley related one account of a movie being filmed that called for an attack on a wagon train with three hundred bareback riders on horseback. Thirty of the riders were to be paid an extra dollar for falling from their horses. But at the crack of the first volley, all three hundred riders fell from their horses. It seemed every local man wanted to claim that bonus.[117] From the 1920s through the 1940s, westerns, including *The Deadwood Coach* (1924) and *Western Union* (1941), were filmed on location in Kane County. Cecil B. DeMille made *Union Pacific* (1939) in the Kanab area. John Wayne came to Kane County to star in *In Old Oklahoma* (1943).[118]

Instead of opposition to federal grazing policies, ranchers in the Grand Staircase and Escalante River country appear to have focused their efforts more towards limiting grazing competition on their own allotments. That meant eliminating some "competition" from wildlife, semidomesticated bison and burros, and the substantial wild horse herd that grazed on the Arizona Strip. Removing the wild horse problem resulted in a strange Old West-New West

FIGURE 5.12. This Kanab hotel was operated by the Rust family, who were early promoters of tourism in Kane County and the Arizona Strip. Dave Rust served a time as mayor of Kanab, as well as a noted guide to tourists, scientists, and famous dignitaries. Photograph courtesy of Homer Jones Collection (ph9b3f1i2), Barbara A. Matheson Special Collections, Gerald R. Sherratt Library, Southern Utah University, Cedar City.

scenario in 1937 when fifty cowboys on horseback were joined by two airplanes. The spectacle attracted hundreds of spectators and a film crew to document the roundup of a thousand head of wild horses near Cane Spring. Upon hearing the airplane engines, however, the stallions scattered their bands "right and left and even the experienced cowboys could only gather a few." As one report noted, "grazing officials" at the scene "are now inclined to think that the only way to get the mustangs off the range is to shoot them."[119]

FIGURE 5.13. Actors Deanna Durbin (center right) and Robert Paige (right) review a new scene in the 1944 musical *Can't Help Singing*, filmed near Kanab. Photograph courtesy of Movies Made in Utah Collection (Folder 3, No. 6, 39222005035519), Utah State Historical Society.

A large herd of wild burros in the Dry Valley area was also eliminated this way. Recalling stories his father had related, Deloy Dutton said sheepmen would catch the burros and break them to be pack animals to move their sheep camps. In the winter, the burros were released to return to their wild ways. "When they put the Taylor Grazing Act in effect and made the grazing permits . . . the BLM went out there and shot them all."[120]

The attempts to reduce the House Rock Valley bison herd also involved killing animals. Charley Lewis and William Crosby were put in charge of identifying which of the 173 bison would be culled. They then herded them from their winter range at the south end of House Rock Valley towards a group of twelve hunters at Kane Springs who had drawn permits from the Arizona game warden. With one exception, the hunters were exclusively Arizona residents.[121]

A recurring conflict in the mid-1930s involved livestock operators who were at odds with game management advocates and hunters over acceptable sizes of the deer and elk populations. The Taylor Grazing Act of 1934 had ensured that wildlife interests would have a say on the grazing advisory boards, but

Utah ranchers on those boards dragged their feet on that provision, and at least two years passed before wildlife advocates got a seat at the table.[122] Livestock operators wanted to be compensated for the damages to their fields caused by wildlife. They also demanded an end to the practice of private landowners creating wildlife sanctuaries where the number of animals could not be controlled through the annual deer hunts. Finally, they wanted assurances that if they reduced the number of livestock to protect the range that those reductions would not be offset by increases in deer and elk.[123]

Ranchers seemingly had a real problem on that latter point, enough so that the acrimony between them and game proponents prompted Utah Governor Henry H. Blood to call a meeting of the two sides in spring 1935 to resolve their differences. At that time, statewide deer populations were at 80,000, compared to only 11,000 deer in 1920. And the elk herd had grown from 684 to 3,700. During that same time, the number of sheep on the ranges had fallen from 756,000 to 642,000, and the number of cattle from 169,000 to 115,000.[124] Wildlife interests acquiesced to the demands of the livestock men, and in return they got a seat on the grazing board.

Beefing Up

The Japanese attack on Pearl Harbor in December 1941 was a galvanizing event that unified southern Utah in common cause with the rest of the nation. Most young men joined the armed forces, as did many young women, and some communities saw 10 to 20 percent of their overall populations deploy to the Pacific or Europe. Additionally, many young women migrated to urban areas to work in defense industries and other tasks to support the war effort. For the first time in the Euro-American history of the region, a substantial portion of the adult population experienced life outside the narrow social constructs of a traditional small village.

Helma Richards Haas and her friend Rella Ott Alvey left Tropic in 1942, catching a ride with a fruit peddler to St. George and then a bus to Southern California. Helma worked for the Red Cross, married that same year, and raised her family in California. "I did anything I could for the war effort," she recalled. Rella was employed at Lockheed, working in an aircraft manufacturing plant; she returned to Tropic after the war. Other friends left to work in a parachute manufacturing plant in Manti. "I made so many dear friends down there," Rella said. "They were from all over Utah and everywhere."[125]

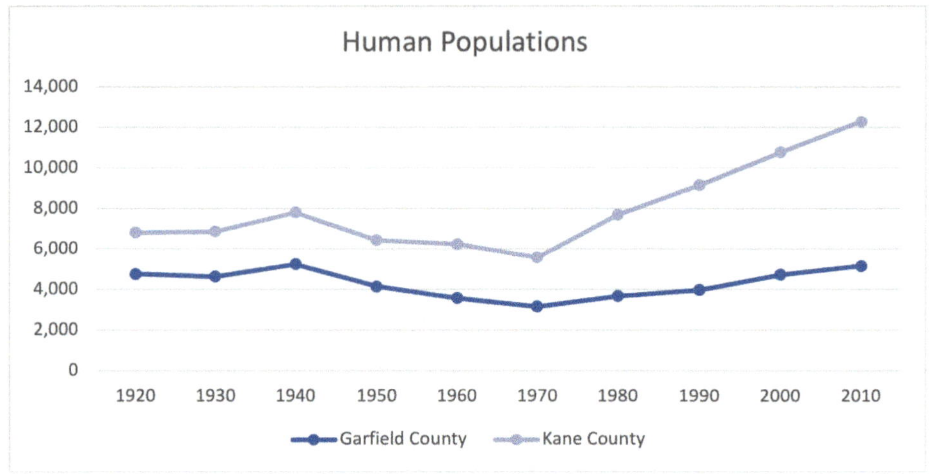

FIGURE 5.14. Population trends in Garfield County and Kane County. Data derived from US Census 1920–2010.

United States Census records suggest that many of these young people decided not to return to an agricultural way of life, believing that their economic prospects were brighter elsewhere. In the year before the war, Garfield County population stood at 5,253, an all-time high. Five years after the end of the war, the count was 4,151 people—a 21 percent decline.[126] The population decrease in Kane County was not as precipitous—10 percent during that same period—but it dropped nonetheless, and the county would not experience substantial growth again until 1980 (see Figure 5.14).

In terms of the ranching history of the region, the World War II years were characterized by increased national demand for livestock products—meat, leather, wool—and also by a decreased rural workforce that was unable to respond to that demand. According to historians Linda King Newell and Vivian Linford Talbot, some farmers responded to the labor shortage by trucking in crews of Navajos. All children not old enough to enlist in the armed forces worked the fields and likely tended herds and flocks.[127] As discussed earlier, raising sheep was more labor-intensive, requiring constant effort. But without young men to watch flocks, some Utah sheepmen at the time shifted to less-labor-intensive cattle ranching.[128]

Area sheepmen had been through this conundrum before. During World War I, demand for mutton and wool was high and prices were good, but the labor shortage made it nearly impossible to find anyone to tend the flocks. Interviewed in 1941 as part of the Utah Writers Project, W. J. Thornley recalled:

> During the war we had trouble getting sheepherders and had to pay as high as $125 a month for bums and scum that hadn't been called to the army. It was almost impossible to get a good sheepherder; there were a few foreigners, Basques and Mexicans, but not enough to go around.[129]

Those monthly wages were the equivalent of about $2,000 a month in 2017 dollars.[130] In coming decades, well into the Cold War, federal guest worker programs were instigated to bring foreign sheep herders (mostly Basques but also Mexicans) to America. As evident from Thornley's comments, Basques were seen as the cream of the crop as far as sheepherders were concerned.[131]

The shift from raising sheep to raising cattle also is evident in the U.S. Agricultural Census records at the time. In Kane and Garfield counties, there were 19,463 cows in 1940, the year before the U.S. entered the war. By the end of the war in 1945, the count was 24,342—a 25 percent increase. Those numbers would remain stable through 1950 and then jumped by 40 percent to 33,269 in 1954—the highest cattle population ever recorded in the area. An identical trend was observed on the Arizona Strip. In 1940, the cow population stood at 67,596. By the end of the war, it had grown to 72,649—a 7.5 percent increase. The numbers remained stable through 1950, and then increased by 30 percent to 96,527 in 1954—also an all-time high (see Figure 5.15).

When cattle numbers are considered in aggregate with the declining numbers of sheep on the range, the gross numbers would seem to suggest a proportionate decline in the use of public ranges, but this was not the case. As discussed earlier, the amount of forage consumed by a cow is about five times that of a sheep. An increase in cattle of 40,000 head between 1940 and 1954, as occurred in Kane and Garfield Counties and the Arizona Strip, would be equivalent to the forage needs of 200,000 head of sheep. But sheep populations decreased by only 139,000 head during that same time. As such, actual forage being consumed on public ranges *increased* even though overall livestock numbers *decreased*. This trend is a direct reflection of producers' preference for raising cattle.

The shift from sheep to cattle in Grand Staircase and Escalante River country can be traced to the winter of 1936–1937—an unusually wet winter that blanketed the mountains and canyons in the heaviest snowfall since 1902.[132] The snowstorms made travel impossible and stranded tens of thousands of sheep

FIGURE 5.15. Cattle populations in southern Utah and northern Arizona; data from USDA Census of Agriculture Historical Archive, 1930–1959.

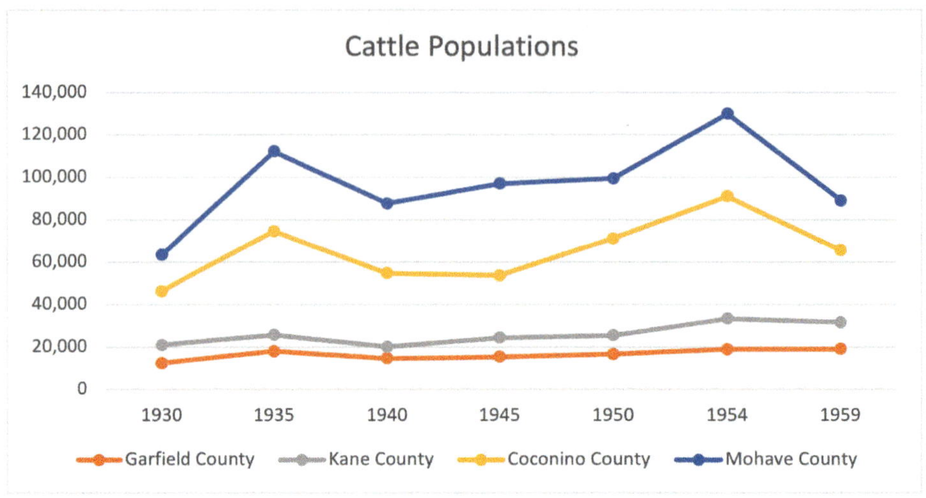

and cows. Trevor Leach recalled that, as a mere sixteen-year-old, he rode to the Paria Plateau to relieve the wranglers and allow them to spend Christmas with their families. While tending the family herd of 4,300 head, it started to snow on December 27, 1936, and "I never saw a person until the second day of February."[133] Many ranchers in Kane and Garfield Counties suffered losses that reached 50 percent for sheep and goats and only slightly less for cattle.[134] The economic losses across the region were devastating, yet another blow to the family rancher.

But the heavy snows also had saturated the rangelands, and by March 1937, the region was brimming in optimism. As tough as the massive losses were to individual ranchers, those losses also reduced supply, which led to higher prices. A new feedlot had opened in Cedar City, reducing transportation costs. The range forage was making a remarkable comeback. Precipitation during the first three months of 1937 was 132 percent of normal. In fact, the range was in better condition in 1937 than any time in the previous ten years.[135] The quality of grazing land had greatly improved for what herds remained, setting up what should have been ideal conditions for an industry expansion.

Only the expansion never happened. The sheep industry would continue its downward spiral, and cattle populations remained more or less at 1935 levels. In effect, the extended Southwest droughts had established the *de facto* maximum carrying capacity of the public ranges, and cattle populations would remain relatively consistent in most years that followed.

In 1935, nearly 112,000 cattle grazed on the ranges in Kane and Garfield Counties and on the Arizona Strip. By 1940, the year before America entered World War II, the number had dipped to 87,000 head, only to rebound to almost 97,000 head by the end of the war, a level that, with one notable exception in 1954, remained stable until 1997. This trend mirrored the cattle industry across the state of Utah.

As World War II came to an end and the U.S. entered the Cold War, cattle ranching was once again king in Grand Staircase, Escalante River, and Arizona Strip country. Yet, the possibility loomed as to whether the southern Utah cattle industry would suffer a fate similar to that of the sheep industry—a complete collapse into irrelevancy. As we discuss in greater detail in Chapter 7, traditional cattle ranching is now experiencing the same economic pressures that destroyed the sheep industry: changing consumer demands away from red meat towards healthier poultry and fish, declining demand for real leather products, the proliferation of cheaper synthetic materials with leather-like characteristics, and increased global competition from foreign cattle producers, especially those in South America.

The Great Depression ushered in a period of great economic and social hardship for residents of southern Utah and the Arizona Strip. Rural families enmeshed in the farming and ranching economy were able to grow or barter for their food, enabling them to survive. While locals generally were opposed to government intervention and welfare programs, President Roosevelt's New Deal programs proved popular in Grand Staircase and Escalante River country. Its relief checks and work programs enabled rural citizens to persevere through the hard times. While flawed, the landmark Taylor Grazing Act of 1934 finally put public grazing lands under meaningful scientific management. Area ranchers played a central role in establishing local range policies. Men and women working for federal agencies—particularly the CCC, WPA, and the PWA—built roads, trails, and park infrastructure that serve as the bedrock of the tourist industry in southern Utah and northern Arizona to the present day. World War II pulled the U.S. out of the Great Depression and proved a boon to local ranchers and businesses reliant on their trade. In 1945, the long-term impacts of foreign markets and new federal grazing regulations on the livestock industry remained to be seen, yet southern Utahns looked forward to a glorious future in the post-World War II world.

FIGURE 6.1. The Grand Canyon had become one of the crown jewels of the National Park system by the 1940s. The public recoiled at the thought such treasures would be transferred to the individual states. Photograph by Dan Bauer.

6 Booms, Busts, and Battlefields, 1946–1995

World War II ended when Japan surrendered in August 1945. Although fought on faraway shores, the war forever changed the lives of men and women of Grand Staircase and Escalante River country. Kane County historian Martha Sontagg Bradley observed that the decades after World War II were years of "shifting values, economies, and social systems" as technologies created new media for interacting with a broader world and families found new ways to earn a living.[1] As detailed in Chapter 5, a good percentage of young people did not return to their homes in Kane and Garfield Counties after the war, opting instead for greater economic opportunities elsewhere, particularly in the urban environments of the Wasatch Front and in California. One of the immediate effects of the soon-to-be booming economies of the West was reopening the question of federal ownership of natural resources.

Choices were fairly limited for those who did return to rural Utah. Many could resume cattle ranching, but as previously covered, the option of raising sheep was largely a thing of the past at this point. Others could work for the federal government (primarily the U.S. Forest Service, and later the Bureau of Land Management), or if lucky enough to own property along U.S. 89, perhaps tap into the tourist industry that blossomed in postwar years. Many residents of southern Utah were forced to do a little bit of everything and anything to survive economically. Sometimes employment was unavailable, at least not locally. "I jobbed around quite a lot," said Vergene Porter, recalling nearly twenty years of odd jobs in Provo and later construction work on the Glen Canyon Dam before he found steady employment as a custodian for the local school district in Garfield County.[2]

In the years right after World War II, internal population growth was high, and once children came of age they were forced to look elsewhere to build their own lives. This conundrum evoked the oft-repeated lament, "our biggest export is our children." For many returning veterans, who had learned valuable trade skills in the military, life somewhere else with good wages was a whole lot more attractive than the drudgery and uncertainty of farm life.

The decades from the end of World War II to the establishment of the Grand Staircase-Escalante National Monument were the most momentous in the history of livestock grazing in southern Utah and northern Arizona. Cattle ranching remained the dominant industry for many of these decades, but fewer families made their living raising cattle and sheep. With some ups and downs, the overall trend was towards a reduction in cattle numbers on the public ranges, with sheep raising collapsing completely as a viable economic pursuit. Combined with economically disadvantageous trends at the national and international levels, increased environmental activism and federal regulations led to a decline in the importance of livestock raising to average citizens of the region. In contrast, the recreation industry experienced an upsurge, with more and more residents reliant upon tourist dollars for a living. The completion of Glen Canyon Dam in the early 1960s, as well as regrets about its negative environmental impacts, helped galvanize the modern environmental movement. A slew of environmental laws followed, impacting the once largely unrestricted grazing of public lands by area ranchers. A tug-of-war emerged in arid southern Utah and northern Arizona over questions regarding the best use of public lands and whose voices should count in deciding their fate.

Since the implementation of the Taylor Grazing Act of 1934, ranchers needed a "home base" to qualify for federal grazing permits. But private lands were in short supply, and as discussed later in this chapter, if a rancher decided to sell out, neighboring ranchers were waiting to buy these lands, eager to expand their own home base. A process of land consolidation occurred in Grand Staircase and Escalante country. As families sold out to their neighbors, the total number of families raising livestock steadily dwindled in postwar decades, even though the number of livestock grazing on public land remained relatively stable through this time.

In other words, a young man might take over his parents' cattle operation, but he would find it next to impossible to start one of his own. If he had brothers or sisters, there was no way that all of them could marry and raise families on that single "home base," usually only a few hundred acres of pasturelands. Typical of this scenario was Garfield County rancher Burns Black, who had permits to graze cattle in the Johns Valley area and the Griffin Top. Once he returned from the Pacific Theater, he married, and in the years that followed, he fathered eight children. Seven of those children moved away to raise their own families in larger urban areas; one son remained to continue the family ranching tradition.

The Taylor Grazing Act of 1934 withdrew most of the available public domain from homesteading, yet there already was scarcely an acre of viable farmland in southern Utah or northern Arizona that settlers had not patented by that time. The lack of available private lands hampered the ability of young men and women to strike off on their own. In Kane County, the amount of private land totals 11 percent; in Garfield County, it is only 5 percent.[3] With the exception of seasonal tourism jobs, the absence of significant economic growth in other sectors limited the number of local jobs. As a result, the populations of Kane and Garfield Counties reached an equilibrium that was maintained through perpetual out-migration.

Many areas of the West shared southern Utah's liability of having most of its lands owned by the federal government. At the national level, some Western congressmen decided the time was ripe to try to take control of public lands, making up for the lost opportunity offered by President Hoover to turn over these lands to the states during the early years of the Great Depression. In 1946, Wyoming Senator E. V. Robertson, a sheepman, introduced a bill to transfer all public lands, including lands held by the National Park Service, to the states. Powerful Nevada Senator Pat McCarran, who had been mercilessly attacking the Grazing Service for years, also backed the plan. An advocate for his sheep-ranching constituents, McCarran and others were tired of the federal government telling them what to do. Earlier in 1945, Senator McCarran had held hearings in Salt Lake City on public lands management. Here, L. C. Montgomery, chair of the Utah Cattle and Horse Growers Association, challenged statements by the federal range management chief, forcing him to admit proposed stock reductions could reduce herds by 30–50 percent. In this heated atmosphere, one privatization bill actually passed the House.

In a spark that would lead to the full-blown environmental movement in later years, famous conservationist and cofounder of the Wilderness Society, Aldo Leopold, came out against what was being dubbed the greatest "land grab" in all of United States history. Native Utahan, essayist, and historian Bernard DeVoto, who was often critical of conservative Utah culture, used his column "Easy Chair" in *Harper's Magazine* and other forums to argue against the privatization drive. In retrospect, advocates of the land grab clearly went too far, wanting all U.S. Forest Service and National Park Service lands transferred to the states. These lands were too dearly loved by the American public, and the effort ultimately failed to be enacted into law.[4]

An outgrowth of the attempted land grab was it united the previously loosely aligned conservation-oriented groups in America. Prior to World War II, conservation efforts usually centered around one or two issues. The Sierra Club represented hikers and nature lovers, the Audubon Society represented birders and wildlife watchers, and the Wilderness Society represented people who wanted backcountry preservation. Few individuals thought of conserving the public lands as a whole. William Voigt Jr., who was active in environmental politics at the time with the Izaak Walton League, recalls that these organizations came together to establish the Natural Resources Council to coordinate efforts, including efforts to curb overgrazing on public lands. The land grab served to rally many constituencies to the cause. Even the magazines *Sports Afield* and *Field and Stream* opposed the Western congressional effort. The Dude Ranchers Association rallied to the opposition, as well.

Secretary of Agriculture Ezra Taft Benson, who would later become a Mormon apostle and church president, said that letters to his agency ran 100 to 1 against the ranching industry.[5] The public's growing appreciation for wilderness and nature preservation happened to run counter to long-held Mormon beliefs—and perhaps Benson's personal beliefs, although he didn't mention that—stemming from scripture about taming the wilderness. An often-quoted Mormon text stated that once humankind had irrigated the land and brought it under human control, "the wilderness and the solitary place shall be glad for them: and the desert shall rejoice, and blossom as the rose."[6]

In the immediate postwar decades, southern Utah's high percentage of government-owned land prompted county officials to explore the development of other economies, as Bradley observed, to "entice young people to stay in the county rather than leave for better jobs and economic security elsewhere."[7] Economic development options included timber harvesting, coal mining, uranium mining, and to a lesser extent oil and gas exploration. Some officials looked to tourism, although then usually viewing it as a supplemental source of family income. By the 1950s, many local leaders undoubtedly and reluctantly acknowledged that ranching was not and never would be a growth industry. The ranges were already at capacity.

As detailed in this chapter, the ranching history of Grand Staircase and Escalante River country in the decades following World War II was intertwined with a series of events occurring throughout the region, as well as trends occurring nationally. The postwar economic prosperity enjoyed by most of the nation was minimal or nonexistent in southern Utah and northern Arizona. Cattle ranching resumed its dominance of the livestock industry throughout the region, but the number of ranching families dwindled through time. But, as noted previously, overall herd sizes remained comparatively stable. In effect, there were fewer ranchers, each with larger herds than a generation before.

In the 1950s, a short-lived expansion in livestock numbers saw cattle herds reach all-time highs. But by the 1970s, cattle numbers on the public ranges began slowly sliding downward, the result of greater federal oversight, increased activism by environmental organizations, and economic shifts that made family livestock operations less and less viable in a national marketplace.

The construction of the monumental Glen Canyon Dam in the late 1950s and early 1960s garnered people in Kane and Garfield Counties high-paying jobs for a few years, but it also further reduced the amount of rangeland available to permittees, first through inundation of winter rangelands along the Colorado River, and later by National Park Service management approaches that favored recreation at the expense of livestock grazing. More importantly, the dam also shifted local economies even more towards recreation. Growing populations in Kane County after 1970 flowed, at least in part, from the emergence of a new recreation-based economy.

A national conservation movement emerged in the 1960s, galvanized in large part by its well-publicized failure to stop the construction of Glen Canyon Dam and the subsequent flooding of the spectacular canyons of the region. Determined never to let it happen again, the Sierra Club and other groups organized, campaigned, and litigated to force federal land managers to manage public lands for all uses, not just extractive ones. This effort eventually led to passage of the National Environmental Policy Act of 1969 and the Federal Land Policy and Management Act of 1976, both of which afforded greater public participation to "outsiders" who did not actually live and work on those lands.

Finally, increased costs and reduced profit margins prompted the largest American livestock producers to concentrate production at bigger, more economically efficient operations elsewhere. The process of rising economies of scale marginalized the profitability of small family ranchers who did not

FIGURE 6.2. Kodachrome Basin, Garfield County. Photograph by Dan Bauer.

possess enough capital and hence could not compete with the larger operators. Foreign imports of cheaper beef also made family cattle operations less competitive through time.

Red Meat

Young men who returned to Kane and Garfield Counties from World War II found a homeland not much different than the one they had left—still poor, geographically isolated, and largely dependent on subsistence agriculture. Rationing to support the war effort had limited the availability of basic necessities, and even if families had money during the war, there was little they could purchase. The end of hostilities, however, brought a wave of optimism and a short-term flurry of spending, as well as an unprecedented connection to the outside world. The two newspapers of the Grand Staircase and Escalante region, the *Garfield County News* and the *Kane County Standard*, later to become the *Kane County News*, expanded to offer readers national and international news. Most families had radios that connected them to Salt Lake City, itself linked to a bigger world, and by the early 1950s those in the larger southern Utah communities had television, albeit with limited programing.

State and federal infrastructure spending resulted in better roads. More families purchased automobiles that connected them to far-flung family and friends. But roads and motor vehicles also changed how ranchers moved cattle and sheep. It was no longer necessary to spend days in the saddle moving herds between summer and winter ranges, or trailing them to railheads or auctions.

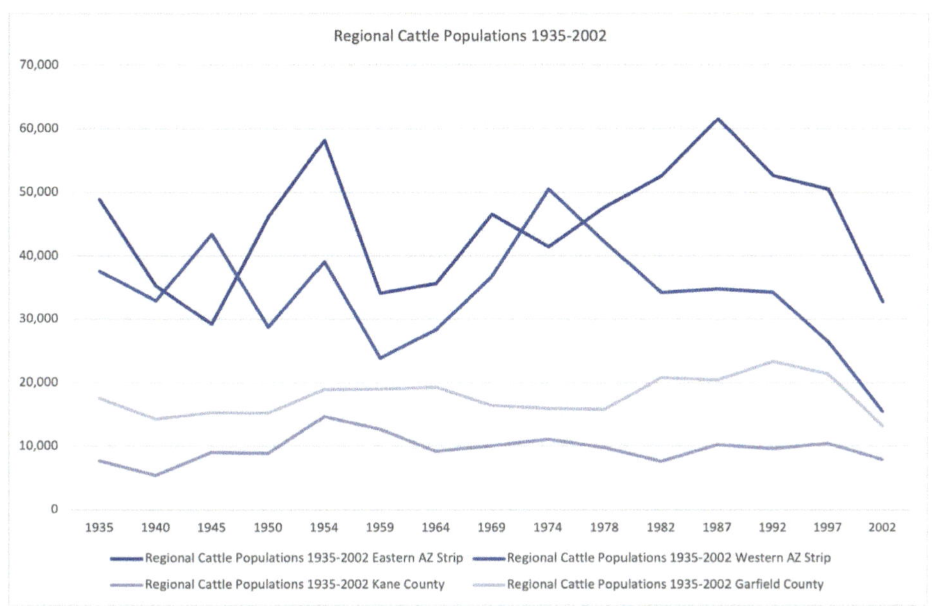

FIGURE 6.3. Total cattle populations in the Kane-Garfield region and Arizona Strip. All numbers derived from USDA Census of Agriculture Historical Archive, 1935–2002.

Dick Yardley, whose family still runs cattle in Garfield County, remembered they first started using bobtailed trucks to move cattle in the late 1940s, "and then in semi-trucks, which we are still doing today."[8] For most operations, the days of the long cattle drives were over.[9]

Those who returned to their ranching homes in 1945 found the existing cattle herds had swollen to nearly one hundred thousand head in Kane and Garfield Counties and on the Arizona Strip—a 10 percent increase from 1940. The numbers increased by only about two thousand head by 1950, suggesting stable range conditions and minimal increase in demand for beef in the years after the war.[10] Overall, cattle populations increased dramatically in the mid-1950s, next retracted to 1940 levels for the next decade, and then stabilized between 110,000 and 129,000 head through the 1997 agricultural census (see Figure 6.3).

The overall stability in cattle populations after World War II obscures the demographic trends occurring in the Grand Staircase, Escalante River, and Arizona Strip regions—fewer ranchers but larger herds. The year before the war started, cow farms in Kane County had an average of twenty-eight cows, and Garfield County cow farms had thirty-six (compared to a state average of fourteen). By 1945, average herd sizes had climbed in Kane County to sixty-three and in Garfield County to forty-six. Over the next half century, the herd

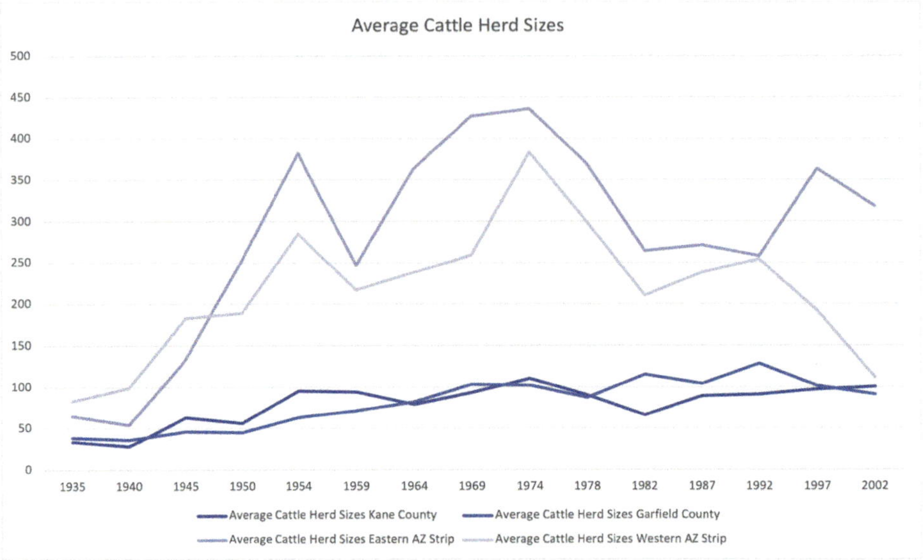

Average Cattle Herd Sizes

Average Cattle Herd Sizes Kane County
Average Cattle Herd Sizes Garfield County
Average Cattle Herd Sizes Eastern AZ Strip
Average Cattle Herd Sizes Western AZ Strip

FIGURE 6.4. Average herd sizes (total cattle divided by total cattle farms) reported in USDA Census of Agriculture Historical Archive for 1935–2002.

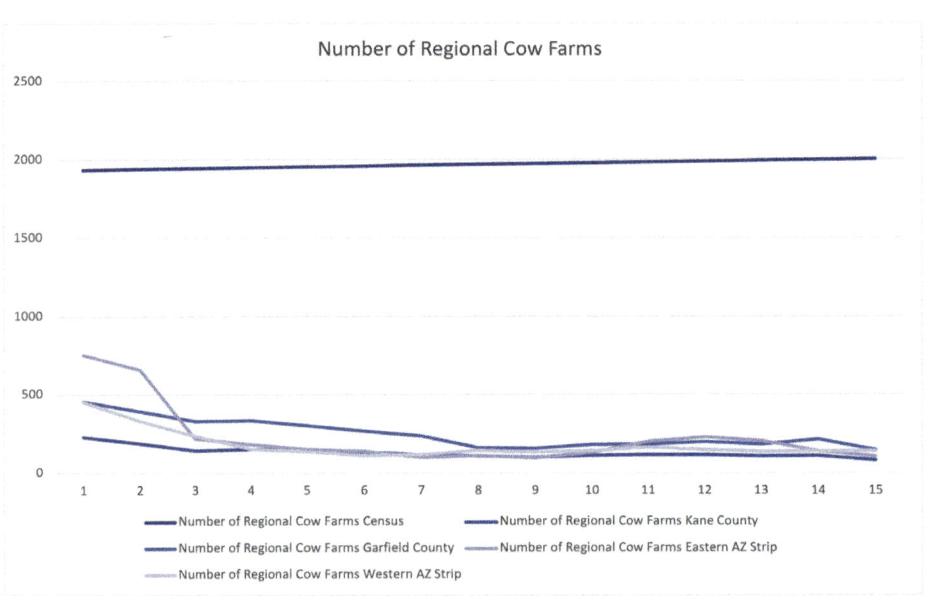

FIGURE 6.5. Number of "cow farms" reported in USDA Census of Agriculture Historical Archive for 1935–2002.

sizes rose by threefold over 1940 averages, while at the same time the number of cattle farms declined by 76 percent (see Figures 6.4 and 6.5).

Several trends in an overall-declining sheep industry also emerged. Regional sheep populations had plummeted by nearly half between 1940 and 1945, from 187,000 head to 98,000 head. But during the first five years after the war, those populations decreased only marginally. It is important to note that even though overall sheep populations held steady, the average size of individual flocks dropped. In Kane County, flocks fell from an average of 489 sheep in 1945 to 387 sheep in 1950, and in Garfield County, from 940 to 262. These statistics suggest that more families were raising sheep, but their individual flocks were substantially smaller.

In 1940, Garfield County had approximately ninety-four sheep farms. Ten years after that, the number of sheep farms had dropped to eighty-six, a 9 percent decline. In contrast, in Kane County, the number of sheep farms increased, from forty-two in 1940 to forty-seven in 1950. The growth occurred even as the number of sheep fell by more than 50 percent in both areas. This trend is inconsistent with a common belief that regional sheep ranchers switched to cattle ranching during World War II. The number of sheep farms actually remained relatively stable, suggesting individual sheep ranchers were simply raising far fewer sheep than they had before the war, adding cattle to their herds in the process. But they were still raising sheep.

For returning war veterans, starting a new cattle or sheep operation was not a realistic dream. The number of ranches was actually declining at this time, even as cattle herds were getting larger and sheep flocks were getting smaller. Veterans would have to look elsewhere for local employment, either in the emerging lumber industry with its thriving mills in Fredonia, Kanab, Panguitch, and Escalante, or in the expanding coal mines in Alton.[11]

The Red Scare

News accounts during the several years following World War II rarely mentioned the livestock industry other than an occasional comment on range conditions, cattle prices, and ongoing soil conservation measures. The annual movement of twenty thousand head of cattle or more to the Dixie National Forest summer range, however, was an annual spectacle that usually warranted some notice in the newspapers.[12]

FIGURE 6.6. The lumber industry on the national forests in southern Utah and northern Arizona created rural jobs in the post-World War II era. But most operations were small and undercapitalized, the timber that could be harvested was limited, and transportation costs remained high. This U.S. Forest Service photo is of the Mammoth Lumber Company of Hatch, Garfield County. Photograph courtesy of J. Willard Marriott Library Special Collections Repository (39222000581764), University of Utah, Salt Lake City.

The generally conservative and highly patriotic citizens of the Grand Staircase and Escalante River region had other things on their minds as the entire state and nation was enveloped in nationalist fervor. Far more articles in the local newspapers reported the communist threat to the free world and the imminent prospects of World War III. This was the Atomic Age, made more frightening after 1949 when the Soviet Union exploded its first nuclear bomb and America lost its nuclear monopoly. FBI Director J. Edgar Hoover fanned the flames of mass hysteria by claiming that 540,000 "native-born communists and sympathizers" were embedded across the United States.[13] Wisconsin Senator Joseph McCarthy also threw gasoline on the fire by accusing hundreds of government employees of communist subversion.

In the early 1950s, powerful Nevada Senator Pat McCarran and Vice President Richard Nixon gained national followings by holding hearings and accusing individuals of communist sympathies. Future Mormon Church President Ezra Taft Benson, secretary of agriculture during the Eisenhower Presidency, was a private supporter of the ultraconservative John Birch Society that also led the crusade against supposed internal communist subversion.[14] Fears were further stoked by the Soviet-backed communist invasion of South Korea in 1950 and the dread that sons and fathers would again be called to war.[15]

In 1951, with the nuclear arms race at full speed, the government began aboveground nuclear testing in Nevada, which showered southern Utah in radiation. Former Utah Governor Scott Matheson recalled:

> People in southern Utah were mainly concerned with making a living, and I don't recall anyone being too upset about the brilliant flashes and thunder-like blasts.... People were concerned about the sheep deaths that occurred in May 1953, but when the [Atomic Energy Commission] said there was nothing to worry about, we all just shrugged our shoulders. No one really accepted the malnutrition rationale, but we were used to accepting whatever the government said, especially during that very nationalistic period.[16]

FIGURE 6.7. Anti-Communist fervor swept the nation in post-World War II years even as the national economy boomed and a thriving American middle class emerged. This image by an uncredited artist appeared on the cover of a 1947 propaganda comic book published by the Catechetical Guild Education Society.

Residents paid a steep price for their allegiance. Clem Griffin of Escalante lost a wife and daughter to cancers attributed to the radiation fallout. He recalled, "I talked to guys that worked for the government down on the uranium mines, down on the Burr Trail, sayin' that their Geiger counters would ... go wild sometimes, just from the fallout that was runnin' through there." Leola Mangum Catterly Shoenfeld lost her husband, Graydon Catterly, a turkey farmer and dairy man, to bone cancer. His dairy cows were so afflicted by radiation poisoning they lost their udders. "They [cows] got it too," Shoenfeld said. "We lost a lot of people to cancer."[17]

The uranium mining boom of the 1940s and 1950s impacted the eastern fringes of the Escalante River country. Hopeful uranium millionaires plowed miles of dirt roads on once trackless public lands in the region. In the interest of winning the Cold War, federal funds were allocated to construct highways in southern and eastern Utah to facilitate uranium mining. But while Moab blossomed for a time from the industry, small towns like Escalante and Boulder saw few long-term benefits. The hoped-for new bonanza industry had fizzled by the 1980s in the face of foreign competition and low ore prices.[18]

The Cold War and its "hot" Korean conflict impacted the ranching industry in the region. As they had done in previous wars, local men responded to the nation's call. More than ninety men from Escalante alone served in the Korean War[19]—estimated to be more than 50 percent of its adult male population at the time.[20] Similar communities made disproportionately high commitments to the war effort—something that reduced the available labor pool in the short term. Yet more were sent to Europe to face down the threat of a Soviet invasion.

Tropic rancher DeRell Sudweeks found it ironic that his two brothers had fought the Germans in World War II, one of whom lost both legs in combat, but when it came time for him to serve "they shipped us into Germany to protect Germans" from the Soviet Union.[21] In effect, the U.S. military was one of the largest single employers of southern Utah's unemployed or underemployed young men in the early 1950s.

When the Korean War ended in 1953, the returning soldiers again found few jobs awaiting them. "I wasn't here very long 'til I left for Salt Lake because there was no employment here," recalled Calvin Schow of Escalante: "There was nothing here. What was here was already occupied, somebody else had the job."[22] Schow was not alone as hundreds of Garfield County residents left for better opportunities elsewhere. Other parts of the region continued to bleed population, as well. According to U.S. Census records, Garfield County's population fell from 4,151 in 1950 to 3,577 in 1960, a 13.8 percent drop in ten years (and 32 percent below the record high recorded in 1940). Many of those who left might have been rancher families getting out of the business. The number of Garfield County cow farms declined from 338 in 1950 to 214 in 1960—a 37 percent decline in ten years.

Kane County, however, experienced growth during this same period, from 2,299 residents in 1950 to 2,667 in 1960, a 16 percent increase. This rise reflects better economic opportunities outside of ranching. Sawmills were doing a booming business, coal jobs were available in Alton, workers were needed to construct the Glen Canyon Dam, and tourism was exploding. At that same time, the number of Kane County cow farms continued to dwindle, from 152 in 1950 to 133 by 1960, even though average herd sizes were 86 percent greater than they were in 1950.[23]

Grazing Policies and Politics

Little evidence suggests that local ranchers were much concerned with federal grazing policies at the end of World War II. But this political issue was most certainly a major one on the national stage. As the war neared its end, the U.S. Grazing Service began to look at ways to revive its conservation priorities, especially range studies and improvement projects. This effort stirred the embers of a long-running battle with the U.S. Congress that ultimately led to the demise of the federal agency and left its successor, the Bureau of Land Management (BLM), unable to manage grazing policy effectively.

Among the reforms the Grazing Service advocated was an increase in the existing grazing fee of 5 cents per animal unit month (AUM) charged to ranchers.[24] That proposal met with fierce opposition from Western congressional delegations, but it had strong support in the House Appropriations Committee. The Grazing Service was caught between a rock and a hard place: Western lawmakers warned against a fee increase while at the same time the House Appropriations Committee demanded a fee increase to at least cover the costs of the program. The Grazing Service eventually chose to drop the fee-increase proposal altogether.[25]

In 1946, the Grazing Service's relationship with the U.S. Congress continued to worsen, and it saw its budget cut in half, forcing it to close eleven of its sixty offices and lay off nearly two-thirds of its employees. To salvage what remained of the federal grazing program, Democratic President Harry S. Truman proposed merging the General Land Office and the U.S. Grazing Service into the new BLM. The merger was completed on July 16, 1946. As BLM historians James Muhn and Hanson R. Stuart noted: "The first years found the agency struggling to survive. It was hindered in its organization effort and haunted by the Grazing Service's fee increase debacle. There was serious question as to whether the agency would survive."

Congressional budget cuts had left the new agency with only eighty-six range management employees to oversee 150 million acres of rangeland, and it was ill-equipped to process grazing applications, monitor grazing conditions, prevent trespass, or make range improvements.[26] Even a grazing fee increase in 1947 from 5 to 8 cents per AUM did not ameliorate the funding problem.[27] The situation became so dire that local grazing advisory boards actually began paying the salaries of BLM range employees, creating a situation where the regulators were beholden to those they were supposed to be regulating.[28] Paul F. Starrs, a geographer who has written extensively on the cattle industry in the West, concluded that these conditions resulted in the BLM largely following traditional policies of allowing locals much control over the agency's functioning.[29]

The situation began to improve in 1948 with the appointment of Marion Clawson as the new BLM director. He pushed for the decentralization of the agency's functions to regional districts (Utah was in District 4, along with Colorado, whereas the Arizona Strip was part of District 5, along with the rest of Arizona, New Mexico, Texas, and Oklahoma). Clawson also pushed to hire more scientifically trained range managers. He gained another grazing fee increase, this time to 12 cents per AUM, which allowed the agency to hire additional employees, including many with college degrees in fields such as range management.[30] The rate hike also allowed the BLM to implement range improvement programs such as the development of water sources, fencing, reseeding, soil erosion control, and reductions in AUMs where rangelands had been depleted.

Also noteworthy, Clawson's 1948–53 tenure at the BLM marked the emergence of multiple use management.[31] This strategy prompted the BLM to inventory and classify public lands to determine "best and highest priority uses." Multiple use of public lands remains a fundamental component of BLM land management to this day, albeit one enveloped in controversy as different uses have become increasingly competitive with one another.

During the BLM's formative years, local livestock and soil conservation associations assumed greater influence over local grazing matters, including range improvements and efforts to improve herd quality.[32] For example, the Panguitch Lake Cattlemen's Association issued rules that all permit holders' bulls must be Grade B or better, and only Hereford and Durham bulls would be allowed on the Dixie National Forest.[33]

Apart from the BLM, the U.S. Forest Service used a different formula to arrive at grazing fees based on a sliding scale tied to beef and lamb/wool prices the previous year. In 1949, southern Utah stockmen paid record high prices for their grazing permits, but in 1950 the fees were reduced by 7 or 8 cents per head of cattle per month and a half-cent per head of sheep per month.[34] The BLM would eventually shift to a sliding scale in the late 1950s.

BLM attitudes toward management of grazing experienced another fundamental shift in 1953 following the election of Dwight D. Eisenhower, the first Republican president in twenty years. Edward Woozley, an Idaho state lands manager, was named to head the BLM, and he brought to the job a commitment to states' rights and support for business and industry. His mantra was "the full worth of the valuable resources on the public lands may be realized with minimum exposure to the taxpayer and that through careful cooperation with private enterprise, these lands can produce the products on which local, state, and national economy depend."[35]

Woozley again reorganized the BLM, creating individual state offices with satellite field offices. Ten field offices were established in Utah, including one in Kanab housed in an old Civilian Conservation Corps (CCC) barracks, which had responsibility for 2.68 million acres of public lands.[36] He also changed the year-to-year grazing lease policy to allow most range users to secure ten-year leases, initiated a new "appraisal" process to determine the carrying capacity of the ranges, and oversaw grazing fee increases. The latter rose from the existing 12 cents per AUM of the previous administration to 15 cents per AUM in 1955, 19 cents per AUM in 1958, and 22 cents per AUM in 1959; all of the increases were tied to the prices ranchers received for their livestock at market.[37]

The BLM's official history suggests conflicts with ranchers were constant during this period and much centered on land managers' efforts to reduce herd sizes. Muhn and Stuart state:

> BLM grazing district managers with hard and cold facts in hand, often reduced range use to levels more compatible with the new carrying capacity determinations. Stockraisers did not like the cuts and resisted BLM's efforts to impose them. BLM, however, did what it could to work out the disagreements and was usually successful in reducing range use where it was needed.[38]

BLM-directed herd reductions were not apparent in Grand Staircase and Escalante River country. Available records indicate federal land managers responded too slowly to immediate climate-related range conditions. Woozley's tenure coincided with the largest *increase* in cattle populations in the twentieth century, despite the fact the rangelands had been subjected to punishing droughts at that time. In 1950, the combined cattle populations in the Arizona Strip, Kane County, and Garfield County stood at 97,732. By 1954, it had risen to 129,796—a 33 percent increase in just five years. The cattle population fell to 89,087 in 1959 and 92,126 in 1964 before rebounding in 1969 and holding relatively consistent between 108,000 and 127,000 cows through 1997.

The specific reasons why cattle populations were so high in 1955 are unclear. Bradley indicates the region was hit by two crippling droughts, one in 1949 and another in 1952. These prompted the Farmers Home Administration to declare the region a disaster area, which in turn facilitated federal loans to ranchers in financial trouble. Between 1952 and 1953, the region received only 2.55 inches of total rainfall; Kanab typically averages 15 inches of total precipitation annually and Tropic receives 11 inches annually. Bradley noted that the "area rangeland was producing much less feed than normal."[39] Any BLM reappraisal of range conditions at that time should have revealed the rangelands were distressed and the number of livestock would have been reduced to its carrying capacity. Instead, 32,000 additional cattle were added to ranchers' inventories.

In 1957, the region received more rain in one year than it had any other year for the past fifty years—the drought was finally over and the rangelands were recovering.[40] Even so, the cattle population plummeted by nearly 40,000, likely because of a belated attempt by BLM officials to reduce stock on the damaged range or perhaps a response to declining demand for beef.

Contrast of Values: The Sixties

The 1960s was a turbulent time in the United States caused, in part, by a collision of basic values. On one hand, there were traditionalists who were pro-development, largely conservative, and fiercely capitalist. On the other hand, there were reformists who, for the most part, were liberal, advocated for civil rights, opposed American intervention in foreign conflicts, and sought fundamental changes to social, political, and economic practices, often through marches and protests. Tradition-minded Americans collectively referred to these individuals as "radicals." This collision of values resulted in significant, although sometimes indirect effects on the livestock industry in southern Utah and northern Arizona. The region was buffeted as both sides of the national culture wars would stake their claim to these rangelands, with most on each side not actually having been there.

Three events would figure prominently in the history of livestock grazing in the region: (1) the Vietnam War and the decidedly different response of young men in the region to that conflict, (2) the construction of the Glen Canyon Dam, which gave birth to a highly organized environmental movement that was determined to never allow such developments again, and (3) the election of progressive presidential administrations that embraced the concept that public lands belonged to all Americans, not only to grazers, miners, and timbermen, as well as the belief that all Americans had a fundamental right to clean air, clean water, and open spaces.

Most young men in Kane County and Garfield County had always been fiercely patriotic, responding enthusiastically to their nation's call to service during World War I, World War II, and the Korean War. Perhaps 50 percent of the adult male population served in the Korean War, but the Vietnam War was different. The conflict between communist North Vietnam and pro-Western South Vietnam had simmered in the background since 1955 before exploding in 1964 when the United States retaliated for trumped up attacks on its Navy destroyers. The nation began drafting large numbers of men into military service that same year, and over the next 10 years, 2.2 million Americans would be drafted to serve in Vietnam.[41]

For some, the Vietnam War was a way to leave behind rural Utah and the limited economic opportunities found there. Recalled Brent Owens, "When I graduated from Panguitch High School, if you had offered me the best farm in the valley I would have told you, 'no thank you.' I was ready to leave Panguitch Valley, do something else and go on to other things. The world looked pretty big to me." Owens enlisted in the Marine Corps and flew CH53 helicopters in the war.[42]

Many young men in rural Utah perceived the Vietnam War differently than their fathers and grandfathers had viewed the wars before, including the faraway Korean conflict that erupted early in the Cold War that ended largely in a stalemate. Rodney Black of Garfield County, who served as an infantryman in Vietnam in 1969, remembered the war "had a very bad reputation, something none of us wanted any part of." By the mid- to late-1960s, he and his classmates were doing everything they could to avoid the draft, or at least delay it. Young men could get a two-year deferment if they served a Mormon Church mission, and then the deferment would be extended if they enrolled in and remained in college. Some stayed in college until after they were twenty-seven and too old for the draft. Black served a mission to Samoa and then promptly enrolled in college. But when he dropped out one summer to help on the family ranch, the draft board representative, Duane Luke, "showed up in Antimony and said I was next to be drafted."[43]

Of course, such a system favored the more well-to-do, those who could afford to send their sons to college and cloister them there for years on end. But even poorer families would borrow and mortgage their farms to pay college tuitions, a ransom, of sorts, to protect their sons. Rodney Black estimated only about 15 percent of his male classmates were actually drafted. The net result was a generation of young men who were highly educated, some of them with advanced degrees and most of whom would not return to rural Utah. Said Black, "the farms were not big enough to support families, and everybody was poor. There was never any money until the cattle were sold or the potatoes harvested in the fall. You get a [college] education and you have more opportunities. I left because of the opportunity to make a better living for my family."

The out-migration that characterized the mid-1960s to mid-1970s mirrored similar migrations that had followed previous wars. Both Kane and Garfield Counties experienced population declines in the 1960s (Garfield County experienced a twentieth century low point in 1970), although decennial censuses do not reflect momentary population bursts. One of these occurred in the late 1950s and early 1960s with the construction of the Glen Canyon Dam, which also resulted in direct effects on grazing in Kane County as ranchers with permits along the Colorado River were displaced.

The indirect effects of the massive public works project on regional grazing were much, much greater. First, the filling of Lake Powell refocused public attention on the grandeurs of the canyon country and its recreational opportunities, and Kane County was quick to capitalize on new tourism opportunities. Second, the inundation of Glen Canyon and its stunning environment that few had ever seen beyond photographs served as a rallying cry to the nation's environmental activists who were determined to protect the Colorado Plateau by thwarting similar developments in the future. In fact, with the Sierra Club's book *The Place No One Knew*, the loss of the magical Glen Canyon labyrinth became a central rallying point for the growing environmental movement.[44] Part of the public awakening to the beauty of the region resulted in the establishment of Canyonlands National Park, created the year after the waters of Lake Powell began to rise.[45]

The Glen Canyon area had been eyed as a potential Colorado River dam site since 1922 when six of seven states ratified the Colorado River Compact (Arizona would not join until 1944). But it was not a preferred site due to its geographical isolation, absence of a transportation system to move equipment and materials, and various engineering and logistical challenges. The preferred site was in Echo Park near the confluence of the Yampa River with the Green River—an area already part of Dinosaur National Monument. David Brower of the Sierra Club led a dramatic come-from-behind campaign to save Echo Park based largely on the argument a dam at that location would impinge upon an existing national monument. He drew upon the public's consciousness of the Hetch Hetchy controversy of the early twentieth century when this spectacular canyon in Yosemite National Park, the "sister valley" to Yosemite Valley, was lost after a dam was built to supply San Francisco with water. Brower could not make the national park argument to save Glen Canyon and conservationists acquiesced—a failure that haunted Brower the rest of his life.[46]

On October 15, 1956, President Dwight D. Eisenhower symbolically set off the blasts to signal the start of the Upper Colorado River Storage Project and construction of the Glen Canyon Dam, as well as Flaming Gorge Dam on the Utah-Wyoming border.[47] As historian Adonis Findlay Robinson wrote, "Kanab, the County seat and nearest town to the dam site before Glen Canyon City, doubled its population in three months. The Bureau of Reclamation moved its offices into the vacated Kanab school house, where all bids for future contracts were opened. Cash registers rang up increased sales as tourists, contractors, and salesmen for construction materials crowded into the booming town. Five new classrooms were added to the elementary school house to accommodate the increased school enrollment. Kanab property owners voted to bond for a new water system and sewage disposal plant."[48]

Building Glen Canyon Dam meant good-paying jobs for the sons and daughters of ranch families, something that would last until 1963 when the dam was completed and Lake Powell began filling behind the behemoth structure. But it appears that nothing was written about the ranchers who had permits along the 150 mi of Colorado River to be inundated and whether they were compensated for the lost range lands now under Lake Powell. Who were they? Bradley hints that one of them might have been Floyd Maddox, a "local stockman" who had guided Federal Power Commissioners Merrill MacDonald and William J. Smirl to the proposed dam site in February 1954.[49]

Probably others also were running livestock along the Colorado River, some below the Kaiparowits Plateau and others at the mouth of the Escalante River. But this country is exceptionally rugged and remote, and very few cows ever were grazed in that country.[50] As Bill Wolverton noted, "the cold hard reality is that it is more trouble than [the cattle] are worth to find them and get them out of there." The area was also so remote that federal officials had a long history of ignoring grazing practices there. No one seemed to care if a rancher was running more cattle than he was permitted or if the cows even stayed within the allotments.[51]

Perhaps a bigger issue to the ranchers in the Glen Canyon region was the reality that Lake Powell was later designated a "national recreation area" under the administration of the National Park Service. Whereas the BLM had a mandate to manage public lands for grazing, the Park Service's mandate was preservation, and it was no cheerleader for the livestock industry. Any time a National Park Service unit was announced, local ranchers became concerned. In all but a few cases in its history, the Park Service banned grazing in park boundaries and even "grandfathered in" allotments that were slated for eventual retirement. Established by an act of the U.S. Congress in 1972, however, the enabling legislation for Glen Canyon National Recreational Area authorized grazing.[52]

Limited grazing thus continues in this national recreation area, but there is less of it, and what remains is the subject of opposition by conservationists and activists. Inspired by Edward Abbey's *The Monkey Wrench Gang*,[53] at times activists have taken matters into their own hands. In 1990, someone shot twenty-one cows and burned line shacks belonging to rancher Ard Lyman. Lyman had enough and approached the Park Service about buying him out. Two years later, the Park Service paid Lyman $100,000 and then permanently retired the permits.[54]

A more lasting impact to ranchers in the area than national parks and recreation areas was the emergence of highly organized and well-funded environmental organizations that began to challenge not just major developments such as dams and coal mines, but all federal land management policies, including grazing in Kane County, Garfield County, and on the Arizona Strip. This activism was initially led by the Sierra Club and the Wilderness Society, but in the years that followed, particularly the late 1960s and early 1970s, other voices joined the cause, among them Earth First!, the National Resources Defense Council, the Environmental Defense Fund, the Sierra Club Legal Defense Fund (now Earthjustice), the Native American Rights Fund, Friends of Dixie, Grand Canyon Trust, and the Southern Utah Wilderness Alliance (SUWA).[55] Local ranchers commonly attribute the subsequent decline of cattle ranching to environmental obstructionism, or in the local vernacular "damned environmentalists" or just simply "enviros." Overall, they are seen as "outsiders," as young idealistic (naïve) liberals or affluent leisure-seekers naturally opposed to local interests. The reality is that all environmental issues had emerged as a major national concern by the end of the 1960s, and as Muhn and Stuart noted, "the public became a permanent player in the game and demonstrated that it was no longer willing to entrust the job entirely to land managers, to House committees, or to anyone else to the exclusion of others."[56]

University of California, Berkeley, environmental scientist Sally Fairfax observed that, "government idealists" had led the conservation struggle since the early 1900s. But, she said, the 1960s were "years of profound questioning and resisting of the established order. Techniques of political activism developed in

FIGURE 6.8. Completed in the early 1960s, Glen Canyon Dam marked the genesis of a coordinated environmental movement and the birth of a new recreation-based economy. Photograph by Dan Bauer.

the civil rights movement and refined in the antiwar movement were employed in the environmental cause." Federal agencies were no longer "leading the movement, and toward the end of the decade they were being attacked by it."[57] As detailed hereafter, the Department of Interior's attempts to implement reforms to address the new wave of environmental concerns evoked the consternation and hostility of ranchers and Western politicians that persists to this day.

A Rebel Yell

The 1960s and 1970s were decades of comparative stability in the southern Utah cattle industry. Regional cattle populations fluctuated from a low of 92,126 in 1964 to a high of 120,805 in 1974, continuing the trend of growth in individual cattle herd sizes and towards larger operations rather than small family ranches. Kane and Garfield sheep populations also continued to slide precipitously, dropping to only 7,033 sheep by 1978. During those two decades, many locals had the perception that cattle ranching always would be the backbone of the area agricultural economy. Even though there were fewer individual ranchers, the number of cattle was the same as any time before with the exception of the record high in 1954.

But changing public policy would have profound effects on livestock operations throughout the West. The "multiple use" philosophy was tested as more voices demanded a say in land uses in the once isolated Grand Staircase and Escalante River country of southern Utah. As Bradley noted:

> Other Americans, their elected representatives, and various agency directors began to pay more attention to public lands. The agencies that earlier had essentially tried to facilitate use of the land by ranchers or timbermen were now asked to foster and accommodate other uses, including growing recreational uses and an environmental conservation movement.[58]

The shift away from the 1950s Eisenhower Administration's pro-industry and pro-business approaches to public lands was undoubtedly rooted in fundamental philosophical differences that were spotlighted with the election of Democratic President John F. Kennedy in 1960. Kennedy stated that public lands were suffering from "uncontrolled use and a lack of proper management." Stewart Udall, his new secretary of the interior, was himself of Mormon heritage, a descendant of Levi Stewart, a founder of Kanab. He grew up in the high desert community of St. Johns, Arizona. Under Kennedy's direction, though, he came to embrace a more aggressive multiple use mandate for public lands that emphasized planning, sustainability, and public involvement, something Udall called the nation's "Third Conservation Wave."[59] This led to special management designations for lands with unique attributes, such as primitive areas, conservation areas, and natural areas—each with proscriptions to protect certain resources. National and state advisory boards were expanded to include representation from conservation groups, forest and mining interests, and the oil and gas industry.

In time, southern Utah and northern Arizona were swept into national debates stemming from two major demographic and ideological changes in the 1950s and 1960s. The first was the aforementioned shifting ideologies about the environment and humankind's place in the natural world. A key moment occurred in 1949 when Aldo Leopold published a soon-to-be classic, *A Sand County Almanac,* in which he proposed a "land ethic," an ecological ethos that sought to place limits on human's freedom of action regarding nature. He asked people to see themselves as part of nature, as "a member of a community of interdependent parts."[60]

At the same historical moment, many people relocated to the Southwest and an "amenities belt" developed as well, with thousands of people and businesses migrating to the region because of its natural attractions and sunny climate. These benefits outweighed traditional barriers such as its isolation from the coasts and its increased costs of doing business. Newcomers demanded more of a say in how their cherished environment was managed.[61]

The growing counterculture of the 1960s adopted ideas of wilderness and ecology, in a new form of environmentalism that promoted the idea that humans were part of nature, with a biological and ecological connection that bound humans with all life on earth. These individuals often embraced Indigenous spirituality—both real and ersatz—that supported Leopold's science-based ideas. These concepts became intertwined with popular culture, epitomized by the "peace and love" movement of the late 1960s that promulgated ideas that horrified conservatives. If traditional conservatives, farmers and ranchers among them, needed a villain in the culture wars they found easy targets among the long-haired, bead-wearing, rock music-loving, war-protesting, pot-smoking "hippies."[62]

By the end of the 1960s the concept of "Spaceship Earth" emerged. The famous "Earthrise" photograph taken from the moon in 1968 made many people see how fragile and small the earth appeared from space. The words "ecology" and "environment" emerged as slogans in the youth movement, connecting humankind's "quality of life" and even survival itself with maintaining a healthy environment and balance with nature.[63]

During the 1960s quite simply, a radical rethinking took place that would reshape Western land policies that had been entrenched for nearly a century. The new ethic generally promoted the idea that public lands belonged to all Americans, not just the select few who had worked those lands. As articulated by BLM Director Charles H. Stoddard (1963–66), "we hope to acquaint every American with the thought that he is part owner of a great national treasure—which is becoming ever more valuable as our population grows."[64] Some of Stoddard's allies in the private sector wanted to eliminate the "archaic" Taylor Grazing Act that they felt hampered effective land management. Particularly troubling to these individuals was the law's emphasis on home ranches and existing rights tied to allotments. William Voigt Jr. recalled that Stoddard's stance made the ranching industry "furious," something that contributed to Stoddard's leaving his post earlier than intended.[65]

The new land ethic was bolstered by the passage of several federal laws. The Classification and Multiple Use Act of 1964 expanded the land use planning process to include concerns over wildlife, recreation, soil, and water resources. The Wilderness Act of 1964 set up a process to identify and protect lands that remained in a condition "untrammeled by man." The National Historic Preservation Act of 1966 created a mechanism for protecting archaeological sites on public lands, and later required federal agencies to consider the impacts of various land uses on those resources. And the National Environmental Policy Act (NEPA) of 1969 required all federal agencies to consider the potential environmental impacts of all activities permitted by the government.

Looking at the Wilderness Act and its progeny reveals competing ideologies that are difficult to reconcile in places like Grand Staircase and Escalante River country. Noted attorney and environmental historian Charles F. Wilkinson has written that the concept of government-protected wilderness is one of "America's greatest contributions to intellectual history." To him, they create a place where human spirit and values can be rejuvenated. By federal law, a wilderness area is one "untrammeled by man," where man is but a visitor. Clearly lands set aside as wilderness are, by definition, places where local ranchers and their traditions are not welcome. Since these places are set aside for spiritual and humanistic renewal, ranchers' presence is akin to fouling a sacred space.[66]

A key issue in designating wilderness areas is whether an area in question is "roadless." An 1866 mining law allowed use of right-of-ways across federal lands for access to deposits. While a 1976 law repealed this provision, it grandfathered rights to existing roads, many of which were little more than jeep tracks or in the case of the Paria River in Kane County, the meandering gravel-filled streambed. As historian Jedediah S. Rogers noted when examining the region's history, these feeble tracks were not just roadbeds, but human creations steeped in historical and cultural meaning. They were part of local Mormon and cowboy heritage, symbols of man overcoming wilderness. Rights to maintain them thus became central to battles over land use in Grand Staircase and Escalante River country.[67]

Even though the Wilderness Act specifically allowed grazing, each new environmental law would, to a greater or lesser degree, directly impact grazing practices on public lands. Perhaps the most far-reaching legislation was the Federal Land Policy and Management Act (FLPMA) of 1976 that reemphasized multiple use mandates, called for an inventory of public lands suitable for wilderness designation, implemented additional studies on grazing fees, and allowed for the creation of areas of critical environmental concern to be subjected to more intense management, among myriad other changes. One provision that would bite ranchers in the pocketbook, however, was a requirement that the federal government receive fair market value for use of public lands—a mandate that would mean substantial grazing fee increases.

Udall earlier had initiated grazing reforms that emphasized multiple use of the public lands, as well as new rangeland practices such as rest-and-rotation and deferred grazing systems that would foster range recovery. BLM managers subsequently worked with ranchers to develop goals for forage, soil stabilization, and recreation, and progress towards those goals was reviewed annually. Udall also provoked widespread outrage among ranchers when he pushed through grazing fee increases, first to 19 cents per AUM in 1961, then 30 cents in 1963, 33 cents in 1966, and 44 cents in 1969.

In the 1960s, grazing fees emerged as a flash-point issue between environmentalists and ranchers. Stock raisers insisted they were already paying too much, while conservationists insisted the AUM rates were well below fair market value and American taxpayers were subsidizing the industry. "Welfare Ranchers" became a popular term that stung conservative cattlemen who generally opposed social welfare programs. Fueling this debate was the disparity between fees charged by the Forest Service (72 cents per AUM) and fees charged by the BLM (33 cents per AUM). An interagency technical committee was assigned to study those differences in 1968. The committee found no justification for the fee differences and also determined that *both* agencies were charging far less than fair market value, which the committee set at $1.23 per AUM. The U.S. Congress balked at such a large increase, deciding to phase it in over ten years, 9 cents a year for the BLM and 7.2 cents a year for the Forest Service.[68]

In 1973, the National Resources Defense Council (NRDC) sued the BLM, claiming the issuing of grazing permits and licenses constituted significant federal actions that warranted local environmental impact statements required under NEPA. The federal court agreed with the NRDC, setting off a flurry of environmental studies throughout the 1970s.[69] At the same time, grazing fees continued to rise incrementally each year towards the $1.23 target established in 1968 (the target amount also rose as inflation was taken into account). By 1976, the grazing fee stood at $1.51 per AUM—five times what it had been just 10 years before. By 1980, it had risen again to $2.36 per AUM—another 56 percent increase in just four years.

Western ranchers and their powerful congressional allies cried foul. But the outrage over grazing fee increases seemed to have diverted attention from the fundamental policy changes occurring in the Department of Interior, changes that were significantly less industry-friendly. Since 1934, rangelands had been specifically managed for livestock (and to a lesser degree timber harvesting and mining). Ranchers worked closely with BLM range managers to determine proper carrying capacities, and although grazing permits afforded no legal property rights, familes who had used lands for generations perceived that grazing permits gave them exclusive rights to those areas.

Secretary of the Interior Udall had turned that assumption on its head by advocating that public lands belonged to all Americans, not just the few who used the land for their livelihoods. Through provisions of NEPA, all Americans were invited to participate in the environmental planning process. State and national environmental groups embraced this invitation with gusto. Decisions that were once a matter of agreement between a rancher and a range manager would now be subjected to intense scrutiny by attorneys, economists, political scientists, riparian experts, and others representing an array of constituencies with a smorgasbord of concerns.

In the Mormon cultural area of Kane and Garfield Counties, the interjection of forceful outside voices in land management decisions represented a unique variant in Western politics. While BLM and U.S. Forest Service agents often were locals sympathetic to livestock interests, the fact they worked for the federal government represented an outsider presence in the Mormon region. As geographer D. W. Meinig observed, the federal government is by far the most visible and powerful outside presence in Mormon-dominated areas. Battles over land management policies in Grand Staircase and Escalante country promised religious baggage not seen in areas outside the Mormon cultural area.[70]

In a very real sense, the 1960s and early 1970s battles over public lands represented a confrontation of values and ideologies. On one hand, the Republican pro-development contingent advocated for more dams, more highways, and more power plants to feed the energy needs of a growing nation and to spur economic development of the West. It is sometimes unrecognized, however, that many Democratic members of the U.S. Congress from the West joined their Republican counterparts on these issues. On the other hand, greater environmental protection became somewhat of a bipartisan issue outside the West. The presidential administrations of Democrats John Kennedy (1961–1963) and Lyndon Johnson (1963–1969), Republican Richard Nixon (1969–1974), and Democrat Jimmy Carter (1977–1981) all embraced environmental reforms, arguing Americans had a fundamental right to clean air, clean water, and open spaces for solitude and recreation.

By the mid-1970s the BLM was literally caught in the middle, struggling to balance all these competing interests. Used to having the ear of the agency, local ranchers battled perceived threats from many parties. They also seemed to have conflicting feelings about the local presence of the BLM. Kanab-based *Southern Utah News* warned about the "anti-hunting movement" led by groups like the Humane Society that were seeking to end cherished family traditions in the area.

Local news sources also raised the alarm about another perceived threat from Indigenous Americans in Arizona at the time. As part of a land settlement involving the Hopis and Navajos, the government agreed in 1975 to swap lands lost by the Navajo to the Hopis on the Navajo Nation for BLM lands in other areas. The Navajo Nation government wanted to claim 250,000 acres in House Rock Valley as grazing land, to which a group of local ranchers protested and threatened to fight in court. The group headed by Mack Frost of Kanab even proposed calling for an environmental impact statement (EIS), apparently seeing no irony in the request, to prevent the swap. At the same time, most area residents cheered as the BLM helped to facilitate what was being dubbed as a $3.5 billion coal mine project on the Kaiparowits Plateau. Showing the conflicting sentiments, when a proposal emerged in 1975 to reconfigure the BLM and potentially move its local office from Kanab, residents reacted in opposition. U.S. Senator Jake Garn, a Utah Republican, stated: "once again the appointed bureaucracy has ignored the wishes of elected officials, both local and national, and the wishes of the people in the area concerned."[71]

As to ongoing environmental issues, the Utah situation was complicated by the religious beliefs of many local Mormons. In a rarely noted phenomenon, Mormon beliefs in the coming Millennium may impact Utah positions toward difficult conservation measures. Geographer John B. Wright found that many Latter-day Saints wait for a "Millennial rescue" upon God's return and reign of His people on earth. At that point, they believe, God will repair the land and create a new earthly paradise. This belief, of course, may work against efforts to protect the environment in the present, especially when devout members feel the "end times" are imminent. Wright quotes a high official in one of Utah's state land management agencies who told him: "I feel that the Millennium is a real event that's coming soon. And when God comes to Utah, he'll bring with him all the Lost Tribes and all the Mormons who have passed on. And you know, we're going to need the room."[72]

At the national level, public opinion, once firmly on the side of development, shifted dramatically to conservation values by the late 1960s and early 1970s. Proposals to dam the Colorado River in Grand Canyon and to build a coal-fired power plant next to Capitol Reef National Park lost resoundingly in the court of public opinion. And a proposal to construct a coal mine and power plant complex on the Kaiparowits Plateau—what was intended to be the largest coal-fired power plant in the nation—was abandoned after thirteen years of planning and development due largely to concerns over effects of air pollution on the Grand Canyon. As Wilkinson observed, "Kaiparowits was proof positive that the context had fundamentally changed."[73]

The fact that some individuals would challenge the benefits of the proposed coal mine was beyond the scope of reason for many local Utahns. For generations it was accepted dogma that the Kaiparowits coal mine could bring nothing but blessings to residents of the southern part of the state.[74] Local anger toward outside environmental groups increased even before the coal project was canceled. In 1975, *Southern Utah News* blamed them for the slow progress on the project, quoting William R. Gould, then executive vice president of Southern California Edison, as saying: "the delays stem from objections by environmental groups and lengthy approval processes."[75]

These new social and political developments would have few immediate impacts on grazing in the region in the 1970s, but that was about to change. The public participation provisions of NEPA enabled (or emboldened) environmental groups to begin challenging traditional grazing practices. The impact of grazing on riparian areas and the resulting deterioration of water quality and watersheds became a repeated concern. Others challenged the fees charged to grazers because they were less than fair market value calling them "subsidies," and yet others questioned BLM determinations of appropriate carrying capacity. Increasingly environmental organizations took to the federal courts to push their agendas.

The conflict over how best to manage public rangelands reached a fever pitch in the late 1970s when rancher opposition to federal lands policies rebranded itself with a catchy, media-ready name—the Sagebrush Rebellion. Colorado Governor Richard Lamm, himself no fan of the federal land policies, wrote in 1982 that it was "part hypocrisy, part demagoguery, partly the honest anger of honest people, it is a movement of confusion and hysteria and terrifyingly destructive potential," all rooted in opposition to and suspicion of federal authority.[76] Geographer William L. Graf makes a compelling case that the 1970s–1980s rebellion was not the first, but simply the latest in a series of rebellions rooted in Westerners' discontent and distrust of the government that reared its head every ten or fifteen years stretching back to the late 1800s.[77]

Like those that came before, the 1970s–1980s "rebellion" was stoked by the uneasy relationship between Western states like Utah and Nevada and the federal government. In the twentieth century, local politicians had voraciously courted federal funds and subsidies for a host of economic activities, yet were angry at the high level of federal controls over millions of acres of lands within their borders. The first volley in this latest iteration of the Sagebrush Rebellion was a bill that passed the Nevada state legislature in 1979 declaring that the state had a right to own and to manage 49 million federal acres within Nevada. This declaration was purely symbolic and had no force of law. But Utah Senator Orrin Hatch soon called the nascent rebellion the "second American Revolution." As environmentalists and citizens outside the Great Basin organized to resist the newfound "land grab," rhetoric heated up on both sides. The next year, the Utah Legislature passed a bill almost identical to the bill from Nevada. Democratic governor Scott Matheson signed the bill into state law, although he privately admitted he was worried over the potential costs of such a measure to the state should it come to pass in federal law.[78]

The seeds of the Sagebrush Rebellion had been planted in the early 1960s when Stewart Udall implemented policies of multiple use following his philosophy that public lands belonged to all Americans. The rebellion, however, really picked up steam in the early 1970s with implementation of NEPA and the public participation that ensued, bringing to the decision-making table a wide array of interested parties, including environmentalists. It exploded in the mid- to late-1970s in the wake of two watershed events: (1) the successful 1973 lawsuit by the Natural Resources Defense Council that required federal agencies to prepare 144 site-specific environmental impact statements that examined the

FIGURE 6.9. Ronald Reagan, a transplant to the West and film star-turned president, became an articulate voice for a growing "rebellion" that sought to overturn the environmental agenda that had taken root in the 1960s. This image was first published in 1980 in Paonia, Colorado-based *High Country News* and reprinted in the *High Country News* on January 14, 2016. The original source of the image is not determined.

deleterious environmental impacts of grazing on public lands, and (2) passage in 1976 of the Federal Land Policy and Management Act, which strengthened multiple-use mandates, shifted priorities from maximizing extraction to preservation, and gave environmental and recreation interests legal equality alongside traditional extraction interests such as mining and grazing.[79]

At the local level in Grand Staircase and Escalante country, mounting grievances, whether blamed on the correct causes or not, served to fan the flames. Bradley reported that Roland Esplin, who had run sheep for years in southern Utah, sold about one half of his herd of 6,000, shipping them to Oregon, while blaming increased federal regulations for his "quitting" the business, particularly the fact he felt he could no longer protect his sheep from coyotes and mountain lions. That same year, angry ranchers met Fred Howard, the BLM district manager based in Kanab, to express fears of a conspiracy led by "expert" outsiders to run their cattle off the land.[80] In a book about their lives growing up on the large family-owned Lazy B cattle ranch in southern Arizona, former U.S. Supreme Court Justice Sandra Day O'Connor and her brother Alan Day, who ran the operation for decades with both private land and public leases, came to feel the BLM was ruining the cattle business. As they noted, the BLM increased

> its staff and the number of paper-pushing bureaucrats. Development of new rules and regulations became the top priority instead of on-site range improvement. At the same time, the ability of the rancher to produce a profit declined. The increase in grazing fees and monthly expenses more than offset the improvements in the land and the grass.[81]

The Endangered Species Act of 1973 became a particularly effective weapon in the conservation movement's arsenal, something that rankled many local ranchers. Both Lisa Force, a regional coordinator for the Center for Biological Diversity, and Andrew Fahlund, a high-ranking official at American Rivers, have admitted that they have no qualms about bringing lawsuits to achieve their goals.[82] By the late 1970s, many conservative ranchers in southern Utah could sense that many former youth movement leaders of the turbulent 1960s had segued into roles as professional environmental lobbyists and legal advocates. With their crisp suits and very non-hippie-like grasp of policy, former "Left" radicals clearly had learned to play by political rules in the post-1960s decades. Most had gravitated to the Democratic Party as well.[83]

For rural Utahns, in particular, endangered species protections were seen as an existential threat. Many failed to see why animals were elevated above human concerns. As noted historian Donald Worster has found, many Americans, even those in urban areas, have trouble comprehending the legal and abstract notion that animals have "rights."[84] In rural southern Utah, many people sensed that politics and federal pork barrel spending were involved in campaigns that cost millions of taxpayer dollars to preserve small animals that they viewed as having little or no value.

In southern Utah and northern Arizona, rural residents often bemoaned what seemed to them absurd cases involving endangered species and non-native species. It seemed every animal had its own special interest group. Non-native wild horses and burros had special legislation passed to protect their range, often at the expense of both native wildlife and cattle.[85] Howls of protest and derision erupted in Kane County when the U.S. Fish and Wildlife Service listed the Kanab ambersnail (*Oxyloma haydeni kanabense*), found in wetlands about 6 mi north of Kanab, as an endangered species in the 1990s.[86] The Utah prairie dog, considered in many quarters a "varmint" and pest, was once almost poisoned out of existence. It became a *cause célèbre* for species recovery after it was listed as threatened under the Endangered Species Act in 1973. Development was often halted once a prairie dog colony was discovered, causing local resentment. Water development was questioned if it could negatively impact several species of endangered native chubs and suckers in the Virgin River watershed or at isolated springs in the region.[87]

Federal efforts to protect the Mexican spotted owl proved highly contentious in the Grand Staircase and Escalante River country. The Mexican spotted owl (*Strix occidentalis lucida*) is one of three subspecies of the spotted owl. It is closely related to its more famous relative the northern spotted owl (*Strix occidentalis caurina*). The northern spotted owl, native to the Pacific Northwest, was at the center of an acrid 1990s battle between the timber industry and national environmental groups after it was listed as threatened under the Endangered Species Act in 1990. Because it nested in old growth forests, timber sales of large tracts of ancient woodlands were halted. The press reported that between 12,000 and 60,000 jobs were predicted to be lost as a result.

While the validity of these projections was debated, many residents of Southern Utah dependent on extractive industries were concerned over the Mexican spotted owl, whose habitat included southern Utah, Arizona, New

Mexico, and northern Mexico. The Mexican subspecies also needed old growth forests to survive. While most of the old forests of southern Utah and northern Arizona had been previously logged, Mark Hughes of the Sierra Club Legal Defense Fund and Robin Silver, one of the founders of the Center for Biological Diversity, became concerned that timber companies would soon target the remaining pockets in southern Utah, including particularly difficult-to- access old growth pine and fir forests hidden in the steep canyons of the region. These environmental groups and several others were successful in getting the federal government to list the Mexican spotted owl as threatened in 1993. Ken Rait, director of SUWA at that time, was also involved; he had earlier claimed that the U.S. Forest Service was not doing enough to protect the owl. Other wildlife advocates argued that, in addition to the loss of old growth forest, the Mexican spotted owl also was threatened because of habitat fragmentation, grazing, ATV use, and fires.[88]

As the United States Fish and Wildlife Service began studies to designate areas of critical habitat, observers began to predict adverse impacts on future timber sales in southern Utah. Like many advocates of the lumber industry in the American Southwest, Fredonia mayor Brent Mackelprang blamed the Mexican spotted owl for the loss of hundreds of jobs in the Kanab region.

Overall, representatives of extractive industries in the West reacted in a way that was swift and vociferous from the start. Shouts of "federal colonialism" grew ever louder, and demands that the federal government transfer public lands to the states became a rallying cry for influential Western lawmakers, such as Utah's Orrin Hatch, Arizona's Barry Goldwater, and Alaska's Ted Stevens. Funded in large part by corporate interests, several advocacy groups were created to counter the preservation messages of the well-organized environmental movement.

As far as locals were concerned, they were quite irritated that environmental writer and iconoclast Edward Abbey had gained such a national profile through his association with southern and eastern Utah. His classic works *Desert Solitaire* and *The Monkey Wrench Gang* were set, in part, in the region. Abbey had floated down Glen Canyon in 1959, and for the rest of his life he bemoaned its loss. *The Monkey Wrench Gang* centered upon a fictitious group of eco-warriors who planned to blow up Glen Canyon Dam. The novel inspired a real "monkey wrenching" movement in the group Earth First!, whose first public relations stunt occurred in spring 1981 when members unfurled a 300-foot black ribbon down the face of the dam that from afar looked like a giant crack. Afterward, the Sierra Club began a campaign to drain Lake Powell, a proposition seen as sacrilege to many local residents. In time, some devotees began calling southern and eastern Utah "Abbey's Country" to replace other slogans, including "Zane Grey Country," an ode to the Old West writer.[89] Abbey and some of his academic allies were among the first to portray ranchers as despoilers of the public lands and destroyers of the perceived "Garden of Eden" that existed before their arrival.[90]

FIGURE 6.10. Edward Abbey, author of classics like *Desert Solitaire* and *The Monkey Wrench Gang*, became the much-despised face of the radical environmental movement in southern Utah. But he was a beloved icon outside of rural Utah and also the first writer-in-residence at the University of Utah. Photograph courtesy of J. Willard Marriott Library Special Collections Repository (P0305 Faculty Photos), University of Utah, Salt Lake City.

All the pent-up rage against federal oversight and outside agitators like Edward Abbey meant that many southern Utahns were hearty supporters of the Sagebrush Rebellion. Rogers reports that the climax of the Sagebrush Rebellion in Utah occurred in southeastern Utah in and around Moab in summer 1980. Increasingly angry and frustrated over the Democratic administration of Jimmy Carter and its strong enforcement of endangered species protections, FLPMA rules, and designation of thousands of Utah acres as wilderness study areas (WSA), residents erupted into open defiance. On July 4, 1980, a protest group, organized and led by Grand County commissioners, decorated a bulldozer with "Sagebrush Rebel" signs, moved onto a proposed wilderness area en masse, and symbolically graded a part of an old roadbed. As previously noted, "roadless" areas were important to future WSA designation, and whether an historic road existed or not became a central question. As about eighty vehicles snaked up a canyon behind the bulldozer, a counterprotest was also occurring in nearby Moab led by Dave Foreman, who had recently cofounded Earth First! At the event, spokespersons for the Utah chapter of the Sierra Club and other groups decried the "lawless" actions sponsored by the county commissioners. While no violence occurred as it had in nearby states, clearly the issues that sparked the Sagebrush Rebellion and opposition to it resonated in Utah.[91] Bradley reports that most residents of Kane Country were sympathetic to the movement.[92]

The creation of WSAs or their proposed establishment served as flashpoints for area ranchers for decades, and they ignite anger to the present day. Rancher Clare Ramsay noted their impacts in an interview in 2004.

> This wilderness debate goes on, it seems, forever and environmentalists, we have to fight them at every turn. The WSAs, wilderness study areas, they were created back in the sixties [or] seventies maybe, but the

> BLM studied the whole state. They inventoried the whole state and they came up with 3.2 million acres. That's wilderness study areas ... that's ridiculous.

He and others recognize, however, that the push for WSAs did not come simply from groups outside the state:

> What they don't understand along the Wasatch Front, I've been up there and seen on their lawns ... "Save Our Lands" [placards] and so forth, signs on their lawns. What they don't understand is if this land is ever locked up as wilderness, it's locked up to them too. The only way they can get to it is to walk. They think it's just going to be a playground for them ... [but] they're going to have to walk into it, because that means no wheels! No wheels, no helicopters can land there, no airplanes.[93]

The rebellion achieved many of its short-term goals after the 1980 election of President Ronald Reagan and his subsequent appointment of Secretary of Interior James Watt, a self-described antienvironmentalist.[94] Regulations were rolled back and promises were made to give greater weight to local interests in federal decision-making. As journalist Jonathan Thompson noted, "there was suddenly far less to rebel against, at least for the extractive industries and their allies."[95] During this period, grazing fees began to fall, from $2.31 per AUM in 1981 to $1.86 in 1982, $1.40 in 1983, $1.37 in 1984, and $1.35 in 1985.[96]

To assume the underlying principles of the Sagebrush Rebellion ever went away would be a mistake. These issues would again rear their heads in the mid- to late-1980s, in the late 1990s, and in 2014 in the armed standoffs with Nevada rancher Cliven Bundy, who ran cattle on the western border of the Arizona Strip without paying federal grazing fees. The prosecution of San Juan County Commissioner Phil Lyman on trespass charges in 2016 for entering an area closed to vehicles on public land, and the armed occupation of the Malheur National Wildlife Refuge led by several of Bundy's sons, also in 2016, fanned the resistance. In effect, Western opposition to federal land management policies has simmered unabated for four decades, exploding into angry rhetoric and occasional violence every decade or so.

The ideological and moral chasm that emerged dividing livestock raisers and environmental advocates into competing camps had been forming since the mid-1960s. Noted historian Richard White has identified a major perceptual trend that has gained momentum since—environmentalists increasingly denigrate ranching work, labor done with a man or woman's hands, while elevating work by college-educated individuals in urban workplaces. This class-based dichotomy obviously rankles the largely working-class ranching culture of southern Utah as it does elsewhere in the West.[97] White argues that some environmentalists' beliefs stem from their romantic views of the land and a desire to return it to a state "before man" or the original "Eden." White has found that "most environmentalists disdain and distrust those who most obviously work in nature," and that they see this work as destructive to a perceived "wilderness" state that often never was. As he concludes:

> Nature has become an arena of human play and leisure . . . environmentalists so often seem self-righteous, privileged, and arrogant because they so readily consent to identifying nature with play and making it by definition a place where leisured humans come only to visit and not to work, stay, and live.[98]

It should also be noted that the cyclical nature of Western discontent coincides with the cyclical nature of litigation by environmental groups to challenge or reverse the policies of administrations more sympathetic to Westerners, such as policies promulgated by Reagan, George H. W. Bush, and George W. Bush. As researcher Shawn Regan observed, the rebellion was "born out of a federal grazing system that encourages conflict, not negotiation. Competing user groups often have no way of coming together to resolve conflicting demands except through top-down political or judicial means."[99]

A good example of this situation occurred in the early 1990s with a campaign by environmental groups to eliminate grazing on public lands. Armed with catchy slogans like "No Moo in '92" and "Cattle Free by '93," the campaign appropriated the expertise of a wide range of economists, rangeland scientists, riparian specialists, biologists, and experts in recreation and wildlife management to make a convincing argument that the cost to taxpayers to manage grazing was more than three times greater than the revenue the grazing fees generated. In other words, the federal grazing program was a massive government subsidy to ranchers at the expense of riparian areas, water quality, wildlife, and recreation.[100] Environmentalists referred to them as "welfare ranchers."

These campaigns hit a chord with many urban Americans, especially those outside the West, who have an aesthetic dislike for cows, both their physical bodies and their messy tendencies in the outdoors.[101] These individuals view cows as unnatural on the land and believe they need to be removed.[102] It did not help that areas favored by tourists and hard-core backpackers were often the same areas favored by cattle. Especially in arid country like southern Utah, cattle prefer riparian areas because they produce twenty-five times more vegetation per unit of land than upland sites. In these fragile environments, cattle tear up the banks, creating avenues for runoff and gullying. They chew up moist willow and cottonwood shoots, stymying their efforts to regenerate over time. Through these processes, former marshy areas dry up and become devoid of their once-lush streamside vegetation.[103]

Riparian areas are also the source of the greatest biodiversity per acre in arid regions. A 1999 Grand Staircase-Escalante National Monument visitor survey found that 68 percent of backcountry travelers reported that cattle detracted from their visit, with over one half saying that cattle were "unacceptable" in areas once they were categorized as wilderness.[104]

FIGURE 6.11. Environmental organizations organized against grazing on public lands in the late 1980s to mid-1990s. *How Not to be Cowed* was published in 1991 by the Natural Resource Defense Council as a primer for local activists.

One of the emerging realities that has been hard for some to grasp is the fact that the "enemy" of the local ranching tradition is often "us" in Utah. In the post-World War II era, the state became one of the most urbanized in the entire nation, with over 90 percent of residents residing along the Wasatch Front in northern Utah. This trend was a national one, and by 2012, only about 15 percent of Americans resided in rural areas.[105] As early as the 1980 Sagebrush Rebellion bulldozer protest near Moab, Rogers found that reaction to that event was overwhelmingly negative in the northern Utah-based press of the time.[106] By the 1990s at the national level, Starrs noted a marked shift in public opinion regarding rural ranching and farming traditions. While previous surveys routinely found a strong tendency to support these activities, the U.S. public now had taken a decided turn against them, especially on public lands.

Even though gerrymandering meant that a Democrat who supported environmental causes could rarely win a congressional or local government seat, urban Utahns increasingly demanded their voices be heard. Many of these individuals took a keen interest in public policies toward southern and eastern Utah—the canyon country became highly symbolic of a place for them to escape to the seeming primeval wilderness. Protests and "land grabs" of the Sagebrush Rebellion years had awakened many Utahns to the possibility they might lose access to cherished public lands throughout the state.[107] As historian Patricia Nelson Limerick and other scholars have noted, the West had long been a place of great national symbolic importance wrapped in ideas of the frontier and freedom. But ultimately the region is mainly unique as a place that people call home. So questions about who can claim this unique and beautiful place remain central to the future of southern Utah's canyon country.[108]

Some researchers have defended ranchers with their own studies that argued that rangelands were healthier with grazing, that grazing improvement projects benefited wildlife, that riparian deterioration could be managed, that traditional values should not be ignored in economic models, and that "many of the communities that thrive in the sparsely populated portions of the West would be uninhabited if it were not for a viable livestock industry."[109] Starrs has concluded that because of improved ranching practices and federal regulations federal lands were in better shape in the late 1990s than they had been in the World War II years. He also pointed out that public lands ranchers receive far less in federal subsidies than other industries such as dairy, tobacco, rice, and cotton farmers.[110]

It is probably not coincidence that the campaign to eliminate grazing was waged just as President Bill Clinton took office, ending twelve years of Republican control and sparking hope among environmentalists that new Secretary of Interior Bruce Babbitt would advocate comprehensive grazing reforms. In August 1995, Babbitt implemented a new set of regulations under the title "Rangeland Reform '94" that succeeded in angering both sides of the debate. The reforms left in place federal subsidies, but also implemented a "command and control" approach that mandated national standards to assess the impacts of livestock on land, soil, air, water, plants, and wildlife.[111] For all intents and purposes, the reforms diffused the environmentalists' campaign to end grazing altogether; clearly the Clinton Administration and the president himself, a committed centrist, had no stomach for such a fight.

Changing Realities

Federal grazing regulations and environmental activism continue to be cited as the twin reasons for the decline in the southern Utah cattle industry since 1970. But a third cause is rarely mentioned: the changing nature of the industry nationally, particularly its rise in scale and consolidation, and the plummeting consumer demand for beef since 1970. As of 2013, 85 percent of all beef in the United States was being produced by only four companies (Tyson Foods, JBS, Cargill, and Smithfield Foods), all of which centralized production in feedlots with 16,000 to 32,000 head of cattle each. Even though the United States produces more beef than ever before, beef operations experienced a 175,000 decline in cattle operations over the past decade, 144,000 of which were small outfits with fewer than fifty head.[112]

As detailed earlier, the trend towards fewer cow farms with larger herds began shortly after World War II. This trend continued in the 1970s and 1980s as more and more small operators sold out to larger outfits. As one economic study observed, "a 100 cow herd does not provide enough cash flow or profit to support a family," yet as of 1978, nearly 75 percent of all cattle operations on BLM lands had permits to run fewer than one hundred cows.[113] Added to this trend was a profound shift for large operations to move production to the humid pastures of the Southeastern states, where most beef was raised by the late 1990s. By this time, only 2–3 percent of the nation's cattle were grown on public lands, lands that were mainly in the West.[114]

Added to these factors hampering the beef industry in southern Utah and northern Arizona was the fact that cattle had to be generally smaller and rangier than cattle that thrived on eastern, well-watered pastures.[115] And raising a cattle crop in the rough canyon country was difficult. A long-time rancher from Escalante who was born in 1909, Neal Liston recalled some of these trials: "Sometimes it would take, oh, a good month gathering [the cattle] off the mountain because they'd drift in different places so bad. And it was the same way on the desert, they'd drift clear to Hole in the Rock, to the Colorado River."

Often the cattle brought in were in bad shape, having survived in such arid conditions.[116]

Small cattle operators also found themselves squeezed by the high cost of beef production. One 1986 government study of costs and returns for cow-calf operations on U.S. Forest Service lands determined ranchers were losing between $259 and $586 per animal.[117] At the same time, increased mechanization and improved nutritional practices, among other factors, had increased economic returns at the largest feedlot and packing operations.[118] Whether they grazed their animals on public lands or private pastures in Grand Staircase and Escalante River country or elsewhere, small cattle operators were increasingly noncompetitive in a commodities marketplace that favored centralization. One Utah State University study found that "declining profitability of cattle ranching on both public and private lands, accompanied with increasing production costs, appears to represent the greatest threat to livestock grazing."[119]

Changing consumer preferences also have played a role in the decline of the beef industry. In 1937, during the Great Depression, Americans consumed 56 lb of beef per person each year. Forty years later in 1977, the amount consumed per capita peaked at 94.3 lb annually before beginning a precipitous freefall. Today, consumption is only about 55 lb per person. This amount is only slightly more than the 50 lb of pork per year consumed by every American and only a shadow of the nearly 97-lb-per-person consumption of chicken each year.[120]

Why the growing disparity? Economists point to two primary factors. First, increased health concerns over red meat (cholesterol and heart disease) prompted consumers to switch to fish and chicken. Second, the high cost of beef production has kept store prices high and consumers have opted for much less expensive alternatives such as pork and poultry. In fact, cattle are the most expensive stock to raise.[121]

The effect of global economics on U.S. beef production is not as clear-cut as the factors causing the sheep industry decline discussed earlier in this book. The United States is the world's largest beef producer and the largest exporter of beef. But it also imports significant quantities of beef. This seeming inconsistency rests in the quality of beef being produced. According to the U.S. Department of Agriculture, the vast majority of American beef is grain-fed, producing the highest quality cuts demanded not only by American consumers but by higher-end consumers in Mexico, Canada, and Asia. In contrast, beef imported to the United States consists primarily of lower-quality, grass-fed cattle used to make hamburger.[122]

A fact about cattle grazing on public rangelands, like those in the Grand Staircase and Escalante River country, is that these cows are grass-fed and are of lower quality with far less desirable fat covering (e.g., choice, select, standard, or commercial grades). Given that cattle are sold by weight, rangeland ranchers are therefore left with only two options. First, they can raise their animals to optimal weight and then sell their lower grade steers and heifers at much lower prices in direct competition with inexpensive foreign imports. Or alternately, they can sell their lighter-weight yearling calves to intermediaries, called "stockers," at a lower price because the animals have not achieved significant market weight. Cow-calf operations in southern Utah and northern Arizona almost exclusively reflect the second option.[123]

Although small, family-owned cattle ranchers have dwindled dramatically during the last half century in southern Utah, northern Arizona, and nationally, the beef industry thus has not suffered the same fate as the sheep industry. Given Americans' love of hamburgers, a similar collapse is probably not imminent. But two realities of today's consumer preferences are eerily similar to what befell the sheep industry. The first parallel is the nature of American meat consumption. Prior to World War II, mutton and lamb were staples in the American diet. After the war, no one seemed to want much to do with mutton. Consumer preferences quickly shifted to beef, a trend evidenced by the proliferation of fast-food hamburger chains across America such as McDonald's, founded in 1955. Americans nearly doubled their per-person consumption of beef in the decades after the war.

From 2000 to 2020, red meat consumption, which includes lamb and pork, has dropped by nearly a third as people took notice of health warnings that red meat contributes to certain cancers, kidney failure, diabetes, heart disease, and colon disease. Doctors now routinely recommend diets weighted far more towards fish and poultry, and a growing number of Americans are vegetarians or vegans, with 37 percent of adults indicating they always or sometimes eat vegetarian meals when dining out.[124] Not only are these options healthier, but also they are less expensive—itself a powerful economic motivator in consumer choices and one that does not portend well for the long-term viability of the beef industry.

The second parallel to what befell the sheep industry is changing consumer preferences regarding animal products for apparel. Animal hides for leather have traditionally been a valuable byproduct of beef processing, producing materials for shoes, furniture, automobile upholstery, wallets and purses, coats, and myriad other products. Many of the early industries in southern Utah's Kane and Garfield Counties derived from tannery products. But just as wool was replaced by synthetic fibers, leather is now being replaced by lesser-cost synthetics with comparable durability, easier maintenance, and broader consumer appeal. For example, athletic shoes (sneakers, tennis shoes, running shoes, basketball shoes, and even hiking shoes) are the best-selling footwear today with annual sales in the United States alone of $22.3 billion in 2023, but almost none of these contain leather. The trend away from leather products might seem to have little relevance to southern Utah and northern Arizona cow-calf operations. But even an indirect impact could facilitate even lower prices paid to cattle producers, and if the value to end-users is less, the prices paid at each intermediate level of the production process would also be lower. With the faded sheep industry as a backdrop, cattle ranching in the arid West faces an uncertain future.

FIGURE 7.1. Grosvenor Arch near Cannonville was an attraction largely unknown outside the local area. The designation of the Grand Staircase-Escalante National Monument in 1996 suddenly gave it a national audience. Photograph by Dan Bauer.

7 Monumental Changes, 1996–2022

On September 18, 1996, President William Jefferson Clinton stood on the South Rim of the Grand Canyon and, with a flowery speech and the stroke of a pen, issued Proclamation 6920 creating the 1.7-million-acre Grand Staircase-Escalante National Monument encompassing the lion's share of federal land in Kane and Garfield counties.[1] The Grand Canyon chasm that yawned behind his back provided a physical and symbolic safe haven for the president from locals in Utah outraged upon hearing about the declaration—in some cases, just hours before.

To southern Utahns, "locking up" these public lands was bad enough, but the fact that the president did not consult with local politicians beforehand—and, in fact, had worked in the shadows—went against a local sense of manhood and the Western way.[2] To many residents, especially Republicans, Clinton was living up to his reputation behind the nickname, "Slick Willy." As Vance Esplin, a former Kane County commissioner noted: "This whole thing burns me up. Clinton didn't even have enough guts to come up here. He stayed 70 miles away."[3] In Kanab, they served up "Clinton Burgers" made of "100 percent chicken." In Escalante, they burned both Clinton and his Secretary of Interior Bruce Babbitt in effigy on the town's Main Street. Babbitt, whose family owns a massive cattle operation in and around Flagstaff all the way to the Grand Canyon, was seen as the mastermind of the designation.[4] Indignant Utah politicians scrambled to find microphones, with powerful Senator Orrin Hatch calling the monument designation the "mother of all land grabs."[5]

According to the wording of the proclamation, the monument was created to protect geologic, paleontological, archaeological, and scenic treasures of national significance. But motivations were political as well, not the least of which was currying political favor among liberals and environmentalists in Clinton's rocky reelection bid. Clinton gave them what they wanted. In a speech later that day, he said, "I am concerned about a large coal mine proposed for the area. Mining jobs are good jobs, and mining is important to our national economy and to our national security. But we can't have mines everywhere, and we shouldn't have mines that threaten our national treasures."[6] The proclamation had, for all intents and purposes, killed yet another mining proposal, this one by the Dutch company Andalex Resources, to extract vast coal reserves on the Kaiparowits Plateau. And with the stroke of a pen, Clinton had quashed the dreams of Kane County residents for those good-paying mining jobs.[7]

By all accounts, the Clinton administration had expected fierce opposition from local residents and Utah's Republican delegation. But they also knew they had nothing to lose. Only a small number of rural Utahns ever voted Democratic in presidential elections and there was not a snowball's chance in Hades that Utah's Electoral College votes would ever swing in Clinton's favor anyway. The national monument designation did not help his cause in southern Utah—Clinton received only 298 votes in Kane County in 1996, compared to Republican Bob Dole's 1,653 and third-party candidate Ross Perot's 286.[8]

Clinton, however, really did not need or care to curry favor in southern Utah's red rock country. The Republican-dominated Utah delegation had opposed the Clinton administration at every turn, so there was no risk in thumbing his nose at Utah Republicans.[9] There was certainly confidence that the president's use of the Antiquities Act would weather any and all legal challenges, even if the new monument dwarfed in size any other single monument in the lower forty-eight states.[10] As legal scholar Eric C. Rusnak observed, "to date, it has been impossible, in the view of the courts, for a president to abuse his power under the Antiquities Act," because the act itself placed few limits on the president's authority.[11]

Local Republican leaders were not consulted as to plans for the new Grand Staircase-Escalante National Monument, but had they known more about the actual behind-the-scenes political intrigue they would have been even more angry. Years later, in a 2011 interview, well-known legal expert and writer, Charles Wilkinson, reported that he and a small group of fifteen people under John Leshy, solicitor for the Department of the Interior, were working on it in "absolute secret." Wilkinson personally loved the area and wanted to fulfil his dream of finally establishing the once-proposed and massive "Escalante National Monument" from a half century before. But as he recalled, "If Orrin Hatch had known . . . there wouldn't be a monument." In another interview in

FIGURE 7.2. With the Grand Canyon at his back, President Bill Clinton signs an executive order in 1996 creating the Grand Staircase-Escalante National Monument. Vice President Al Gore stands behind him. National Archives.

2015, Babbitt noted that Dick Morris, Clinton's poll-crazy advisor, was "looking for a big splash production at the front end of the '96 election" and polling told him that "soccer moms" were into the environment. Babbitt stated that President Clinton just decided he did not want a debate about the monument proposal and went forward in secrecy.[12]

As the plan for the monument went forward within the "top secret" group, Babbitt and others debated which agency would administer the new unit. Traditionally, national monuments were managed by the National Park Service. But attuned to the local sentiments from his own ranching heritage in the Southwest, Babbitt feared how this would be perceived. Another option would be the Bureau of Land Management, but he also questioned the wisdom of this possibility. As he recalled, "It was a very traditional place. Their traditional mission, as they see it, is collaboratory with the locals to maximize resources production . . . What, we can't cut timber anymore? No coal mines! And the ORV guys will be unhappy."[13]

Wilkinson remembered that Babbitt had the brilliant insight of a new conservation approach which he called "working landscapes." These protected lands would be under federal environmental protections while allowing some traditional economic uses. He recalled that neither agency was involved with the planning. Babbitt chose to have the BLM manage the new monument feeling local Utahns and Arizonans would be more comfortable with this arrangement. Wilkinson remembers that when they found out: "The Park Service was furious. To them, monuments are Park Service, not BLM." Babbitt later went on to establish a nongovernmental organization around his newly conceived "working landscapes" idea, with the group helping to draft the proposal for the controversial Bears Ears National Monument in nearby southeastern Utah in subsequent years.[14]

Following Babbitt's idea, President Clinton extended an olive branch, of sorts, to local residents by inserting language in the proclamation that guaranteed that traditional uses of federal lands within the BLM-administered monument would continue, and grazing was specifically identified as one of those uses. The proclamation specifies:

> Nothing in this proclamation shall be deemed to affect existing permits or leases for, or levels of, livestock grazing on Federal lands within the monument; existing grazing uses shall continue to be governed by applicable laws and regulations other than this proclamation.[15]

Also avoiding a potential sticking point, hunting was allowed in the monument, something that is quite rare in other parklands.

But such assurances were met with skepticism. Ranchers were only a few years removed from the "No Moo in '92" and "Cattle Free in '93" campaigns where conservationists had sought to remove all livestock from public ranges. Secretary Babbitt's 1995 rangeland reforms had left them seething at the top-down management approach to decisions they believed were best left to local managers. And a monument managed for protection could only mean one thing: the federal government had aligned itself with the hated environmentalists who demanded nothing short of a ban on livestock grazing on public lands.[16] Many southern Utah residents felt the designation was just another step towards complete eradication of their traditional way of life. Former Garfield County Commissioner Louise Liston summed up the local disgust at the time when she said:

> I think this land is going to be a victim. People will do a lot of damage that cattle and cowboys never did. You can't preserve this land and kick off the people. Rural values are the salvation of this country. I hate to see that go. We all do.[17]

With the establishment of the Grand Staircase-Escalante National Monument, rhetoric used by residents supporting traditional grazing (and other extractive industries) and environmentalists became increasingly polarized. Kane County Commissioner Joe Judd stated that a "war" was being waged against local residents by the federal government. Others pointed out correctly that the manner that the national monument was created was not in any way in keeping with the "democratic process." A pervasive belief in the region was that federal decision-makers cared little about local needs or concerns.[18] In a guest editorial in Kanab-based *Southern Utah News*, Dellas Sorensen, a Vietnam veteran, wrote that for the first time he could understand the domestic terrorist attack on the federal building in Oklahoma City, that he could see why people "consider the federal government the enemy." He noted that President Clinton had never set foot in Kane County and only listened to a small number of outsiders, "those who have never worked this land." He ended by saying, "today, I believe the newest and fastest growing religion in America is Radical Environmentalism; the Earth is their god, and their well-paid ministers cry, 'Save the earth, the plants, the animals,' while they sit under a tree and count the easy money."[19]

Others decried the loss of the aforementioned coal mine widely reported as having a $200 billion value, as well as future jobs from other extractive industries. Kanab resident JoAnne Honey highlighted another thread of discord that entered the debate, remarking on a man who supported the monument, "he, like many newcomers, are experts on how we should live."[20] Famed actor and environmental activist Robert Redford and the Sierra Club became favorite targets of attack for their roles in the monument's creation. Statements by some locals showed clear anti-intellectualism, their archconservative attacks on liberal academics harkening back to the era of Senator Joseph McCarthy in the 1950s.[21] Lingering resentment showed its face in rhetoric attacking outside experts in ivory towers with only book-learning and university degrees to their credit. In short order, the Kane County Commission passed a resolution against the monument, neatly summarizing the feelings of many in the county, saying they were against "its adverse effects on the people, lands, resources, economic stability, culture, and way of life of Kane County."[22]

As identified by environmental historian James R. Skillen, the West's latest "sagebrush rebellion" was well underway by 1996, in what he labeled "The War for the West." Clinton's one-sided declaration of the monument added fuel to its fired-up constituency. The Republican Party already was taking a hard right turn. After incumbent President George H. W. Bush's defeat in 1992 to what many perceived as an upstart Southern Democrat, many Republican leaders believed that they could not win with a moderate platform, such as that put forth by Bush. They instead embraced the tough rhetoric and often conspiratorial theories of leaders such as Georgia Congressman Newt Gingrich, who launched his "Contract with America" in 1994. Anger at a seemingly heavy-handed federal government inspired a conservative coalition that in spirit, and sometimes also in action, backed the Utah rebels against the new Grand Staircase-Escalante National Monument. Supporters included a broad swath of conservative Christians, Latter-day Saints, private property rights advocates, corporate leaders, gun rights supporters, and white nationalists against a "common" foe: environmentalists and their federal backers.[23]

While most conservative leaders in the "War for the West" were not averse to utilizing harsh language and linking tenuous causes to their campaigns, monument advocates also invoked inflammatory rhetoric and came out strongly against traditional land uses in southern Utah. Environmental activists, such as Babbitt, had shown no desire to work with local officials or Utah politicians, and their public words and actions admitted that fact. Ken Rait, a leader of SUWA, a local environmental organization which had filed lawsuits to stop the Andalex operation before the monument designation, accused "foreign mining" corporations of stripping national resources and leaving destruction behind.[24] Other groups decried coal-fired, air-polluting plants in Southern Utah and Northern Arizona that would merely provide electricity for urban sprawl in California. Rallying against Californians was seen as a way to gain local Utah support.

The environmental groups seemed to welcome the ranchers' incendiary rhetoric. An academic at the University of Utah admitted that the "Sagebrush Rebellion" screeds of local Utahns only served to pour money into the Sierra Club's fundraising campaigns.[25] The environmental debate became so polarized that many southern Utahns even opposed the generally popular reintroduction of the critically endangered California condor in southern Utah in subsequent years.[26] In the press, the only clear point of agreement between environmentalists and ranching interests in southern Utah was that both felt they were taking a stand on the Grand Staircase issue "for our children" and the "future."

Noted Western historian Richard White has written about a growing chasm that emerged in the 1970s between environmentalists and ranchers over different conceptions of work and ways of life. Livestock growers in rural environments felt increasingly besieged by urban environmentalists who, they knew, denigrated their working-class upbringing and ways of making a living, especially their often-gritty, dirty work with cows. Part of the cowboy identity in the West—and firmly established in southern Utah—is a pride in doing hard manual work with animals on rugged western lands. To ranchers and their admirers, this labor is seen as heroic, constructed as antithetical to white collar, urban work in sanitary high-rises.[27]

The subculture of the area, so influenced by Mormonism, also affected local opinion. The communal aspects of Mormon society and unique land stewardship ideals had largely been forgotten by the twentieth century, replaced by a zealous embrace of industriousness and devotion to hard work. Mormon leaders generally separated business issues from moral concerns, and widely embraced conservative politics.[28] As historian Jedediah Rogers concluded, modern environmental concerns were not widely embraced by church leaders. While teaching at Brigham Young University in the late 1990s, historian George B. Handley found that younger church members with environmental concerns often felt isolated in the church and uncomfortable in speaking out about conservation issues.[29]

Vocal outsiders who moved to southern Utah and espoused environmental causes were subjected to local harassment and even threats of violence. Julian Hatch, a person of Mormon heritage, moved to Boulder, Utah, in 1983. He formed the Boulder Regional Group and worked toward ending cattle trespass on town lands. He began to advocate that all cattle should be taken off Boulder Mountain, and that the government could pay to retire their allotments. These actions did not make Hatch welcome in the small town. He reported that when he went away for a week, he returned to find that someone had cut the fence enclosing his garden and that cows had destroyed it. He accused a local cattleman of driving his cows into the garden. According to Hatch, when a local lawman came to investigate, the officer said flatly that Hatch had cut the fence himself to incite conflict. The next week, the son of the accused rancher came up to Hatch in town and shot and killed his dog right in front of him. According to Hatch, he screamed, "This is what you get, environmentalist!"

Patrick Diehl—who holds degrees from the University of California-Berkeley, Harvard University, and Oxford University—also reported extreme abuse at the hands of area residents. When he and his partner Tori Woodard moved to Escalante in 1998, they at first were welcomed by the local Mormon-dominated community. He even sang in the Mormon Church choir. But once Diehl started speaking out against a proposed reservoir that would promote growth and against cattle grazing in Wilderness Areas, he felt people distancing themselves from him and his partner; when Diehl uttered the ultimate heresy—potentially draining Lake Powell, "immediately doors that had been open to us closed."[30] He reported that one night someone opened the irrigation pipe on his property and flooded an excavation site for his planned community for people suffering from chemical sensitivity. The local irrigation district then sued him for the value of the lost water. He spent thousands fighting this accusation in court, believing that locals were trying to drive him out of town. "The situation became one of profound hostility between the town and us," he noted. His front door was kicked in, his windows were smashed, and his phone lines were cut. He received death threats. Animosity ran so deep that Diehl felt that even local environmentalists distanced themselves from him, turning their backs on him and his partner.[31]

The monument issue is often disguised by secular language that pits the ranching industry and conservative values against liberal politics. But Mormon culture itself not only buttressed opposition to the monument, but also to land management efforts that predated the designation of Grand Staircase-Escalante National Monument. After conducting a major study of environmental politics in Utah and Colorado up to 1993, geographer John B. Wright wrote that, "Mormon theology has made Utah the most arduous cultural terrain in the Rocky Mountain West for land conservationists." He finds that the people's emphasis on an impending second coming of Christ has thwarted long-range planning. According to Wright, Latter-day Saints await a "Millennial rescue" when God will return to earth and rule as a divine monarch. In the process, God will perfect the land of Zion and rule for a thousand years. Utah will be remade into paradise for the Saints. Many modern Mormons believe that large families, boundless economic expansion, and personal accumulation of wealth are signs to God that they are true believers. Any party that argues against these beliefs, or wants to place limits on them, is contravening these deeply-held religious tenets. If a politician in the state dared to advocate limits on these traditions, it would amount to political suicide.[32]

Seen as self-righteous outsiders, many local Mormons view environmentalists as a serious threat to their religious values and way of life. And thus it is no surprise that southern Utahns espoused antienvironmental views in protests over the land grab involving the monument. In 1996, Honey, mentioned previously, wrote a letter to the Kanab newspaper stating: "The environmentalists must be a different breed than the rest of us. We have to work for a living—to buy food and other necessities, but they only work to destroy our country ... is it possible they can live off scenery?"[33] To local stock raisers and their friends, out-of-town environmentalists and tourists were elites with loads of cash to spread around, interested in their home simply as "landscapes of leisure," an envisioned "Garden of Eden" that never was.

One guiding question cannot be easily answered but nonetheless has inflamed debates surrounding who has the best claim to the public lands in the West. Locals in southern Utah believe that first claim to use the land belongs to them as they are fifth and sixth generation ranchers descended from "pioneer ancestors." As previously noted, this issue was not a major problem during the years that public land agencies worked closely with permit-holders to make decisions. But with the multiple use philosophy and a BLM-managed national monument, locals felt even more threatened by outside forces potentially deciding what was the best use of their home country.

Many Kane County residents also expressed valid concerns that the monument designation would only increase visitor traffic and actually hurt the environment. This claim was made in the age before the Internet. But since the early 2000s, photo posts on the Internet have led to a deluge of visitors throughout southern Utah and Arizona in once-hidden places. Many people clearly believed that calling their home country a "national monument" only promised a surge in tourists. Ron Hamblin of southern Utah wrote to the Kanab paper: "Which is worse—a coal mine on the Kaiparowits Plateau, or a visitor's center, large over-crowded campgrounds, RV dumps, millions of visitors, more roads and trails, etc ... since when has the Park Service ever preserved an area?"[34] Today's visitors to congested Zion National Park would have a hard time arguing with some of Hamblin's points. Closer to the Grand Staircase-Escalante National Monument, a once obscure sandstone formation known as "The Wave" on the Utah-Arizona border east of Kanab brought a throng of visitors attracted by Internet posts. In late December 2017, rangers reported that one day 400 people applied to visit the site, while only ten permits were issued. That year alone, 160,000 people applied for permits to visit "The Wave," although only a few thousands received one.[35]

Right after the monument was declared, a group calling itself the Western States Coalition announced plans to sue the Clinton Administration, saying it violated the 1906 Antiquities Act's mandate to set aside the "smallest area" possible and that the president had acted unilaterally without local input.[36] Throughout 1996, some coalition members hurled insults at Clinton and Babbitt. The coalition hosted a summit in Salt Lake City in late 1996, with more than 250 lawmakers, loggers, ranchers, and others in attendance.[37]

In contrast to the prevailing local concerns was a growing caucus of powerful environmental groups, buoyed by a largely supportive public, that backed efforts to create public lands safeguards. A 1993 study of people in western Colorado, itself a far cry from being a hotbed of environmental activism, showed that 60 percent of respondents believed that ranchers had "overgrazed" the public lands. According to 86 percent of those surveyed, water quality had declined on the western ranges, while 34 percent said that public grazing should be banned.[38]

Although local ranchers felt like they were the victims of public policy generated outside the region, many backers of environmental preservation felt the opposite. A 1999 study conducted by the BLM on the Grand Staircase-Escalante National Monument found that many respondents viewed local ranchers as part of a "special interest" group that was favored by federal policy, and the group's "special uses" were not good for the land.[39] This perception tied into long-held American beliefs that the public lands should be for the "little man" and not special interests. Many felt that agencies such as the BLM were in the pocket of local resource users, not regulating them effectively and providing "welfare" through low fees.[40]

To view "the environmentalists" as a monolithic group is an error. Great differences exist among various groups and individuals. Many activists disagree about how to preserve the awe-inspiring landscapes and diverse ecology of Grand Staircase and Escalante River country. One example is the "Cattle Free" movement so despised by many in southern Utah. As historian Mike Hudak notes, SUWA was not a vocal supporter of Patrick Diehl's efforts to have cattle removed from wilderness areas.

On the other hand, the Grand Canyon Trust accelerated its own campaign to remove cattle from fragile Colorado Plateau landscapes by purchasing grazing permits from willing sellers and then working with BLM to permanently "retire" the permits. However, when the Grand Canyon Trust purchased grazing permits inside the new monument, local ranchers and county commissioners struck back in the courts. In a nutshell, they argued that grazing permits could not be permanently retired, and if unused they can be claimed by other ranchers. In response, the Grand Canyon Trust purchased cattle to graze the disputed allotments, and as Raymond B. Wrabley, a political scientist at the University of Pittsburgh, wrote: "they were now in the livestock business." Utah State Representative Mike Noel, summarized the irony of it all: "We turned them from environmentalists into cowboys. I guess what they can do is get their cows and start losing money like the rest of us."[41]

The Grand Staircase-Escalante National Monument proclamation specifically guaranteed that existing grazing leases would be respected, but few local ranchers trusted government promises. As the years passed under BLM management, many ranchers came to the conclusion that regulations were aimed at running them off the land. Hal Hamblin, a fifth-generation stock raiser out of Kanab, was one of them. He asserted that the issue had more to do with restrictions on rangeland "improvements" than it did in limiting herd sizes. In 2015, he told a reporter that he still has the same number of permits on the Grand Staircase-Escalante National Monument, but he is only able to run about one-half the number of cattle that he did before 1996.

In the short term, Hamblin felt that "the rules and regulations that they've put in place are destroying the land." He added that he could not make "improvements" such as moving water lines that disperse cattle and reduce localized overgrazing. Hamblin also noted that he could not cut cedar posts to fence off sensitive riparian areas or use machinery to remove brush to improve water flows.[42] Adding urgency to the rumors the federal government wanted ranchers off the land, in 2015 Utah Senator Orrin Hatch claimed the BLM was considering eliminating grazing completely on monument lands and vowed to fight that policy.[43]

Many environmentalists, however, rejected ranchers' arguments that they improve range conditions in southern Utah. Jim Catlin, a Sierra Club volunteer and director emeritus of the Wild Utah Project, told a reporter in 2015: "there has been a lack of stewardship on their part." Catlin further questioned ranchers' continuing place on the fragile landscape. He noted that livestock raisers now were a minority in the region and had a small economic impact. He also echoed other environmentalists' arguments that cattle were very destructive to the land, eradicating plants, degrading soils, and trampling riparian areas.[44]

A long-time coach at Tropic's high school who received his education degree from Brigham Young University in the early 1960s, Clare Ramsay still ran cattle after the Grand Staircase-Escalante National Monument was created. When he was interviewed in 2004 in the midst of an epic drought that gripped the region (and grew worse into 2022), he recognized multiple factors that were negatively impacting the cattle industry. "This drought has really hurt people," he said. "It's caused them to cut back on their numbers and the feed isn't good." He noted that many ranchers just sold out and got out of the business. As he related:

> The other thing that's discouraged a lot of people, a lot of us, is the dealings with the federal government. The BLM and the Forest Service have been hard to live with on a number of issues and seems like they're just looking for excuses to move people off the range.

Ramsay felt that the agencies made too many cutbacks on grazing permits, largely to push their weight around. "They want to let you know they're in control of things," he said.

Ramsay and others blamed politicians, especially state politicians' failure to seek input from locals, as a major factor contributing to the region's economic hardships. He further noted:

> This dog-gone monument got created and that further hurt us. Then our governor got with Bruce Babbitt, the secretary of the interior, and hurt us further when he traded out those state sections so he traded out 176,000 acres in Garfield and Kane counties. That hurt to lose those state sections. It hurt especially in that we have no chance now of development. If there's any methane gas or coal or anything out there that could and would develop someday, it's tied up now.

Ramsay had heard that county commissioners had been working with an energy company to potentially exploit gas resources east of the Cockscomb, and then Utah Governor Mike Leavitt and federal officials working with him on issues regarding state lands inside the new monument just pulled the rug out on them without any warning.[45]

The Great Drought

By happenstance, the creation of the Grand Staircase-Escalante National Monument coincided with the beginning of the worst drought to hit the Southwest since the late AD 1500s, worse than the droughts of the Dust Bowl era and the Great Depression.[46] In 1996, grass was sparse across the West, springs dried up, and ranchers dumped their inventories, creating a market glut that lowered cattle prices. Ranchers everywhere were devastated as the drought refused to loosen its grip for nearly nine years. The U.S. Department of Agriculture Economic Research Service summarized the drought in clinical terms.

> Dry conditions that began in 1996 and persisted from 1998 through 2003 held down the retention of heifers until forage conditions improved. By late 2003 and 2004, grazing conditions had improved and ended a nine-year cyclical liquidation of cattle inventories. This change, together with strong feeder calf prices, began the process of herd expansion through the addition of heifers and calves. The expansion lasted until 2007; then inventories began declining because of increasing feed and energy prices.[47]

Rangelands in the monument were especially hard-hit, and ranchers scrambled to sell their herds. In Garfield County, the number of cows fell by 38 percent between 1997 and 2002 to its lowest level since 1930. In Kane County, the cow population fell by 24 percent to the lowest point since 1982, and before that since 1940. Cattle numbers have been inching upward since 2002, but have yet to recover to pre-drought levels reported in the 1997 U.S. Agricultural Census, even as market conditions and herd sizes have improved nationally. This slow recovery stoked recurrent fears that once grazing was voluntarily reduced to accommodate drought-stricken rangelands, then federal managers would never allow herd sizes to rise to pre-drought levels. Many Americans have been keen on conspiracy theories, and some local ranchers were sure there was an ultimate-but-secret Washington agenda to eliminate grazing altogether.

Lonnie Pollack, who ranches in the Grand Staircase-Escalante National Monument, provides a local perspective on the the waves of drought. In 2003, he stated in an interview:

> About twenty years ago my brother and I decided to delve into the cow business a little bit because we like it and like the lifestyle and thought it might be something to work at . . . That was the plan, but the drought, and oh, restrictions, and prices and things complicate that a little bit.

He also reported on the ongoing dry conditions.

> It's like this drought, we've sold off about 60 to 70 percent of our cattle and you try to hang on to a few so that when you bring new cattle in and hopefully if the drought ends that those other cattle can take your new cattle and teach them your range.[48]

A public relations blunder in 2000 did nothing to alleviate those concerns. Responding to the persistent drought and a flurry of rangeland fires, monument manager Kate Cannon ordered ranchers on the Kaiparowits Plateau to remove their livestock earlier in the season than their grazing permits required. Of the 116 permit-holders, all but three complied. Three permittees—Quinn Griffith, his uncle Gene, and Mary Bulloch—refused. They disagreed vehemently with the BLM's assessment that the droughts had exhausted the range. When they remained defiant, federal employees in November of that year rounded up the trespassing livestock and impounded them at an auction house in Salina in central Utah. Outraged at this federal "atrocity," a group of ranchers "rustled back" the cattle as the Sevier County sheriff looked on, unwilling or unable to do anything to stop them.[49]

The standoff over the Kaiparowits cattle seemed to confirm many ranchers' worst fears. The incident elevated the already-inflammatory local rhetoric to a fevered pitch that federal authorities were implementing their plan to end grazing. The talk obscured the fact that 97.4 percent of permittees complied with the government's request to remove livestock earlier than normal. They might not have agreed with the rangeland assessments, but they could not deny that springs had dried up and the ground was parched. Even some locals rolled their eyes at the antics of the most vociferous protesters, although most agreed in principle. When Mary Bulloch drove around town with the severed head of one of her cows in her pickup, her fellow grazers certainly felt sympathy, as well as agreed that the new breed of federal managers who accompanied the monument designation were not their friends and allies.[50]

Cannon acknowledged at the time that the situation had escalated far beyond what it should have, wincing that this particular controversy became a "line in the sand" regarding the future of grazing in the monument. Cannon insisted she had extended deadlines, hauled feed and water on the ranchers' behalf, and offered other assistance that was rejected. According to her, Bulloch and the others still defied the orders to remove the livestock. The monument manager believed she had no other choice but to impound the cattle. As she told the *Denver Post,* "it's the job of the BLM to be the caretaker of the land, to manage grazing so the land remains healthy and productive for all uses."[51]

Cannon's increasingly antagonistic relationship with local ranchers underscored larger trends occurring within the BLM. As early as the 1930s, grazing agencies were hiring more and more employees trained at colleges in scientific range management and related fields. Because they lived in isolated rural communities, they developed "cozy" relationships nonetheless with local stock raisers they ostensibly were there to regulate and oversee. The birth of "multiple use" principles in the 1960s had strained these relationships. By the 1990s, employees of both the U.S. Forest Service and BLM increasingly came not from local communities, but as geographer Paul Starrs says, were "enthusiastic city people" who were college-educated but lacked any grounding in the "cowboy culture" of places like southern Utah. These nonlocals were largely pragmatic and diplomatic in temperament, not crusaders or activists, but as the cultural lines were drawn, they increasingly found themselves at odds with the people with whom they lived and worked.[52]

Even so, some ranchers like Pollack tried to take a balanced approach to BLM oversight. He reported that in the first years since the monument's designation, ranchers found it hard to operate because of uncertainty about the new management. But as he remarked in 2003, "actually, at the local level they've been pretty darn good to work with. Our local managers and range techs have been real understanding and helpful and tried to help us out." He does worry about what he refers to as "the big bureaucracy," lamenting that "there's a lot more paperwork" with complying with the Endangered Species Act and other laws and regulations.[53]

As the culture wars heated up, cattle populations in both counties plummeted by a third during the drought years of 1997 to 2003 before recovering somewhat by 2012. With the exception of a few single years, the 2012 combined Kane-Garfield cattle population of 25,899 was still the lowest it had been since 1950. Ranchers attributed this slow recovery to the unwillingness of federal land managers to allow full use of permits, a pattern evident not only in Grand Staircase but throughout the West. During testimony to a congressional oversight committee, Randy Parker, CEO of the Utah Farm Bureau Federation, decried the "slow, methodical and systematic attack on critical multiple use components and functions that underpin successful family livestock ranches on public lands." One product of the anti-grazing federal agenda, he asserted, has been that "cuts in grazing permits and the federal agencies abusing nonuse and suspended-use classification for reducing livestock grazing AUMs has [sic] become far too commonplace in Utah and across the West."[54]

Ranch Consolidation: Farm Size Matters

As discussed in Chapter 6, a trend emerged in the decades after World War II with fewer and fewer families involved in cattle ranching, but having larger and larger herds. This shift seems to have continued after the 1996 creation of Grand Staircase-Escalante National Monument, although there are subtle differences between what happened in Garfield County and Kane County. In Kane County, thirteen households heavily depended on cattle ranching as reported on the 1997 U.S. Census of Agriculture.[55] By 2012, the total had dropped by more than half to only six cow farms. During that same period, the number of cattle in Kane County fell by 21 percent. This decrease probably reflected the aforementioned drought conditions where the larger operators (200 or more head) reduced their herds, and medium-sized (50–199 head) and small ranches (less than 50 head) reduced or suspended operations due to the high cost of providing feed during that period.[56]

Garfield County appears to have been much more dependent on cattle ranching than Kane County with more than double the number of cows. Again, the largest cattle operators were responsible for most of the cattle production. Thirty-six large operators owned 62 percent of the cattle in 1997; by 2012, that number fell to only eighteen large operators (12 percent of all cow farms), but these were responsible for 78 percent of all cattle in the county (see Table 7.1).

Overall, apart from any potential issues related to Grand Staircase-Escalante National Monument, ranch consolidation continued apace. A closer review of cow farms by herd size reveals that the percentage of large operators and medium-sized operators also has steadily declined in both counties since 1996. In Kane County, these operations constituted 42 percent of all cow farms in the 1997 census. By 2012, they represented just 32 percent.

In Garfield County, large- and medium-sized operators represented 43 percent of all cow farms in 1997; by 2012 this number had fallen to 28 percent. During that same period of time, the cattle herds owned by those large and medium-size operators in Garfield County increased by more than one thousand head, a 9 percent rise over 1997 levels. In short, there were fewer ranch

TABLE 7.1. Numbers for Largest Cattle Producers for 1992–2012.

Largest Cattle Operations					
Kane County			**Garfield County**		
1992	Total primary farms	13	1992	Total primary farms	33
	Percent of total cow farms	12		Percent of total cow farms	18
	Total cattle	5,321		Total cattle	14,576
	Percent of total cattle	55		Percent of total cattle	62
1997	Total primary farms	13	1997	Total primary farms	36
	Percent of total cow farms	12		Percent of total cow farms	25
	Total cattle	5,361		Total cattle	12,603
	Percent of total cattle	51		Percent of total cattle	58
2002	Total primary farms	10	2002	Total primary farms	17
	Percent of total cow farms	13		Percent of total cow farms	11
	Total cattle	n/a		Total cattle	8,066
	Percent of total cattle	n/a		Percent of total cattle	61
2007	Total primary farms	8	2007	Total primary farms	13
	Percent of total cow farms	9		Percent of total cow farms	8
	Total cattle	4,082		Total cattle	9,160
	Percent of total cattle	60		Percent of total cattle	60
2012	Total primary farms	6	2012	Total primary farms	18
	Percent of total cow farms	5		Percent of total cow farms	12
	Total cattle	n/a		Total cattle	13,746
	Percent of total cattle	n/a		Percent of total cattle	78

Note: Data derived from agricultural census reports from 1992 to 2012, available at the USDA Census of Agriculture Historical Archive.

families but just as many or more cattle. Complete census data for Kane County is lacking, but in Garfield County 12 percent of cattle ranches now produce 78 percent of the cattle. A similar trend is likely for its neighbor to the south.

The agricultural census data also point to another trend that has emerged since the monument's creation—so-called "hobby ranches" that have proliferated in southern Utah and most of the American West. These very small ranches get their name because the size of the herds is never sufficient to sustain a family, but livestock sales can supplement income from nonagricultural sectors. Hobby ranches also can provide beef for personal consumption, sales to family and neighbors, and sales in the growing niche market for organic grass-fed beef. Hobby ranches are viable if the owner has enough private pasture, but become less so if the ranchers have to lease pastures and purchase hay.[57] Many of these "hobbyists" raise cattle for the prestige involved, so that they can claim to be cowboys and become part of a storied tradition and lore of the Old West.[58] For this study, a "hobby ranch" is any operation with fewer than fifty cows.

TABLE 7.2. Percentage of Cow Farms by Size per County.

Kane County Cow Farms by Size (Percentages)					
Census Year	**1992**	**1997**	**2002**	**2007**	**2012**
Hobby ranches (1–49)	54	59	57	70	68
Subsistence ranches (50–199)	34	29	30	19	27
Primary ranches (200+)	12	13	13	11	6

Kane County Cattle by Farm Size (Percentages)					
Census Year	**1992**	**1997**	**2002**	**2007**	**2012**
Hobby ranches (1–50)	10	14	n/a	18	18
Subsistence ranches (51–199)	35	34	30	22	22
Primary ranches (200+)	55	51	n/a	60	60

Garfield County Farms by Size (Percentages)					
Census Year	**1992**	**1997**	**2002**	**2007**	**2012**
Hobby ranches (1–50)	43	47	63	64	73
Subsistence ranches (51–199)	38	36	26	28	16
Primary ranches (200+)	18	17	12	8	12

Garfield County Cattle by Farm Size (Percentages)					
Census Year	**1992**	**1997**	**2002**	**2007**	**2012**
Hobby ranches (1–50)	7	10	13	12	10
Subsistence ranches (51–199)	31	33	32	28	12
Primary ranches (200+)	62	58	69	60	78

Note: Data derived from agricultural census reports from 1992 to 2012, available at the USDA Census of Agriculture Historical Archive.

In Kane County, the total number of cow farms actually increased from 107 in 1997 to 116 in 2012, even as the number of larger operators declined. In 1996, the hobby rancher constituted 54 percent of all Kane County cow farms. By 2012, it had risen to 68 percent. While many were operated by longtime ranching families, two out of every three cattle operations in Kane County were "hobby ranches," or small, part-time affairs that represented a small contribution to the family income (see Table 7.2).[59]

In Garfield County, the shift to small hobby ranching is even more striking. In 1997, about 47 percent of all cow farms were small-time affairs with fifty cows or fewer. By 2012, almost three out of every four cow farms (73 percent) could be considered a hobby ranch where livestock sales merely supplemented outside income. Hobby ranchers owned 10 percent of the total cattle population in Garfield County in 1996 and 2012. The actual number of hobby ranches, however, increased from 101 cow farms in 1997 to 111 in 2012, a modest 10 percent increase. This trend also suggests that growth in cattle numbers in Garfield County was primarily concentrated among the largest operators.

While not a flashpoint as important to locals as the Grand Staircase-Escalante National Monument, they warily eye a growing number of subdivisions and "ranchettes" as an impending threat to traditional ways of life. Throughout the West, scholars have noted the ill effects of this phenomenon. Scientists are in agreement that land carved into 1–10 acre ranchettes is far more detrimental to ecology than traditional ranching (if managed correctly). Ranchette subdivisions perhaps appear semi-"open" and "natural," apart from various cabins and vacation homes that dot these developments, but the human presence impoverishes wildlife, both in the number of species and actual numbers of animals except for a few human-adapted animals like raccoons and sparrows that thrive among people. These developments negatively impact movement of species, wildlife's access to water sources, and native plant diversity. They also help spread invasive plant species and disturb wild animals through pet activity.[60] Oscar Judd, who has ranched east of Kanab for decades, worries about the impacts of new subdivisions on his livelihood. In 2004, he noted the incursion of several larger subdivisions at Elk Ridge and the Divide with big wells. "If they hit the aquifer then they will keep draining it," and it will dry up his reservoir, he said.[61]

Economic Engine or Grand Illusion?

The economic impact of cattle ranching has been analyzed in myriad professional and general interest publications with pro-industry forces marshaling economists on their side and environmental groups doing the same on their side. The result of these various studies is bewildering, to say the least, because the methodologies are different and certain economic assumptions used in the models are suspect.[62] It is also beyond the scope of this history to develop our own model to tease out the economic importance of cattle ranching to local economies. Instead, this analysis relies exclusively on U.S. Census of Agriculture data from 1992 (four years before the monument designation) to 2012, a twenty-year span.

As already established, this period includes a great drought that began in 1996 and continues into 2022 when ranchers throughout the West liquidated a good share of their inventory and prices were low. Scientists now recognize that 1996 was the beginning of a much more serious "megadrought" that impacts much of the American Southwest, caused in large part by the effects of man-made climate change resulting from carbon emissions.[63]

Census data include the total number of cattle sold during the previous year in each individual county, as well as the total value of those sales. These statistics allowed us to arrive at a *relative* per animal value (total value divided by cattle sold). This relative value also permits us to calculate the relative wealth of ranch operations in the region. For example, at $770 per head, the value of Garfield County cattle herds in 2012 would have been $13.6 million. The average value per cow in Kane County was slightly less, but the total value of the herds there in 2012 was about $6.2 million. Each county is discussed separately below.

Kane County has far fewer cow farms, typically half, than Garfield County. The cattle sales and total value of cattle in Kane County is but a shadow compared to its neighbor to the north. In the 1992 census, 9,603 cattle were reported in the county divided among 106 cow farms, or an average of ninety-one cows per farm. A total of 4,543 cows were sold, generating $6.4 million in revenue, with cattle on average bringing $450 per head. Five years later, at the beginning

TABLE 7.3. Total Cattle and Total Cattle Sold from 1992–2012.

Kane County Cattle and Sales Revenue							
Census Year	Total Cow Farms	Total Cows	Average Per Farm	Total Cows Sold	Value of Sales ($)	Per Cow Price ($)	Inventory Value ($)
1992	106	9,603	91	4543	2,039,000	450	4,321,000
1997	107	10,436	98	5581	2,572,000	460	4,801,000
2002	79	7,920	100	6839	3,182,000	465	3,683,000
2007	91	6,786	75	5564	2,398,000	430	2,918,000
2012	116	8,213	71	5021	3,749,000	745	6,119,000
Garfield County Cattle and Sales Revenue							
Census Year	Total Cow Farms	Total Cows	Average Per Farm	Total Cows Sold	Value of Sales ($)	Per Cow Price ($)	Inventory Value ($)
1992	182	23,525	129	13,743	6,338,00	460	10,822,000
1997	213	21,791	102	11,017	4,828,000	440	9,588,000
2002	145	13,214	91	11,831	4,952,000	420	5,550,000
2007	159	15,326	96	7,293	4,623,000	635	9,732,000
2012	153	17,717	116	10,425	8,012,000	770	13,642,000

Note: Data derived or averages calculated from agricultural census reports from 1992 to 2012, available at the USDA Census of Agriculture Historical Archive.

of the mega-drought, 10,436 cattle were divided among 107 cow farms, or an average of ninety-eight cows per farm. A total of 5,581 cows were sold, generating roughly $2.6 million, with cattle on average bringing $460 per head. In effect, there was little difference in number of animals or their value in the years leading up to the drought (see Table 7.3).

By 2002, the cattle numbers reflected a sell-off of inventory, as ranchers were doing across the West. Kane County had far fewer cattle with only 7,920 reported in the 2002 census, a 24 percent decline from five years before, and the number of cattle sold at market was 6,839, or 23 percent more. These sales generated $3.2 million in revenue to Kane County ranchers, with cattle bringing an on-average price of $465 per head. In 2007, after several years of lessened drought, total cattle populations continued to decline another 14 percent. Cattle sales also declined by 19 percent, with revenues dropping to $2.4 million as average cattle prices fell to $430 per head. Little evidence supports that Kane ranchers were rebuilding their herds. Instead, they were shedding inventory in the face of low cattle prices and a resurgence of severe drought conditions after 2007.

By 2012, cattle populations had surged to their highest level since 1997 with 8,213 cows reported at 116 cow farms, or an average of seventy-one cows per farm, a number still far below what it had been before the drought years. But cattle prices had rebounded remarkably. Kane County cattle sales in 2012 were 10 percent less compared to five years before, but the average price per cow had risen 73 percent to $745, generating 56 percent more revenue to ranchers than in previous years.

In summary, the value of Kane County cattle sales over the twenty years considered here ranges from $2 million to $3.7 million annually. In theory, with the higher cattle prices evident in 2012, even small operators selling off only twenty-five or so head could generate nearly $20,000 in revenue to supplement outside family incomes. In bad years, the same operator would generate about half that amount. Census data also indicates that farming is very expensive in Kane County, with the average dollar amount of expenses per farm more than doubling since 1992, and in one instance in 2007, nearly tripling.

In this light, Kane County farmers have rarely made enough money to support a family on farming income alone. But things have gotten worse for many ranchers in the past twenty years. As production expenses have risen, average

TABLE 7.4. Farm Expenses and Net Income by County.

Kane County Farm Expenses and Net Income		
Census	Average Per Farm Expenses ($)	Per Farm Average Net Income ($)
1992	17,785	4,195
1997	16,305	3,854
2002	26,885	1,711
2007	68,660	21
2012	44,602	−3851
Garfield County Farm Expenses and Net Income		
Census	Average Per Farm Expenses ($)	Per Farm Average Net Income ($)
1992	28,025	4,711
1997	23,761	1,467
2002	29,659	−6926
2007	32,219	−6067
2012	44,602	658

Note: Averages calculated from USDA Census of Agriculture Historical Archive report data from 1992 to 2012.

net income per farm has declined to the point that the average farm in Kane County now loses almost $4,000 a year (see Table 7.4 above).[64]

The Kane County experience plays out similarly in Garfield County, but on a larger scale. In 1992, before the drought, 23,529 total cows were divided among 182 cow farms, or an average of 129 cows per farm. The census also reported 13,743 cows had been sold at an average price of $460 per cow, generating $6.4 million in revenue to ranchers. Five years later, at the beginning of the drought, slightly fewer cows (21,791) were divided among more cow farms, which reduced the average number of cows per farm to 102. Twenty percent fewer cattle were sold in 1997, all at a lower average price, and total revenues to Garfield ranchers dropped by 24 percent to $4.8 million (see Tables 7.3 and 7.4).

The 2002 census reflects a massive sell-off of Garfield County cattle. Total cattle populations here decreased by 39 percent to 13,214, with the number of cattle sold at market increasing 23 percent. More cattle were sold but cattle prices remained low, averaging $420 per cow, and the total revenue to Garfield ranchers was just under $5 million (only slightly more than it had been five years before). Cattle prices rebounded in 2007 (earlier than in Kane County) to an average per-cow price of $635. By 2012, it had soared to an average of $770 per cow. The 2007 census data suggest that total cattle populations had increased by 6 percent and that ranchers were rebuilding their herds overall. Total revenue to Garfield ranchers in 2007 was $4.6 million.

By 2012, Garfield ranchers were taking full advantage of higher cattle prices and selling off stock. Total cattle populations continued to increase another 16 percent over 2007, at the same time that the number of cattle sold increased by 43 percent. Higher cattle prices produced a record windfall of $8 million in local revenue, most of which went to the largest cattle operators, who owned 78 percent of the cattle in Garfield County at the time. In theory, all cow farms should have enjoyed the higher cattle prices, but in the census data, net farm income for the *entire* county was reported at $184,000 with the average farm earning only $658. Still, the prices were quite an improvement over 2007 when local ranchers lost a combined $1.7 million and the farmers lost on average just over $6,000 (see Table 7.4).

In summary, Garfield County cattle numbers rebounded somewhat since 2004 even as drought conditions worsened. But as of 2012, they had yet to return to 1997 levels. Cattle sales in 2012, however, were near 1997 levels, and 2012 cattle prices were 75 percent greater. Despite these increased cattle prices, Garfield ranchers, who reported losing money in 2002 and 2007, turned only a small net profit in 2012 with the average net income of $658 per farm. This income was barely breaking even. As in Kane County, increased production costs seem to have eroded any gains brought by increased cattle prices. In fact, expenses in 2012 were nearly 60 percent higher than they were twenty years before.

Ranchers cite several reasons for the increased production costs, including purchasing hay and leasing pastures during drought conditions, increased transportation costs, and higher equipment costs. They also point to investments in range improvements and higher grazing fees on non-BLM lands. Some of these costs were offset by federal subsidies and drought relief payments. In Kane County, the average farmer might have lost $3,851 in 2012, but federal payments averaged $11,283 and resulted in a per farm net profit of $7,432. In Garfield County, as noted above, the average farmer made a net return of $658 per farm, and when that figure is added to federal subsidies averaging $5,125, the profit actually totaled $5,783. In neither case would this amount of profit be sufficient to raise a family on farm income alone. Federal subsidies quantified in the censuses are summarized in Table 7.5.

TABLE 7.5. Per Farm Average Federal Subsidies

Per Farm Average Federal Subsidies		
Census	**Kane County ($)**	**Garfield County ($)**
2002	8,799	3,270
2007	12,044	6,932
2012	11,283	5,125

Note: Data from agricultural census reports from 2002, 2007, and 2012, available at the USDA Census of Agriculture Historical Archive.

Sacred Cows, Sacred Lands

Scholars and journalists who have reported on grazing after the creation of the monument in 1996 have noted the ongoing, vitriolic mudslinging by both sides in the battle over cattle grazing on these lands. Even so, ranchers and environmentalists have more in common than is generally acknowledged. Both cattle growers and conservationists tend to be idealistic, with a hint of romanticism, with a deep connection to the strange and haunting landscapes of southern Utah.

When Clinton unilaterally designated the Grand Staircase-Escalante National Monument, the rhetoric coming from southern Utah made it seem as if violent conflict might erupt. After twenty-five years of BLM management under the "working landscapes" concept, however, residents of the area had settled into a begrudging acceptance of the monument. But when Republican President Donald Trump signed an executive order vastly reducing the size of the Grand Staircase-Escalante National Monument, while gutting the Obama-era Bears Ears National Monument in southeast Utah, local politicians in Kane and Garfield counties and the entire Republican-dominated Utah congressional delegation cheered. Traditional dreams resurfaced of cash-generating coal mines, oil and gas development, and lands opened to less-regulated grazing. Local politicians had lobbied for these reductions, so the Trump actions were no accident. However, the joy that met his executive orders revealed that simmering anger and resentment over the monument still ran strong.

Desmond Twitchell, who was about eighty years old when he was interviewed in 2001, echoed this resentment. He noted that he got a permit to run cattle on Sheep Flat years before. "At that time, it would not support 50 head of cattle," Twitchell told an interviewer, adding that his outfit took out pinyon and juniper and cleared brush "and planted some new grasses, crested wheat grass, now it will support up to 500 head." Yet, as he says, "the environmentalists say that we are not doing the right thing. They say it is being depleted. The livestock should be taken off." Twitchell felt that the big issue is that environmentalists do not live in the area and see it as some sort of "Wild West." He added, "the environmentalists say they want to save it for future generations; well they don't even think about our generations."

Twitchell's opinions touch upon some of the central issues in ongoing rancorous debates about public lands. He said:

> We would like to maintain it for ourselves and pass it to the future generations. But that is not the idea of some of these environmentalists. They come from back east, most of them. They got their education from these books and people back there.

As Twitchell concludes: "They come out here and try to change our methods of doing things. Their methods are not as good as ours, as far as I am concerned."[65]

Seemingly influenced by Edward Abbey's monkey-wrenching idea, some activisits have done more than just donate funds for new parklands. Twitchell told an interviewer he has seen actual destruction, and he still feared violence in 2001. "They have proven that some of the environmentalists have shot a lot of cattle, burned some of the cabins," he said. Like many rural Westerners, he views environmentalists and ecotourists as either young, fit, and idealistic or older elitists with no regard for local residents' livelihoods. According to Twitchell:

> They want to throw this wide open for the few people who come in here with a pack on their back and hike around . . . if it goes through like they want it to with closing all the roads and what not . . . there are not too many people that [can] walk" into these places.[66]

Twitchell references a still-ongoing source of controversy over Grand Staircase-Escalante National Monument and other public lands in the region: the closure of roads and declaration of wilderness areas. If local county commissioners could not prevent the establishment of Grand Staircase-Escalante National Monument, they could at least hold out for possibilities for future development in the area, and that meant keeping existing roads open. In a more immediate sense, roads made ranching easier. Kane County officials

FIGURE 7.3. ATV use has exploded on public lands throughout southern Utah and northern Arizona. Land managers have struggled to convince users to stay on existing trails. The tire-track scars of this noncompliance can last for years. Photograph by Jerry D. Spangler.

battled to designate the Paria riverbed a traditional road, arguing it was a major wagon route in the 1870s. Historian Jedediah Rogers reported that they asserted their rights in court, while doing some monkey-wrenching of their own at the local level, removing or replacing BLM "road closed" signs while encouraging locals to create road tracks to maintain a legal sense of their usage. In the late 1990s, the Sierra Club charged local officials with using a bulldozer to blade a debated roadway on the Kaiparowits Plateau. The powerful all-terrain vehicle (ATV) lobby entered the fray as well, with egalitarian and antielitist arguments that motorized travel was the only way most common and elderly people could see their public lands.[67]

The huge increase in ATV use in the years since the monument was created in 1996 has been remarkable, especially in Kane County where ATV rental shops have sprouted like dandelions. The increasing demand for vehicular access to public lands has put BLM managers between a rock and a hard place. With the powerful backing of the governor's office, the counties claim all of the roads as their own, whereas the BLM tries to balance those assertions with its mandate to protect natural resources against unregulated ATV use. One study found that some ATV routes on the Wygaret Terrace actually led to and through ancient Indigenous villages that all had been severely looted. In fact, the only purpose for the routes was to facilitate the looting.[68]

Some area ranchers like Lonnie Pollack, who runs stock on monument lands in the remote country south of Cannonville all the way to Wahweap, expressed more moderate positions on land use and changes after the monument's creation in 1996. He was aware that tourists and environmentalists do not like cattle but thinks it stems from their own lack of knowledge. "I think a lot of them, they're misinformed, they don't understand," he said. "They think the livestock destroy the land instead of just use it as a renewable resource so they look at it that way." Pollack's statement has some truth. When managed correctly, scientists are recognizing that many landscapes, especially grasslands, evolved with grazing by hoofed animals. If kept out of some riparian areas and rotated on and off certain ranges, grazed landscapes are healthier with grazing than without.[69] The problem is that, in decades past, cash-strapped ranchers had not proven good stewards of fragile Western rangelands, prioritizing immediate profits rather than sustainable grazing practices just to make ends meet. Pollack wants others to see that ranchers have changed. "I think most of your stockmen, they're pretty much environmentalists. You know they take care of the land. They have to. If they don't, they lose their means of making a livelihood."

While Twitchell worried about restrictions on development like roads, Pollack worried about the opposite.

> I love to see it the way it is. That's why to begin with, the monument really upset me because I thought, oh you know we're going to have more roads and campgrounds and maybe some of that would be good but I wanted to see it stay the same, where we run cattle, and it stayed the way it was, wild and untamed.

Pollack added, however, that his fears about overdevelopment in the remote parts of the monument proved unfounded.[70]

The secret way the monument was established—especially President Clinton's collusion with outside environmental groups and the lack of local support for it—only spurred local belief that environmentalists were their enemies and held largely "un-American" values that were incompatible with the views of Utah ranchers. As Clare Ramsay noted in 2004: "I don't even like to mention my name alongside the word 'environmentalist.'" As Ramsay told an interviewer:

> I've asked environmentalists, I've said, "Okay, you don't want any drilling, no mining, no logging, no cattle on the range. What is your agenda? If that's all gone, what do you want?" And they can't answer it . . . [they are] a destructive force in our country.

Ramsay concludes, "It's really kind of a selfish, self-centered philosophy."[71]

Many environmental advocates rejected the arguments of ranchers like Clare Ramsay, with hard data pointing to the ill effects of livestock on fragile western landscapes. They also highlighted decades of traditional government favoritism toward the industry. As previously noted, ranchers historically pursued short-term economic gains at the expense of preserving arid rangelands. Collectively their decisions resulted in denuded grasslands, severe erosion, and the loss of native wildlife. Overgrazing led to the silting of rivers, extreme and all too common "one-hundred-year" flood events, and loss of important riparian habitats. Environmental degradation, in turn, opened the door for noxious weeds and invasive plant species such as Russian thistle (tumbleweed), cheat grass, and Russian olive.

It is well-established that federal policies and laws have favored western livestock interests. In the nineteenth century, "free grass" and cheap homesteads encouraged thousands of settlers to move to the American West. Subsequent federal policies, including livestock subsidies previously referenced in this chapter, helped some ranchers survive when raw economics would have ended their operations. Laws and federal tax breaks continue to favor the industry, often bolstering livestock raisers in marginal areas increasingly unfit for stock-raising because of man-made climate change.[72]

Buying Local?

Seeing that the Grand Staircase and Escalante River region is ranching country, the economics of cattle raising impact the regional economy, yet not nearly as much as is popularly perceived. All revenue generated by ranchers contributes to the overall economy even if the rancher is losing money. A rancher still needs to maintain equipment, put gas in trucks, repair fences, and tend to sick cattle regardless of what a cow sells for at market. Some economists use multipliers to suggest that every dollar spent by a farmer or rancher generates two or three times that amount as it is passed from one source (farmer) to another (merchant) to another (supplier). When used to project economic contributions to rural communities, such models assume that farmers are using revenue from their sales to purchase goods and services locally. Such assumptions are tenuous in Kane County and Garfield County where certain goods and services related to livestock production are hard to find, thus requiring ranchers to travel to larger communities such as Richfield, Cedar City, and St. George. Added to this regional reality, most goods a rancher might need can now be purchased on the Internet (sometimes with free shipping), and those online sales rarely return any additional benefit to the local economy.

If actual livestock sales are an accurate indication of the economic significance of the industry, then livestock revenue totals in southern Utah should reflect a significant part of the overall local revenue stream. But this is not the case. Tourism has overtaken stock raising in significance in Grand Staircase and Escalante country. In Kane County, total livestock sales amounted to only about 8 percent of receipts compared to those collected by county hotels and restaurants, and only 5 percent of revenues compared to Kane County retail stores. In Garfield County, total livestock sales amounted to 13 percent of the sales reported by county hotels and restaurants, and 28 percent of the sum spent at county retail establishments.[73] In total, recreation/service and retail sectors each produce ten to twenty times more revenue than do livestock sales in Kane County, and the disparity is only slightly less in Garfield County. In terms of economic importance, total agricultural sales comprise only 3 percent of the Kane County economy and 11 percent of the Garfield County economy (see Table 7.6). These figures challenge persistent claims that either county is "predominantly" agricultural or that ranching is the economic backbone of the region.

These surprising conclusions contrast with the findings of a 2015 study by Gil Miller, an economic consultant to Kane County, and Kevin Heaton, of the Utah State University Extension in Panguitch, that found that livestock is a significant force in the economy. They used a combination of interviews with past and present grazing permittees on the Grand Staircase-Escalante National Monument, and then used government data and computer modeling (IMPLAN V3)

TABLE 7.6. Economic Profiles of Garfield and Kane Counties. *Note:* Data derived from 2012 county profiles in the USDA Census of Agriculture Historical Archive and U.S. Census Bureau Quick Facts for Kane County and Garfield County.

Economic Profiles (2012)			
		Kane County ($)	Garfield County ($)
Total agricultural sales		4,683,000	12,043,000
	Total livestock sales	3,894,000	8,426,000
	Livestock/percent of agricultural sales	83	70
	Gross income per farm	25,591	43,165
Hotel/restaurant sales		47,940,000	62,859,000
Total retail sales		77,065,000	29,909,000
Other nonagricultural Sales		19,642,000	2,142,000

to determine total economic contributions to Kane and Garfield Counties. They concluded that 2015 levels of grazing on the monument contributed $11.9 million in direct economic benefits to the counties and $23.4 million in combined direct and indirect effects. They reported that if monument managers allowed full use of suspended AUMs, then the direct effects would rise by nearly 40 percent to $16.6 million, and the direct and indirect effects would increase by a similar percentage to $32.5 million. Miller and Heaton stated that nonuse of grazing permits was costing the local economy $9.1 million a year.[74]

Their report indicated that current grazing practices on the monument have created the equivalent of 111 full-time ranching jobs and 208 direct and indirect jobs. If the ranchers were allowed full use of the AUMs, they predicted direct employment would rise to 155 jobs and direct and indirect employment would rise to 289 jobs. This analysis is intriguing (and problematic) on several key points.

The report maintains that 2015 grazing levels account for 111 full-time livestock grazing jobs and another 97 jobs created indirectly through ranch expenditures in the local communities. But family ranchers in southern Utah rarely receive actual wages or salaries. Instead, ranchers typically take out operating loans and live off borrowed money until their livestock is actually sold.[75] With few exceptions, ranch employees are unpaid family members who would have no ranch wages to spend in the local communities, and therefore the economic ripple effect would be nonexistent. A hallmark of the family cattle ranch involves unpaid family members working together for the economic good of the family, something that is not realized until the cattle are actually sold. The largest of the cattle operations occasionally hire seasonal cowboys to help move the herds to and from allotments and to maintain hay fields, but this rarely involves full-time employment.

Miller and Heaton's computer modeling indicates a nearly 50 percent increase in ranch jobs if full grazing were allowed. But the AUMs in question are seasonal, usually only a few months at a time, and any jobs created would be limited to part-time employment, perhaps only a few months or even just weeks of the year. Grazing of public ranges requires intensive labor only during two brief periods, each lasting about a week or two. One week involves transporting cattle to the allotment, dispersing cows on the allotment, and ensuring adequate salt and access to water. The other week involves returning to round up the cattle and hauling them to the "home base" or to a different allotment. Given the economies of scale, a larger herd would probably require the same level of "employment" as needed to move a somewhat smaller herd and thus little or no rise in employment or overall labor income. Any increased indirect benefits would also be minimal or nonexistent because the employment would not have changed (or changed only minimally), and the employees would have the same amount of money to spend as they did working the smaller herd.

The report also concludes, however, that ranching jobs are economically inferior options to the often-dismissed tourism jobs of the region. Miller and Heaton use labor income statistics that reflect that of the 111 full-time-equivalent ranch employees ranching on monument lands. Each received annual wages of $8,776, or on average $4.21 per hour for a standard forty-hour week. In a region that discounts tourist jobs as low paid and seasonal, hiring on with a rancher would appear to offer 40 percent less compensation than the most menial tourist job.

Another consideration involving ranching's impact on the Grand Staircase and Escalante River region is the use of multipliers to measure the economic ripple effects of sales and wages. This long-standing approach is valid *if* it can be demonstrated that the revenue actually remains in the local community. The Miller-Heaton approach used multipliers to account for the ripple effect of ranchers being paid for their cattle, then spending the money at local businesses, and those businesses in turn spending the money to hire more employees who then spend more money in the local community.

Regarding local spending, a clear disconnect extends between popular perception and reality. Permittees interviewed for the report indicated that they spend 95 percent of all revenues in their local communities. This assertion differed from a Utah State University analysis that found relatively few local purchases related to agricultural production in the counties where the Grand Staircase-Escalante National Monument is located.[76] Informal discussions with area residents suggested they do spend a fair amount of their revenue locally. There are two ranch supply stores in Kanab, and area ranchers prefer to buy their hay from farmers in Panguitch or Richfield. They also buy most of their equipment from other ranchers in the area. But if they need new, generally high-priced equipment or specialty items or services, they are forced by necessity to find them at larger and more specialized businesses in Cedar City or St. George.

Even seeing these economic realities, the public perception that livestock grazing is an important—if not the most important—economic contributor to their local economies is slow to change, sometimes stemming from the Miller-Heaton study. Misinformation about stock-raising's importance contributes to popular folklore and sayings in southern Utah. One oft-repeated joke about environmental-oriented tourists, especially backpackers, is that they arrive in southern Utah with a twenty-dollar bill in their wallets and one pair of underwear, they spend a week, and do not change either one the entire time. When interviewed by Nicole Croft, one elected Kane County official insisted grazing provides "about 20 million-plus a year in county domestic product. It exceeds the tourism dollar."[77] The interviewee was referring to the $23 million economic contribution noted in the Miller-Heaton study, which includes multipliers to reflect the economic ripple effects of spending. Sales at Kane County restaurants and hotels at the same time totaled nearly $48 million *before* any multipliers were added.

Where the Grass is Greener

Throughout the previous chapters, the majority of highlighted grazing practices occurred on public lands. The reason why stemmed from the fact there are minimal private lands in either county (11 percent in Kane County and 5 percent in Garfield County) and certainly not enough private land to accommodate livestock herds of any size. The predominance of public lands grazing continued through at least the mid-1970s or early 1980s when the BLM initiated more aggressive range management and implemented range health evaluations that resulted in grazing reductions in some areas.

But grazing practices in Grand Staircase and Escalante River country have changed over the past twenty-five years. According to a Utah State University study, more and more ranchers have relinquished their federal grazing permits in favor of grazing on private lands and state lands. Even those with federal grazing permits have increasingly turned to private pastures as a significant source of at least some livestock forage. This shift coincides with a steady reduction in AUMs allowed on both U.S. Forest Service and BLM lands, a trend that began in the 1940s and continues today.[78] Researchers noted that AUMs on Forest Service lands statewide fell from just over a million in the 1940s to about half that amount in the 2000s.

BLM lands had 1.8 million AUMs statewide in the 1940s, whereas only 1.2 million AUMs in 2006.[79] Collectively, the reduced numbers of permits to graze livestock have fueled suspicions that federal regulators are hell-bent on eliminating grazing altogether.[80]

In Kane and Garfield Counties, cattle ranchers have adapted by diversifying their grazing sources. Those without federal grazing permits indicated in the USU study that 51 percent of their feed came from pastures and 39 percent from grazing on state lands, with the remainder coming from other sources. Of these, 52 percent had previously held BLM permits and 38 percent had held Forest Service permits. They cited frustration with agency administrators as a major reason for relinquishing the permits, and none of them indicated any willingness to have federal grazing permits in the future. Of note, non-permittees have made greater use of state lands where the cost of AUMs on isolated sections is $5.72, or more than three times the federal rate of $1.87 per AUM. Ranchers with federal permits in the area rely on federal rangelands more so than in any other region of the state, with federal lands providing 55 percent of forage needs.[81]

In Grand Staircase and Escalante River country, ranchers placed the highest value on Forest Service summer grazing permits that allowed producers to remove livestock from private lands during the hay-growing season. The Escalante Ranger District and the Powell Ranger District manage thirty-three allotments with fifty-eight permittees. There are 41,210 authorized AUMs for cattle and another 2,150 for sheep. None of the permits are currently in voluntary nonuse, and nonuse of AUMs has occurred only rarely in recent years due to isolated personal and administrative issues.[82]

Ranchers placed the lowest value on BLM rangelands. Most BLM lands in the Kane-Garfield area are part of the Grand Staircase-Escalante National

FIGURE 7.4. Paria River country. Photograph by Dan Bauer.

Monument, although there are some non-monument BLM lands managed by the Kanab Field Office and limited grazing in the Glen Canyon National Recreation Area. Within the monument, there are seventy-nine allotments with ninety-one permittees authorized to graze cattle. The BLM has three categories of AUMs: authorized, active, and actually used. The monument currently has 106,645 authorized AUMs, of which 76,957 are active (72 percent). This total is almost the same as when the monument was created in 1996.[83]

The point of contention with county officials and some producers is the "actual use" numbers. The BLM can and does request voluntary nonuse of the grazing permits to respond to specific range conditions such as persistent drought. It can also make requests to restore damaged riparian areas and to reduce conflicts with other uses. Monument officials maintain that actual use levels have averaged just over 41,000 AUMs annually, and, "there is no evidence of sharp or precipitous declines in grazing on the Monument since designation."[84] The roughly 35,000 unused AUMs are the source of the Miller-Heaton findings discussed above that make the case that voluntary withdrawals are costing county businesses and producers $9 million a year in lost revenues.[85]

Into the Sunset

Grazing in southern Utah and northern Arizona has enjoyed a long and colorful history. But as the number of family ranches continues to dwindle, serious questions remain as to whether cattle ranching will survive as a viable industry in the area, or whether it will follow the path of the sheep industry into steep decline. Outside factors have generally had detrimental impacts on the local cattle industry, including a lack of competitiveness vis-à-vis centralized producers in the Midwest and Southeast, rising production costs, and changing consumer preferences. The future of cattle ranching in the region (and elsewhere in the state) has generated considerable interest among state leaders, economists, and industry associations, but they have reached little consensus as to what can be done to reverse trends that challenge the very existence of the traditional cowboy lifestyle rooted so deeply in the culture of southern Utah.

Some might argue that the conventional or "real" cowboy lifestyle is almost dead but for a handful of local ranchers who still cherish the traditions of their ancestors in an industry that many see as economically unsustainable. As previously discussed, as much as three-quarters of cattle production in Grand Staircase and Escalante country is now concentrated among fewer than two-dozen large producers, eight in Kane County and thirteen in Garfield County. All agricultural production as a percentage of the local economies has declined precipitously, with farm sales amounting to only 3 percent of Kane County receipts and 11 percent of Garfield County's receipts. For the farmers and ranchers, if they are not losing money year to year then they are scraping by with total annual earnings of less than $5,000, usually far less.

And this begs the question: Why continue to ranch if it makes no economic sense? The answer cannot be measured by economic formulas and computer modeling. Rather, its value is found deeply engrained in the hearts and souls of the people who live there, some of them with roots that extend five and six generations into the past. It is rooted in their sense of place and their time on the land, all wrapped in the deeply religious context of the memories of their ancestors who struggled for their faith and worked this land before them. In the region, still heavily dominated by members of the Church of Jesus Christ of Latter-day Saints, one commonly hears words like "salvation" and "God's gifts" and "callings" when locals talk about their own stewardship of the land. The latter is, in every sense, an immeasurable cultural value that will never show up on balance sheets. Ranching might make no sense economically, but it makes perfect sense to people tied spiritually to the land and to their ancestors long buried in the local cemeteries.

Former Garfield County Commissioner Louise Liston hinted at this different worldview when she told the *High Country News*:

> I love the land, and it's different from an environmentalist's love. We have a deep, abiding love; they have a weekend love affair. Their love is intense and passionate, but it's not an abiding love. That kind of love comes from making a living off the land. They go back to their amenities in their cities, while we continue to eke out an existence.

As Liston makes clear, she would rather struggle to make a living amid God's beauty than chase wealth and happiness somewhere else.

Religion is a fundamental component of how locals view the world around them, as well as how they view anyone without their shared beliefs. As discussed by historian D. Michael Quinn, the Mormon Church thrived in the face of long-standing and repeated persecution because it fostered an "us against them" tribalism with a powerful group-identity defined by its opposition to outsiders.[86] Cliven Bundy, a rancher on the western edge of the Arizona Strip, represents perhaps the most extreme expression of this ethos. Supported by as many as a thousand anti-government diehards, many of them armed militiamen, Bundy framed his 2014 (and still ongoing) opposition to proposed BLM confiscation of his cattle as "a battle between good and evil." Because Bundy claimed his Mormon ancestors had worked the land before any federal regulations or regulators, Cliven felt his rights superseded federal interests.[87]

Croft, citing scores of interviews with long-time Kane County residents, as well as newcomers, makes a convincing argument that the same ethos is firmly entrenched in how locals view land use today, including livestock grazing. This is expressed through beliefs, couched in religious ideology, that the land needs human stewardship to reach its full potential, that humans have a responsibility to extract optimal benefits from the land, and that without human intervention, the land would have no value.[88] In other words, grass not grazed is grass wasted.

Of course, this worldview stands in direct opposition to conservation and environmental philosophies that value landscapes in their natural and "wild" states. In 2010, then-Secretary of the Interior Ken Salazar instructed the BLM to prioritize conservation, ecological connectivity, and science in the management of public lands. One long-time BLM employee in Kanab observed that this mandate created a clash between traditionalists and reformists.

> [To] the older culture of BLM, restoration means getting the environment into a condition that is conducive to grazing. The alternative definition of restoration has to do with maintaining, getting the environment into a place where it has resilience to maintain itself on its own, even with the pressures of climate change and whatever other management, like grazing or recreation, might have on it.[89]

In the final analysis, the economics of livestock ranching in southern Utah present a daunting challenge to future men and women hoping to continue the traditions of their ancestors. But there are really two different issues here. First, can the livestock industry in Grand Staircase and Escalante River country ever be revived to the point that a rancher earns a profit sufficient to actually support a family? And second, can the traditional cowboy way of life expressed by devotion to God, family, and righteous use of the land be preserved as an essential part of our nation's cultural heritage? The answer to both questions is open to debate.

Thinkers, pundits, and experts of various shades have offered myriad ideas for economic and cultural revitalization in light of the region's strong ranching heritage, some bordering on the bizarre, others on the arcane, and still others that can only be characterized as pie-in-the-sky wishful thinking. For example, one expert was hired to advise local stockmen and women on how to market their "Monument" cattle as "riparian-free beef," a reference to management measures to keep livestock out of sensitive riparian areas, even though no mechanism existed to market the area's cattle directly to consumers under a label no one had ever heard of before or did not understand in the context of public lands grazing. Liston and her husband Robert even tried their hand at raising ostriches, but that proved unsuccessful. In the following sections, we review some of the many recommendations, suggestions, and challenges facing ranchers in Kane County and Garfield County.

Diversification

Private ranchers can increase profitability by embracing other economic activities that supplement cattle production. Most private lands also have wildlife and recreation values, which afford opportunities for fee hunting, fee fishing, wildlife viewing, nature tours, guest ranching, and dude ranching that can potentially improve revenue.[90] Several ranchers in the region have already added recreation and tourism elements to their operations. Among the challenges facing ranchers seeking to diversify revenue by adding tourism and recreation are capitalization costs for visitor amenities and inexperience in tourism marketing and management. Challenges also include high insurance costs, additional regulatory oversight, and possible fees if those activities extend onto public lands or involve state-regulated activities such as hunting and fishing.

Niche Marketing

National demand is growing for specialty or "alternative" meat products such as bison, venison, and elk meat, primarily among affluent urban consumers.[91] Such products command much higher prices than traditional beef, offering the potential of much higher returns to the ranchers. Niche marketing, however, has significant challenges. Raising bison, deer, and elk requires capital investment in specialty fencing, as well as oversight by state agencies concerned about diseases infecting wildlife. Considered in tandem with an immature marketing network for specialty products, the region's geographic isolation also would have higher transportation costs. No mechanism is available yet for area ranchers to market directly to urban consumers, especially higher-end restaurants. Greater production costs could be ameliorated by direct marketing to restaurants in southern Utah, but partnerships with regional meat processors probably would be required.[92]

Kevin McLaws, who produces bison at his Zion Mountain Ranch, also indicated that state laws must be tweaked to accommodate alternative livestock. For example, current law requires all livestock to be loaded into trucks and transported to a U.S. Department of Agriculture inspection station before being slaughtered. But bison and elk do not take kindly to being loaded into a cattle trailer. He believes Utah should follow the lead of Texas and other Western states that promote alternative livestock by allowing "field inspections," which lower inspection costs while still ensuring public health standards.[93]

Natural Beef

The public has become increasingly concerned about feedlot practices designed to increase cattle weight and fat marbling prior to slaughter, in particular the use of growth hormones, anabolic steroids, and exotic cattle diets rich in sawdust, chicken wastes, and even plastics.[94] This concern has led to increased demand for more humanely raised, organic, hormone-free, and grass-fed beef. Most grocery stores now have an organic section where consumers are willing to pay prices three to five times more than the cost of regular meats. Cattle in southern Utah are already grass-fed, either on private pastures or on public rangelands, and this region would seem ideally situated to transition to natural beef production. The production costs are greater (it takes cattle longer to reach optimal weight on a grass-only diet), but the return rates are also much higher.

This transition would require a shift in long-held ranching practices from the traditional cow-calf operation where the calves are sold at one year old to be finished elsewhere to one where beef cattle are retained on the ranch for as long as three years until ready for slaughter. Consumer demand for natural beef is currently a very small portion of all beef sales, although demand is expected to grow exponentially in the years to come.[95]

Ethnic Markets

American consumers prefer beef, pork, and chicken, but in most of the world, meat consumption is oriented towards lamb and goats. New Zealand has become a world leader in lamb production by marketing to these populations. Utah producers are unlikely to be able to tap into that world market. But large ethnic populations from Africa, the Middle East, countries around the Mediterranean Sea, and some areas of Asia have immigrated to the United States in recent decades, and these new American residents prefer lamb and goat meat, both of which command store prices two or three times that of beef. This new demand has resulted in increased direct marketing to ethnic consumers, especially for Muslim, Christian, and Jewish celebrations (e.g., Ramadan, Easter, and Passover).[96]

Transportation costs from southern Utah would be a prohibitive obstacle if marketing to consumers in the East, Midwest, or South. But targeted direct marketing to ethnic consumers in western cities such as Salt Lake City, Las Vegas, Denver, and Phoenix could establish a niche market with higher returns than beef production. Focused direct sales to unique ethnic and religious communities would require sales and marketing expertise that has not yet been demonstrated by Utah's sheep industry.

Community Partnerships

As we discussed earlier in this chapter, most beef production in Kane County and Garfield County is concentrated in the hands of relatively few producers who enjoy a higher potential for profitability because of their larger economies of scale. Studies have found that ranchers with herds larger than five hundred head typically have about half the production costs of ranchers with herds of fewer than fifty head. One Utah State University study asserts that if small operators entered into partnerships, they could capture the same economies of scale as the large ranches, including "lower costs, greater access to new technology, the ability to distribute fixed costs over higher levels of production, greater access to markets, and opportunities to secure higher prices." Partnerships, as opposed to consolidation, would better sustain the integrity of the rural communities.[97]

Perhaps in the final analysis, the future of ranching in Grand Staircase and Escalante country may require a return to the past. The viability of community-based livestock partnerships is not without precedent in the Kane-Garfield region. As we discussed in Chapter 3, the livestock industry here became wildly successful in the 1870s and 1880s because of community cooperatives where the costs and benefits of raising cattle and sheep were shared among many small producers. The model worked because of centralized Mormon Church management of the cooperatives (church leaders arbitrated disputes and distributed rangelands). It remains to be seen whether individual ranchers acting in their own self-interests could successfully partner with other ranchers also acting in their own interests.

Epilogue

Ask today's cowboys and cowgirls what they see as the future of the livestock industry in southern Utah and you get answers laced with both optimism and pessimism. Most will acknowledge that the fate of cattle ranching faces myriad challenges, even if they disagree as to what those obstacles or hurdles are. Laura Pollock, who runs cattle with her husband Coot, is optimistic that twenty years from now their family operation will be even bigger than it is today. She said, "I have great hopes for the future and hope to be able to pass it on to the next generation the way my uncles did to me." But she added that the future is also "somewhat scary because of the environmental groups limiting what improvements you can do on the land. If the environmental groups stay out of it, then the viability will be good for years."[1]

Others do not share her optimism and, in some instances, have sold their permits to dissuade their children from getting into the business. Sean Stewart, a direct descendant of Levi Stewart, the first bishop of Kanab, recalled that his grandfather, Reginald Stewart, sold off the family's federal grazing permits in the 1970s to deter his sons from entering the ranching business. His tactic did not work. Today, Sean's brother and father have federal grazing permits, and they supplement the rangeland grasses with alfalfa and pasture from their private lands. Sean works for the BLM as a range specialist and also raises cattle on the family's private lands. There is no way, however, he said, that he would urge his own children to take up saddle and spurs.[2]

A fifth-generation rancher might find it hard to imagine a southern Utah landscape without cows, and even the most pessimistic cowman would probably admit there will always be cattle to some extent. But no one can be certain as food producers embrace new technologies to manufacture alternative protein products that look like, taste like, and have the texture of real beef, chicken, and seafood, all without the demands that livestock place on land, water, and feed. In fact, the biggest threat to livestock ranching probably will not come from environmentalists or more government regulations or the ever-rising costs of doing business. It will come from consumers. If the sheep industry is reflective of fickle consumer preferences, public demand for beef may ebb in future decades much like it did for sheep products.

Any meaningful transition to non-livestock-based meat production might seem unfathomable to some people in the region today, much in the same way that the thought of chemical fibers and plastics created in factories was unfathomable to a wool grower living in Orderville in the 1910s. A world without cattle and sheep and other sources of meat would, in a very real sense, mark a fundamental change in the human experience. Animal husbandry has been a traditional (and respected) part of human cultures for millennia, with cows and sheep and other animals functioning as a form of moveable currency. In fact, the English word "cattle" is rooted in the old French word "chattel," meaning "property." And that word is itself rooted in the old Latin word "capitale," meaning "property" or "stock." For much of recorded history, many cultures have defined individual wealth by the number of livestock a person owned. In a twist of irony perhaps, people today own "stock" in companies like Apple or Google in the same way that people once owned livestock that could be bought, sold, and traded. Will future generations living in Grand Staircase and Escalante country continue to trade livestock for other forms of moveable currency?

Captive to forces beyond their control, whether it be geographic isolation or centralized production, family ranchers in southern Utah have rarely enjoyed much in the way of tangible wealth from their livestock operations. But they always have been proud of their ranching heritage, happy to be part of the region's "cowboy zeitgeist"—centered on ideas of fierce individualism, self-determination, and spiritual integrity etched into their sunburned faces and on the gravestones of their ancestors.

Notes

Notes to Chapter 1

1. Joel C. Janetski et al., "The Paleoarchaic to Early Archaic Transition on the Colorado Plateau: The Archaeology of North Creek Shelter," *American Antiquity* 77, no. 1(2012): 125–59.
2. Stewart B. Koyiyumptewa, Hopi Tribal Preservation Officer, to Vicki Tyler, Grand Staircase-Escalante National Monument Manager, October 26, 2020, Grand Staircase-Escalante National Monument, Kanab, Utah.
3. Ted J. Warner, ed., *The Domínguez-Escalante Journal*, trans. Fray Angelico Chavez (1976; reis., Salt Lake City: University of Utah Press, 1995).
4. Ronald L. Holt, *Beneath These Red Cliffs: An Ethnohistory of the Utah Paiutes* (Logan: Utah State University Press, 2006), 9–10, 19–21.
5. Heidi Roberts, Richard Ahlstrom, and Jerry D. Spangler, eds., *Far Western Basketmaker Beginnings: The Jackson Flat Reservoir Project* (Salt Lake City: University of Utah Press, 2022).
6. Mark Brunson and George Wallace, "Perceptions of Ranching: Public Views, Personal Reflections," in *Ranching West of the 100th Meridian: Culture, Ecology, and Economics*, eds. Richard L. Knight, Wendell C. Gilbert, and Ed Marston (Washington, DC: Island Press, 2002), 91.
7. Adam R. Brown, *Utah Politics and Government: American Democracy among a Unique Electorate* (Lincoln: University of Nebraska Press, 2018), 16–18.
8. Paul F. Starrs, *Let the Cowboy Ride: Cattle Ranching in the American* West (Baltimore, MD: Johns Hopkins University Press, 1998), 7–9; Bob Budd, "Colors and Words," in *Ranching West of the 100th Meridian*, eds. Richard L. Knight, Wendell C. Gilbert, and Ed Marston (Washington, DC: Island Press, 2002), 42–43.
9. Richard White, "Animals and Enterprise," in *The Oxford History of the American West*, eds. Clyde A. Milner II, Carol A. O'Conner, and Martha A. Sandweiss (New York: Oxford University Press, 1994), 258.
10. Thomas G. Alexander, "Lost Memory and Environmentalism: Mormons on the Wasatch Front, 1847–1930," in *The Earth Will Appear as the Garden of*

Eden: Essays on Mormon Environmental History, eds. Jedediah S. Rogers and Matthew C. Godfrey (Salt Lake City: University of Utah Press, 2018), 53.

11. William Cronon, George Miles, and Jay Gitlin, "Becoming West: Toward a New Meaning for Western History," in *Under an Open Sky: Rethinking America's Western Past*, eds. William Cronon, George Miles, and Jay Gitlin (New York: W. W. Norton, 1992), 25.
12. The technical term for moving herds between summer and winter ranges is "transhumance"; Terry G. Jordan, *North American Cattle-Ranching Frontiers: Origins, Diffusion, and Differentiation* (Albuquerque: University of New Mexico Press, 1993), 304–5.
13. Jedediah S. Rogers, *Roads in the Wilderness: Conflict in Canyon Country* (Salt Lake City: University of Utah Press, 2013), 109.
14. William Cronon, *Uncommon Ground: Rethinking the Human Place in Nature* (New York: W. W. Norton, 1996), 39.
15. Jared Farmer, *On Zion's Mount: Mormons, Indians, and the American Landscape* (Cambridge: Harvard University Press, 2008), 9.
16. Nathan F. Sayre, *Ranching, Environmental Species, and Urbanization in the Southwest: Species of Capital* (Tucson: University of Arizona Press, 2002), xxxv.
17. The elevation at Powell Pont on the north is 10,188 ft. The Colorado River's elevation in the Grand Canyon is about 2,800 ft at Nankoweap, and it becomes progressively lower as it flows southwest towards its terminus at the Gulf of California.
18. Clarence Dutton, *Report on the Geology of the High Plateaus of Utah* (Washington, DC: U.S. Geological Survey, 1880).
19. Charles Hunt, *Physiography of the United States* (San Francisco: W. W. Freeman, 1967); Herbert E. Gregory and Raymond C. Moore, *The Kaiparowits Region: A Geographic and Geologic Reconnaissance of Parts of Utah and Arizona*, U.S. Geological Survey Professional Papers 164 (Washington, DC: Government Printing Office, 1931).
20. "Grand Staircase-Escalante National Monument," Bureau of Land Management, accessed September 29, 2020, https//www.blm.gov.
21. Walter Prescott Webb, *The Great Plains* (New York: Grosset and Dunlap, 1931), 206, 227.
22. Walter Nugent, *Into the West: The Story of Its People* (New York: Alfred A. Knopf, 1999), 5–14.
23. Michael E. McGerr, "Is There a Twentieth Century West?" in *Under an Open Sky: Rethinking America's Western Past*, eds. William Cronon, George Miles, and Jay Gitlin (New York: W. W. Norton, 1992), 251–253 (quote, 251).
24. Howard R. Lamar, "Westering in the Twentieth-First Century," in *Under an Open Sky: Rethinking America's Western Past*, eds. William Cronon, George Miles, and Jay Gitlin (New York: W. W. Norton, 1992), 262.
25. Thomas D. Power, *Lost Landscapes and Failed Economies: The Search for a Value of Place* (Washington, DC: Island Press, 1996), Table 8-2.

26. Data from county profiles, Kane County and Garfield County in U.S. Census of Agriculture 2012, available online in USDA Census of Agriculture Historical Archive, Albert R. Mann Library, Cornell University, Ithaca, NY; National Agricultural Statistics Service(NASS), Washington DC, https://agcensus.library.cornell.edu/ (hereafter cited as "Agricultural Census" with relevant date and page number).
27. U.S. Census Bureau, "Quick Facts, Garfield County, Utah," accessed July 5, 2024, www.census.gov/quickfacts/garfieldcountyutah; U.S. Census Bureau, "Quick Facts, Kane County, Utah," accessed July 5, 2024, www.census.gov/quickfacts/kanecountyutah.
28. George Wuerthner and Mollie Matteson, eds., *Welfare Ranching: The Subsidized Destruction of the American West* (New York: Island Press, 2002), 3–12; "Information and Facts," Public Lands Ranching, accessed July 2, 2024, http://www.publiclandsranching.org.
29. Jordan, *North American Cattle-Ranching Frontiers*, 297.
30. Wallace Stegner, *Mormon Country* (1942; reis., Lincoln: University of Nebraska Press, 1981), 108.
31. Andrew Gulliford, *The Woolly West: Colorado's Hidden History of Sheepscapes* (College Station: Texas A&M University Press, 2018), 57–59.
32. Charles S. Peterson and Brian Q. Cannon, *The Awkward State of Utah*, (Salt Lake City: University of Utah Press, 2015), 205–7.
33. Martha J. Sullins et al., "Lay of the Land: Ranch Land and Ranching," in *Ranching West of the 100th Meridian: Culture, Ecology, and Economics*, eds. Richard L. Knight, Wendell C. Gilbert, and Ed Marston (Washington, DC: Island Press, 2002), 25–26.
34. "Points to Make in Your Comments on Grand Staircase-Escalante National Monument," Southern Utah Wilderness Alliance, accessed September 30, 2020, https://suwa.org/points-make-comments-grand-staircase-escalante-national-monument/.
35. Congressional Research Service, "Federal Land Ownership: Overview and Data," updated February 21, 2020, https://sgp.fas.org/crs/misc/R42346.pdf.
36. "Garfield County Economic Development Plan," Garfield County, Utah, January 2019, https://www.garfield.utah.gov/home/showpublisheddocument/1220/637274745016100000; "Kane County, Utah, General Plan," Kane County, Utah, August 2018, https://kane.utah.gov/gov/dept/planning/draft-of-2018-kane-county-general-plan/#; both accessed September 30, 2020.
37. Daniel Kemmis, *This Sovereign Land: A New Vision for Governing the West* (New York: Island Press, 2001), 41–44.

Notes to Chapter 2

1. Martha Sonntag Bradley, *History of Kane County* (Salt Lake City: Utah State Historical Society [hereafter USHS]; Kanab, UT: Kane County Commission, 1999), 60.

2. Adonis Findlay Robinson, *History of Kane County* (Kanab, UT: Kane County Daughters of the Utah Pioneers, 1970), 4.
3. "History," Kanab Heritage House Museum, accessed July 2, 2024, www.kanabheritagehouse.com/history.html; Bradley (*Kane County*) offered a slightly different translation, indicating the word means a willow basket used by Paiute women to carry their infants on their back in Allan Kent Powell's *Encyclopedia of Utah History* (Salt Lake City: University of Utah Press, 1994), 294.
4. Blanche Mace, "Biography of Silas Hoyt," n.d., Special Collections, Kanab City Library, Kanab, UT, 1–7.
5. Mace, "Silas Hoyt," 7–10.
6. U.S. Census Bureau, population schedule, Utah Territory, 1860 United States Federal Census, microfilm publication M653, 1,438 rolls, National Archives and Records Administration, Washington, DC, images reproduced by FamilySearch, Ancestry.com, accessed July 2, 2024.
7. Douglas D. Alder and Karl F. Brooks, *History of Washington County* (USHS; St. George, UT: Washington County Commission, 1998), 28. See also Jacob Hamblin, cited in Hartt Wixom, *Hamblin: A Modern Look at the Frontier Life and Legend of Jacob Hamblin* (Springville, UT: Cedar Fort Incorporated, 1996), 231.
8. W. Paul Reeve, *Making Space on the Western Frontier: Mormons, Miners, and Southern Paiutes* (Urbana: University of Illinois Press, 2006), 119; Mark Reisner, *Cadillac Desert: The American West and Its Disappearing Water* (New York: Penguin Books, 1993), 120.
9. Wixom, *Hamblin*, 128.
10. Robinson, *Kane County*, 4.
11. Robinson, *Kane County*, 1–2.
12. Sondra G. Jones, *Being and Becoming Ute: The Story of an American Indian People* (Salt Lake City: University of Utah Press, 2019), 159.
13. Richard Lyman Bushman, "Making Space for the Mormons," in *The Collected Leonard J. Arrington Mormon History Lectures* (Logan: Utah State University Press, 2004), 35–37.
14. Leonard Arrington, *Great Basin Kingdom* (1958; reis., Lincoln: University of Nebraska Press, 1966), 21. Arrington hints that Brigham Young's decision to take the deal was economically motivated and not rooted in any particular American patriotism. Early Utah historian Hubert Howe Bancroft, however, insisted "Mormons were true-hearted Americans" ready to "answer any call the government might make upon them for service in the field of battle"; Hubert Howe Bancroft, *History of Utah* (Salt Lake City, UT: Bookcraft, 1964), 241.
15. David L. Bigler, *Forgotten Kingdom: The Mormon Theocracy in the American West, 1847–1896* (Logan: Utah State University Press, 1998), 46–49.
16. Philip L. Fradkin, *A River No More: The Colorado River and the American West* (Berkeley: University of California Press, 1996), 148.

17. Bancroft, *History of Utah*, 240.
18. Jeff Nichols, "Before the Boom: Mormons, Livestock, and Stewardship, 1847–1870," in *The Earth Will Appear as the Garden of Eden*, eds. Jedediah S. Rogers and Matthew C. Godfrey (Salt Lake City: University of Utah Press, 2019), 159–60.
19. George W. Rollins, "Land Policies of the United States as Applied to Utah to 1910," *Utah Historical Quarterly* 20, no. 2 (1952): 244.
20. Mormons certainly claimed lands as their own, but these claims were not recognized by the federal government. A legal process to acquire title was not established until 1862 with passage of the Homestead Act, and even then the law applied to only those lands that had been surveyed by official government surveyors. These surveys were slow in coming to southern Utah and northern Arizona, and the rugged nature of the terrain was such that they were among the last tracts of public land to be surveyed in the United States in the early 1900s. In effect, the earliest ranchers in southern Utah and northern Arizona were squatters.
21. Brigham Young, quoted in Levi S. Peterson, "The Development of Utah Livestock Law, 1848–1896," *Utah Historical Quarterly* 32, no. 3 (1964): 200–201.
22. *Journal of Discourses*, quoted in Peterson, "Livestock Law," 200.
23. Bigler, *Forgotten Kingdom*, 51.
24. Peterson, "Livestock Law," 201.
25. Peterson, "Livestock Law," 201–2.
26. Bigler, *Forgotten Kingdom*, 53.
27. Dorothy Fillerup Boyer, *William Derby Johnson Jr. Journal Excerpts, 1850–1894* (Self-published, 2005), 47, Special Collections, Kanab City Library, Kanab, UT.
28. Bradley, *Kane County*, 81–82.
29. Paul H. Peterson, "An Historical Analysis of the Word of Wisdom" (Master's thesis, Brigham Young University, 1972), 1–2, https://scholarsarchive.byu.edu/etd/5039/.
30. Jeff Nichols, "Before the Boom," 155–59.
31. Don D. Walker, "The Cattle Industry of Utah, 1850–1900: A Historical Profile," *Utah Historical Quarterly*, 32, no. 3 (1964): 183.
32. Walker, "Cattle Industry of Utah," 185.
33. Walker, "Cattle Industry of Utah," 184.
34. Brigham A. Riggs, "Early History," February 14, 1941, in Julius S. Dalley, *History of Grazing*, Utah Writer's Project, 1941, MSS B 100, USHS [hereafter Dalley, *History of Grazing*].
35. Edwin G. Woolley, "Expedition to Intercept Navajoe [*sic*] Indians Who Had Stolen Stock from Southern Utah, Feb. 25th to March 12th 1869," *Utah Historical Quarterly* 29, no.2 (1961): 154.
36. William W. Adair, "Interview with Wm. W. Adair," February 4, 1941, in Dalley, *History of Grazing*.

37. Ira W. Hatch, "Statement of Ira W. Hatch Regarding Early Range Conditions in Southern Utah," Special Range Report R-4, September 22, 1940, MSS B 100, USHS.
38. Joseph J. Porter, "Statement of Jos. J. Porter, Concerning Range Conditions on Forest and Public Lands in Southern Utah in the Early Days as Compared with the Present," Special Range Report R-4, September 25, 1940, MSS B 100, USHS.
39. Charlotte Maxwell Webb, "Sketch of the Life of William Bailey Maxwell," Ancestry.com, posted May 4, 2008, accessed July 2, 2024, https://www.ancestry.com/mediaui-viewer/tree/60784447/person/-1348928992/media/eb05f9c4-ff81-4676b0f2-c6c6d0799b64.
40. William Bailey Maxwell, Ancestry.com, accessed July 2, 2024, http://search.ancestry.com/cgi-bin/sse.dll?indiv=1&db=LDSVitalMembership1830-1848&h=59196&tid=&pid=&usePUB=true&_phsrc=xtJ66&_phstart=successSource&usePUBJs=true&rhSource=61157.
41. Lorenzo B. Maxwell, "A Sketch of the Life of William Bailey Maxwell," Ancestry.com, posted May 4, 2008, accessed July 2, 2024, https://www.ancestry.com/mediaui-viewer/tree/60784447/person/-1348928992/media/b94a4cf3-0af9-4ea7ad6f-b40991e731d7.
42. Maxwell, "William Bailey Maxwell."
43. Thomas Cottam Romney, *The Mormon Colonies in Mexico* (Salt Lake City: Deseret Book Company, 1938), 76, 132.
44. William Bailey Maxwell, Ancestry.com; Webb, "William Bailey Maxwell."
45. "Pipe Spring," National Park Service, accessed September 27, 2021, https://www.nps.gov/pisp/planyourvisit/pipe-spring.htm. Not a lot has been written about Robert McIntyre. Some histories refer to him as a "herder" in Dr. Whitmore's employ, another as a ranch foreman, and in one account as being related by marriage to Whitmore. Like Whitmore, McIntyre had come to Utah by way of Texas. He was only nine years old when his mother, Margaret McIntyre Moody, and stepfather, John M. Moody, joined the Mormon Church, migrating to Utah in 1853 (four years before the Whitmores). He is listed on the 1860 census as Robert Moody. He was only twenty-three years old when he was killed at Pipe Springs. Like Whitmore, he is buried in the St. George Cemetery. See Mormon Pioneer Overland Travel Database, accessed July 2, 2024, https://history.lds.org/overlandtravel/pioneers/59175/robert-mc-intyre.
46. Daughters of the Utah Pioneers, *Pioneer Women of Faith and Fortitude,* vol. 4 (Salt Lake City: Daughters of the Utah Pioneers, 1998), 3349.
47. Jerry D. Spangler and Donna Kemp Spangler, *Last Chance Byway: A History of Nine Mile Canyon* (Salt Lake City: University of Utah Press, 2016), 100–101.
48. U.S. Census Bureau, population schedule, *St. George, Washington County, Utah Territory*, 1870 United States Federal Census, microfilm roll *M593_1613*, page

395B. National Archives and Records Administration, Washington, DC, Family History Library film *553112, i*mages reproduced by FamilySearch, Ancestry .com, accessed July 2, 2024.

49. U.S. Census Bureau, population schedule, *St. George, Washington County, Utah,* 1880 United States Federal Census, microfilm roll *1339*, page *359A*, enumeration district *093,* National Archives and Records Administration, Washington, DC, Family History Library film *553112,* images reproduced by FamilySearch, Ancestry.com, accessed July 2, 2024.
50. Spangler and Spangler, *Last Chance Byway*, 102.
51. Robinson, *Kane County*, 2.
52. Bradley, *Kane County*, 61.
53. It is not known whether this is Ezra Strong Sr. or Ezra Strong Jr. The former was one of the earliest converts to Mormonism, enduring the many tribulations of Church followers in Ohio, Missouri, and Illinois. He was a close associate of Joseph Smith and was ordained a high priest by the prophet's brother, Don Carlos. Born in 1788 near Albany, New York, he was living in Santaquin in October 1862 where he was baptized into the Reorganized Church of Jesus Christ of Latter Day Saints, a rival to Brigham Young's claim to divine legitimacy inasmuch as it claimed the title of "prophet" was to be handed down to those in Joseph Smith's lineage. If he indeed started a remote ranch in Kane County in 1862 or 1863, it might have been because he had been banished from the Mormon communities for apostasy. He would have been seventy-four years old at the time. His daughter Priscilla would later become a stalwart of the Orderville experiment discussed in Chapter 3. Ezra was posthumously rebaptized into the Mormon faith more than a hundred years later. He died in 1877 in Washington State with the title "Reverend." Ezra Strong Jr. was also living in Santaquin in 1860 and 1870, and no vital statistics exist to suggest he ever moved to southern Utah. He had moved to Washington State by 1880 and died in Wyoming in 1894. See Ezra Strong Jr, "Find A Grave: Ezra Strong," Ancestry.com, accessed July 2, 2024, http://search.ancestry.com/cgibin/sse.dll ?indiv=1&db=FindAGraveUS&h.
54. Merle H. Graffam, "A Survey of Cowboy Glyphs from the Big Water, Utah, region of Kane County, Utah" (1997): 1. Savage's inscription is found on a butte near Church Wells. If Graffam's claim that Savage arrived in the "early 1860s" is valid, then this might be the oldest cowboy inscription in the region.
55. Alder and Brooks, *Washington County*, 15.
56. Reeve, *Making Space*, 15–17, 85–92.
57. Holt, *Beneath These Red Cliffs:* 2, 8; Isabel T. Kelly, *Southern Paiute Ethnography*, University of Utah Anthropological Papers 69 (Salt Lake City: University of Utah Press, 1964).
58. Farmer, *On Zion's Mount,* 74–91.

59. Franz Kolb, "The Northern Ute Indian Reservation: Established Portrayal and Change" (Master's thesis, Brigham Young University, 1983); Warren R. Metcalf, "A Precarious Balance: The Northern Utes and the Black Hawk War," *Utah Historical Quarterly* 57, no. 1 (1989), 24–35; Virginia McConnell Simmons, *The Ute Indians of Utah, Colorado and New Mexico* (Boulder: University of Colorado Press, 2000). The removal occurred over several years and included all Utah bands of Northern Utes. Southern Paiutes were not part of this removal, and many were probably glad to be rid of the Utes. Wa'kara and his raiders had wreaked havoc on Paiute communities during their enthusiastic participation in the slave trade with the Mexicans in New Mexico and California.
60. Peter Gottfredson, *History of Indian Depravations in Utah* (Salt Lake City: Skelton Publishing, 1919).
61. Jacob Hamblin, cited in Wixom, *Hamblin*, 231–32; Jones, *Being and Becoming Ute*, 68–73, 98–105.
62. Priddy Meeks, "Journal of Priddy Meeks," *Utah Historical Quarterly* 10 (1942): 185.
63. Luella Adams Dalton, *History of Iron County Mission, Parowan, Utah, the Mother Town* (Parowan, UT: Daughters of the Utah Pioneers, 2001), 67.
64. Linda King Newell and Vivian Linford Talbot, *A History of Garfield County* (USHS; Panguitch, UT: Garfield County Commission, 1998), 52.
65. Meeks, "Journal," 187–88.
66. Adair, interview.
67. Dalton, *Iron County Mission*, 149–50.
68. Dalton, *Iron County Mission*, 149–50.
69. Glynn Bennion, "A Pioneer Cattle Venture of the Bennion Family," *Utah Historical Quarterly* 34, no. 4 (1966): 320.
70. Bradley, *Kane County*, 60.
71. Robinson, *Kane County*, 5.
72. It is always possible that Hamblin and his missionary companions ventured into the Kanab area during his tenure as an missionary and that he constructed the dugouts as temporary shelters during his missionary forays to the Kaibab Paiutes. Wixom notes that Hamblin was chastised for making unauthorized missionary trips to outlying bands from 1854 to 1857. By 1858, he had been named president of the Southern [Utah] Indian Mission and was free to go where he wanted, and he immediately initiated expeditions to the Hopi Pueblos. No mention is made of missionary trips to the Kaibab Band at that time.
73. National Park Service, "The Mormon Militia and Pipe Springs," accessed September 27, 2021, http://www.nps.gov/pisp/photosmultimedia/the-mormon-militia-and-pipe-sprin.htm.
74. Robinson, *Kane County*, 18. This might be an alternate spelling for Wahweap, which is located near Crossing of the Fathers at the lower end of Lake Powell.

It would have been directly in the path of Navajo raiding parties. The National Park Service's history of Lee's Ferry indicates that Mormons placed guards at Lee's Ferry (called Pahreah Crossing at the time) and at Crossing of the Fathers to deter Navajo raiders. See "Lees Ferry History," Glen Canyon National Recreation Area, National Park Service, accessed September 27, 2021, https://www.nps.gov/glca/learn/historyculture/leesferryhistory.htm.

75. Jacob Hamblin, letter dated March 1870, cited in Bradley, *Kane County,* 70.
76. Robinson, *Kane County*, 18.
77. Meeks, "Journal," 191–92.
78. His name is spelled Shirts, Shirtz, and Shurtz in various family records, in LDS Church records, and on Ancestry.com, and his father's name was spelled Shertz.
79. Robinson, *Kane County*, 10, 488.
80. S. M. Smith, "History of Peter Shirts," Ancestry.com, accessed October 28, 2016, http://mv.ancestry.com/viewer/2eda31dc-07074ce6-9fb9-63b684b5243c/9356973/6044587404. See also: P. T. Reilly, "Historic Utilization of Paria River," *Utah Historical Quarterly* 45, no. 2 (1977): 189.
81. Smith, "Shirts."
82. "Peter Shirts," Ancestry.com, accessed July 2, 2021, https://www.ancestry.com/mediaui-viewer/tree/6701845/person/975118281/media/678e110a-369e-47f1-9103bd1461d9d384.
83. Smith, "Peter Shirts History." Most in the Shirts family now accept as gospel truth a story told of an old prospector who showed up in Fruitland, New Mexico, in 1882. The prospector became ill and died, and was buried in an unmarked grave there. The family has since erected a monument to Peter Shirts at the Fruitland cemetery. See Ambrose Shirts, "A Biographical Sketch of Peter Shirts," October 7, 1958, accessed July 2, 2024, https://www.familysearch.org/photos/artifacts/424793.
84. Bradley, *Kane County*, 60.
85. Bradley, *Kane County*, 60.
86. James A. Little, *Jacob Hamblin: A Narrative of His Personal Experience as a Frontiersman, Missionary to the Indians and Explorer* (Salt Lake City: Deseret News, 1909), 100. Note: Hamblin was not prone to exaggeration or hyperbole, and the total livestock indicated are probably an accurate indication of what he was told. If the numbers he gives are correct, Kane County settlers were engaged in livestock ranching in a big way. Probably fewer than 100 people were living in the area at the time, or the equivalent of 120 to 150 head of cattle and sheep per person. The herds also possibly belonged to farmers in communities in Iron and Washington County, and reflect aggregated herds in the area.
87. Bradley, *Kane County*, 69.
88. Bradley, *Kane County*, 46–47.

89. George Theobald, "Personal Pioneer Interview," January 25, 1937, Works Progress Administration, Utah Section, Biographical Sketches, ca. 1930–1941, MSS B 289, USHS.
90. Newell and Talbot, *Garfield County*, 57–59. Given the small size of the enclosure, it seems unlikely that the earliest residents of Garfield County brought large numbers of livestock with them. In fact, the earliest efforts of the settlers seem to have been focused primarily on cultivation of crops and construction of irrigation ditches.
91. Newell and Talbot, *Garfield County*, 65.
92. Newell and Talbot, *Garfield County*, 66–67.
93. Newell and Talbot, *Garfield County*, 62.
94. John Louder, in Gottfredson, *Depredations*, 190.
95. Newell and Talbot, *Garfield County*, 66.
96. Lowell J. Mecham, interview exhibit, Bryce Canyon National Park Museum, Bryce Canyon National Park, UT.
97. Mecham, interview exhibit.
98. Wixom, *Hamblin*, 242–46.
99. Bradley, *Kane County*, 69.
100. Juanita Brooks, "Journal of Thales H. Haskell," *Utah Historical Quarterly* 12 (1944), 69.
101. Lamanite is a term from the Book of Mormon that refers to the ancient inhabitants of the New World who had fallen from their enlightened state as taught to them by Jesus Christ.
102. Wixom, *Hamblin,* 13.
103. Brigham Young, letter to Jacob Hamblin, titled "President's Office, Great Salt Lake City, March 5, 1858," transcribed in Little, 55.
104. According to one child survivor of the Mountain Meadows Massacre, Hamblin's Paiute foster son Albert participated in the tragic events (see Wixom, *Hamblin*, 84–85).
105. Bradley, *Kane County*, 70.
106. Bradley, *Kane County*, 67, 99.
107. Hamblin, quoted in Holt, *Beneath These Red Cliffs*, 34–35.
108. Robinson, *Kane County*, 11.
109. Robinson, *Kane County*, 15.
110. There are references to Navajo raiding parties crossing at Pahreah Crossing, which would become Lee's Ferry, but this would have been much more difficult for livestock due to faster-moving waters. The National Park Service's historical interpretation at Lee's Ferry indicates the crossing was first used by Jacob Hamblin in 1864, and that Mormon militiamen guarded the crossing during the Indigenous American hostilities of 1866–69; National Park Service, "Lees Ferry History."

111. Little, *Jacob Hamblin*, 101.
112. Gottfredson, *Depredations*, 184–85.
113. Woolley, "Expedition," 153–54.
114. Gottfredson, *Depredations*.
115. George Theobald, "Personal Pioneer Interview."
116. Editorial, "Little Known Circleville Massacre Is Very Much Worth Remembering," *Salt Lake Tribune*, April 22, 2016, accessed March 25, 2021, http://archive.sltrib.com/article.php?id=3808767&itype=CMSID; Albert Winkler, "The Circleville Massacre: A Brutal Incident in Utah's Black Hawk War," *Utah Historical Quarterly* 55, vol. 1 (1987): 4–21.
117. A complete list of all expedition participants is offered in Gottfredson, *Depredations*, 225.
118. Gottfredson, *Depredations*, 225.
119. Bradley, *Kane County*, 52.
120. Robinson, *Kane County*, 29.
121. Beef cattle prices in the 1860s ranged from $5 per head in Texas to $40 per head in the Midwest, which gave rise to the huge cattle drives of Western lore. Early Utah ranchers raised cattle for milk, leather, tallow, and occasionally consumption, and sheep for wool, both by their own families and as a currency to trade for other goods and services. Very rarely would livestock be sold for cash amongst themselves, as most Utah families of that day had little or none. But the pioneers could demand high prices from outsiders traveling through the territory. Even at a high of $40 per head, Tenney's estimate of a $1 million loss would be the equivalent of 25,000 head of stolen cattle in southern Utah.
122. Charles Kelly, *The Outlaw Trail: A History of Butch Cassidy and His Wild Bunch* (1938; reis., Lincoln: University of Nebraska Press, 1996), 146.
123. Wixom, *Hamblin,* 249.

Notes to Chapter 3

1. Julius S. Dalley, *History of Grazing*, Works Progress Administration, Utah Writers Project (1941), 3; MSS B 100, USHS.
2. The federal government's campaign against the stalwarts of the Mormon religion was the second time the Utah faithful had felt betrayed by the United States (the first was the invasion of Salt Lake City during the 1857 Utah War). Many practicing polygamists in Kane and Garfield counties were arrested and imprisoned, and local communities developed early warning systems that alerted the faithful of the approach of U.S. marshals. The antipolygamy crusade fostered a seething resentment towards the federal government that persists to this day, one that plays out in public lands issues. Mark E. Miller, "St. Johns' Saints: Interethnic Conflict in Northeastern Arizona, 1880–1885," *Journal of Mormon History* 23 (1997), 84–92; Bigler, *Forgotten Kingdom*, 317–36; Bradley, *Kane County*, 148.

3. This "great" colonization was to be the last one organized and directed by Mormon Church leaders, but it was not the last land rush in Utah. The great Uinta Basin land rush of 1905–06 resulted from the opening of the Ute Reservation to homesteaders, many of whom were young Mormon families hopeful of acquiring their own farms. Many grown children of families from Kane and Garfield Counties participated in the Uinta Basin land rush in hopes of acquiring their own farms. This land rush was coordinated by the federal government, and church involvement was limited to encouraging its members to participate in the lottery for homestead parcels. This encouragement was apparently successful as all subsequent communities in the Uinta Basin were predominantly Mormon. David Rich Lewis, *Neither Wolf Nor Dog: American Indians, Environment, and Agrarian Change* (New York: Oxford University Press, 1994), 53–60.
4. Dee Brown and Martin F. Schmitt, *Trail Driving Days* (New York: Charles Scribner's Sons, 1974), 1–6; John F. Ptak, "On the Early Imagery and Definition of the 'Cowboy,'" JF Ptak Science Books Post 3836, April 2020, http://longstreet.typepad.com/thesciencebookstore/2020/04/on-the-history-of-the-word-cowboy.html.
5. Charles S. Peterson, "Grazing in Utah: A Historical Perspective," *Utah Historical Quarterly* 57, no. 4 (1989): 302–3.
6. Peterson, "Grazing," 306
7. Peterson, "Grazing," 306.
8. Bennion, "Pioneer Cattle Venture," 315–25.
9. Stephen Vandiver Jones, quoted in Richard E. Turley Jr. and Eric C. Olson, "Fame Meets Infamy: The Powell Survey and Mountain Meadows Participants, 1870–1873," *Utah Historical Quarterly* 81, no. 1 (2013): 6–26.
10. Turley and Olson, "Fame Meets Infamy," 15–16. There are no General Land Office records indicating that the Adair family ever filed a patent on these lands.
11. Newell and Talbot, *Garfield County,* 61.
12. The lead author wishes to thank the many southern Utah cowboys who accompanied him on expeditions deep into the wilderness and who assisted with this history with the help of whiskey tucked in saddle bags. As promised, you will remain unnamed.
13. Peterson, "Historical Analysis," 311.
14. Arthur L. Thomas, *Report of the Governor of Utah to the Secretary of the Interior, 1890* (Washington, DC: U.S. Government Printing Office, 1890). See also Peterson, "Livestock Law," 202–3.
15. Walker, "Cattle Industry of Utah," 186. Note the railhead in California was actually in Oakland.
16. Inflation Calculator, accessed March 26, 2021, http://www.westegg.com/inflation.

17. Frank Hamblin, "An Interview with Frank Hamblin," February 17, 1941, in Dalley, *History of Grazing*.
18. Brown and Schmitt, *Trail Driving Days*, 7–8.
19. John William Malone, *An Album of the American Cowboy* (New York: Franklin Watts, 1971), 46–47.
20. Andrew Amundsen, quoted in Andrea Aker, "A Little History Behind Arizona's Early Mormon Missions," Arizona Oddities, accessed July 29, 2021, https://arizonaoddities.com/2010/09/a-little-history-behind-arizonas-early-mormon-missions/; Miller, "St. Johns' Saints," 68–71.
21. Alder and Brooks, *Washington County*, 215.
22. Jerry D. Spangler and Matthew Zweifel, *Risky Business: Farming and Travel in the Upper Paria River Corridor* (Ogden: Colorado Plateau Archaeological Alliance, 2012).
23. Miller, "St. John's Saints," 66–99; Pearl Udall Nelson, "Eliza Luella Stewart Udall," in *Pioneer Women of Arizona,* eds. Roberta Flake Clayton, Catherine H. Ellis, and David F. Boone, 737–40 (1969; reis., Salt Lake City: Deseret Book, 2017), 737–740.
24. John W. Mangum, "History of John W. Mangum," interviewed by Layton J. Ott, February 20, 1939, Works Progress Administration, Federal Writers' Project, USHS. In 1941, Brigham A. Riggs indicated that he was guarding the fort at the time and his brother Charles H. Riggs was also present and planting crops before Stewart arrived. John A. Riggs had also brought a herd of forty-two cattle in 1870.
25. Levi Stewart, "I, Levi Stewart," testimony as told to Norene Robinson, n.d., Special Collections, Kanab City Library, Kanab, UT.
26. Bradley, *Kane County*, 73.
27. Robert H. Webb, Spence S. Smith, and V. Alexander S. McCord, *Historic Channel Change of Kanab Creek, Southern Utah and Northern Arizona*, Grand Canyon Natural History Association Monograph 9 (1991). See also Jonathan E. Harvey, Joel L. Pederson, and Tammy M. Rittenour, "Exploring Relations Between Arroyo Cycles and Canyon Paleoflood Records in Buckskin Wash, Utah," *GSA Bulletin* 123 no. 11–12 (2011):2266–76.
28. Turley and Olson, "Fame Meets Infamy," 6.
29. Juanita Brooks, *Emma Lee* (Logan: Utah State University Press, 1984), 46–47.
30. Turley and Olson, "Fame Meets Infamy," 4–6. William Dame, the first mayor of Parowan, was also indicted and arrested for his involvement in the Mountain Meadows Massacre. He never went to trial. Will Bagley, *Blood of the Prophets: Brigham Young and the Massacre at Mountain Meadows* (Norman: University of Oklahoma Press, 2002), 283, 290, 300–301.
31. It is certainly possible Powell or someone else in his party informed authorities about John D. Lee and William Dame operating with impunity, but the

journal references of the Powell Expedition participants all express dismay that either man could have been involved, stating that they were all agreeable and hospitable. According to their journals, the participants in the 1871 expedition down the Colorado River were warmly welcomed at Lee's ranch at the mouth of the Paria River, and they helped out with ranching and gardening chores while awaiting resupply.

32. Brooks, *Emma Lee*, 57, 65–70, 83–85; Newell and Talbot, *Garfield County*, 80–81.
33. Brigham Young's "call" to settle rural parts of the state was, to faithful members of the Church, the word and will of God, and refusal was not an option. There were instances where individuals avoided the calling by paying someone else to take their place.
34. U.S. Census Bureau, population schedule, Kanab, Kane County, Utah Territory, 1870 United States Federal Census, microfilm roll M593_1611, page 447B, image 349581, National Archives and Records Administration, Washington, DC, Family History Library Film 553110, images reproduced by FamilySearch, accessed July 2, 2024, Ancestry.com. Levi Stewart was part of Brigham Young's contingent that had visited Fort Kanab in April 1870.
35. Robinson, *Kane County,* 21.
36. "Autobiography of John Franklin Brown, as told to Blanche Mace," n.d., Special Collections, Kanab City Library, Kanab, UT. Brown is probably referring to Anson P. Winsor, who arrived in 1870 to manage Mormon Church livestock at Pipe Spring.
37. Clarice Stewart Anderson, "A Sketch of the Life of My Parents John Riley and Elizabeth Stevenson Stewart," n.d., Special Collections, Kanab City Library, Kanab, UT; Bradley, *Kane County*, 76–78.
38. Willis Little, "Interview with Willis Little," February 17, 1941, in Dalley, *History of Grazing*. See also Robinson, *Kane County*, 23.
39. Brigham Young, quoted in Turley and Olson, "Fame Meets Infamy," 7. Brigham Young's expedition was joined by members of the Powell Expedition somewhere on the Markagunt Plateau between Paragonah and Panguitch. Brigham Young and John Wesley Powell, as well as Powell's expeditioners, enjoyed an exceptionally cordial and cooperative relationship in light of the federal government's campaign against Mormon polygamy. Beginning in the winter of 1871–72, Powell's survey would be based out of Kanab. Francis Marion Bishop, a Civil War veteran and cartographer on the 1871–72 Powell Expedition, remained in Utah, converted to Mormonism, married the daughter of Mormon Apostle Orson Pratt, and became a professor at the University of Deseret, now the University of Utah.
40. Moses Franklin Farnsworth, "Autobiography of Moses Franklin Farnsworth," n.d., Special Collections, Kanab City Library, Kanab, UT.

41. Robinson, *Kane County*, 458–59.
42. The 1870 Census lists their surname as "Janbreon" and the first names of the males all have Nordic spellings, such as Jahl, Lael, and Almvrn; U.S. Census Bureau, population schedule, Belview, Kane County, Utah Territory, 1870 United States Federal Census, microfilm roll M593_1611, page 467A, image 350498, National Archives and Records Administration, Washington, DC, Family History Library Film 553110, images reproduced by FamilySearch, Ancestry.com, accessed July 2, 2024. William "Willie" Johnson was also implicated in the Mountain Meadows Massacre but was never charged.
43. Robinson, *Kane County*, 486–87. Brigham Young had "discovered" Johnson Canyon during his 1870 expedition to explore the upper Sevier River country (see Turley and Olson, "Fame Meets Infamy").
44. Citing Joel Johnson's journal, Robinson says the Johnsons arrived in spring 1871. How long Joel remained is uncertain, but he was gone by 1880. Very little information about the other Johnson brothers is available on Ancestry.com, and which of them, or their families, moved to Johnson Canyon is uncertain. U.S. Census records indicate his brother William and family were still there in 1880.
45. The brothers' descendants are said to comprise the largest family in the Mormon Church today. They were early converts to Mormonism and confidants of early Church leaders. One sister became a plural wife to Church founder Joseph Smith, and two other sisters were sealed to him in temple rites. Joel is credited with writing the words to the Mormon anthem "High on the Mountain Top," still sung by congregations to this day. See R. D. Johnson, *J. E. J.: The Trail to Sundown, Casadaga to Casa Grande* (Salt Lake City, UT: Joseph Ellis Johnson Family Committee, 1961).
46. Alvin Judd, "An Interview with Alvin Judd," February 13, 1941, in Dalley, *History of Grazing*.
47. Bradley, *Kane County*, 84.
48. Bradley, *Kane County*, 96. Note that Robinson's history states the Moapa Valley (Nevada) settlers arrived in 1869, but this information is inconsistent with other histories, nor is it reflected in U.S. Census records.
49. Bradley, *Kane County*, 83.
50. Jack Chynoweth, interview by Marsha Holland, Southern Utah Oral History Project, May 13, 2003, Matheson Special Collections, Southern Utah University, Cedar City (hereafter SUU).
51. Bradley, *Kane County*, 85. This number might well include the large church herds and Orderville United Order herds at that time grazing on the Arizona Strip. These herds were managed out of Kanab and Orderville, respectively.
52. Dalley, *History of Grazing*, 5.
53. Little, interview; Frank Hamblin, interview.

54. Little, interview. Little also noted that the harsh winter of 1879–80 wiped out much of Andrus-Mansfield herd. James Andrus was superintendent of the church-owned New Canaan cattle cooperative at this same time. Whether the Skutumpah herds were part of New Canaan or were Andrus's private investment is unknown.
55. Frank Hamblin, interview.
56. Riggs, "Early History"; William McAllister, "An Interview with Mr. and Mrs. William McAllister," February 5, 1941, in Dalley, *History of Grazing*.
57. Little, interview.
58. Adair, interview.
59. Riggs, "Early History."
60. Riggs, "Early History."
61. U.S. Census Bureau, Kanab 1870.
62. Dalley, *History of Grazing*, 2. The numbers of sheep and cattle were probably much greater than indicated. Kanab-area ranchers used ranges in Arizona and Utah and therefore would have to pay taxes in both states. Often ranchers claimed half of their livestock in one state and half in the other.
63. Bradley, *Kane County*, 82. The 20-acre estimate was clearly inaccurate inasmuch as Long Valley had not been resettled at the time of the 1870 federal census, and farms continued to be developed there in 1871 and 1872.
64. Bradley, *Kane County*, 84.
65. Bradley, *Kane County*, 19.
66. Newell and Talbot, *Garfield County*, 79.
67. Bradley, *Kane County*, 136.
68. Oscar Judd, interview by Marsha Holland, Southern Utah Oral History Project, February 24, 2004, SUU.
69. Bradley, *Kane County*, 85.
70. F. A. Hammond, *Deseret News*, April 29, 1885. See also Arrington, *Great Basin Kingdom*, 354.
71. Alexander, "Lost Memory and Environmentalism," 47–68.
72. Arrington, *Great Basin Kingdom*, 354.
73. Bradley, *Kane County*, 82.
74. Newell and Talbot, *Garfield County*, 59.
75. The Andrus contingent appears to have traveled up the Paria River, or at least a good portion of it. The bottom of the Paria River is relatively flat and gravel-packed, something that made it attractive as a major wagon route in the 1870s for Mormons bound for new colonies in Arizona. The axle-grease inscriptions of these pioneers are still evident on the canyon walls here.
76. Newell and Talbot, *Garfield County*, 71. Andrus himself would return to Kane County to become a cattle rancher. Escalante was originally called "Potato Valley" because of the wild potatoes that once grew there in abundance.

Militiaman John S. Adams wrote in 1866 that he cooked a bunch and "they were somewhat like the cultivated potato but smaller," quoted in Gottfredson, *Depredations*, 233.

77. Jones, *Being and Becoming Ute*, 172; Hatch, "Statement."
78. Newell and Talbot, *Garfield County*, 113.
79. C. C. Anderson, *Yesterday and Today* (Salt Lake City: Utah Writers Project, Works Progress Administration, 1940): 2.
80. E. A. Griffin, "Statement of E. A. Griffin, Concerning Range Conditions on Forest and Public Lands in Southern Utah, as It Was in Early Days and as It Is Now," in *Special Range Report R-4*, compiled by Carl H. Dopp, September 25, 1940. MSS B 100, USHS.
81. Newell and Talbot, *Garfield County*, 117.
82. Arrington, *Great Basin Kingdom*, 314.
83. Arrington, *Great Basin Kingdom*, 315.
84. Arrington, *Great Basin Kingdom*, 321.
85. Andrew Karl Larson, *I Was Called to Dixie: The Virgin River Basin, Unique Experiences in Mormon Pioneering* (Salt Lake City: Deseret Press, 1961).
86. According to LDS Church biographical sketches, Anson P. Winsor was an early convert to Mormonism in 1842 and was a close associate of Church founder Joseph Smith, serving as a bodyguard to the Mormon prophet. He migrated to Utah and was prominent in the Utah War of 1857. In 1861, he was sent to southern Utah to be bishop of the Grafton Ward before being called to settle Kanab and Pipe Spring. Winsor in Long Valley (now Mount Carmel) was named after him. Andrew Jenson, *LDS Biographical Encyclopedia: A Compilation of Biographical Sketches of Prominent Men and Women in the Church of Jesus Christ of Latter Day Saints* (Salt Lake City: Andrew Jenson History Co., 1901).
87. Robert W. Olsen, "The Powell Survey Kanab Base Line," *Utah Historical Quarterly* 37, no. 2 (1969): 19.
88. Robinson, *Kane County*, 491–492. Pipe Spring would seem an odd location for a large-scale dairy operation due to the transportation challenges. Possibly dairy products were shipped to nearby Kanab, although there were other large dairy operations near Kanab (Dairy Canyon was so named because of a large-scale dairy there). St. George and its surrounding communities would have been a ready market, but the dairy products would have been transported 60 mi. The distances, the suffocating heat, and the lack of refrigeration would have posed significant obstacles. See Juanita Brooks, "The Arizona Strip," *Pacific Spectator* 3 (1949): 290–301.
89. A. P. Winsor, letter to Brigham Young, April 9, 1866, datelined "Grafton, Kane County," Brigham Young Office Files Reel 43, Box 31, Folder 17, Special Collections, J. Willard Marriott Library, Salt Lake City.

90. *U.S., Register of Civil, Military, and Naval Service, 1863–1959*, online database, Ancestry.com, accessed December 1, 2021. Both the father, Abraham Perry Winsor, and the son, Anson Perry Winsor, went by "A. P.," but the historical events in southern Utah are all attributed to the son, Anson.
91. Arrington, *Great Basin Kingdom*, 221.
92. "Pine Valley Chapel," Washington County Historical Society, accessed March 29, 2021, https://wchsutah.org/churches/pine-valley-chapel.php.
93. Brooks, "Arizona Strip."
94. Jeffrey H. Altschul and Helen C. Fairley, *Man, Models, and Management: An Overview of the Archaeology of the Arizona Strip and the Management of Its Cultural Resources* (St. George, UT: Arizona Strip Field Office, Bureau of Land Management, 1989), 187.
95. Sarah Blanche Robinson, "Reminiscences," told to Louise Haycock, n.d., Special Collections, Kanab City Library, Kanab, Utah.
96. Robinson, *Kane County*, 460.
97. Arrington, *Great Basin Kingdom*, 355.
98. Riggs, "Early History."
99. Bradley, *Kane County*, 148.
100. The sell-off of the New Canaan assets coincided with the "release" of Elizabeth Whitmore, the widow of James Whitmore who was killed at Pipe Spring in 1866, from her southern Utah mission. The Whitmore family history indicates she returned to Salt Lake City in 1883 trailing a large herd of cattle. At about that same time, her sons began a large cattle operation in the West Tavaputs Plateau of eastern Utah that ran about ten thousand head of cattle. Elizabeth self-identified on the 1880 Census as a "stock raiser," but there is no mention of Whitmore herds on the Arizona Strip after the death of her husband. The timing of her "release" and the simultaneous emergence of massive Whitmore herds in eastern Utah suggest the possibility that Elizabeth was a major shareholder in New Canaan, or that church herds were transferred to her ownership to avoid their confiscation by federal authorities.
101. Riggs, "Early History."
102. Newell and Talbot, *Garfield County*, 115.
103. William Berry was one of the original settlers of Long Valley in the 1860s, and with his extended family, the community was known as Berryville. During the Black Hawk War, two brothers and a sister-in-law were killed, and William Berry and other families abandoned Long Valley on Brigham Young's orders. At the end of hostilities, Long Valley was "given" to economic refugees from the Muddy Mission in Nevada. When some of the original settlers returned to reclaim their farms, they found their cabins and farm lands had already been appropriated by the Muddy Mission settlers. Berry was later murdered by a mob in Tennessee while serving a Church mission. See Shauna Timpson Johnson, "Early Latter-day Saint Martyrs: The Jesse Woods and Armela Shanks Berry Family," *Religious Educator* 19, no. 2 (2018): 152–71.

104. Ida Chidester and Eleanor Bruhn, *Golden Nuggets of Pioneer Days: A History of Garfield County* (Panguitch: Daughters of the Utah Pioneers, 1989), 33.
105. Raymond Devar Pollock, interview, n.d., Visitor Center Museum, Bryce Canyon National Park, Bryce, Utah.
106. Newell and Talbot, *Garfield County*, 127–28, 143. Isaac Riddle would build a ranch in this area later in the 1870s at what would become known as the community of Widtsoe. Riddle was part of Jacob Hamblin's missionary campaign to the Hopis in 1860, and he accompanied Hamblin on an 1874 expedition to Grass Valley with a Navajo delegation to investigate the killing of young Navajos who had gone there to trade. He would later move to Escalante in the 1870s and built a flour mill there in 1892. The name of Riddle's livestock cooperative is not indicated in the history of Garfield County.
107. Walker, "Cattle Industry," 188.
108. Walker, "Cattle Industry," 189.
109. Arrington, *Great Basin Kingdom*, 323.
110. Arrington, *Great Basin Kingdom*, 323–24. The panic occurred the same year Congress passed the Coinage Act of 1873, which shifted the United States to the gold standard and demonetized silver, making it impossible for silver mine owners to have their silver minted. The value of silver plummeted, and silver mines closed across the West. See United States Mint, "U.S. Mint History: The Crime of 1873," March 22, 2017, https://www.usmint.gov/news/inside-the-mint/mint-history-crime-of-1873.
111. Arrington, *Great Basin Kingdom*, 324.
112. E. M. Webb, "Manuscript History of Kanab Stake," LDS Church Archives, Salt Lake City, Utah.
113. Arrington, *Great Basin Kingdom*, 324.
114. Boyer, *William Derby Johnson Jr. Journal.*
115. Arrington, *Great Basin Kingdom*, 326.
116. P. T. Reilly, "Kanab United Order: The President's Nephew and the Bishop," *Utah Historical Quarterly* 42, no. 2 (1974): 144–64. Reilly indicates a census was taken that revealed 261 members of the Kanab Order, thirty-nine in the Johnson Order and sixty-seven in the Pahreah Order; the membership totals of the other orders were not indicated (p. 149).
117. Angus Woodbury, "A History of Utah and its National Parks," *Utah Historical Quarterly* 12, nos. 3–4 (1944): 184.
118. Stegner, *Mormon Country*, 108–120.
119. Arrington, *Great Basin Kingdom*, 334.
120. Brooks, *Emma Lee*, 67–69.
121. Adair, interview. Adair claims no other ranchers were in the area when he arrived in January 1878, but this seems unlikely. New Canaan herds had been running in House Rock Valley for years, as had the K herds out of Kanab.
122. Adair, interview. This statement suggests that outside encroachment had emerged by 1880.

123. Mark A. Pendleton, "The Orderville United Order of Zion," *Utah Historical Quarterly* 7, no. 4 (1939): 149.
124. Altschul and Fairley, *Man, Models, and Management*, 190–91.
125. Altschul and Fairley, *Man, Models, and Management*, 191; Larson, *Called to Dixie*, 306.
126. U.S. Census Bureau, population schedule, Orderville, Kane County, Utah, 1880 United States Federal Census, microfilm roll *1336,* page 452C, enumeration district 029, National Archives and Records Administration, Washington, DC, Family History Library film 1255336, images reproduced by Family Search, accessed July 2, 2024, Ancestry.com.
127. Warren Foote, quoted in Bradley, *Kane County*, 95.
128. Altschul and Fairley, *Man, Models, and Management,* 191.
129. Adair, interview.
130. Chidester and Bruhn, *Golden Nuggets*, 93.
131. Gregory C. Crampton, *Mormon Colonization in Southern Utah and Adjoining Parts of Arizona and Nevada, 1851–1900* (Grand Canyon Village, AZ: Grand Canyon National Park Library, 1965).
132. F. M. Hodgin, "History of the North Kaibab, Kaibab National Forest" (Williams, AZ: Kaibab National Forest, 1962).
133. Robert G. Cleland and Juanita Brooks, *A Mormon Chronicle: The Diaries of John D. Lee, 1848–1876* (San Marino, CA: Huntington Library, 1983).
134. R. E. Gery and John A. Smith, *Report on Lieu Selections on that Portion of Arizona Line North and West of the Colorado River* (Washington, DC: U.S. Department of Agriculture, 1915).
135. Byrd H. Granger, *Arizona's Names: X Marks the Place* (Tucson, AZ: Falconer Press, 1983). The 1880 U.S. Census records for the Orderville precinct do not include anyone named Thompson or Van Slack.
136. Altschul and Fairley, *Man, Models, and Management*, 191; Woodbury, "National Parks," 190.
137. John Franklin Brown, quoted in Wesley P. Larsen, *Stories from the Arizona Strip* (Salt Lake City: Utah State Historical Society, 1998), 78.
138. Adair, interview.
139. Bradley, *Kane County*, 90–91.
140. Arrington, *Great Basin Kingdom*, 334–336.
141. Bradley, *Kane County*, 127.
142. Altschul and Fairley, *Man, Models, and Management*, 188.
143. Newell and Talbot, *Garfield County*, 119–120.
144. Newell and Talbot, *Garfield County*, 83.
145. John B. Wright, *Rocky Mountain Divide: Selling and Saving the West* (Austin: University of Texas Press, 1993), 160.
146. Wright, *Rocky Mountain Divide*, 166–167, 174.

147. Arrington, *Great Basin Kingdom*, 367.
148. Larsen, *Arizona Strip*, 60–61.
149. Effie Dean Rich, *Buckskin History, Kaibab Plateau and Grand Canyon* (1941), 5–6; manuscript on file, USHS.
150. Secretary's Department to Bros. Edwin D. Woolley and D. Seegmiller, January 29, 1887; A. W. Ivins, Memorandum of Agreement with Edwin D. Woolley and Daniel Seegmiller, March 1, 1894, box 4, folder 1, MS 36, Edwin D. Woolley Collection (henceforth Woolley Collection), SUU.
151. Larsen, *Arizona Strip*, 60–61.
152. Peterson, "Grazing," 309.
153. Altschul and Fairley, *Man, Models, and Management*, 192–193; Adair, interview.
154. H. E. Borrowman, letter to D. Seegmiller, November 14, 1891, MS 36 B4F1, Woolley Collection, SUU.
155. Altschul and Fairley, *Man, Models, and Management*, 193.
156. Secretary's Department, Salt Lake and Ft. Douglass Railway, letter to Bros. Woolley and Seegmiller, January 29, 1887, MS 36 B4F1, Woolley Collection, SUU.
157. Bradley, *Kane County*, 132.
158. Deidre M. Paulsen, "Stories and Storytelling Techniques of Rowland W. Rider, Cowboy on the Arizona Strip in the Early 1900s" (Master's thesis, Brigham Young University, 1975), 53.
159. Larson, *Called to Dixie*, 247.
160. Woodbury, "National Parks," 190.
161. Walter G. Mann, *The Kaibab Deer: A Brief History and Present Plan of Management* (Williams, AZ: Kaibab National Forest, 1941), 8.
162. Ivins, Memorandum of Agreement.
163. Anthony W. Ivins, "The Anthony W. Ivins Papers, 1875–1934," Register of the Collection at the Utah State Historical Society, Salt Lake City, 2001.
164. Ivins, Memorandum of Agreement.
165. Michael Belshaw and Eli Peplow Jr., *Historic Resources Study, Lake Mead National Recreation Area, Arizona* (Tucson, AZ: National Park Service, 1978).
166. "Ivins Papers," 4–7.
167. Anthony W. Ivins, *An Address Delivered by President Anthony W. Ivins Upon Completion of the Union Pacific Lodge at Grand Canyon* (Salt Lake City: Union Pacific System, 1935), 7–9, Anthony W. Ivins Collection, USHS.
168. Newell and Talbot, *Garfield County*, 224.
169. Kelly, *Outlaw Trail*, 16; Robinson, *Kane County*, 60–62.
170. Kelly, *Outlaw Trail*, 16–28; Robinson, *Kane County*, 60–62.
171. Miller, "Saint Johns' Saints," 70–78. This article details how David King Udall's second wife, Ida Hunt Udall, often ran family operations during David's long absences.

172. Richard Patterson, *Butch Cassidy: A Biography* (Lincoln: University of Nebraska Press, 1998), 5.
173. Patterson, *Butch Cassidy*, 7.
174. Patterson, *Butch Cassidy*, 7. Charles Kelly offered a different account of the Marshall Ranch, saying Max Parker bought the ranch in what is now Bryce Canyon National Park, which for some time had been a headquarters for a gang of horse thieves and cattle rustlers. Max kept one of the rustlers, Mike Cassidy, on as a hired hand. This account is not consistent with other histories.
175. Kelly, *Outlaw Trail*, 6.
176. Peterson, "Livestock Law," 209.
177. "Cattle Thieves: How They Do Business in Southern Utah," *Salt Lake Tribune*, September 16, 1882.
178. Odie B. Faulk, *Arizona: A Short History* (Norman: University of Oklahoma Press, 1970), 161.
179. White, "Animals and Enterprise," 262; "Cattle Thieves: How They Do Business in Southern Utah," *Salt Lake Tribune*, September 16, 1882.
180. Cited in Peterson, "Livestock Law," 209.
181. Peterson, "Livestock Law," 209.
182. "John A. 'Jack' Watson—Soldier, Blacksmith, Texas Ranger, Outlaw, Lawman, Private Investigator and Friend to Cyrus 'Doc' Shores—A Man to Cross Rivers With," accessed July 2, 2024, http://freepages.genealogy.rootsweb.ancestry.com/~hookersbend/bio_john_a_watson.htm.
183. Kelly, *Outlaw Trail*, 22–23; Matt Warner, *Last of the Bandit Riders . . . Revisited* (Salt Lake City: Big Moon Traders, 2000), 36.
184. Warner, *Bandit Riders*, 36.
185. Pearl Baker, *The Wild Bunch at Robbers Roost* (Lincoln: University of Nebraska Press, 1971), 147.
186. Frank Hamblin, interview.
187. Mangum, "History."
188. Warner, *Bandit Riders*, 43.
189. Patterson, *Butch Cassidy*, 236.
190. Newell and Talbot, *Garfield County*, 229.
191. Frederick S. Dellenbaugh, *A Canyon Voyage: the Narrative of the Second Powell Expedition Down the Green Colorado River from Wyoming, and the Explorations on Land in the Years 1871 and 1872* (New Haven, Connecticut: Yale University Press, 1908), 167.
192. Isabel Kelly, "Southern Paiute Ethnography."
193. Gottfredson, *Depredations*.
194. Anthony W. Ivins, *Cowboy Apostle: The Diaries of Anthony W. Ivins, 1875–1932*, ed. Elizabeth Oberdick Anderson (Salt Lake City, UT: Signature Books, 2013), 105–6.

195. Holt, *Beneath These Red Cliffs*, 33–35.
196. Holt, *Beneath These Red Cliffs*, 33–35.
197. Don D. Fowler and Catherine S. Fowler, eds., *Anthropology of the Numa* (Washington, DC: Smithsonian Institution, 1971).
198. J. W. Powell and G. W. Ingalls, *Report of Special Commissioners J. W. Powell and G. W. Ingalls on the Condition of the Ute Indians of Utah; the Pai-utes of Utah, Northern Arizona, Southern Nevada, and Southeastern California; the Go-si Utes of Utah and Nevada; the Northwestern Shoshones of Idaho and Utah; and the Western Shoshones of Nevada* (Washington, DC: Bureau of Indian Affairs, 1873).
199. Holt, *Beneath These Red Cliffs*, 105–6.
200. Paiute Tribe of Utah, accessed March 26, 2021, www.utahpaiutes.org.

Notes to Chapter 4

1. Utah Division of Water Resources, *Drought in Utah: Learning from the Past—Preparing for the Future*, State Water Plan 14 (Salt Lake City: Utah Division of Water Resources, 2017), 14.
2. Lenora Hall LeFevre, *Boulder Country and Its People: A History of the People of Boulder and the Surrounding Country, One Hundred Years, 1872–1973* (Springville, UT: Art City Publishing, 1973), 237.
3. Newell and Talbot, *Garfield County*, 219.
4. The term "tragedy of the commons" was first coined in 1833 by British economist William Forster Lloyd to describe unregulated grazing on common lands, referred to in Britain as "the commons." If an individual herder put out more cattle than he was allotted, the herder would benefit personally, but the other users of the commons would suffer as the resource was depleted. The term gained widespread attention in 1968 when ecologist Garrett Hardin expanded the concept to include all shared and unregulated resources such as oceans, rivers, and even air. The theory continues to enjoy favor in modern discussions about sustainable development, particularly as it relates to air quality, climate change, the depletion of fisheries and forests, habitat destruction, and human population growth. See Garrett Hardin, "Tragedy of the Commons," *Science* 162, no. 3859: 1243–48.
5. Wright, *Rocky Mountain Divide*, 170.
6. White, "Animals and Enterprise," 256.
7. Peterson, "Grazing," 306.
8. Agricultural Census, 1920, vol. 5, 692.
9. Heifers can be bred as early as fifteen months with the first calf produced at twenty-four months, but it requires skilled animal husbandry and ideal range conditions whereby the heifers can achieve minimum body weights for reproduction. Herefords reach puberty at 357 days and under ideal conditions could

produce a calf by the end of the second year of life. See: Stephen B. Blezinger, "Heifer Development Program Important to Ranch Management," *Cattle Today Online*, October 2013, http://www.cattletoday.com/archive/2003/October/CT295.shtml.

10. Starrs, *Let the Cowboy Ride,* 75; Gil Miller and Kevin Heaton, *Livestock Grazing on the Grand Staircase-Escalante National Monument: The Historical and Cultural Importance to the Region*, (Logan: USU-Agriculture Extension, 2015).
11. Judd, interview.
12. Chidester and Bruhn, *Golden Nuggets*, 161.
13. Bennion, "Pioneer Cattle Venture," 316.
14. William G. Robbins, *Lumberjacks and Legislators: Political Economy of the U.S. Lumber Industry, 1890–1941* (College Station: Texas A&M University Press, 1982), 23.
15. Walker, "Cattle Industry," 191. Garfield County did not exist in 1880 as a legal entity, but cattle certainly were there at the time, and these totals would have been lumped into Iron County.
16. Agricultural Census, 1935, vol. 1, pt 3, 886.
17. Rowland Rider relates an account where he helped instigate an incident where ten thousand head of sheep jumped to their deaths, or were forced to jump, trying to get to Colorado River water. See Paulsen, "Stories and Storytelling," 104.
18. Peterson, "Livestock Law," 305.
19. Robbins, *Lumberjacks and Legislators*, 12, 19, 22–25, 26–27.
20. Wright, *Rocky Mountain Divide*, 167–69.
21. H. F. Heady et al., "Livestock Grazing on Federal Lands in the 11 Western States," *Journal of Range Management*, 27, no. 3 (1974): 180.
22. Altschul and Fairley, *Man, Models, and Management,* 193.
23. Preston Nutter to J. N. Darling, Chief of the Bureau of Biological Survey, Washington, DC, 1935, USHS.
24. Brooks, "The Arizona Strip," 297.
25. Reed and Grace Mathis, Oral History #98-012, Dixie Pioneers and Story Tellers Oral History Collection (USHS, 1998), 9.
26. Rowland Rider, *The Rollaway Saloon: Cowboy Tales of the Arizona Strip* (Logan: Utah State University Press, 1985), 28, 42.
27. Edwin D. Woolley to Reid Smoot, October 28, 1903, box 4, fd 9, MS 36, SUU.
28. One notable exception was the San Rafael Desert country known as Robbers Roost. This area was teeming with rustlers, and ranchers in this area either formed an alliance with the "Roosters" for protection or they found their herds pilfered mercilessly. One rancher in the Green River Desert lost his entire herd of five hundred cattle in one year.
29. Paulsen, "Stories and Storytelling," 56.
30. "Men Who Have Made Utah Famous," *Salt Lake Telegram*, July 16, 1906.

31. Gery and Smith, *Lieu Selections.*
32. Robinson, *Kane County*, 113.
33. Rider, *Rollaway Saloon*, 50–51.
34. Gretchen Younghan and Katrina Rogers, "A Short History of Kane Ranch," on file with the Grand Canyon Trust, Flagstaff, AZ, n.d., 7.
35. Mann, *Kaibab Deer.*
36. Federal census records prior to 1900 do not allow for a more exact determination of the number of livestock on the Arizona Strip. Livestock populations were not separated out of state totals or they were lumped in with other counties south of the Colorado River.
37. Woolley to Smoot, October 28, 1903.
38. Peterson and Cannon, *Awkward State*, 186–87.
39. C. John Burk, "The Kaibab Deer Incident: A Long-Persisting Myth," *Bioscience* 23, no. 2 (1973), 113.
40. Burk, "Kaibab Deer Incident," 113.
41. David E. Brown, *The Grizzly in the Southwest* (Norman: University of Oklahoma Press, 1996), 123–26; David E. Brown, *The Wolf in the Southwest: The Making of an Endangered Species* (Tucson: University of Arizona Press, 1984), 24, 173.
42. Neil Prendergast, "Tracking the Kaibab Deer into Western History," *Western Historical Quarterly*, vol. 39, no. 4 (2008), 413–414; Aldo Leopold, "Deer Irruptions," paper completed for the National Resources Committee, Wisconsin Academy of Sciences, Arts and Letters, accessed April 19, 2022, https://localinannarbor.com/wp-content/uploads/2015/02/wi-wt1943-aleopold.pdf.
43. Donald Worster, *An Unsettled Country: Changing Landscapes of the American West* (Albuquerque: University of New Mexico Press, 1994), 73–75.
44. White, "Animals and Enterprise," 271. Some notable male writers of the day—including Grinnel himself, Theodore Roosevelt, Liberty Hyde Bailey, and Ernest Thompson Seton—validated both nature study and nature hunting.
45. Woolley to Smoot, October 28, 1903; Lorum Pratt to Reed Smoot, July 17, 1903; Woolley to Reed Smoot, August 26, 1909; latter two both box 4, fd 2, MS 36; all SUU.
46. Rider, *Rollaway Saloon*, 47.
47. David Lavender, *The Southwest* (Albuquerque: University of New Mexico Press, 1980), 218.
48. Bradley, *Kane County*, 70.
49. Peterson, "Grazing," 309.
50. Rider, *Rollaway Saloon*, 47.
51. H. E. Borrowman to Edwin D. Woolley, November 14, 1891, box 4, fd 1, MS 36, SUU.
52. Rider, *Rollaway Saloon*, 48; Altschul and Fairley, *Man, Models, and Management*, 196.

53. P. T. Reilly, "Road Across Buckskin Mountain," *Journal of Arizona History* 19 (1978): 402.
54. Rider, *Rollaway Saloon*, 64.
55. Rider, *Rollaway Saloon*, 49–51.
56. "Navajo Bridge," Glen Canyon National Recreation Area, accessed October 21, 2020, https://nps.gov/glca/historyculture/navajobridge.htm.
57. Paulsen, "Stories and Storytelling," 197.
58. Altschul and Fairley, *Man, Models, and Management*, 197.
59. Ruth L. Cunningham, "Pioneers of the Arizona Strip," 1996, Special Collections, Kanab City Library, Kanab, Utah.
60. Peterson and Cannon, *Awkward State*, 185, 192.
61. Quoted in Paulsen, "Stories and Storytelling," 57.
62. Altschul and Fairley, *Man, Models, and Management*, 196.
63. The Kaiparowits Plateau was probably "discovered" in the 1860s during the Black Hawk campaigns, but the first references are in the late 1870s when Mormon settlers arrived in Escalante. Along with Boulder Mountain, the Kaiparowits became ideal summer range for the Escalante ranchers. It is not yet known for certain whether they shared the southern Kaiparowits with their Mormon brethren from Kanab who used the adjacent Glen Canyon country near Wahweap.
64. James H. Beckstead, *Cowboying: A Tough Job in a Hard Land* (Salt Lake City: University of Utah Press, 1991), 58.
65. Roy Webb, *Register of the Records of the Preston Nutter Corporation (1876–1981)*, 1987, Manuscript Collection, Special Collections, J. Willard Marriott Library, University of Utah, Salt Lake City, 11.
66. Virginia N. Price, and John T. Darby, "Preston Nutter: Utah Cattleman, 1886–1936," *Utah Historical Quarterly* 32, no. 3 (1964): 238.
67. Webb, *Register of the Records*, 12; Janet Taylor, "A Tough Cattleman in a Tough Land: Preston Nutter," *Outlaw Trail Journal* (Summer 2007): 39.
68. Peterson, "Grazing," 306.
69. "The Last Great Cattle King," *Salt Lake Telegram*, January 28, 1936, 10. In a roundabout way, Nutter bought the Arizona Strip assets from the Mormon Church. Even though the LDS Church had renounced polygamy in 1890, church assets had been seized by the federal government as part of its campaign against polygamy. But the Church had retained its livestock herds using unindicted surrogates like Ivins. Today, the LDS Church owns one of the nation's largest cattle operations, the Deseret Land and Livestock Company, which was started in 1891.
70. Price and Darby, "Preston Nutter," 244.
71. Jerry D. Spangler, *Vermilion Dreamers and Sagebrush Schemers: An Overview of Human Occupation in the House Rock Valley and Eastern Arizona Strip* (Flagstaff, AZ: Grand Canyon Trust, 2007).

72. Price and Darby, "Preston Nutter," 244.
73. Webb, *Register of the Records*, 12.
74. Beckstead, *Cowboying*, 58; "Reservation Cattle," *Salt Lake Tribune*, August 7, 1894.
75. Preston Nutter, quoted in Price and Darby, "Preston Nutter," 243.
76. Jones, *Being and Becoming Ute*, 241–42.
77. Price and Darby, "Preston Nutter," 245.
78. Spangler and Spangler, *Last Chance Byway*, 186–87.
79. Walker, "Cattle Industry," 191. Ranchers big and small typically underrepresented the number of livestock they owned. Property taxes were levied on livestock, and by keeping the numbers low they could keep property taxes low. An example of this practice was Preston Nutter, who claimed to Carbon County that he only had a few hundred head of cattle there when it was widely known he had many thousand head. Nutter's claim provoked guffaws from county officials and the media, who usually lionized Nutter (see Spangler and Spangler, *Last Chance Byway*, 181).
80. Newell and Talbot, *Garfield County*, 224.
81. Robert McNamara, "Meaning and History of the Term Robber Baron," Thought Co., Humanities: History and Culture, last updated on March 2, 2021, https://thoughtco.com/robber-baron-definition-1773342.
82. Warner, *Bandit Riders*, 43.
83. Newell and Talbot, *Garfield County*, 228; Kelly, *Outlaw Trail*, 168–169. Ogden later helped Butch Cassidy evade a posse by giving him a fresh mount, and Cassidy gave Ogden a hundred-dollar bill and his tired mount.
84. Price and Darby, "Preston Nutter," 241.
85. Spangler and Spangler, *Last Chance Byway*, 165. Pete Nelson's son, Lee Sage, hints that his father continued to steal from Nutter throughout his employment.
86. Nutter, quoted in Price and Darby, "Preston Nutter," 249.
87. Southern Utah and Northern Arizona Cattlemen's Association, meeting minutes, January 17, 1906, box 2, fd 2, MS 36, SUU.
88. Southern Utah and Northern Arizona Cattlemen's Association, minutes.
89. B. F. Saunders to Edwin Woolley, April 19, 1905, box 2, fd 2, MS 36, SUU.
90. "A Man to Cross Rivers With," 2.
91. Doc Shores is a notable historical character in his own right. He worked from time to time for the Pinkerton Detective Agency, including one stint where his partner was famed assassin Tom Horn. He later became chief of police in Salt Lake City.
92. "A Man to Cross Rivers," 2; "Jack Watson Killed," *Salt Lake Tribune*, July 24, 1898; "From Monday's Daily July 25," *Deseret News*, July 30, 1898. Watson's biography does not indicate whether the killings occurred in Utah or the Arizona Strip.

93. Bradley, *Kane County*, 163–64.
94. Robinson, *Kane County*, 112.
95. Anderson, "John Riley and Eliza Stevenson Stewart."
96. Bennion, "A Pioneer Cattle Venture, 315–25.
97. Paul F. Starrs, "Transhumance as Antidote for Modern Sedentary Stock Raising," *Rangeland Ecology & Management* 71, no. 5 (2018): 592–602.
98. Rollins, "Land Policies," 248.
99. Dick Yardley, email to Matthew Zweifel, Grand Staircase-Escalante National Monument, August 10, 2017, copy in authors' possession. James Gilbert "Gib" Yardley was killed in France in World War I.
100. Yardley, email to Zweifel.
101. Adair, interview.
102. Chidester and Bruhn, *Golden Nuggets*, 161.
103. Newell and Talbot, *Garfield County*, 216. Some Panguitch ranchers continue to use the Wahweap area as winter ranges.
104. Veda Moosman Behunin, interview by Jay Hammon, July 10, 1997, Southern Utah Oral History Project, SUU.
105. Heber Hall, interview by Jay Hammon, July 14, 1998, Southern Utah Oral History Project, SUU.
106. Arrington, *Great Basin Kingdom*, 399–400.
107. Daniel Glass, "A History of Bullion Canyon," Marysvale, Utah Chamber of Commerce, 2010, accessed July 5, 2024, http://www.marysvaleutah.org/informationaboutmarysvale/history/59-a-history-of-bullion-canyon-marysvale-utahpiute-county.html. The railroad no longer exists, and portions of the railroad bed have been converted to bicycle trails.
108. Quoted in Newell and Talbot, *Garfield County*, 216.
109. Bradley, *Kane County*, 165; Robinson, *Kane County*, 112.
110. "Progress at Modena," *Salt Lake Tribune*, May 1, 1899. See also, Leonard J. Arrington, *David Eccles, Pioneer Western Industrialist* (Logan: Utah State University Press, 1975).
111. Donald F. Kraack, "Strip Country," *Frontier Times* (1965): 38–39.
112. Alder and Brooks, *Washington County*, 214.
113. Bradley, *Kane County*, 190.
114. G. Sutherland to Edwin Woolley, August 6, 1908, and Edwin Woolley to Gov. William Spry, April 1, 1910, box 4, fd 6, MS 36, SUU.
115. J. H. Manderfield to Edwin D. Woolley, August 13, 1913, box 4, fd 7, MS 36, SUU.
116. Bradley, *Kane County*, 204–5.
117. Dixie Shakespear, interview by Magaret Shakespear, October 21, 1999, SUU.
118. Behunin, interview.
119. White, "Animals and Enterprise," 267.

120. Neal Liston, interview by Jay Hammond, November 5, 1998, SUU.
121. Liston, interview.
122. Boyer, *William Derby Johnson Journal*, 173.
123. Oscar Judd, interview.
124. Robert Easton and Mackenzie Brown, *Lord of the Beasts: The Saga of Buffalo Jones* (Tucson: University of Arizona Press, 1961), 133.
125. Cited in Bradley, *Kane County*, 165.
126. Neaf Hamblin, "An Interview with Neaf Hamblin," February 21, 1941, in Dalley, *History of Grazing*.
127. Agricultural Census, 1935, 891–892.
128. Lorum Pratt to Edwin Woolley, July 17, 1903, box 4, fd 2, MS 36, SUU.
129. Bowman and Company to Reed Smoot, December 6, 1907, box 4, fd 2, MS 36, SUU.
130. Bradley, *Kane County*, 166; Altschul and Fairley, *Man, Models, and Management*, 195.
131. Sharlot Hall, *Sharlot Hall of the Arizona Strip: A Diary of a Journey Through Northern Arizona in 1911*, ed. C. Gregory Crampton (Flagstaff, AZ: Northland Press, 1975), 57; Arizona Memory Project, "Sharlot M. Hall—Arizona's Curator," accessed November 16, 2020, https://azmemory.azlibrary.gov/nodes/view/216.
132. Rich, "Buckskin History," 15.
133. Larsen, *Arizona Strip*, 100.
134. Tracie Welton, "A Very Brief History of the Kaibab Plateau and House-rock Valley," n.d., manuscript on file with Kaibab National Forest, Prescott, Arizona, 8.
135. Bradley, *Kane County*, 154–60.
136. Orson Hyde, quoted in Peterson, "Grazing," 316–17.
137. Peterson, "Grazing," 317.
138. Forest Reserve Act of 1891, Public Law 51-561, 16 U.S.C. ch. 2, subch 1, § 471 et seq.
139. Roosevelt's aggressive protection of forest lands was curtailed in 1907 when Congress limited the president's authority to designate new reserves and Congress changed the name of existing reserves to National Forests.
140. Samuel P. Hays, *Beauty, Health, and Permanence: Environmental Politics in the United States, 1955–1985* (New York: Cambridge University Press, 1987), 100–101; William Voight, Jr., *Public Grazing Lands: Use and Misuse by Industry and Government* (New Brunswick, NJ: Rutgers University Press, 1976), 52.
141. Peterson, "Grazing," 318.
142. Newell and Talbot, *Garfield County*, 218.
143. Rider, *Rollaway Saloon*, 28–29.
144. Gulliford, *Woolly West*, 79.

145. Starrs, *Let the Cowboy Ride*, 29.
146. Chidester and Bruhn, *Golden Nuggets*, 250–56.
147. Bradley, *Kane County*, 169.
148. Samuel P. Hays, *Conservation and the Gospel of Efficiency: The Progressive Conservation Movement, 1890–1920* (Cambridge, MA: Harvard University Press, 1959). Wendi Kane, "The U.S. Environmental Movement 1890–2002: Discourse, Divisions, Environmental Crisis Events, and Strategic Concessions" (PhD diss., University of Central Florida, 2014).
149. Wayne K. Hinton, "Getting Along: The Significance of Cooperation in the Development of Zion National Park," *Utah Historical Quarterly* 68, no. 4 (2000): 314.
150. Hal Rothman, "Shaping the Nature of a Controversy: The Park Service, the Forest Service, and the Cedar Breaks Proposal," *Utah Historical Quarterly* 55, no. 3 (1987): 215–16.
151. Hinton, "Getting Along," 316.
152. Hinton, "Getting Along," 316. Not all ranchers in southern Utah were opposed to the federal land designations. Residents living near what would become Zion National Park actually welcomed the National Park Service and "cheerfully" removed their cattle from the canyon when requested to do so (see Hinton, "Getting Along," and Betsy Gaines Quammen, "American Zion: Mormon Culture and the Creation of a National Park," in *The Earth Will Appear as a Garden of Eden: Essays on Mormon Environmental History*, eds. Jedediah S. Rogers and Matthew C. Godfrey, (Salt Lake City: University of Utah Press, 2019), 131–51.
153. Antiquities Act of 1906, 16 U.S.C. §§ 431-433.
154. Reed Smoot to Edwin Woolley, March 30, 1906, box 4, fd 5, MS 36, SUU.
155. "Petition" from the residents of Kanab and Freedonia," 1906, box 4, fd 5, MS 36, SUU.
156. Hal Rothman, "Second-Class Sites: National Monuments and the Growth of the National Park System," *Environmental Review* 10, no. 1 (1986): 44–47.
157. "Attempting to Make National Park of Kaibab Would Do Great Injury to Cattle and Sheep Industries," *Kane County Independent*, September 5, 1912.
158. "Legalized Robbery," *Kane County Independent*, October 24, 1912.
159. Anthony W. Ivins, *Cowboy Apostle: The Diaries of Anthony W. Ivins, 1875–1932*, ed. Elizabeth Oberdick Anderson (Salt Lake City, UT: Signature Books, 2013), 105–6.
160. Anthony Ivins to A. B. Farrow, August 10, 1925 and A.B. Farrow to Anthony Ivins, box 14, fd. 13, MSS B2, Anthony W. Ivins Papers, USHS; Frederick Hoxie, "From Prison to Homeland: The Cheyenne River Indian Reservation before World War I," *South Dakota History* 10 (1979): 1–24.
161. William Palmer to Dr. Farrow, August 25, 1925, box 11, fd. 41, Palmer Collection, SUU.

162. William Palmer to Hazel Brockbank, August 17, 1935, box 11, fd. 35, Palmer Collection, SUU.
163. Unknown author, "Indian Reservation," unpublished manuscript, box 14, fd. 11, MSS B2, Ivins Papers, USHS.
164. Ivins to Farrow, August 10, 1925.
165. Kathleen L. McKoy, *Pipe Spring: Cultures at a Crossroads: An Administrative History*, Cultural Resource Selections No. 15 (2000), National Park Service Intermountain Region, accessed April 5, 2021, https://nps.gov/parkhistory/online_books/pisp/adhi/adhin.htm#243.
166. James R. Garfield to Reed Smoot, October 1908, cited in McKoy, *Pipe Spring*.
167. McKoy, *Pipe Spring*.
168. R. A. Ward to Commissioner of Indian Affairs, October 23, 1912, cited in McKoy, *Pipe Spring*.
169. U.S. Census Bureau, Twenty-second Census Taken in the Year 2000. Washington, DC: U.S. Printing Office, 2002.
170. Chidester and Bruhn, *Golden Nuggets*, 261.
171. Newell and Talbot, *Garfield County*, 219.
172. Porter, "Statement." Porter's estimate is probably an exaggeration, although not by much. The 1930 U.S. Agricultural Census noted nearly 131,000 sheep in all of Garfield County.
173. Griffin, "Statement."
174. Iker Saitua, *Basque Immigrants and Nevada's Sheep Industry: Geopolitics and the Making of an Agricultural Workforce, 1880–1954* (Reno: University of Nevada Press, 2019), 104.
175. *Kane County Independent*, October 3, 1912.
176. Bradley, *Kane County*, 217.
177. Rollins, "Land Policies," 249.
178. Price and Darby, "Preston Nutter," 250. Nutter's view was widespread across the West, especially in Nevada where the problem of "tramp" sheepherders was common. See also Starrs, *Let the Cowboy Ride*, 59.
179. Utah Congressman Don Colton was a major architect of the Taylor Grazing Act. Colton was a former resident of Vernal near Nutter's ranch headquarters in Nine Mile Canyon, and Nutter was probably well acquainted with him.
180. Woolley to Spry.
181. Gary Topping, "Zane Grey in Zion: An Examination of His Supposed Anti-Mormonism," *BYU Studies Quarterly* 18, no. 4 (1978), article 2, accessed April 24, 2002, https://scholarsarchive.byu.edu/byusq/vol18/iss4/2/.
182. Bradley, *Kane County*, 182, 189–200.
183. Saitua, *Basque Immigrants*, 128–30.
184. Bradley, *Kane County*, 194–95.
185. Newell and Talbot, *Garfield County*, 285.
186. Gulliford, *Woolly West*, 145.

187. Peterson and Cannon, *Awkward State*, 203–4.
188. Warren Foote, interview by Marsha Holland, August 24, 2016, Southern Utah Oral History Project, SUU.
189. Jean Bybee Syrett, interview by Marsha Holland, January 15, 2003, Southern Utah Oral History Project, SUU.
190. Newell and Talbot, *Garfield County*, 291–92.
191. Charles Wilkinson, *Fire on the Plateau: Conflict and Endurance in the American Southwest* (Washington, DC: Island Press/Shearwater Books, 1999), 93–94.
192. Gulliford, *Woolly West*, 178–79.
193. David Lavender, *Colorado River Country* (New York: E.P. Dutton, 1982), 150.
194. McAllister, interview.
195. Walker, "Cattle Industry," 197.
196. Neaf Hamblin, interview.

Notes to Chapter 5

1. Peterson and Cannon, *Awkward State*, 264–66.
2. "Modern City," *Kane County Standard*, June 5, 1931.
3. Trevor Leach, interview by Marsha Holland, July 17, 2002, Southern Utah Oral History Project, SUU.
4. Melda Davis, interview by Marsha Holland, April 11, 2002, Southern Utah Oral History Project, SUU.
5. Clare Ramsay, interview by Marsha Holland, April 15, 2004, Southern Utah Oral History Project, SUU.
6. Helma Richards Haas, interview by Marsha Holland, October 10, 2001, Southern Utah Oral History Project, SUU.
7. Newell and Talbot, *Garfield County*, 290.
8. Peterson and Cannon, *Awkward State*, 274.
9. Brian Q. Cannon, "Struggle Against Great Odds: Challenges in Utah's Marginal Agricultural Areas, 1925–30," *Utah Historical Quarterly* 54, no. 4 (1986), 317.
10. Cannon, "Struggle," 315.
11. All sheep and cattle numbers used in this chapter are derived from numbers indicated in the U.S. Census of Agriculture reports compiled every five years. The methods of calculating these numbers were not always consistent from one census to the next. For example, some years the total number of sheep was tallied and in others only the number of sheep shorn. In the case of cattle, some totals include cows and calves, and other years include only adult cows. These totals also were revised from one census to another so that 1935 numbers indicated in the 1935 census might be different when revised for the 1940 census. We attempt to use "total numbers" whenever possible, and we defer to revised

numbers in later reports when available. The reports used in this chapter are all available online at the previously cited USDA Census of Agriculture Historical Archive and cited as "Agricultural Census" with the relevant date and page number.

12. Peterson and Cannon, *Awkward State*, 274.
13. Erin Carlyle, "Beyond California: The Worst Droughts in American History," *Forbes*, May 13,2015, https://www.forbes.com/sites/erincarlyle/2015/05/13/forget-california-north-america-has-faced-far-worst-droughts/. The Dust Bowl droughts and their economic fallout were the subject of John Steinbeck's classic novel *The Grapes of Wrath*.
14. Donald Worster, *Dust Bowl: The Southern Plains in the 1930s* (New York: Oxford University Press, 1979), 185.
15. "Utah in Focus," *Utah Historical Quarterly* 89, no. 2 (2021): 176. By all accounts, Governor Dern was extremely well-liked by Republicans and Democrats. He was a native of Nebraska who had come to Utah to join his father in the operations of the Mercur Gold Mining and Milling Company, rising to become a manager and developer of a new mining process that still bears his name. His 1924 surprise upset of incumbent Governor Charles Mabey was remarkable at the time, but Dern has since been largely forgotten and ignored by history. As Stanford John Layton wrote: "Neither candidate showed any imagination in text or technique and both were exceedingly polite to one another. With only slight exception, the voters were simply faced with the matter of a good-looking Tweedledum versus a good-looking Tweedledee"; Stanford John Layton, "Governor Charles R. Mabey and the Utah Election of 1924" (Master's thesis, University of Utah, 1969), 49. Today, George Dern is better known as the grandfather of Academy Award-nominated actor Bruce Dern and the great grandfather of Academy Award-winner Laura Dern.
16. Worster, *Dust Bowl*, 185.
17. U.S. Department of Agriculture, "The Western Range," 74th Congress, Senate Document No. 199, April 24, 1936.
18. Dalley, *History of Grazing*, 32.
19. Cannon, "Struggle," 320.
20. Cannon, "Struggle," 320.
21. Peterson and Cannon, *Awkward State*, 301.
22. Library of Congress Photographic Collection, Washington, DC.
23. Andrew M. Honker, "Been Grazed Almost to Extinction: The Environment, Human Action, and Utah Flooding, 1900–1940," *Utah Historical Quarterly* 67, no. 1 (1999), 27.
24. Taylor Grazing Act (1934). PL 73-482; 48 Stat. 1269.
25. Shawn Regan, "Managing Conflicts Over US Federal Rangelands," in *Ranching Realities in the 21st Century*," edited by Holly Fretwell and Mark

Milke (Vancouver, Canada: Fraser Institute, 2016), 39–63. https://www.fraserinstitute.org/sites/default/files/ranching-realities-in-the-21st-century.pdf. Note: The Taylor Grazing Act is named after Colorado congressman Edward Thomas Taylor, but for years the fight had been led by Utah Republican Representative Don B. Colton. When Colton left the House of Representatives, Taylor took on the cause.

26. Gulliford, *Woolly West*, 25.
27. Dalley, *History of Grazing*, 32.
28. Nutter, quoted in Price and Darby, "Preston Nutter," 250.
29. Jack Welter, "Taylor Grazing Act Protects Livestock Men," *Kane County Standard*, December 25, 1936.
30. John Muir, quoted in Gulliford, *Woolly West*, 6; Roosevelt, quoted in Saitua, *Basque Immigrants*, 88.
31. Gulliford, *Woolly West*, 80.
32. Liston, interview.
33. Ramsay, interview.
34. "Grazing Act Affects a Large Number," *Kane County Standard*, August 10, 1934. This article was published word-for-word in every rural newspaper in the state.
35. J. M. Macfarlane, quoted in "Utah Scores Arizona Strip Grazing Move," *Kane County Standard*, September 21, 1934.
36. "Arizona Fights Importation of Grazing Stock," *Kane County Standard*, November 9, 1934.
37. "Notice Given to Stockmen of Kane and Garfield Co.," *Kane County Standard*, May 31, 1935.
38. "Stockmen of Kane, Garfield Counties Meet at Kanab," *Kane County Standard*, June 7, 1935.
39. "Deadline for Filing Applications for Grazing Permits," *Kane County Standard*, July 19, 1935; "Fourth Advisory Board Passes Resolutions," *Kane County Standard*, September 13, 1935.
40. "Stockmen Are Greatly Concerned," *Kane County Standard*, August 16, 1935.
41. Dalley, *History of Grazing*, 5.
42. Arnold Alvey, interview by Marsha Holland, August 2007, Southern Utah Oral History Project, SUU.
43. "Fourth Advisory Board Passes Resolutions," *Kane County Standard*, September 13, 1935.
44. Original settlers interviewed in the 1930s and early 1940s as part of the Utah Writers Project and the Federal Writers Project were unanimous in their views that predators were never much of a problem until the large flocks of sheep swarmed the region beginning in the 1890s. Wolves were mentioned as fairly

common then, and these would occasionally prey on all types of livestock. Coyotes and cougars were said to have been uncommon. If these observations are correct, predator populations might have grown exponentially due to the abundance of livestock.

45. "Grazing District No. Four Effect Action on Rules," *Kane County Standard*, December 13, 1935.
46. Gulliford, *Woolly West*, 3.
47. Willis Sears, interview (interviewer not recorded), January 8, 1964, Gerald R. Sherratt Library, SUU; White, "Animals and Enterprise," 269.
48. Sears, interview.
49. Gulliford, *Woolly West*, 112.
50. "Fined for Unlicensed Grazing of Cattle," *Kane County Standard*, February 18, 1938.
51. Lee Mace, interview by Matthew Zweifel, December 11, 2003, Grand Staircase Escalante National Monument, Kanab, Utah.
52. Edith McInelly Barker, interview by Marsha Holland, January 2016, Southern Utah Oral History Project, SUU.
53. Peterson and Cannon, *Awkward State*, 268.
54. Peterson and Cannon, *Awkward State*, 290–291.
55. Claude Glazier, interview by Jay Hammond, March 4, 1999, Southern Utah Oral History Project, SUU.
56. Chenowyth, interview.
57. Jon Thiem and Deborah Dimon, *Rabbit Creek Country: Three Ranching Lives in the Mountain West* (Albuquerque: University of New Mexico Press, 2008), 208.
58. "Government Cattle Buying Plan Explained," *Kane County Standard*, July 13, 1934.
59. "Federal Sheep Buying Program Is Explained," *Kane County Standard*, August 10, 1934.
60. "1700 Cattle Have Been Shipped From County," *Garfield County News*, August 24, 1934.
61. "Advisory Com. Meet on Cattle Relief," *Kane County Standard*, August 3, 1934.
62. Utah to Purchase Ten Million Goats," *Garfield County News*, December 14, 1934.
63. Chenowyth, interview.
64. C. Roger Lambert, "The Drought Cattle Purchase, 1934–1935: Problems and Complaints," *Agricultural History* 45, no. 2 (1971): 91.
65. "Cattle and Sheep Purchasing May Be Resumed Soon," *Kane County Standard*, October 26, 1934.

66. "Organization Will Improve Livestock," *Kane County Standard*, August 4, 1939.
67. Worster, *Dust Bowl*, 113.
68. Anson B. Call Jr., "Set Up Range Program," *Kane County Standard*, October 16, 1936.
69. William Peterson, quoted in *Kane County Standard*, "Set Up Range Program," 1936.
70. "Government Pays Millions to Farmers," *Kane County Standard*, July 30, 1937.
71. Peterson and Cannon, *Awkward State*, 304.
72. "Government Offers Loans to Woolmen," *Kane County Standard*, March 18, 1938.
73. "2500 to be Issued in Grants to Relieve Livestock Owners," *Kane County Standard*, February 19, 1937.
74. Bradley, *Kane County*, 223.
75. Wayne K. Hinton and Elizabeth A. Green, *With Picks, Shovels, and Hope: The CCC and Its Legacy on the Colorado Plateau* (Missoula, MT: Mountain Press Publishing, 2008), 94–95.
76. "CCC Opens up Road to 25,000 Head of Livestock," *Kane County Standard*, February 19, 1937.
77. Peterson and Cannon, *Awkward State*, 293.
78. The Living New Deal, "Highway 12 'The Million Dollar Road'—Garfield County, UT,", accessed May 10, 2021, https://livingnewdeal.org/projects/highway-12-million-dollar-road-escalante-national-monument-ut/.
79. Mark E. DeGiovanni Miller, "Timeline: Bryce Canyon National Park," *Bryce Canyon Memories: A Multi-Media Documentation of the Oral History of Bryce Canyon National Park*, DVD (Bryce, UT: National Park Service and the Bryce Canyon Association, 2016).
80. The federal government during this period seemed to be acutely aware of underlying Western hostilities toward a top-down management strategy originating in Washington, DC. In the specific instances we identified, Utah State Agricultural College Extension offices staffed with Utah experts would act as the federal surrogate, or the federal agency would hire a respected local livestock man to administer the program. This approach seemed to diffuse suspicions that the conservation programs had nefarious motives.
81. Bradley, *Kane County*, 226.
82. Bernard DeVoto, "The West Against Itself, *Harper's*, January 1947.
83. Lambert, "Drought Cattle," 93.
84. Bradley, *Kane County*, 226.
85. Newell and Talbot, *Garfield County*, 286.
86. Vernon Davies and Arthur L. Beeley, "The Survey of Relief and Rehabilitation in Garfield County, Utah: Results and Implications," *Proceedings of the Utah*

Academy of Sciences, Arts, and Letters (1939): 103; cited in Newell and Talbot, *Garfield County*, 286.

87. Stegner, *Mormon Country*, 345.
88. Bradley, *Kane County*, 229–30, 257–59.
89. E. Bruce Godfrey, "Livestock Grazing in Utah: History and Status," Report to the Utah Governor's Public Lands Policy Coordination Office (Salt Lake City, 2008), 7.
90. Agricultural Census 1935, 891. Note: The ratio of sheep to beef cattle statewide was actually much higher, about 10.6 sheep per cow. Typically, five sheep are considered equivalent to one cow in terms of forage requirements (see Godfrey, "Livestock Grazing," 9).
91. Luke Runyon, "The Long, Slow Decline of the U.S. Sheep Industry," Harvest Public Media, Nebraska Public Media, October 15, 2013, https://nebraskapublicmedia.org/en/news/news-articles/the-long-slow-decline-of-the-us-sheep-industry.
92. Agricultural Census 1935, 891. Note: The 1930 census indicates the number of sheep shorn but not the total number of sheep, which was probably somewhat higher.
93. Agricultural Census 1940, 453.
94. Agricultural Census 1930, 349–50, 379; 1935, 880, 891.
95. Agricultural Census 1945, 48.
96. "No Lowering of Tariff on Wool," *Garfield County News*, February 9, 1934.
97. Ramsay, interview.
98. Ramsay, interview.
99. Ramsay, interview.
100. M. Polasek, "U.S. Wool Policy and Its Effects on Apparel Wool Imports," *Australian Journal of Agricultural Economics* 6, no. 2 (1962), 9.
101. Agricultural Census 1940, 453; 1950, 52.
102. Polasek, "Wool Policy," 13. See also, "End the Wool and Mohair Subsidy," U.S. Department of Agriculture, accessed July 2, 2024, https://govinfo.library.unt.edu/npr/library/reports/ag01.html.
103. Polasek, "Wool Policy," 15.
104. Runyon, "Slow Decline," 2.
105. "Changes in the Sheep Industry in the United States: Making the Transition from Tradition," National Academies, 2008, https://nap.nationalacademies.org/catalog/12245/changes-in-the-sheep-industry-in-the-united-states-making.
106. Gulliford, *Woolly West*, 205–6.
107. Gulliford, *Woolly West*, 205–6.
108. "Dollars and Cents," Sheep101.info, accessed July 2, 2024, http://www.sheep101.info/farm.html.
109. Polasek, "Wool Policy," 9–15.

110. "Fourth Advisory Board Passes Resolutions," *Kane County Standard*, September 13, 1935.
111. "Capitol Reef Natl. Monument is Added to Scenic Attractions," *Kane County Standard*, October 1, 1937.
112. Ezra C. Knowlton, *History of Highway Development in Utah* (Salt Lake City: Utah State Road Commission, n.d.), 25–26.
113. Miller, "Timeline."
114. Elmo R. Richardson, "The Escalante National Monument Controversy of 1935–1940," *Utah Historical Quarterly* 33, no. 2 (1965): 109–133. Richardson states the proposal was named Escalante National Park (or Monument) because planners believed it lay across the route used by Spanish friar Silvestre Vélez de Escalante during his landmark explorations of Utah in 1776. In fact, Escalante's route did not pass anywhere near the proposed national park.
115. Redd, quoted in Jared Farmer, *Glen Canyon Dammed* (Tucson: University of Arizona Press, 2004), 19; Gulliford, *Woolly West*, 172–73.
116. "Escalante," Glen Canyon National Recreation Area, National Park Service, accessed November 25, 2020, https://www.nps.gov/glca/planyourvisit/escalante.htm.
117. Bradley, *Kane County*, 233–34. Local rancher Trevor Leach said he was one of the horsemen who fell from his horse for the $1 bonus. The Parry Lodge in Kanab, where all of the cast and crew stayed during filming, still keeps the original Hollywood history alive with scores of signed photos from stars and starlets.
118. Stephen B. Armstrong, "Kanab: Utah's Little Hollywood," Utah Film Commission (blog), accessed November 17, 2020, film.utah.gov/blog/littlehollywood.
119. "Airplanes, Punchers Gather Mustangs," *Kane County Standard*, June 25, 1937. "Mustang Drive Not Too Successful," *Kane County Standard*, July 2, 1937.
120. Deloy Dutton, interview by Marsha Holland, March 9, 2012, Southern Utah Oral History Project, SUU.
121. "Dates Are Set for Buffalo Hunt," *Kane County Standard*, January 21, 1938.
122. "Game Chief Hits Grazing Director," *Kane County Standard*, Feb. 7, 1936.
123. "Livestock Men Oppose the Big Game Games [*sic*] Increase," *Kane County Standard*, March 1, 1935; "Stock Raisers and Game Men Reach Accord," *Kane County Standard*, May 10, 1935.
124. "Reach Accord," *Kane County Standard*.
125. Haas, interview; Rella Ott Alvey, interview by Marsha Holland, February 6, 2002, Southern Utah Oral History Project, SUU.
126. Newell and Talbot, *Garfield County*, 308.
127. Newell and Talbot, *Garfield County*, 312.
128. Godfrey, "Livestock Grazing," 9.
129. W. J. Thornley, quoted in Dalley, *History of Grazing*, 69.

130. U.S. Inflation Calculator, accessed July 5, 2024, http://www.usinflationcalculator.com/.
131. Saitua, *Basque Immigrants*, 214–220.
132. "Snow Causes Loss in Livestock," *Kane County Standard*, January 22, 1937.
133. Leach, interview.
134. "Winter Losses Totaled," *Kane County Standard*, June 4, 1937.
135. "Range Feed Good," *Kane County Standard*, April 23, 1937; "Range Conditions Good," *Kane County Standard,* December 31, 1937; "More Moisture Encourages AAA," *Kane County Standard*, May 21, 1937.

Notes to Chapter 6

1. Bradley, *Kane County*, 253.
2. Vergene Porter, interviewed by Marsha Holland, August 2007, Southern Utah Oral History Project, SUU.
3. Godfrey, "Livestock Grazing," 21.
4. William Voigt Jr., *Public Grazing Lands: Use and Misuse by Industry and Government* (New Brunswick, NJ: Rutgers University Press, 1976), 6–7, 79; David Rich Lewis, "Bernard DeVoto's Utah," in *Utah in the Twentieth Century*, eds. Brian Q. Cannon and Jessie L. Embry (Logan: Utah State University Press, 2009), 91, 101–2; Gulliford, *Woolly West*, 206–210; Adam M. Sowards, "Sometimes, the West Must Be Protected from Itself," *High Country News*, July 28, 2016.
5. Voigt, *Public Grazing Lands*, 102–113.
6. Quoted in Fradkin, *River No More*, 133.
7. Bradley, *Kane County*, 253.
8. Yardley to Zweifel, email.
9. The shift to motorized transportation of livestock probably did not save much in production costs because the purchase or rental of trucks would have added to the overall cost of doing business. But trucks did give ranchers much greater flexibility in the timing of their livestock sales, allowing them to wait out short-term market downturns or to respond almost instantly to better market prices for their animals.
10. Agricultural Census, 1940–1997; this data reflects total livestock numbers, which would have included animals grazed on private lands. In light of the fact there was so little private land in Kane and Garfield counties, and even less on the Arizona Strip, it can be assumed that most of the total livestock grazed on public lands at least part of the year.
11. Bradley, *Kane County*, 268–69. On March 3, 1960, *Southern Utah News* reported that the Kaibab Lumber Company's annual payroll was $1 million with three quarters of its employees living in Kanab. The demise of the local lumber industry is attributed locally to federal protections for the endangered Mexican spotted owl.

12. "Dixie Forest Grazing is Big Business," *Garfield County News* February 9, 1950; "Livestock Trek to Mountain Grazing Grounds," *Garfield County News*, June 22, 1950.
13. "J. Edgar Hoover Says Potential Fifth Column of 540,000 in U.S.," *Garfield County News*, June 29, 1950. In 1950, the nation's population stood at 151 million. Hoover's claims of a "fifth column" of native-born communists and sympathizers in the United States at that time would suggest that as many as a third of the nation's population worked for or sympathized with the Soviet Union.
14. Richard M. Fried, *Nightmare in Red: The McCarthy Era in Perspective* (New York: Oxford University Press, 1990), 145, 193–95.
15. "United States Ground Forces Sent into Korea; Uneasy World Fears Crisis May Lead to New World War," *Garfield County News*, July 20, 1950.
16. Scott M. Matheson, quoted in Janet Burton Seegmiller, "Nuclear Testing and the Downwinders," accessed June 19, 2024, http://historytogo.utah.gov/downwinders.
17. Clem Griffin, interviewed by Marsha Holland, April 2004, Southern Utah Oral History Project, SUU; Leola Mangum Catterly Shoenfeld, interviewed by Marsha Holland, September 19, 2002, Southern Utah Oral History Project, SUU.
18. Ken Krahulec, "Energy News: A New Uranium Boom?" Utah Geological Survey, May 2008, https://geology.utah.gov/map-pub/survey-notes/energy-news/energy-news-may-2008/; Farmer, *Glen Canyon Dammed*, 22–32. Also see: Raye C. Ringholz, *Uranium Frenzy: Saga of the Nuclear West* (Logan: Utah State University Press, 2002).
19. Newell and Talbot, *Garfield County*, 346–47.
20. Escalante had a population of 773 in 1950. The percentage was calculated based on an assumption that half of the residents might have been adults and half of those would have been men. Given the large number of children in Garfield County households, the ratio of adults to children might have been substantially less, making the percentage of adult males in military service even greater than the 50 percent of adults estimated here.
21. DeRell Sudweeks, interviewed by Marsha Holland, March 2015, Southern Utah Oral History Project, SUU.
22. Calvin Schow, interviewed by Marsha Holland, April 2004, Southern Utah Oral History Project, SUU.
23. The fact that populations increased in Kane County but declined in Garfield County cannot be readily explained. Both counties had thriving sawmills, both experienced increased tourism due to proximity to national parks, and both had some mining (coal mining in Kane County and uranium mining in Garfield County). The only substantial difference was that Kane County enjoyed the economic benefits of the ongoing construction of Glen Canyon Dam in the late 1950s.

24. An AUM, or animal unit month, is the amount of forage consumed in any given month by one cow and one calf, one horse, or five sheep or goats.
25. James Muhn and Hanson R. Stuart, *Opportunity and Challenge: The Story of the BLM* (Washington, DC: Bureau of Land Management, 1988), 47–48.
26. Muhn and Stuart, *Opportunity and Challenge*, 54.
27. The 8-cent fee is the equivalent of $1 per AUM in 2017 dollars (see U.S. Inflation Calculator, accessed July 5, 2024, http://www.usinflationcalculator.com/). Ranchers agreed to the fee increase on the condition that 2 cents of the new 8-cent per AUM fee would be dedicated to range improvements. The rest would be distributed between the states and the federal treasury. At the end of the day, the BLM had no more money in its budget than it had before the fee increase.
28. Muhn and Stuart, *Opportunity and Challenge*, 57.
29. Starrs, *Let the Cowboy Ride*, 59.
30. Muhn and Stuart, *Opportunity and Challenge*, 64. The 12-cent fee is the equivalent of $1.22 per AUM in 2017 dollars (U.S. Inflation Calculator).
31. Marion Clawson, quoted in Muhn and Stuart, *Opportunity and Challenge*, 62.
32. "Local Soil Conservation District Reports on Accomplishments," *Garfield County News*, January 12, 1950; "County Federal Agencies Will Promote Reseeding Program," *Kane County Standard*, February 3, 1950.
33. "Cattlemen Take Bull by Horns," *Garfield County News*, March 9, 1950.
34. "Forest Grazing Fees Reduced," *Garfield County News*, March 2, 1950.
35. Edward Woozley, quoted in Muhn and Stuart, *Opportunity and Challenge*, 76–77.
36. Bradley, *Kane County*, 297.
37. Muhn and Stuart, *Opportunity and Challenge*, 81.
38. Muhn and Stuart, *Opportunity and Challenge*, 80.
39. Bradley, *Kane County*, 264–65.
40. Bradley, 265.
41. All American men between ages eighteen and twenty-six had been required to register for the draft as far back as the Civil War. Young men had been drafted throughout the Cold War, the most famous being Elvis Presley, who was drafted in 1957. In 1964, President Lyndon B. Johnson requested and received congressional approval to build up U.S. forces, now referred to as the Gulf of Tonkin Resolution. Local draft boards determined who was called up, a process rife with cronyism and favoritism that resulted in a disproportionate number of poor people, many of them from rural towns and farming communities, being inducted. In 1969, the Selective Service implemented a lottery system intended to ameliorate abuses. See Vietnam War Draft Lottery, accessed July 2, 2024, http://www.vietnamwardraftlottery.com.
42. Brent Owens, interview by Marsha Holland, Southern Utah Oral History Project, SUU.

43. Rodney Black, interviewed by Jerry D. Spangler, July 13, 2017, notes in the possession of the author.
44. Fradkin, *River No More*, 195.
45. As early as 1936, Secretary of Interior Harold Ickes had envisioned an Escalante National Monument of 4.5 million acres that would have encompassed everything south of Green River, Utah, and include much of which is now protected by Canyonlands National Park, Glen Canyon National Recreation Area, and Grand Staircase-Escalante National Monument. See National Parks Traveler, accessed July 2, 2024, https://www.nationalparkstraveler.org/parks/canyonlands-national-park.
46. Gary Topping, *Glen Canyon and the San Juan Country*, (Moscow: University of Idaho Press, 1997), 338–39; Jon M. Cosco, *Echo Park: Struggle for Preservation* (Boulder, CO: Johnson Books, 1995), 107–115; Byron E. Pearson, *Still the Wild River Runs: Congress, the Sierra Club, and the Fight to Save Grand Canyon* (Tucson: University of Arizona Press, 2002), xiv, 5–6, 19–23.
47. James M. Aton, *The River Knows Everything: Desolation Canyon and the Green* (Logan: Utah State University Press, 2009), 154–61; Farmer, *Glen Canyon Dammed*, 144–45.
48. Robinson, *Kane County*, 198. Kanab had always been an isolated and homogenous community, almost entirely Mormon and white. Very little was written at the time about sociocultural effects of so many outsiders—non-Mormons and people of color—arriving in Kanab who did not share the same pioneer values of the native residents.
49. Bradley, *Kane County*, 265.
50. Wilkinson, *Fire on the Plateau*, 325.
51. Bill Wolverton, interview by Marsha Holland, January 2016, Southern Utah Oral History Project, SUU.
52. National Park Service, "Grazing," Glen Canyon National Recreation Area, accessed November 17, 2020, https://nps.gov/glca/learn/nature/grazing.htm.
53. Edward Abbey, *The Monkey Wrench Gang* (Philadelphia: J. B. Lippincott, 1975).
54. National Park Service, "Grazing." The transaction to permanently retire grazing permits might have been the first of its kind and perhaps one of the last. The rules were later changed to make it nearly impossible for federal agencies to permanently retire permits. This point was illustrated by the Grand Canyon Trust's purchase of the Kane Ranch in House Rock Valley. The Trust had hoped to retire the grazing permits, but now it must graze some cattle on the allotment or risk having the permits sold to someone else.
55. Wilkinson, *Fire on the Plateau*, 233.
56. Muhn and Stuart, *Opportunity and Challenge*, 153; Brian Q. Cannon and Jessie L. Embry, eds., *Utah in the Twentieth Century* (Logan: Utah State University Press, 2009), 305–311.
57. Sally Fairfax, quoted in Muhn and Stuart, *Opportunity and Challenge*, 153.

58. Bradley, *Kane County*, 297.
59. John F. Kennedy, quoted in Stuart and Muhn, *Opportunity and Challenge*, 104. On Udall family, see Miller, "Saint John's Saints," 66–80.
60. Aldo Leopold, *A Sand County Almanac* (New York: Ballantine Books, 1986), 238–39.
61. Carl Abbott, *The Metropolitan Frontier: Cities in the Modern American West* (Tucson: University of Arizona Press, 1993), 157.
62. The lead author here was a preteen in the late 1960s and remembers being taught in Sunday School as gospel truth that the peace symbol of the day was not representative of the foot of a dove, a universal symbol of peace, but rather it was an upside-down, broken Christian cross representing Satan worship.
63. Roderick Nash, *Wilderness and the American Mind* (New Haven, CT: Yale University Press, 1982), 254–55.
64. Charles H. Stoddard, quoted in Muhn and Stuart, *Opportunity and Challenge*, 105.
65. Voigt, *Public Grazing Lands*, 303–4.
66. Charles F. Wilkinson, *Crossing the Next Meridian: Lands, Water, and the Future of the West* (Washington, DC: Island Press, 2013), 16.
67. Rogers, *Roads in the Wilderness*, 4–6, 134.
68. Muhn and Stuart, *Opportunity and Challenge*, 136–37.
69. Muhn and Stuart, *Opportunity and Challenge*, 207.
70. D. W. Meinig, "The Mormon Culture Region: Strategies and Patterns in the Geography of the American West, 1847–1964," *Annals of the Association of American Geographers* 55 no. 2 (1965), 215. See also Paul F. Starrs, "Meetinghouses in the Mormon Mind: Ideology, Architecture, and Turbulent Streams of an Expanding Church," *Geographical Review* 99, no. 3 (2009): 323–55.
71. "The Sportsmen vs. the Anti-Hunting Movement," *Southern Utah News*, December 18, 1975; "Navajo Tribe Looks at House Rock Valley," *Southern Utah News*, July 10, 1975; "BLM Rolls Rough Shod Over All, says Garn," *Southern Utah News*, July 10, 1975.
72. Wright, *Rocky Mountain Divide*, 247.
73. Wilkinson, *Fire on the Plateau*, 231–33.
74. Fradkin, *River No More*, 140.
75. "Regulatory Delays, Uncertainties Force Delay of Kaiparowits Project," *Southern Utah News*, Dec. 18, 1975.
76. Richard Lamm, quoted in Jonathan Thompson, "The First Sagebrush Rebellion: What Sparked It and How It Ended," *High Country News*, January 14, 2016.
77. William L. Graf, *Wilderness Preservation and the Sagebrush Rebellions* (Savage, MD: Rowman & Littlefield, 1990), 3–9.
78. Jedediah S. Rogers, "The Volatile Sagebrush Rebellion," in *Utah in the Twentieth Century*, eds. Brian Q. Cannon and Jessie L. Embry (Logan: Utah State University Press, 2009), 367–68.

79. Frank Gregg, "Implementing FLPMA," in Muhn and Stuart, *Opportunity and Challenge*, 206.
80. Bradley, *Kane County*, 299–300.
81. Sandra Day O'Connor and H. Alan Day, *Lazy B: Growing Up on a Cattle Ranch in the American Southwest* (New York: Random House, 2002), 264–65.
82. Andrew Fahlund, interview by Mark E. D. Miller, November 30, 2018; Lisa Force, interview by Mark E. D. Miller, November 29, 2018; interview notes in possession of author.
83. Todd Gitlin, *The Sixties: Years of Hope, Days of Rage* (New York: Bantam Books, 1987), 421–23.
84. Worster, *Unsettled Country,* 56.
85. Gulliford, *Woolly West*, 238.
86. Federal Register, January 6, 2020, Document No. 2019-28352. In 2020, the U.S. Fish and Wildlife Service proposed to delist the Kanab ambersnail after genetic studies determined the snails were actually closely related to a different species that was not endangered.
87. "Frustrated Officials and Citizens Hold a 'Loss of Rights' Rally," *Southern Utah News*, September 25, 1996.
88. "Forest Service Will Begin Study of Utah's Spotted Owl," *Deseret News*, March 27, 1990; "Mexican Spotted Owl," Zion National Park, National Park Service, accessed March 9, 2022, https://nps.gov/zion/learn/nature/mexicanspottedowl.htm; "Fight Over Another Owl Takes Flight," *Deseret News*, November 1, 1991.
89. Bradley, *Kane County*, 332; Farmer, *Glen Canyon Dammed*, xiii–xxi.
90. Starrs, *Let the Cowboy Ride*, 20.
91. Rogers, "Volatile Sagebrush," 372–78.
92. Bradley, *Kane County*, 332–33.
93. Ramsay, interview.
94. Most Western state legislatures passed resolutions demanding the federal government transfer federal lands to the states. See Thompson, "Sagebrush Rebellion," 4.
95. Thompson, "Sagebrush Rebellion," 5.
96. Muhn and Stuart, *Opportunity and Challenge*, 239.
97. Richard White, "Are You an Environmentalist or Do You Work for a Living?: Work and Nature," in *Uncommon Ground: Rethinking the Human Place in Nature*, ed. William Cronon, (New York: W. W. Norton, 1996), 171–73.
98. White, "Are You an Environmentalist," 171–72.
99. Regan, "Managing Conflicts."
100. E. Bruce Godfrey and C. Arden Pope, "The Trouble with Livestock Grazing on Public Lands" (1990; reis. *Southern Utah Wilderness Alliance Newsletter*, Winter 1991/1992; Paul F. Starrs, "'Cattle Free By '93' & the Imperatives of Environmental Radicalism," *Ubique: Notes from the American Geographical Society* 14, no. 1 (1994), 1–4.

101. Starrs, *Let the Cowboy Ride*, 21.
102. Thiem and Dimon, *Rabbit Creek Country*, 221.
103. Wilkinson, *Crossing the Next Meridian*, 76–80.
104. Brunson and Wallace, "Perceptions of Ranching," 96.
105. Michael Hibbard and Susan Lurie, "The New Natural Resource Economy: A Framework for Community Resilience," in *Bridging the Distance: Common Issues of the Rural West*, ed. David B. Danbom (Salt Lake City: University of Utah Press, 2015), 192.
106. Rogers, "Volatile Sagebrush," 377.
107. Rogers, "Volatile Sagebrush," 217.
108. Patricia Nelson Limerick, "Making the Most of Words," in *Under a Western Sky: Rethinking America's Western Past*, eds. William Cronon, George Miles, and Jay Gitlin (W. W. Norton & Co., 1992), 182.
109. Thomas M. Quigley and E. T. Bartlett, "Livestock on Public Lands: Yes!" (1990; *Southern Utah Wilderness Alliance Newsletter*, Winter 1991/1992).
110. Starrs, *Let the Cowboy Ride*, 74–75.
111. Karl Hess Jr., "The Status of Range Reform," accessed July 5, 2024, http://www.ti.org/rangeref.html.
112. Arrowquip, "Timeline of Changes: Beef Cattle Farming in North America," posted on June 6, 2017, https://arrowquip.com/blog/timeline-of-changes-beef-cattle-north-america. The U.S. Department of Agriculture reported in 2017 that the average cow-calf beef herd was forty head, although operations of this size were typically supplemental to off-farm employment.
113. Godfrey and Pope, "Trouble with Livestock," 5.
114. Starrs, *Let the Cowboy Ride*, 11, 69.
115. Lonnie Pollack, interview by Marsha Holland, March 14, 2003, Southern Utah Oral History Project, SUU.
116. Liston, interview.
117. W. F. Hahn, T. L. Crawford, K. E. Nelson, and R. A. Bowl, *Estimating Forage Values for Grazing National Forest Lands*, United States Department of Agriculture Staff Report No. 89-51, Washington, DC, 1989.
118. "Timeline of Changes."
119. Ellie Leydsman McGinty, Ben Baldwin, and Roger Banner, *A Review of Livestock Grazing and Range Management in Utah*, Report to the Governor's Public Lands Policy Coordination Office (Logan: Utah State University Press, 2009), 7.
120. National Chicken Council. "Per Capita Consumption of Poultry and Livestock, 1960 to Forecast 2024, in Pounds," accessed August 3, 2021, http://www.nationalchickencouncil.org/statistics/per-capita-consumption-poultry/.
121. Starrs, *Let the Cowboy Ride*, 3.
122. Economic Research Service, "Cattle & Beef," U.S. Department of Agriculture, Washington, DC, last updated August 30, 2023, https://www.ers.usda.gov/topics/animal-products/cattle-beef/background.aspx.

123. Agricultural Marketing Service, "Slaughter Cattle Grades and Standards," U.S. Department of Agriculture, accessed August 3, 2021, https://www.ams.usda.gov/grades-standards/slaughter-cattle-grades-and-standards. Beef calves are weaned at six to ten months of age when they weigh 450 to 700 lb. They are typically sent to a "backgrounder" or "stocker" who continues to graze them on grass or alfalfa until they are twelve to sixteen months old, usually on private pastures with higher quality "roughage." The animals are then sent to a feedlot where they are fed a grain-based diet until they reach a market weight of 1,200 to 1,400 lb. Cow-calf operators with ample home base pastures might seek to "cut out the middleman" and sell directly to feedlots when the cows reach twelve to sixteen months, but this would involve substantial feed costs during the winter and keeping them on the public range a second season, reducing the permits available for a new crop of calves. There are inconsistencies in the age of the animal at the time of slaughter. The USDA says thirty to forty-two months.

124. Honor Whiteman, "Red Meat: Good or Bad for Health," *Medical News Today*, January 25, 2017, https://www.medicalnewstoday.com/articles/315449.

Notes to Chapter 7

1. The acreage was expanded to 1.9 million acres through a subsequent trade with the state of Utah for isolated state school sections within the national monument boundary. In return, the state received developable lands around thriving communities that have since returned significant profits to the School Learning and Nuturing Development (LAND) Trust.
2. Lindsey Raisa Feldman, "Good Hands and True Grit: Making a Ranching Identity in the Altar Valley, Arizona," *Journal of the Southwest* 58, no. 1 (2016), 98–99.
3. Carol Sullivan, "Former Commissioner Esplin Thinks Rait Is in the SUWA," *Southern Utah News* 65, no. 33, September 25, 1996.
4. The selection of Grand Staircase, Kaiparowits Plateau, and Escalante Canyon as the newest national monument caught most observers by surprise. It was widely assumed at the time that Clinton would make a grand environmental gesture to secure support from conservationists, many of whom had defected to Green Party candidate Ralph Nader. Most thought the president would protect Cedar Mesa in southeastern Utah, a region rich in archaeological treasures that had been on conservationists' wish list for decades. Twenty years later, President Barack Obama protected Cedar Mesa through a proclamation designating Bears Ears National Monument, something that elicited identical howls of protest from rural Utahns that echoed back to Grand Staircase two decades before.
5. Senator Orrin Hatch, speaking on S. 477, 105th Congress, 1st sess., *Congressional Record* 143, no. 36 (March 19, 1997): S 2563. Of course, the designation was

not a land "grab" in any literal sense. These lands were federally administered before the designation, and they remained so afterwards. But the perception remains that the monument appropriated private lands.

6. William J. Clinton, "Remarks Announcing the Establishment of the Grand Staircase-Escalante National Monument at Grand Canyon National Park, Arizona," September 18, 1996, The American Presidency Project, https://www.presidency.ucsb.edu/documents/remarks-announcing-the-establishment-the-grand-staircase-escalante-national-monument-grand.
7. These coal deposits are the same ones that were targeted for development in the 1960s and 1970s in what was intended to be the largest coal mine and power plant in the world, prompting conservationists to organize in such fierce opposition that it led to the abandonment of the project. The Andalex proposal was much smaller in scale, but nonetheless faced steep environmental hurdles. Clinton's designation recognized existing leases and therefore did not kill the Andalex proposal outright. But it certainly added onerous regulatory obstacles that prompted Andalex to abandon the project soon after the designation.
8. Dixie Brunner, "Kane County Demonstrates Frustration with President Clinton," *Southern Utah News*, November 13, 1996.
9. U.S. Representative Bill Orton, whose district encompassed the new monument, was the only Democrat in the Utah delegation at the time. The popular, conservative "Blue Dog" Democrat lost his reelection bid later in 1996, a defeat largely attributed to Clinton's monument designation.
10. Contrary to often-repeated claims, Grand Staircase-Escalante is not the largest national monument ever created by presidential proclamation. In 1978, President Jimmy Carter used the Antiquities Act to simultaneously designate fifteen Alaskan national monuments totaling 56 million acres. These designations were later repealed by the U.S. Congress, which also added a condition that no future monuments could be created in Alaska without congressional approval. Wyoming has a similar congressional escape clause that resulted from local outrage over the creation of Grand Teton National Monument, now Grand Teton National Park. Congress later designated some of Carter's Alaska monuments as national parks, national preserves, and wilderness areas.
11. Eric C. Rusnak, "The Straw that Broke the Camel's Back? Grand Staircase-Escalante National Monument Antiquates the Antiquities Act," *Ohio State Law Journal* 64 (2003): 681. Most national monument designations have been opposed by local and state governments, and many designations were subject to unsuccessful legal challenges, including such icons as Grand Canyon and Grand Teton.
12. Bruce Babbitt, interview by Marsha Holland, November, 13, 2015, Southern Utah Oral History Project, SUU; Charles Wilkinson, interview by Marsha Holland, February 25, 2011, Southern Utah Oral History Project, SUU.
13. Babbitt, interview.

14. Babbitt, interview; Wilkinson, interview.
15. William J. Clinton, "Proclamation 6920—Establishment of the Grand Staircase-Escalante National Monument," September 18, 1996, American Presidency Project, https://www.presidency.ucsb.edu/documents/proclamation-6920-establishment-the-grand-staircase-escalante-national-monument.
16. Julie Cart, "Amid Drought, a Range War Erupts in Utah Over Grazing Restrictions," *Los Angeles Times*, December 26, 2000.
17. Louise Liston, quoted in Paul Larmer, "Beauty and the Beast: The President's New Monument Forces Southern Utah to Face Its Tourism Future," *High Country News*, April 14, 1997.
18. Bradley, *Kane County*, 349–57.
19. Dellas Sorenson, "I Once Was a Proud American," guest editorial, *Southern Utah News*, January 29, 1997.
20. JoAnne Honey, letter to the editor, *Southern Utah News*, October 23, 1996.
21. Fried, *Nightmare in Red*, 162.
22. Dixie Brunner, "Commission Declares War over N.M. Designation," *Southern Utah News*, October 9, 1996.
23. James R. Skillen, *This Land is My Land: Rebellion in the West* (New York City: Oxford University Press, 2020), 109–117, 129–130.
24. Rogers, *Roads in the Wilderness*, 136.
25. Bradley, *Kane County*, 344–57.
26. Bradley, *Kane County*, 348.
27. White, "'Are You an Environmentalist,'' 172–74; Feldman, "Good Hands and True Grit," 110–17.
28. Nichols, "Before the Boom," 2–5.
29. Jedediah S. Rogers, "History, Nature, and Mormons in Historiography," in *The Earth Will Appear as the Garden of Eden*, eds. Jedediah S. Rogers and Matthew C. Godfrey (Salt Lake City: University of Utah Press, 2019), 7–8; George B. Handley, "On the Moral Lessons of Mormon Environmental History," in *Earth Will Appear*, 253–54.
30. Mike Hudak, *Western Turf Wars: The Politics of Public Lands Ranching* (Binghampton, NY: Biome Books, 2013), 211.
31. Hudak, *Western Turf Wars*, 215–16.
32. Wright, *Rocky Mountain Divide*, 244, 247.
33. Honey, letter to the editor.
34. Ron Hamblin, letter to the editor, *Southern Utah News*, September 18, 1996.
35. Erin Alberty, "More than 160,000 People Applied to Hike The Wave Last Year. Only a Few Thousand Got In," *The Salt Lake Tribune*, February 14, 2018.
36. "Western States Sue Clinton," *Southern Utah News,* November 6, 1996.
37. "Western States Coalition Tones Down Radical Rhetoric," *Las Vegas Sun*, November 15, 1996, https://lasvegassun.com/news/1996/nov/15/western-states-coalition-tones-down-radical-rhetor/.

38. Brunson and Wallace, "Perceptions of Ranching," 95–97.
39. Brunson and Wallace, "Perceptions of Ranching," 95–97.
40. Wilkinson, *Crossing the Next Meridian*, 20–22.
41. Raymond B. Wrabley Jr., "Managing the Monument: Cows and Conservation in the Grand Staircase-Escalante National Monument," *Journal of Land Resources and Environmental Law* 29 (2009), 279–80.
42. Jamie Hawley, "Ranching around Monuments in Southern Utah," *Progressive Cattle,* February 24, 2017, https://www.agproud.com/articles/49465-ranching-around-monuments-in-southern-utah.
43. Cami Cox Jim, "Battle over Cattle: Controversy at Grand Staircase-Escalante National Monument," *St. George News*, July 6, 2015.
44. Jim, "Battle over Cattle."
45. Ramsay, interview.
46. A. Park Williams et al., "Large Contribution from Anthropogenic Warming to an Emerging North American Megadrought," *Science* 368, no. 6488 (2020): 314–18.
47. Economic Research Service, "Cattle & Beef."
48. Pollack, interview.
49. Cart, "Amid Drought." Although the forced removal was viewed as heavy-handed, the government was acting according to long-standing practices that had previously provoked minimal public interest. BLM procedures typically include rounding up the trespass animals using horses and helicopters, and if that approach is unsuccessful, then the trespass animals would be killed. In 1990, Dennis Willis led a posse of BLM rangers that shot and killed seventeen trespass cattle in Desolation Canyon (see Aton, *The River Knows Everything*, 172). And the issue of impounding and killing trespass cattle has again emerged in the much-publicized and ongoing Cliven Bundy case in Nevada.
50. Julie V. Brugger, "Public Land and American Democratic Imaginaries: A Case Study of Conflict over the Management of Grand Staircase-Escalante National Monument" (PhD diss., University of Washington, 2009), 145.
51. Electa Draper, "Rancher Draws Line in Grazing Fight," *Denver Post*, November 26, 2000.
52. Starrs, *Let the Cowboy Ride,* 190, 202–214.
53. Pollack, interview.
54. Randy N. Parker, "Threats to Grazing from Federal Regulatory Overreach," statement of the Utah Farm Bureau Federation and Thirteen Western State Farm Bureaus to the U.S. House of Representatives Committee on Oversight and Government Reform, Subcommittee on Interior, August 6, 2015: 4, 6, https://oversight.house.gov/wp-content/uploads/2015/08/Parker-Statement-8-6-Wyoming-Grazing.pdf.
55. The official agricultural censuses divide ranching into seven categories organized by the size of the herd. The average size of most herds in Utah is forty

to fifty animals, and various studies have demonstrated that cattle ranching is not profitable with a herd size of less than one hundred cows and it remains marginal even at that level. We have therefore organized the seven census categories into three categories: (1) *hobby ranching*, or small operations of less than 50 cows where ranching is a minor supplement to off-ranch income; (2) *subsistence ranching*, or medium operations of 50 to 199 cows, where ranching is a major supplement to off-ranch income; and (3) *primary ranching*, or large operations of 200 or more cows where ranching is probably the primary source of income.

56. Data from Agricultural Census, 1997, 2002, 2007, and 2012. Some Kane County cattle numbers are missing for 2002 and 2012, disallowing comparisons of population increases or decreases by herd sizes.
57. A general rule of thumb in cattle production is that twenty acres of pastureland are needed to raise one cow. With private lands in short supply in both counties, it is probable that most hobby ranchers have insufficient private lands to support more than a few cows and are therefore forced to lease additional pasturelands or purchase hay. Hay prices typically spike during drought conditions, which would make hobby ranching increasingly risky. There is no clear evidence that hobby ranching declined significantly during the drought of 1996 to 2004, although there was a surge after that time even though the drought persists.
58. Starrs, *Let the Cowboy Ride*, 232.
59. The percentage of total cattle owned by Kane County hobby ranchers could not be determined because certain census data were missing for 2012. In 1997, it was 14 percent, and by 2007 it had climbed to 18 percent, much higher percentages than in Garfield County. Agricultural Census, 1997, 2007, 2012.
60. Wyoming Game and Fish Department, "Rural Subdivision," accessed June 24, 2021, https://wgfd.wyo.gov.
61. Oscar Judd, interview.
62. Perhaps the most "bizarre" twisting of data occurred when former Utah Commissioner of Agriculture Cary Peterson tried to make the political case that agriculture was by far Utah's most significant economic contributor. To do so, he asserted that all grocery store sales were agriculture revenue and all grocery store employees were agriculture workers.
63. Williams et al., "Anthropogenic Warming," 314–18; see also Joan Meiners, "Cedar City to Host Annual Water Festival Saturday," *Spectrum and Daily News*, June 25, 2021. A megadrought is defined as a drought lasting twenty years or longer.
64. We cannot explain why the costs of doing business in 2012 were nearly half what they were five years before. Nor can we understand how, if costs of doing business were so much lower in 2012 and the prices paid for cattle were so high,

the net received by farmers was exponentially less than the amount when costs were higher.

65. Desmond Twitchell, interview by Marsha Holland, October 16, 2001, Southern Utah Oral History Collection, SUU.
66. Twitchell, interview.
67. Rogers, *Roads in the Wilderness*, 134, 149, 141, 152.
68. Jerry D. Spangler and Andrew T. Yentsch, *Cultural Resource Inventories along OHV Routes in Kane, Wayne, and San Juan Counties, Southern Utah* (Ogden, UT: Colorado Plateau Archaeological Alliance, 2010).
69. Page Lambert, "An Intimate Look at the Heart of the Radical Center," and Richard L. Knight, "The Ecology of Ranching," in *Ranching West of the 100th Meridian: Culture, Ecology, and Economics*, eds. Richard L. Knight, Wendell C. Gilbert, and Ed Marston, (Washington, DC: Island Press, 2002), 60, 127.
70. Raymond Pollock, interview.
71. Ramsay, interview.
72. Sayre, *Ranching, Endangered Species, and Urbanization*, xxv, 31, 117.
73. "Quick Facts," U.S. Census Bureau.
74. Miller and Heaton, "Livestock Grazing"; Gil Miller, telephone interview with Jerry D. Spangler to explain methods and definitions, August 31, 2017, notes in possession of Spangler.
75. The labor income statistics used in the Miller and Heaton report were derived in part from interviews with grazing permittees. Given that ranch employment of nonfamily members would be seasonal and quite temporary, and the employment number reflects the equivalent of 111 full-time employees, several hundred "cowboys" might have been hired during the course of the year.
76. Godfrey, "Livestock Grazing." The USU study lumped Wayne County with Kane County and Garfield County in its analysis.
77. Official quoted in Nicole Croft, "All Locked Up: Understanding Conflict in the Communities of the Grand Staircase-Escalante National Monument" (Master's thesis, Westminster College, Salt Lake City, UT, 2015): 43. Participants in her study were granted anonymity.
78. As discussed in Chapter 6, an AUM is unit of measure defined as the amount of forage consumed by a cow and her calf in a given month, or five sheep.
79. Godfrey, "Livestock Grazing," 18.
80. Parker, "Threats to Grazing," 4. See also, Tay Wiles and Brooke Warren, "Federal-Lands Ranching: A Half Century of Decline," *High County News*, June 13, 2016.
81. Godfrey, "Livestock Grazing," 37–38. Non-permittees indicated that 6 percent of their forage came from federal lands, but we are uncertain how this could be the case if they held no federal permits.
82. Jessie Warner, Escalante District, U.S. Forest Service, telephone interview with Jerry D. Spangler, August 31, 2017, notes in possession of Spangler.

83. Bureau of Land Management (BLM), "Grazing on the Monument: Facts and Figures," accessed July 5, 2024, https://www.blm.gov/sites/blm.gov/files/uploads/programs_planning-and-nepa_utah_GSENM-grazing-plan-amendment_grazing-eis-factsheet.pdf.
84. BLM, "Grazing on the Monument."
85. Miller and Heaton, "Livestock Grazing," 1–2.
86. D. Michael Quinn, "Us-Them Tribalism and Early Mormonism," *The John Whitmer Historical Association* 29 (2009): 94–114.
87. "Cliven Bundy to St. George Gathering: Fed Standoff Was a Spiritual Battle," *Associated Press*, August 3, 2014. See also, "BLM Backs Off Confrontation with Nevada Rancher," *Salt Lake Tribune*, April 12, 2014.
88. Croft, "All Locked Up," 35–36.
89. Cited in Croft, "All Locked Up," 54. See also, Christopher Ketchan, "Grand Staircase-Escalante Was Set Up to Fail," *High County News*, July 10, 2017.
90. McGinty et al., *Review of Livestock Grazing*, 9.
91. McGinty et al., *Review of Livestock Grazing*, 9.
92. The biggest challenge might be finding a meat packer willing to gear production towards bison, deer, or elk, especially if the quantities being processed are small compared to other sources.
93. Kevin McLaws, telephone interview with Marsha Holland, September 9, 2017, transcript in possession of Holland.
94. Jeremy Rifkin, "Cattle and Capitalism," accessed July 5, 2024, http://www.columbia.edu/~lnp3/mydocs/ecology/cattle.htm.
95. "Organic Beef," Agricultural Marketing Resource Center, revised November 2021, https://www.agmrc.org/commodities-products/livestock-dairy-poultry/beef/organic-beef.
96. Andrew Larson and Evelyn Thompson, "Direct Marketing Lamb to Niche and Ethnic Markets," IDEA, University of Illinois Extension, n.d., accessed June 22, 2024, https://www.researchgate.net/publication/237102779_Direct_Marketing_Lamb_to_Niche_and_Ethnic_Markets. With its high number of former Mormon missionaries fluent in the culture and language of many of these countries, Utah would seem to be better situated to take advantage of the ethnic market for lamb and goats.
97. McGinty et al., *Review of Livestock Grazing*, 9.

Notes to Epilogue

1. Laura Pollock, email communication with Marsha Holland, September 20, 2017, forwarded copy on file with the authors.
2. Sean Stewart, email communication with Marsha Holland, September 13, 2017, forwarded copy on file with the authors.

Bibliography

Abbey, Edward. *The Monkey Wrench Gang*. Philadelphia: J. B. Lippincott, 1975.

Abbott, Carl. *The Metropolitan Frontier: Cities in the Modern American West.* Tucson: University of Arizona Press, 1993.

Adair, William W. "Interview with Wm. W. Adair." In *History of Grazing*, by Julius S. Dalley. Utah Writer's Project, February 4, 1941. MSS B 100. Utah State Historical Society, Salt Lake City.

Agricultural Marketing Resource Center. "Organic Beef." U.S. Department of Agriculture, Washington, DC. Revised November 2021. https://www.agmrc.org/commodities-products/livestock-dairy-poultry/beef/organic-beef.

Agricultural Marketing Service. "Slaughter Cattle Grades and Standards." U.S. Department of Agriculture, Washington, DC. Accessed August 3, 2021. https://www.ams.usda.gov/grades-standards/slaughter-cattle-grades-and-standards.

Aker, Andrea. "A Little History Behind Arizona's Early Mormon Missions." Arizona Oddities, September 6, 2010. https://arizonaoddities.com/2010/09/a-little-history-behind-arizonas-early-mormon-missions/.

Alder, Douglas D., and Karl F. Brooks. *History of Washington County.* Salt Lake City: Utah State Historical Society; St. George: Washington County Commission, 1998.

Alexander, Thomas G. "Lost Memory and Environmentalism: Mormons on the Wasatch Front, 1847–1930." In *The Earth Will Appear as the Garden of Eden: Essays on Mormon Environmental History,* edited by Jedediah S. Rogers and Matthew C. Godfrey, 47–68. Salt Lake City: University of Utah Press, 2018.

Altschul, Jeffrey H., and Helen C. Fairley. *Man, Models, and Management: An Overview of the Archaeology of the Arizona Strip and the Management of Its Cultural Resources.* St. George, UT: Arizona Strip Field Office, Bureau of Land Management, 1989.

Anderson, C. C. *Yesterday and Today*. Ogden: Utah Writers Project, Works Progress Administration, 1940.

Anderson, Clarice Steward. *A Sketch of the Life of My Parents John Riley and Elizabeth Stevenson Stewart*. N.d. Special Collections, Kanab City Library, Kanab, UT.

Arizona Memory Project. "Sharlot M. Hall—Arizona's Curator." Accessed November 16, 2020. https://azmemory.azlibrary.gov/nodes/view/216.

Armstrong, Stephen B. "Kanab: Utah's Little Hollywood." Utah Film Commission (blog). Accessed November 17, 2020. https://film.utah.gov/blog/littlehollywood.

Arrington, Leonard J. *David Eccles, Pioneer Western Industrialist.* Logan: Utah State University Press, 1975.

Arrington, Leonard J. *Great Basin Kingdom: An Economic History of Latter-Day Saints, 1830–1900.* Lincoln: University of Nebraska Press, 1966. First published by Harvard University Press, 1958.

Arrowquip. "Timeline of Changes: Beef Cattle Farming in North America." Posted June 6, 2017. Accessed June 1, 2024. https://arrowquip.com/blog/timeline-of-changes-beef-cattle-north-america.

Aton, James M. *The River Knows Everything: Desolation Canyon and the Green.* Logan: Utah State University Press, 2009.

Bagley, Will. *Blood of the Prophets: Brigham Young and the Massacre at Mountain Meadows.* Norman: University of Oklahoma Press, 2002.

Baker, Pearl. *The Wild Bunch at Robbers Roost.* Lincoln: University of Nebraska Press, 1971.

Bancroft, Hubert Howe. *History of Utah.* Salt Lake City, UT: Bookcraft, 1964.

Beckstead, James H. *Cowboying: A Tough Job in a Hard Land.* Salt Lake City: University of Utah Press, 1991.

Belshaw, Michael, and Eli Peplow Jr. *Historic Resources Study, Lake Mead National Recreation Area, Arizona.* Tucson, AZ: National Park Service, 1978.

Bennion, Glynn. "A Pioneer Cattle Venture of the Bennion Family." *Utah Historical Quarterly* 34, no. 4 (1966): 315–25.

Bigler, David L. *Forgotten Kingdom: The Mormon Theocracy in the American West, 1847–1896.* Logan: Utah State University Press, 1998.

Black, Rodney. Interview by Jerry D. Spangler. July 13, 2017. Notes in possession of Spangler.

Blezinger, Steven B. "Heifer Development Program Important to Ranch Management." *Cattle Today,* October 2013. http://www.cattletoday.com/archive/2003/October/CT295.shtml.

Boyer, Dorothy Fillerup. *William Derby Johnson Jr. Journal Excerpts, 1850–1894.* Kanab, UT: Self-published, 2005. Special Collections, Kanab City Library.

Bradley, Martha Sonntag. *History of Kane County.* Salt Lake City: Utah State Historical Society; Kanab, UT: Kane County Commission, 1999.

Brooks, Juanita. "The Arizona Strip." *Pacific Spectator* 3 (1949): 290–301.

Brooks, Juanita. *Emma Lee.* Logan: Utah State University Press, 1984.

Brooks, Juanita. "Journal of Thales H. Haskell." *Utah Historical Quarterly* 12, no. 1 (1944): 68–98.

Brown, Adam R. *Utah Politics and Government: American Democracy among a Unique Electorate*. Lincoln: University of Nebraska Press, 2018.

Brown, David E. *The Grizzly in the Southwest.* Norman: University of Oklahoma Press, 1996.

Brown, David E. *The Wolf in the Southwest: The Making of an Endangered Species.* Tucson: University of Arizona Press, 1984.

Brown, Dee, and Martin F. Schmitt. *Trail Driving Days.* New York: Charles Scribner's Sons, 1974. First published 1952 by MacMillan.

Brown, John Franklin. "Autobiography of John Franklin Brown, as told to Blanche Mace." N.d. Special Collections, Kanab City Library, Kanab, UT.

Brugger, Julie V. "Public Land and American Democratic Imaginaries: A Case Study of Conflict over the Management of Grand Staircase-Escalante National Monument." PhD diss., University of Washington, 2009.

Brunson, Mark, and George Wallace. "Perceptions of Ranching: Public Views, Personal Reflections." In *Ranching West of the 100th Meridian: Culture, Ecology, and Economics*, edited by Richard L. Knight, Wendell C. Gilbert, and Ed Marston, 91–105. Washington, DC: Island Press, 2002).

Budd, Bob. "Colors and Words." In *Ranching West of the 100th Meridian: Culture, Ecology, and Economics,* edited by Richard L. Knight, Wendell C. Gilbert, and Ed Marston, 37–45. Washington, DC: Island Press, 2002.

Bureau of Land Management. "Grand Staircase-Escalante National Monument." Accessed September 29, 2020. https://www.blm.gov/office/grand-staircase-escalante-national-monument.

Bureau of Land Management. "Grazing on the Monument: Facts and Figures." Accessed July 5, 2024. https://www.blm.gov/sites/blm.gov/files/uploads/programs_planning-and-nepa_utah_GSENM-grazing-plan-amendment_grazing-eis-factsheet.pdf.

Burk, C. John. "The Kaibab Deer Incident: A Long-Persisting Myth." *BioScience* 23, no. 2 (1973): 113–14.

Bushman, Richard Lyman. "Making Space for the Mormons." In *The Collected Leonard J. Arrington Mormon History Lectures,* 31–54. Logan: Utah State University Press, 2004.

Cannon, Brian Q. "Struggle Against Great Odds: Challenges in Utah's Marginal Agricultural Areas, 1925–30." *Utah Historical Quarterly* 54, no. 4 (1986): 308–27.

Cannon Brian Q., and Jessie L. Embry, eds. *Utah in the Twentieth Century*. Logan: Utah State University Press, 2009.

Carlyle, Erin. "Beyond California: The Worst Droughts in American History." *Forbes*, May 13,2015, https://www.forbes.com/sites/erincarlyle/2015/05/13/forget-california-north-america-has-faced-far-worst-droughts/.

Chidester, Ida, and Eleanor Bruhn. *Golden Nuggets of Pioneer Days: A History of Garfield County.* Panguitch: Daughters of the Utah Pioneers, 1989.

Church of Jesus Christ of Latter-day Saints. "Mormon Pioneer Overland Travel Database." Accessed July 2, 2024. https://history.lds.org/overlandtravel.

Cleland, Robert G., and Juanita Brooks. *A Mormon Chronicle: The Diaries of John D. Lee, 1848–1876.* San Marino, CA: Huntington Library, 1983.

Clinton, William J. "Proclamation 6920—Establishment of the Grand Staircase-Escalante National Monument." September 18, 1996. American Presidency Project. https://www.presidency.ucsb.edu/documents/proclamation-6920-establishment-the-grand-staircase-escalante-national-monument.

Congressional Research Service. "Federal Land Ownership: Overview and Data." Updated February 21, 2020, accessed December 1, 2020. https://sgp.fas.org/crs/misc/R42346.pdf.

Cosco, Jon M. *Echo Park: Struggle for Preservation.* Boulder, CO: Johnson Books, 1995.

Crampton, Gregory C. *Mormon Colonization in Southern Utah and Adjoining Parts of Arizona and Nevada, 1851–1900.* Grand Canyon Village, AZ: Grand Canyon National Park Library, 1965.

Croft, Nicole. "All Locked Up: Understanding Conflict in the Communities of the Grand Staircase-Escalante National Monument." Master's thesis, Westminster College, Salt Lake City, UT, 2015.

Cronon, William, ed. *Uncommon Ground: Rethinking the Human Place in Nature.* New York: W. W. Norton, 1996.

Cronon, William, George Miles, and Jay Gitlin. "Becoming West: Toward a New Meaning for Western History." In *Under an Open Sky: Rethinking America's Western Past,* edited by William Cronon, George Miles, and Jay Gitlin, 3–27. New York: W. W. Norton, 1992.

Cunningham, Ruth L. "Pioneers of the Arizona Strip." 1996. Special Collections, Kanab City Library, Kanab, Utah.

Dalley, Julius S. *History of Grazing.* Utah Writers Project, 1941. MSS B 100. Utah State Historical Society, Salt Lake City.

Dalton, Luella Adams. *History of Iron County Mission and Parowan, the Mother Town.* Parowan: Daughters of the Utah Pioneers, 2001.

Daughters of the Utah Pioneers. *Pioneer Women of Faith and Fortitude.* Vol. 4. Salt Lake City: Daughters of the Utah Pioneers, 1998.

Davies, Vernon, and Arthur L. Beeley. "The Survey of Relief and Rehabilitation in Garfield County, Utah: Results and Implications." *Proceedings of the Utah Academy of Sciences, Arts, and Letters* (1939).

Dellenbaugh, Frederick S. *A Canyon Voyage: the Narrative of the Second Powell Expedition Down the Green Colorado River from Wyoming, and the Explorations on Land in the Years 1871 and 1872.* New Haven, CT: Yale University Press, 1908.

DeVoto, Bernard. "The West Against Itself." *Harper's* Magazine, January 1947.

Dutton, Clarence. *Report on the Geology of the High Plateaus of Utah.* Washington, DC: U.S. Geological Survey, 1880.

Easton, Robert, and Mackenzie Brown. *Lord of the Beasts: The Saga of Buffalo Jones*. Tucson: University of Arizona Press, 1961.

Economic Research Service. "Cattle & Beef." U.S. Department of Agriculture, Washington, DC. Last updated August 30, 2023. https://www.ers.usda.gov/topics/animal-products/cattle-beef/background.aspx.

Fahlund, Andrew. Interview by Mark E. D. Miller. November 30, 2018. Interview notes in the possession of the authors.

Farmer, Jared. *Glen Canyon Dammed: Inventing Lake Powell and the Canyon County*. Tucson: University of Arizona Press, 2004.

Farmer, Jared. *On Zion's Mount: Mormons, Indians, and the American Landscape*. Cambridge, MA: Harvard University Press, 2010.

Farnsworth, Moses Franklin. "Autobiography of Moses Franklin Farnsworth." N.d. Special Collections, Kanab City Library, Kanab, UT.

Faulk, Odie B. *Arizona: A Short History*. Norman: University of Oklahoma Press, 1970.

Federal Register, January 6, 2020, Document No. 2019-28352.

Feldman, Lindsey Raisa. "Good Hands and True Grit: Making a Ranching Identity Work in the Altar Valley, Arizona." *Journal of the Southwest* 58, no. 1 (2016): 97–133.

Force, Lisa. Interview by Mark E. D. Miller. November 29, 2018. Interview notes in the possession of the authors.

Fowler, Don D., and Catherine S. Fowler, eds. *Anthropology of the Numa*. Washington, DC: Smithsonian Institution, 1971.

Fradkin, Philip L. *A River No More: The Colorado River and the American West*. Berkeley: University of California Press, 1996.

Fried, Richard M. *Nightmare in Red: The McCarthy Era in Perspective*. New York: Oxford University Press, 1990.

Garfield County, Utah. "Garfield County Economic Development Plan." January 2019. Accessed September 30, 2020. https://www.garfield.utah.gov/home/showpublisheddocument/1220/637274745016100000.

Gery, R. E., and John A. Smith. *Report on Lieu Selections on That Portion of Arizona Line North and West of the Colorado River*. Washington, DC: U.S. Department of Agriculture, 1915.

Gitlin, Todd. *The Sixties: Years of Hope, Days of Rage*. New York: Bantam Books, 1987.

Glass, Daniel. "A History of Bullion Canyon." Maryville County Chamber of Commerce, 2010. Accessed July 5, 2024. http://www.marysvaleutah.org/informationaboutmarysvale/history/59-a-history-of-bullion-canyon-marysvale-utahpiute-county.html.

Godfrey, E. Bruce. "Livestock Grazing in Utah: History and Status." Report to the Utah Governor's Public Lands Policy Coordination Office. Salt Lake City, 2008.

Godfrey, E. Bruce, and C. Arden Pope. "The Trouble with Livestock Grazing on Public Lands." *Southern Utah Wilderness Alliance Newsletter*, Winter 1991/1992. First published 1990, *Current Issues in Rangeland Resource Economics*.

Gottfredson, Peter. *History of Indian Depredations in Utah*. Salt Lake City, UT: Skelton Publishing, 1919.

Graf, William L. *Wilderness Preservation and the Sagebrush Rebellions*. Savage, MD: Rowman & Littlefield, 1990.

Graffam, Merle H. "A Survey of Cowboy Glyphs from the Big Water, Utah, Region of Kane County, Utah." 1997. Manuscript on file, Grand Staircase-Escalante National Monument, Kanab, UT.

Granger, Byrd H. *Arizona's Names: X Marks the Place*. Treasure Chest Pubns, 1983.

Gregg, Frank. "Implementing FLPMA." In *Opportunity and Challenge: The Story of the BLM*, edited by James Muhn and Hanson R. Stuart, 206. Washington, DC: Bureau of Land Management, 1988.

Gregory, Herbert E., and Raymond C. Moore. *The Kaiparowits Region: A Geographic and Geologic Reconnaissance of Parts of Utah and Arizona*. U.S. Geological Survey Professional Papers 164. Washington, DC: Government Printing Office, 1931.

Griffin, E. A. "Statement of E. A. Griffin Concerning Range Conditions on Forest and Public Lands in Southern Utah, as It Was in Early Days and as It Is Now." In *Special Range Report R-4*, compiled by Carl H. Dopp, September 25, 1940. MSS B 100. Utah State Historical Society, Salt Lake City.

Gulliford, Andrew. *The Woolly West: Colorado's Hidden History of Sheepscapes*. College Station: Texas A&M University Press, 2018.

Hahn, W. F., T. L. Crawford, K. E. Nelson, and R. A. Bowl. *Estimating Forage Values for Grazing National Forest Lands*. United States Department of Agriculture Staff Report No. 89-51. Washington, DC, 1989.

Hall, Sharlot. *Sharlot Hall of the Arizona Strip: A Diary of a Journey through Northern Arizona in 1911*. Edited by C. Gregory Crampton. Flagstaff, AZ: Northland Press, 1975.

Hamblin, Frank. "An Interview with Frank Hamblin." February 21, 1941. In Julius S. Dalley, *History of Grazing*. Utah Writers Project, 1941. MSS B 100, Utah State Historical Society, Salt Lake City.

Hamblin, Neaf. "An Interview with Neaf Hamblin." February 21, 1941. In Julius S. Dalley, *History of Grazing*. Utah Writers Project, 1941. MSS B 100, Utah State Historical Society, Salt Lake City.

Handley, George B. "On the Moral Lessons of Mormon Environmental History." In *The Earth Will Appear as the Garden of Eden*, edited by Jedediah S. Rogers and Matthew C. Godfrey, 253–61. Salt Lake City: University of Utah Press, 2019.

Hardin, Garrett. "Tragedy of the Commons." *Science* 162, no. 3859: 1243–48.

Harvey, Jonathan E., Joel L. Pederson, and Tammy M Rittenour. "Exploring Relations Between Arroyo Cycles and Canyon Paleoflood Records in Buckskin Wash, Utah." *GSA Bulletin* 123 no. 11–12 (2011): 2266–76.

Hatch, Ira W. "Statement of Ira W. Hatch Regarding Early Range Conditions in Southern Utah." Special Range Report R-4, September 22, 1940. MSS B 100. Utah State Historical Society, Salt Lake City.

Hatch, Orrin. Speaking on S. 477. 105th Congress, 1st sess. *Congressional Record* 143, no. 36 (March 19, 1997): S 2563.

Hawley, Jamie. "Ranching around Monuments in Southern Utah." *Progressive Cattle,* February 24, 2017. https://www.agproud.com/articles/49465-ranching-around-monuments-in-southern-utah.

Hays, Samuel P. *Beauty, Health, and Permanence: Environmental Politics in the United States, 1955–1985.* New York: Cambridge University Press, 1987.

Hays, Samuel P. *Conservation and the Gospel of Efficiency: The Progressive Conservation Movement, 1890–1920.* Cambridge, MA: Harvard University Press, 1959.

Heady, H. F., T. W. Box, J. E. Butcher, et al. "Livestock Grazing on Federal Lands in the 11 Western States." *Journal of Range Management*, 27, no. 3 (1974): 174–81.

Hess, Karl, Jr. "The Status of Range Reform." Accessed July 5, 2024. http://www.ti.org/rangeref.html.

Hibbard, Michael, and Susan Lurie. "The New Natural Resource Economy: A Framework for Community Resilience." In *Bridging the Distance: Common Issues of the Rural West*, edited by David B. Danbom, 192–210. Salt Lake City: University of Utah Press, 2015. E-book.

Hinton, Wayne K. "Getting Along: The Significance of Cooperation in the Development of Zion National Park." *Utah Historical Quarterly* 68, no. 4 (2000): 313–31.

Hinton, Wayne K., and Elizabeth A. Green. *With Picks, Shovels, and Hope: The CCC and Its Legacy on the Colorado Plateau.* Missoula, MT: Mountain Press Publishing, 2008.

Hodgin, F. M. *History of the North Kaibab, Kaibab National Forest.* Williams, AZ: Kaibab National Forest, 1962.

Holt, Ronald L. *Beneath These Red Cliffs: An Ethnohistory of the Utah Paiutes.* Logan: Utah State University Press, 2006.

Honker, Andrew M. "Been Grazed Almost to Extinction: The Environment, Human Action, and Utah Flooding, 1900–1940." *Utah Historical Quarterly* 67, no. 1 (1999): 23–47.

Hoxie, Frederick. "From Prison to Homeland: The Cheyenne River Indian Reservation before World War I." *South Dakota History* 10 (1979): 1–24.

Hudak, Mike. *Western Turf Wars: The Politics of Public Lands Ranching.* Binghamton, NY: Biome Books, 2013.

Hunt, Charles. *Physiography of the United States.* San Francisco: W. W. Freeman, 1967.

Inflation Calculator. Accessed March 26, 2021. http://www.westegg.com/inflation/.

Ivins, Anthony W. *An Address Delivered by President Anthony W. Ivins Upon Completion of the Union Pacific Lodge at Grand Canyon.* Salt Lake City, UT: Union Pacific System, 1935.

Ivins, Anthony W. Anthony W. Ivins Papers, 1875–1934. Register of the Collection at the Utah State Historical Society, Salt Lake City, 2001.

Ivins, Anthony W. *Cowboy Apostle: The Diaries of Anthony W. Ivins, 1875–1932.* Edited by Elizabeth Oberdick Anderson. Salt Lake City, UT: Signature Books, 2013.

Janetski, Joel C., Mark L. Bodily, Bradley A. Newbold, and David T. Yoder. "The Paleoarchaic to Early Archaic Transition on the Colorado Plateau: The Archaeology of North Creek Shelter." *American Antiquity* 77, no. 1 (2012): 125–59.

Jenson, Andrew. *LDS Biographical Encyclopedia: A Compilation of Biographical Sketches of Prominent Men and Women in the Church of Jesus Christ of Latter Day Saints.* Salt Lake City: Andrew Jenson History Co., 1901.

"John A. 'Jack' Watson—Soldier, Blacksmith, Texas Ranger, Outlaw, Lawman, Private Investigator and Friend to Cyrus 'Doc' Shores—A Man to Cross Rivers With." Accessed July 2, 2024. http://freepages.genealogy.rootsweb.ancestry.com/~hookersbend/bio_john_a_watson.html.

Johnson, R. D. "J. E. J. : The Trail to Sundown, Casadaga to Casa Grande." Salt Lake City, UT: Joseph Ellis Johnson Family Committee, 1961.

Johnson, Shauna Timpson. "Early Latter-day Saint Martyrs: The Jesse Woods and Armela Shanks Berry Family." *Religious Educator* 19, no. 2 (2018): 152–71.

Jones, Sondra G. *Being and Becoming Ute: The Story of an American Indian People.* Salt Lake City: University of Utah Press, 2019.

Jordan, Terry G. *North American Cattle-Ranching Frontiers: Origins, Diffusion, and Differentiation.* Albuquerque: University of New Mexico Press, 1993.

Judd, Alvin. "An Interview with Alvin Judd." February 13, 1941. In *History of Grazing,* by Julius S. Dalley. Utah Writers Project. MSS B 100, Utah State Historical Society, Salt Lake City.

Kanab Heritage House Museum. "History." Accessed July 2, 2024. www.kanabheritagehouse.com/history.html.

Kane County, Utah. "Kane County, Utah, General Plan." August 2018. Accessed September 30, 2020. https://kane.utah.gov/gov/dept/planning/draft-of-2018-kane-county-general-plan/#.

Kane, Wendi. "The U.S. Environmental Movement 1890–2002: Discourse, Divisions, Environmental Crisis Events, and Strategic Concessions." PhD diss., University of Central Florida, 2014.

Kelly, Charles. *The Outlaw Trail: A History of Butch Cassidy and His Wild Bunch.* Lincoln: University of Nebraska Press, 1996. First published 1938.

Kelly, Isabel T. *Southern Paiute Ethnography*. University of Utah Anthropological Papers 69. Salt Lake City: University of Utah Press, 1964.

Kemmis, Daniel. *This Sovereign Land: A New Vision for Governing the West.* New York: Island Press, 2001.

Knight, Richard L. "The Ecology of Ranching." In *Ranching West of the 100th Meridian: Culture, Ecology, and Economics*, edited by Richard L. Knight, Wendell C. Gilbert, and Ed Marston, 123–44. Washington, DC: Island Press, 2002.

Knowlton, Ezra C. *History of Highway Development in Utah.* Salt Lake City: Utah State Road Commission, n.d.

Kolb, Franz. "The Northern Ute Indian Reservation: Established Portrayal and Change." Master's thesis, Brigham Young University, 1983.

Krahulec, Ken. "Energy News: A New Uranium Boom?" Utah Geological Survey, May 2008. Accessed June 7, 2021. https://geology.utah.gov/map-pub/survey-notes/energy-news/energy-news-may-2008/.

Lamar, Howard R. "Westering in the Twentieth-First Century." In *Under an Open Sky: Rethinking America's Western Past*, edited by William Cronon, George Miles, and Jay Gitlin, 262–63. New York: W. W. Norton, 1992.

Lambert, C. Roger. "The Drought Cattle Purchase, 1934–1935: Problems and Complaints." *Agricultural History* 45, no. 2 (1971): 85–93.

Lambert, Page. "An Intimate Look at the Heart of the Radical Center." In *Ranching West of the 100th Meridian: Culture, Ecology, and Economics*, edited by Richard L. Knight, Wendell C. Gilbert, and Ed Marston, 59–75. Washington, DC: Island Press, 2002.

Larsen, Wesley P. *Stories from the Arizona Strip*. Salt Lake City: Utah State Historical Society, 1998.

Larson, Andrew Karl. *I Was Called to Dixie: The Virgin River Basin, Unique Experiences in Mormon Pioneering.* Salt Lake City: Deseret Press, 1961.

Larson, Andrew, and Evelyn Thompson. "Direct Marketing Lamb to Niche and Ethnic Markets." IDEA, University of Illinois Extension, n.d. Accessed June 22, 2024. https://www.researchgate.net/publication/237102779_Direct_Marketing_Lamb_to_Niche_and_Ethnic_Markets.

Lavender, David. *Colorado River Country*. New York: E. P. Dutton, 1982.

Lavender, David. *The Southwest.* Albuquerque: University of New Mexico Press, 1980.

Layton, Stanford John. "Governor Charles R. Mabey and the Utah Election of 1924." Master's thesis, University of Utah, Salt Lake City, 1969.

LeFevre, Lenora Hall. *Boulder Country and Its People: A History of the People of Boulder and the Surrounding Country, One Hundred Years, 1872–1973*. Springville, UT: Art City Publishing, 1973.

Leopold, Aldo. "Deer Irruptions." Paper completed for the National Resources Committee, Wisconsin Academy of Sciences, Arts and Letters. Accessed

April 19, 2022. https://localinannarbor.com/wp-content/uploads/2015/02/wi-wt1943-aleopold.pdf.
Leopold, Aldo. *A Sand County Almanac.* New York: Ballantine, 1986.
Lewis, David Rich. "Bernard DeVoto's Utah." In *Utah in the Twentieth Century*, edited by Brian Q. Cannon and Jessie L. Embry, 88–107. Logan: Utah State University Press, 2009.
Lewis, David Rich. *Neither Wolf Nor Dog: American Indians, Environment, and Agrarian Change.* New York: Oxford University Press, 1994.
Library of Congress. Prints and Photographs Online Catalog. www.loc.gov/pictures.
Limerick, Patricia Nelson. "Making the Most of Words." In *Under an Open Sky: Rethinking America's Western Past*, edited by William Cronon, George Miles, and Jay Gitlin, 167–84. New York: W. W. Norton, 1992.
Little, James A. *Jacob Hamblin: A Narrative of His Personal Experience as a Frontiersman, Missionary to the Indians and Explorer.* Salt Lake City: Deseret News, 1909.
Little, Willis. "Interview with Willis Little." In *History of Grazing*, by Julius S. Dalley. Utah Writers Project, February 17, 1941. MSS B 100. Utah State Historical Society, Salt Lake City.
Living New Deal. "Highway 12 'The Million Dollar Road'—Garfield County, UT." Accessed May 10, 2021. https://livingnewdeal.org/projects/highway-12-million-dollar-road-escalante-national-monument-ut/.
Mace, Blanche. "Biography of Silas Hoyt." N.d. Special Collections, Kanab City Library, Kanab, UT.
Mace, Lee. Interview by Matthew Zweifel. December 11, 2003. Grand Staircase-Escalante National Monument, Kanab, Utah.
Malone, John William. *An Album of the American Cowboy.* New York: Franklin Watts, 1971.
Mangum, John W. "History of John W. Mangum," by Layton J. Ott. Works Progress Administration, Federal Writers' Project, February 20, 1939. Utah State Historical Society, Salt Lake City.
Mann, Walter G. *The Kaibab Deer: A Brief History and Present Plan of Management.* Williams, AZ: Kaibab National Forest, 1941.
Mathis, Reed, and Grace Mathis. Dixie Pioneers and Story Tellers Oral History Collection. Oral History #98-012. Salt Lake City: Utah State Historical Society, 1998.
Maxwell, Lorenzo B. "A Sketch of the Life of William Bailey Maxwell." Ancestry.com. Posted May 4, 2008. Accessed July 2, 2024. https://www.ancestry.com/mediaui-viewer/tree/6078447/person/-1348928992/media/b94a4cf3-0af9-4ea7ad6f-b40991e731d7.
Maxwell, William Bailey. Ancestry.com. Accessed July 2, 2024. http://search.ancestry.com/cgi-bin/sse.dll?indiv=1&db=LDSVitalMembership1830-1848&h=59196&tid=&pid=&usePUB=true&_phsrc=xtJ66&_phstart=successSource&usePUBJs=true&rhSource=61157.

McAllister, William. "An Interview with Mr. and Mrs. William McAllister." In *History of Grazing*, by Julius S. Dalley. Utah Writers Project, February 5, 1941. MSS B 100. Utah State Historical Society, Salt Lake City.

McGerr, Michael E. "Is There a Twentieth Century West?" In *Under an Open Sky: Rethinking America's Western Past*, edited by William Cronon, George Miles, and Jay Gitlin, 239–56. New York: W. W. Norton, 1992.

McGinty, Ellie Leydsman, Ben Baldwin, and Roger Banner. *A Review of Livestock Grazing and Range Management in Utah*. Report to the Governor's Public Lands Policy Coordination Office. Logan: Utah State University Press, 2009.

McKoy, Kathleen L. *Pipe Spring: Cultures at a Crossroads: An Administrative History*. Cultural Resource Selections No. 15. 2000. National Park Service Intermountain Region. Accessed April 5, 2021. https://nps.gov/parkhistory/online_books/pisp/adhi/adhin.htm#243.

McLaws, Kevin. Telephone interview by Marsha Holland, September 9, 2017. Transcript in possession of Holland.

McNamara, Robert. "Meaning and History of the Term 'Robber Baron.'" Thought Co., Humanities: History and Culture. Last updated March 2, 2021. https://thoughtco.com/robber-baron-definition-1773342.

Mecham, Lowell J. Interview exhibit. Bryce Canyon National Park Museum, Bryce, Utah.

Meeks, Priddy. "Journal of Priddy Meeks." *Utah Historical Quarterly* 10 (1942): 144–223.

Meinig, D. W. "The Mormon Culture Region: Strategies and Patterns in the Geography of the American West." *Annals of the Association of American Geographers* 55, no. 2 (1965): 191–220.

Metcalf, Warren R. "A Precarious Balance: The Northern Utes and the Black Hawk War." *Utah Historical Quarterly* 57, no. 1 (1989): 24–35.

Miller, Gil. Telephone interview by Jerry D. Spangler. August 31, 2017. Notes in possession of Spangler.

Miller, Gil, and Kevin Heaton. *Livestock Grazing on the Grand Staircase-Escalante National Monument: The Historical and Cultural Importance to the Region*. Logan: Utah State University–Agriculture Extension, September 2015.

Miller, Mark E. D. "St. Johns' Saints: Interethnic Conflict in Northeastern Arizona, 1880–1885." *Journal of Mormon History* 23 (1997): 66–99.

Miller, Mark E. D. "Timeline: Bryce Canyon National Park." In *Bryce Canyon Memories: A Multi-Media Documentation of the Oral History of Bryce Canyon National Park*. DVD. National Park Service and the Bryce Canyon Association, 2016.

Muhn, James, and Hanson R. Stuart. *Opportunity and Challenge: The Story of the BLM*. Washington, DC: Bureau of Land Management, 1988.

Nash, Roderick. *Wilderness and the American Mind*. New Haven, CT: Yale University Press, 1982.

National Academies. "Changes in the Sheep Industry in the United States." 2008. https://nap.nationalacademies.org/catalog/12245/changes-in-the-sheep-industry-in-the-united-states-making.

National Chicken Council. "Per Capita Consumption of Poultry and Livestock, 1965 to Estimated 2021, in Pounds." Accessed August 3, 2021. http://www.nationalchickencouncil.org/statistics/per-capita-consumption-poultry/.

National Park Service. "Escalante." Glen Canyon National Recreation Area. Accessed November 25, 2020. https://www.nps.gov/glca/planyourvisit/escalante.htm.

National Park Service. "Grazing." Glen Canyon National Recreation Area. Accessed November 17, 2020. https://nps.gov/glca/learn/nature/grazing.htm.

National Park Service. "Lees Ferry History." Glen Canyon National Recreation Area. Accessed September 27, 2021. https://www.nps.gov/glca/learn/historyculture/leesferryhistory.htm.

National Park Service. "Mexican Spotted Owl." Zion National Park. Accessed March 9, 2022. https://nps.gov/zion/learn/nature/mexicanspottedowl.htm.

National Park Service. "The Mormon Militia and Pipe Spring." Pipe Spring National Monument. Accessed September 27, 2021. http://www.nps.gov/pisp/photosmultimedia/the-mormon-militia-and-pipe-sprin.htm.

National Park Service. "Navajo Bridge." Glen Canyon National Recreation Area. Accessed October 21, 2020. https://nps.gov/glca/historyculture/navajobridge.htm.

National Park Service. "Pipe Spring." Accessed September 27, 2021. https://www.nps.gov/pisp/planyourvisit/pipe-spring.htm.

National Parks Traveler. Accessed July 2, 2024. https://www.nationalparkstraveler.org/parks/canyonlands-national-park.

Nelson, Pearl Udall. "Eliza Luella Stewart Udall." In *Pioneer Women of Arizona*, edited by Roberta Flake Clayton, Catherine H. Ellis, and David F. Boone, 737–40. 2nd ed. Salt Lake City, UT: Deseret Book, 2017. First published 1969.

Newell, Linda King, and Vivian Linford Talbot. *A History of Garfield County.* Salt Lake City: Utah State Historical Society; Panguitch, UT: Garfield County Commission, 1998.

Nichols, Jeff. "Before the Boom: Mormons, Livestock, and Stewardship, 1847–1870." In *The Earth Will Appear as the Garden of Eden,* edited by Jedediah S. Rogers and Matthew C. Godfrey, 155–72. Salt Lake City: University of Utah Press, 2019.

Nugent, Walter. *Into the West: The Story of Its People.* New York: Alfred A. Knopf, 1999.

Nutter, Preston. Preston Nutter to J. N. Darling, Chief of the Bureau of Biological Survey, Washington, DC, 1935. Utah State Historical Society, Salt Lake City.

O'Connor, Sandra Day, and H. Alan Day. *Lazy B: Growing Up on a Cattle Ranch in the American Southwest.* New York: Random House, 2002.

Olsen, Robert W., Jr. "The Powell Survey Kanab Base Line." *Utah Historical Quarterly* 37, no. 2 (1969): 261–68.

Paiute Tribe of Utah. Accessed March 26, 2021. www.utahpaiutes.org.

Palmer, William. William Palmer to Dr. Farrow, August 25, 1925. Box 11, fd. 41. Palmer Collection, Barbara A. Matheson Special Collections, Southern Utah University, Cedar City.

Palmer, William. William Palmer to Hazel Brockbank, August 17, 1935. Box 11, fd. 35. Palmer Collection, Barbara A. Matheson Special Collections, Southern Utah University, Cedar City.

Parker, Randy N. "Threats to Grazing from Federal Regulatory Overreach." Statement of the Utah Farm Bureau Federation and Thirteen Western State Farm Bureaus to the U.S. House of Representatives Committee on Oversight and Government Reform, Subcommittee on Interior. August 6, 2015. https://oversight.house.gov/wp-content/uploads/2015/08/Parker-Statement-8-6-Wyoming-Grazing.pdf.

Patterson, Richard. *Butch Cassidy: A Biography.* Lincoln: University of Nebraska Press, 1998.

Paulsen, Deidre M. "Stories and Storytelling Techniques of Rowland W. Rider, Cowboy on the Arizona Strip in the Early 1900s." Master's thesis, Brigham Young University, Provo, UT, 1975.

Pearson, Byron E. *Still the Wild River Runs: Congress, the Sierra Club, and the Fight to Save Grand Canyon.* Tucson: University of Arizona Press, 2002.

Pendleton, Mark A. "The Orderville United Order of Zion." *Utah Historical Quarterly* 7, no. 4 (1939): 141–59.

Peterson, Charles S. "Grazing in Utah: A Historical Perspective." *Utah Historical Quarterly* 57, no. 4 (1989): 300–319.

Peterson, Charles S., and Brian Q. Cannon. *The Awkward State of Utah*. Salt Lake City: University of Utah Press, 2015.

Peterson, Levi S. "The Development of Utah Livestock Law, 1848–1896." *Utah Historical Quarterly* 32, no. 3 (1964): 198–216.

Peterson, Paul H. "An Historical Analysis of the Word of Wisdom." Master's thesis, Brigham Young University, 1972. https://scholarsarchive.byu.edu/etd/5039/.

Polasek, M. "U.S. Wool Policy and Its Effects on Apparel Wool Imports." *Australian Journal of Agricultural Economics* 6, no. 2 (1962): 9–20.

Pollock, Raymond Devar. Interview, n.d. Visitor Center Museum, Bryce Canyon National Park, Bryce, Utah.

Porter, Joseph J. "Statement of Jos. J. Porter, Concerning Range Conditions on Forest and Public Lands in Southern Utah in the Early Days as Compared with the Present." Special Range Report R-4, September 25, 1940. MSS B 100, Utah State Historical Society, Salt Lake City.

Powell, Allan Kent. *Encyclopedia of Utah History.* Salt Lake City: University of Utah Press, 1994.

Powell, J. W., and G. W. Ingalls. *Report of Special Commissioners J. W. Powell and G. W. Ingalls on the Condition of the Ute Indians of Utah; the Pai-utes of Utah, Northern Arizona, Southern Nevada, and Southeastern California; the Go-si Utes of Utah and Nevada; the Northwestern Shoshones of Idaho and Utah; and the Western Shoshones of Nevada.* Washington, DC: Bureau of Indian Affairs, 1873.

Prendergast, Neil. "Tracking the Kaibab Deer into Western History." *Western Historical Quarterly* 39, no. 4 (2008): 413–38.

Price, Virginia N., and John T. Darby. "Preston Nutter: Utah Cattleman, 1886–1936." *Utah Historical Quarterly* 32, no. 3 (1964): 232–51.

Power, Thomas D. *Lost Landscapes and Failed Economies: The Search for a Value of Place.* Washington, DC: Island Press, 1996.

Ptak, John F. "On the Early Imagery and Definition of the 'Cowboy.'" JF Ptak Science Books Post 3836, April 2020. http://longstreet.typepad.com/thesciencebookstore/2020/04/on-the-history-of-the-word-cowboy.html.

Public Lands Ranching. "Information and Facts." Accessed July 2, 2024. http://www.publiclandsranching.org/.

Quammen, Betsy Gaines. "American Zion: Mormon Culture and the Creation of a National Park." In *The Earth Will Appear as a Garden of Eden: Essays on Mormon Environmental History*, edited by Jedediah S. Rogers and Matthew C. Godfrey, 131–51. Salt Lake City: University of Utah Press, 2019.

Quigley, Thoomas M., and E. T. Bartlett. "Livestock on Public Lands: Yes!" *Southern Utah Wilderness Alliance Newsletter*, Winter 1991/1992. First published 1990, *Current Issues in Rangeland Resource Economics.*

Quinn, D. Michael. "Us-Them Tribalism and Early Mormonism." *John Whitmer Historical Association* 29 (2009): 94–114.

Reeve, W. Paul. *Making Space on the Western Frontier: Mormons, Miners, and Southern Paiutes.* Urbana: University of Illinois Press, 2006.

Regan, Shawn. "Managing Conflicts Over US Federal Rangelands." In *Ranching Realities in the 21st Century*," edited by Holly Fretwell and Mark Milke, 39–63. Vancouver, Canada: Fraser Institute, 2016. https://www.fraserinstitute.org/sites/default/files/ranching-realities-in-the-21st-century.pdf.

Reilly, P. T. "Historic Utilization of Paria River." *Utah Historical Quarterly* 45, no. 2 (1977): 188–201.

Reilly, P. T. "Kanab United Order: The President's Nephew and the Bishop." *Utah Historical Quarterly* 42, no. 2 (1974): 144–164.

Reilly, P. T. "Road Across Buckskin Mountain." *Journal of Arizona History* 19 (1978): 379–402.

Reisner, Mark. *Cadillac Desert: The American West and Its Disappearing Water.* New York: Penguin Books, 1993.

Rich, Effie Dean. *Buckskin History, Kaibab Plateau and Grand Canyon.* 1941. Manuscript on file, Utah State Historical Society, Salt Lake City.

Richardson, Elmo R. "The Escalante National Monument Controversy of 1935–1940." *Utah Historical Quarterly* 33, no. 2 (1965): 109–33.
Rider, Rowland. *The Rollaway Saloon: Cowboy Tales of the Arizona Strip*. Logan: Utah State University Press, 1985.
Rifkin, Jeremy. "Cattle and Capitalism." N.d. Accessed July 5, 2024. http://www.columbia.edu/~lnp3/mydocs/ecology/cattle.htm.
Riggs, Brigham A. "Early History by Brigham A. Riggs." In *History of Grazing*, by Julius S. Dalley. Utah Writers Project, February 14, 1941. MSS B 100. Utah State Historical Society, Salt Lake City.
Ringholz, Raye C. *Uranium Frenzy: Saga of the Nuclear West*. Logan: Utah State University Press, 2002.
Robbins, William G. *Lumberjacks and Legislators: Political Economy of the U.S. Lumber Industry, 1890–1941*. College Station: Texas A&M University Press, 1982.
Roberts, Heidi, Richard V. N. Ahlstrom, and Jerry D. Spangler, eds. *Far Western Basketmaker Beginnings: The Jackson Flat Reservoir Project*. Salt Lake City: University of Utah Press, 2022.
Robinson, Adonis Findlay. *History of Kane County*. Kanab, UT: Kane County Daughters of the Utah Pioneers, 1970.
Robinson, Sarah Blanche. "Reminiscences, Told to Louise Haycock." N.d. Special Collections, Kanab City Library, Kanab, UT.
Rogers, Jedediah S. "History, Nature, and Mormons in Historiography." In *The Earth Will Appear as the Garden of Eden*, edited by Jedediah S. Rogers and Matthew C. Godfrey, 7–25. Salt Lake City: University of Utah Press, 2019.
Rogers, Jedediah S. *Roads in the Wilderness: Conflict in Canyon Country*. Salt Lake City: University of Utah Press, 2013.
Rogers, Jedediah S. "The Volatile Sagebrush Rebellion." In *Utah in the Twentieth Century*, edited by Brian Q. Cannon and Jessie L. Embry, 367–84. Logan: Utah State University Press, 2009.
Rollins, George W. "Land Policies of the United States as Applied to Utah to 1910." *Utah Historical Quarterly* 20, no. 2 (1952): 239–51.
Romney, Thomas Cottam. *The Mormon Colonies in Mexico*. Salt Lake City: Deseret Book Company, 1938.
Rothman, Hal. "Second-Class Sites: National Monuments and the Growth of the National Park System." *Environmental Review* 10, no. 1 (1986): 44–56.
Rothman, Hal. "Shaping the Nature of a Controversy: The Park Service, the Forest Service, and the Cedar Breaks Proposal." *Utah Historical Quarterly* 55, no. 3 (1987): 212–35.
Runyon, Luke. "The Long, Slow Decline of the U.S. Sheep Industry," Harvest Public Media, Nebraska Public Media, October 15, 2013. https://nebraskapublicmedia.org/en/news/news-articles/the-long-slow-decline-of-the-us-sheep-industry/.

Rusnak, Eric C. "The Straw that Broke the Camel's Back? Grand Staircase-Escalante National Monument Antiquates the Antiquities Act." *Ohio State Law Journal* 64 (2003): 669–730.

Saitua, Iker. *Basque Immigrants and Nevada's Sheep Industry: Geopolitics and the Making of an Agricultural Workforce, 1880–1954*. Reno: University of Nevada Press, 2019.

Sayre, Nathan F. *Ranching, Environmental Species, and Urbanization in the Southwest*. Tucson: University of Arizona Press, 2002.

Sears, Willis. Interview (interviewer not recorded). January 8, 1964. Barbara A. Matheson Special Collections, Gerald R. Sherratt Library, Southern Utah University, Cedar City.

Seegmiller, Janet Burton. "Nuclear Testing and the Downwinders." Accessed June 19, 2024. http://historytogo.utah.gov/downwinders.

Sheep101.info. "Dollars and Cents." Accessed July 2, 2024. http://www.sheep101.info/farm.html.

Shirts, Ambrose. "A Biographical Sketch of Peter Shirts." October 7, 1958. Accessed July 5, 2024. https://www.familysearch.org/photos/artifacts/424793.

Shirts, Peter. Ancestry.com. Accessed July 2, 2021. https://www.ancestry.com/mediaui-viewer/tree/6701845/person/975118281/media/678e110a-369e-47f1-9103bd1461d9d384.

Simmons, Virginia McConnell. *The Ute Indians of Utah, Colorado and New Mexico*. Boulder: University of Colorado Press, 2000.

Skillen, James R. *This Land Is My Land: Rebellion in the West*. New York City: Oxford University Press, 2020.

Smith, S. M. "History of Peter Shirts." Ancestry.com, 2006. Accessed October 28, 2016. http://mv.ancestry.com/viewer/2eda31dc-07074ce6-9fb9-63b684b5243c/9356973/6044587404.

Southern Utah and Northern Arizona Cattlemen's Association. Copy of minutes, January 17, 1906. MS 36 B2F2. Barbara A. Matheson Special Collections, Southern Utah University, Cedar City.

Southern Utah Oral History Project. Barbara A. Matheson Special Collections, Southern Utah University, Cedar City.

Southern Utah Wilderness Alliance. "Points to Make in Your Comments on Grand Staircase-Escalante National Monument." Accessed September 30, 2020. https://suwa.org/points-make-comments-grand-staircase-escalante-national-monument/.

Spangler, Jerry D. *Vermilion Dreamers and Sagebrush Schemers: An Overview of Human Occupation in the House Rock Valley and Eastern Arizona Strip*. Flagstaff, AZ: Grand Canyon Trust, 2007.

Spangler, Jerry D., and Donna Kemp Spangler. *Last Chance Byway: A History of Nine Mile Canyon*. Salt Lake City: University of Utah Press, 2016.

Spangler, Jerry D., and Andrew T. Yentsch. *Cultural Resource Inventories along OHV Routes in Kane, Wayne, and San Juan Counties, Southern Utah.* Ogden, UT: Colorado Plateau Archaeological Alliance, 2010.

Spangler, Jerry D., and Matthew Zweifel. *Risky Business: Farming and Travel in the Upper Paria River Corridor*. Ogden, UT: Colorado Plateau Archaeological Alliance, 2012.

Starrs, Paul F. "'Cattle Free By '93' and the Imperatives of Environmental Radicalism." *Ubique: Notes from the American Geographical Society* 14, no. 1 (April 1994): 1–4. Available at: https://www.researchgate.net/profile/Paul-Starrs.

Starrs, Paul F. *Let the Cowboy Ride: Cattle Ranching in the American* West. Baltimore, MD: Johns Hopkins University Press, 1998.

Starrs, Paul F. "Meetinghouses in the Mormon Mind: Ideology, Architecture, and Turbulent Streams of an Expanding Church." *Geographical Review* 99, no. 3 (2009): 323–355.

Starrs, Paul F. "Transhumance as Antidote for Modern Sedentary Stock Raising." *Rangeland Ecology & Management* 71, no. 5 (2018): 592–602.

Stegner, Wallace. *Mormon Country.* Lincoln: University of Nebraska Press, 1981. First published 1942 by Duell, Sloan, and Pearce.

Stewart, Levi. "I, Levi Stewart." Testimony as told to Norene Robinson, n.d. Special Collections, Kanab City Library, Kanab, Utah.

Strong, Ezra, Jr. "Find A Grave: Ezra Strong." Ancestry.com. Accessed July 2, 2024. http://search.ancestry.com/cgibin/sse.dll?indiv=1&db=FindAGraveUS&h.

Sullins, Martha J., David T. Theobald, Jeff R. Jones, and Leah M. Burgess. "Lay of the Land: Ranch Land and Ranching." In *Ranching West of the 100th Meridian*, edited by Richard L. Knight, Wendell C. Gilbert, and Ed Marston, 25–32. New York: Island Press, 2012.

Taylor, Janet. "A Tough Cattleman in a Tough Land: Preston Nutter." *Outlaw Trail Journal* (Summer 2007): 37–44.

Theobald, George. "Personal Pioneer Interview." January 25, 1937. Works Progress Administration, Utah Section, Biographical Sketches, ca. 1930–1941. MSS B 289. Utah Historical Society, Salt Lake City.

Thiem Jon, and Deborah Dimon. *Rabbit Creek Country: Three Ranching Lives in the Mountain West.* Albuquerque: University of New Mexico Press, 2008.

Thomas, Arthur L. *Report of the Governor of Utah to the Secretary of the Interior, 1890.* Washington, DC: U.S. Government Printing Office, 1890.

Topping, Gary. *Glen Canyon and the San Juan Country*. Moscow: University of Idaho Press, 1997.

Topping, Gary. "Zane Grey in Zion: An Examination of His Supposed Anti-Mormonism." *BYU Studies Quarterly* 18, no. 4 (1978), article 2. Accessed April 24, 2022. https://scholarsarchive.byu.edu/byusq/vol18/iss4/2/.

Turley, Richard E., Jr., and Eric C. Olson. "Fame Meets Infamy: The Powell Survey and Mountain Meadows Participants, 1870–1873." *Utah Historical Quarterly* 81, no. 1 (2013): 6–26.

U.S. Census Bureau. Population Schedule, Belview, Kane County, Utah Territory. 1870 United States Federal Census. Microfilm roll M593_1611, page 467A, image 350498. National Archives and Records Administration, Washington, DC. Family History Library film 553110, images reproduced by FamilySearch. Accessed July 2, 2024. Ancestry.com.

U.S. Census Bureau. Population Schedule, Iron County, Utah Territory. 1880 United States Federal Census. Microfilm roll 1336, page 336c, enumeration district 019. National Archives and Records Administration, Washington, DC. Family History Library film 553112, images reproduced by FamilySearch. Accessed July 2, 2024, Ancestry.com.

U.S. Census Bureau. Population Schedule, Kanab, Kane County, Utah Territory. 1870 United States Federal Census. Microfilm roll M593_1611, page 447B, image 349581. National Archives and Records Administration, Washington, DC. Family History Library film 553110, images reproduced by FamilySearch. Accessed July 2, 2024. Ancestry.com.

U.S. Census Bureau. Population Schedule, Orderville, Kane County, Utah Territory. 1880 United States Federal Census. Microfilm roll 1336, page 452C; enumeration District 029. National Archives and Records Administration, Washington, DC. Family History Library film 553112. Images reproduced by FamilySearch. Accessed July 2, 2024. Ancestry.com.

U.S. Census Bureau. Population Schedule, St. George, Washington County, Utah Territory. 1870 United States Federal Census. Microfilm roll M593_1613, page 395B. National Archives and Records Administration, Washington, DC. Family History Library film 553112, images reproduced by FamilySearch. Accessed July 2, 2024. Ancestry.com.

U.S. Census Bureau. Population Schedule, St. George, Washington County, Utah Territory. 1880 United States Federal Census. Microfilm roll 1339, page 359A, enumeration district 093. National Archives and Records Administration, Washington, DC. Family History Library film 553112, images reproduced by FamilySearch. Accessed July 2, 2024. Ancestry.com.

U.S. Census Bureau. Population schedule, Utah Territory. 1860 United States Federal Census. Microfilm publication M653, 1,438 rolls. National Archives and Records Administration, Washington, DC. Images reproduced by FamilySearch. Accessed July 2, 2024. Ancestry.com.

U.S. Census Bureau. Twenty-Second Census Taken in the Year 2000. Washington, DC: U.S. Printing Office, 2002.

U.S. Census Bureau. "Quick Facts, Garfield County, Utah." Accessed July 5, 2024. www.census.gov/quickfacts/garfieldcountyutah.

U.S. Census Bureau. "Quick Facts, Kane County, Utah." Accessed July 5, 2024. www.census.gov/quickfacts/kanecountyutah.
U.S. Department of Agriculture. "End the Wool and Mohair Subsidy." Accessed July 2, 2024. https://govinfo.library.unt.edu/npr/library/reports/ag01.html.
U.S. Department of Agriculture. "The Western Range," U.S. Department of Agriculture, 74th Congress, Senate Document No. 199. April 24, 1936.
U.S. Department of Agriculture (USDA) Census of Agriculture Historical Archive. U.S. Census of Agriculture 1840–2012. Albert R. Mann Library, Cornell University, Ithaca, New York. National Agricultural Statistics Service (NASS). https://agcensus.library.cornell.edu/.
U.S. Inflation Calculator. Accessed July 5, 2024. http://www.usinflationcalculator.com/.
U.S. Mint. "U.S. Mint History: The Crime of 1873." Inside the Mint, March 22, 2017. https://www.usmint.gov/news/inside-the-mint/mint-history-crime-of-1873.
"U.S. Register of Civil, Military, and Naval Service, 1863–1959." Online database. Ancestry.com. Accessed December 1, 2021.
Utah Division of Water Resources. *Drought in Utah: Learning from the Past—Preparing for the Future*. State Water Plan 14. Salt Lake City: Utah Division of Water Resources, 2017.
"Utah in Focus." *Utah Historical Quarterly* 89, no. 2 (2021): 176.
Vietnam War Draft Lottery. Accessed July 2, 2024. https://vietnamwardraftlottery.com/.
Voigt, William, Jr. *Public Grazing Lands: Use and Misuse by Industry and Government*. New Brunswick, NJ: Rutgers University Press, 1976.
Walker, Don D. "The Cattle Industry of Utah, 1850–1900: A Historical Profile." *Utah Historical Quarterly*, 32, no. 3 (1964): 182–97.
Warner, Jessie. Interview with Jessie Warner, Escalante District, U.S. Forest Service, by Jerry D. Spangler. August 31, 2017. Notes in possession of Spangler.
Warner, Matt. *Last of the Bandit Riders . . . Revisited*. Salt Lake City, UT: Big Moon Traders, 2000.
Warner, Ted J., ed. *The Domínguez-Escalante Journal*. Translated by Fray Angelico Chavez. Salt Lake City: University of Utah Press, 1995. First published 1976 by Brigham Young University Press.
Washington County Historical Society. "Pine Valley Chapel." Accessed March 29, 2021. https://wchsutah.org/churches/pine-valley-chapel.php.
Webb, Charlotte Maxwell. "Sketch of the Life of William Bailey Maxwell." Posted May 4, 2008. Accessed July 2, 2024. https://www.ancestry.com/mediaui-viewer/tree/60784447/person/-1348928992/media/eb05f9c4-ff81-4676b0f2-c6c6d0799b64.
Webb, E. M. "Manuscript History of Kanab Stake." N.d. LDS Church Archives, Salt Lake City, Utah.
Webb, Robert H., Spence S. Smith, and V. Alexander S. McCord. *Historic Channel Change of Kanab Creek, Southern Utah and Northern Arizona*. Grand Canyon

Natural History Association Monograph No. 9. Grand Canyon, AZ: Grand Canyon Natural History Association, 1991.

Webb, Roy. *Register of the Records of the Preston Nutter Corporation (1876–1981).* 1987. Manuscript Collection, Special Collections, J. Willard Marriott Library, University of Utah, Salt Lake City.

Webb, Walter Prescott. *The Great Plains.* New York: Grosset and Dunlap, 1931.

Welton, Tracie. "A Very Brief History of the Kaibab Plateau and Houserock Valley." N.d. Manuscript on file with Kaibab National Forest, Prescott, Arizona.

White, Richard. "Animals and Enterprise." In *The Oxford History of the American West,* edited by Clyde A. Milner, Carol A. O'Conner, and Martha A. Sandweiss, 237–73. New York: Oxford University Press, 1994.

White, Richard. "Are You an Environmentalist or Do You Work for a Living?: Work and Nature." In *Uncommon Ground: Rethinking the Human Place in Nature*, edited by William Cronon, 171–85. New York: W. W. Norton, 1996.

Whiteman, Honor. "Red Meat: Good or Bad for Health?" *Medical News Today*, January 25, 2017. https://www.medicalnewstoday.com/articles/315449.

Wilkinson, Charles. *Crossing the Next Meridian: Lands, Water, and the Future of the West.* Washington, DC: Island Press, 2013.

Wilkinson, Charles. *Fire on the Plateau: Conflict and Endurance in the American Southwest.* Washington, DC: Island Press, 1999.

Williams, A. Park, Edward R. Cook, Jason E. Smerdon, Benjamin I. Cook, John T. Abatzoglou, Kasey Bolles, Seung H. Baek, Andrew M. Badger, and Ben Livneh. "Large Contribution from Anthropogenic Warming to an Emerging North American Megadrought." *Science* 368, no. 6488 (2020): 314–18.

Winkler, Albert. "The Circleville Massacre: A Brutal Incident in Utah's Black Hawk War." *Utah Historical Quarterly* 55, no. 1 (1987): 4–21.

Winsor, A. P. A. P. Winsor to Brigham Young, April 9, 1866, datelined Grafton, Kane County. Brigham Young Office Files, Reel 43, Box 31, Folder 17. J. Willard Marriott Library, University of Utah, Salt Lake City.

Wixom, Hartt. *Hamblin: A Modern Look at the Frontier Life and Legend of Jacob Hamblin.* Springville, UT: Cedar Fort, 1996.

Woodbury, Angus. "History of Southern Utah and its National Parks." *Utah Historical Quarterly* 12, nos. 3–4 (1944): 110–209.

Woolley, Edwin D. Edwin D. Woolley Jr. Collection. Barbara A. Matheson Special Collections, Southern Utah University, Cedar City.

Woolley, Edwin G. "Expedition to Intercept Navajoe [*sic*] Indians Who Had Stolen Stock from Southern Utah, Feb. 25th to March 12th 1869." *Utah Historical Quarterly* 29, no.2 (1961): 151–76.

Worster, Donald. *Dust Bowl: The Southern Plains in the 1930s.* New York: Oxford University Press, 1979.

Worster, Donald. *An Unsettled Country: Changing Landscapes of the American West.* Albuquerque: University of New Mexico Press, 1994.

Wrabley, Raymond B., Jr. "Managing the Monument: Cows and Conservation in the Grand Staircase-Escalante National Monument." *Journal of Land Resources and Environmental Law* 29 (2009): 253–80.

Wright, John B. *Rocky Mountain Divide: Selling and Saving the West.* Austin: University of Texas Press, 1993.

Wuerthner, George, and Mollie Matteson, eds. *Welfare Ranching: The Subsidized Destruction of the American West.* New York: Island Press, 2002.

Wyoming Game and Fish Department. "Rural Subdivision." Accessed June 24, 2021. https://wgfd.wyo.gov.

Younghan, Gretchen, and Katrina Rogers. "A Short History of Kane Ranch." N.d. Manuscript on file, Grand Canyon Trust, Flagstaff, AZ.

Federal Laws and Statutes

Agricultural Adjustment Act (1933). 7 U.S.C. ch. 26 § 601 et seq.

Antiquities Act (1906). 16 U.S.C. §§ 431–433 et seq.

Classification and Multiple Use Act (1964). 43 U.S.C. §§ 1411–18.

Endangered Species Act (1973). 16 U.S.C. ch. 35 §§ 1531.

Federal Land Policy and Management Act (1976). 43 U.S.C. ch. 35 § 1701 et seq.

Forest Reserve Act (1891). 16 U.S.C. ch. 2, subch 1. § 471 et seq.

National Environmental Policy Act (1969). 42 U.S.C. § 4321 et seq.

National Historic Preservation Act (1966). 54 U.S.C. §§ 300101-307108. Revised Statute 2477 of 1866. Repealed 1976, Sec. 701, 43 U.S.C. § 1701.

National Wool Act (1948). 80_U.S.C. ch. 488. § 1498. Revised 1954. 83 U.S.C. Sections amended ch. 35a § 1421, ch. 44 § 1781.

Organic Administration Act (1897). 16 U.S.C. § 473 et seq.

Taylor Grazing Act (1934). PL 73-482 and PL-74-827, Title 43 Public Lands, 43 U.S.C. § 315.

Wilderness Act (1964). 16 U.S.C. ch. 23 § 1131 et seq.

Index

Figures, tables, and maps are indicated by italicized page numbers.